OBJECTIVE	CHAPTER
Manipulating Data	**6**
Describe each DML statement	6
Insert rows into a table	6
Update rows in a table	6
Delete rows from a table	6
Merge rows in a table	6
Control transactions	6
Creating and Managing Tables	**7**
Describe the main database objects	7
Create tables	7
Describe the datatypes that can be used when specifying column definition	7
Alter table definitions	7
Drop, rename and truncate tables	7
Including Constraints	**7**
Describe constraints	7
Create and maintain constraints	7
Creating Views	**8**
Describe a view	8
Create, alter the definition, and drop a view	8
Retrieve data through a view	8
Insert, update and delete data through a view	8
Create and use an inline view	8
Perform Top 'N' Analysis	8
Creating Other Database Objects	**9**
Create, maintain and use sequences	9
Create and maintain indexes	9
Create private and public synonyms	9
Controlling User Access	**10**
Create users	10
Create Roles to ease setup and maintenance of the security model	10
Use the GRANT and REVOKE statements to grant and revoke object privileges	10

Exam objectives are subject to change at any time without prior notice and at Oracle's sole discretion. Please visit Oracle's Certification website (`http://www.oracle.com/education/certification/`) for the most current exam objectives listing.

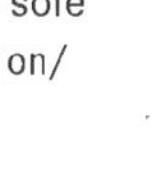

OCA/OCP: Introduction to Oracle9i SQL

Study Guide

OCA/OCP: Introduction to Oracle9i™ SQL

Study Guide

Chip Dawes

Biju Thomas

San Francisco • London

Associate Publishers: Richard Mills and Neil Edde
Acquisitions Editor: Christine McGeever
Developmental Editor: Elizabeth Hurley
Editors: Marilyn Smith and Carol Henry
Production Editor: Leslie E. H. Light
Technical Editors: Ashok Hanumanth and Damir Bersinic
Graphic Illustrator: Tony Jonick
Electronic Publishing Specialist: Jill Niles
Proofreaders: Emily Hsuan, David Nash, Laurie O'Connell, and Nancy Riddiough
Indexer: Ted Laux
CD Coordinator: Dan Mummert
CD Technician: Kevin Ly
Book Designer: Bill Gibson
Cover Designer: Archer Design
Cover Photographer: Photo Researchers

Library of Congress Card Number: 2001099188

ISBN: 0-7821-4062-9

Manufactured in the United States of America

10 9 8 7 6

To Our Valued Readers:

In a CertCities.com article dated December 15, 2001, Oracle certification was ranked #2 in a list of the "10 Hottest Certifications for 2002." This shouldn't come as a surprise, especially when you consider the fact that the OCP program nearly tripled in size (from 30,000 to 80,000) in the last year. Oracle continues to expand its dominance in the database market, and as companies begin integrating Oracle9i systems into their IT infrastructure, you can be assured of high demand for professionals with the Oracle Certified Associate and Oracle Certified Professional certifications.

Sybex is proud to have helped thousands of Oracle certification candidates prepare for the exams over the years, and we are excited about the opportunity to continue to provide professionals like you with the skills needed to succeed in the highly competitive IT industry.

Our authors and editors have worked hard to ensure that the Oracle9i Study Guide you hold in your hands is comprehensive, in-depth, and pedagogically sound. We're confident that this book will meet and exceed the demanding standards of the certification marketplace and help you, the Oracle9i certification candidate, succeed in your endeavors.

Good luck in pursuit of your Oracle9i certification!

Neil Edde
Associate Publisher—Certification
Sybex, Inc.

SYBEX Inc. 1151 Marina Village Parkway, Alameda, CA 94501
Tel: 510/523-8233 Fax: 510/523-2373 HTTP://www.sybex.com

Software License Agreement: Terms and Conditions

The media and/or any online materials accompanying this book that are available now or in the future contain programs and/or text files (the "Software") to be used in connection with the book. SYBEX hereby grants to you a license to use the Software, subject to the terms that follow. Your purchase, acceptance, or use of the Software will constitute your acceptance of such terms.

The Software compilation is the property of SYBEX unless otherwise indicated and is protected by copyright to SYBEX or other copyright owner(s) as indicated in the media files (the "Owner(s)"). You are hereby granted a single-user license to use the Software for your personal, noncommercial use only. You may not reproduce, sell, distribute, publish, circulate, or commercially exploit the Software, or any portion thereof, without the written consent of SYBEX and the specific copyright owner(s) of any component software included on this media.

In the event that the Software or components include specific license requirements or end-user agreements, statements of condition, disclaimers, limitations or warranties ("End-User License"), those End-User Licenses supersede the terms and conditions herein as to that particular Software component. Your purchase, acceptance, or use of the Software will constitute your acceptance of such End-User Licenses.

By purchase, use or acceptance of the Software you further agree to comply with all export laws and regulations of the United States as such laws and regulations may exist from time to time.

Reusable Code in This Book

The authors created reusable code in this publication expressly for reuse for readers. Sybex grants readers permission to reuse for any purpose the code found in this publication or its accompanying CD-ROM so long as all of the authors are attributed in any application containing the reusable code, and the code itself is never sold or commercially exploited as a stand-alone product.

Software Support

Components of the supplemental Software and any offers associated with them may be supported by the specific Owner(s) of that material, but they are not supported by SYBEX. Information regarding any available support may be obtained from the Owner(s) using the information provided in the appropriate read.me files or listed elsewhere on the media.

Should the manufacturer(s) or other Owner(s) cease to offer support or decline to honor any offer, SYBEX bears no responsibility. This notice concerning support for the Software is provided for your information only. SYBEX is not the agent or principal of the Owner(s), and SYBEX is in no way responsible for providing any support for the Software, nor is it liable or responsible for any support provided, or not provided, by the Owner(s).

Warranty

SYBEX warrants the enclosed media to be free of physical defects for a period of ninety (90) days after purchase. The Software is not available from SYBEX in any other form or media than that enclosed herein or posted to `www.sybex.com`. If you discover a defect in the media during this warranty period, you may obtain a replacement of identical format at no charge by sending the defective media, postage prepaid, with proof of purchase to:

SYBEX Inc.
Product Support Department
1151 Marina Village Parkway
Alameda, CA 94501
Web: http://www.sybex.com

After the 90-day period, you can obtain replacement media of identical format by sending us the defective disk, proof of purchase, and a check or money order for $10, payable to SYBEX.

Disclaimer

SYBEX makes no warranty or representation, either expressed or implied, with respect to the Software or its contents, quality, performance, merchantability, or fitness for a particular purpose. In no event will SYBEX, its distributors, or dealers be liable to you or any other party for direct, indirect, special, incidental, consequential, or other damages arising out of the use of or inability to use the Software or its contents even if advised of the possibility of such damage. In the event that the Software includes an online update feature, SYBEX further disclaims any obligation to provide this feature for any specific duration other than the initial posting.

The exclusion of implied warranties is not permitted by some states. Therefore, the above exclusion may not apply to you. This warranty provides you with specific legal rights; there may be other rights that you may have that vary from state to state. The pricing of the book with the Software by SYBEX reflects the allocation of risk and limitations on liability contained in this agreement of Terms and Conditions.

Shareware Distribution

This Software may contain various programs that are distributed as shareware. Copyright laws apply to both shareware and ordinary commercial software, and the copyright Owner(s) retains all rights. If you try a shareware program and continue using it, you are expected to register it. Individual programs differ on details of trial periods, registration, and payment. Please observe the requirements stated in appropriate files.

Copy Protection

The Software in whole or in part may or may not be copy-protected or encrypted. However, in all cases, reselling or redistributing these files without authorization is expressly forbidden except as specifically provided for by the Owner(s) therein.

To my wife, Mary
—Chip Dawes

To my son Joshua, the new light in my life
—Biju Thomas

Acknowledgments

I would like to acknowledge Jerie Dahlman for her help with many of the questions used in this book. Many thanks to the Sybex team—Elizabeth Hurley, Leslie Light, and Marilyn Smith—your skill and efforts have made for a fine book. Lastly, thank you to my family— Mary, Zachary, and Charlie—for giving me the support I needed to complete this book.

—Chip Dawes

Within a couple of days of Oracle announcing the beta exams for Oracle9i certification, Sybex contacted me to inquire about my interest in another project. I'm impressed by the market awareness of Sybex and thank Sybex for considering me for this project.

I would like to thank the following wonderful people at Sybex for their support and patience. Christine McGeever (Acquisition Editor) for getting me started on this project. Her timely call helped me register for the Oracle9i beta exams and get my Oracle9i certification, even before the exams were in production. Elizabeth Hurley (Development Editor) for her support and valuable comments. Leslie Light (Production Editor) for her patience and understanding, and making sure every piece of the book ties together and also keeping us on schedule. I know many more people from Sybex contributed to this book; I thank each one of them for their hard work and the high quality of that work.

I owe Marilyn Smith (Editor) for her hard work. Marilyn, your edits and topic rearrangements definitely improved the quality of the chapters. Thank you. I thank Carol Henry for her edits and comments. I thank Ashok Hanumanth and Damir Bersinic for their technical review and valuable comments. Thank you Chip for your ideas and suggestions, and for taking time to reply to most of the reader comments.

It would not have been possible for me to participate in this project if my parents had not come over to the U.S. from India, to take care of our son Joshua. I thank my parents for taking care of the baby and house for the past five months. Thank you Shiji for your endless support and love.

Last, but not least, I thank my colleagues for their support and friendship. Thank you Wendy for understanding me so well and all the help you provided. Thank you all— you are the best to work with.

—Biju Thomas

Contents at a Glance

Contents

Introduction

There is high demand for professionals in the information technology (IT) industry, and Oracle certifications are the hottest credential in the database world. You have made the right decision to pursue certification, because being Oracle certified will give you a distinct advantage in this highly competitive market.

Many readers may already be familiar with Oracle and do not need an introduction to the Oracle database world. For those who aren't familiar with the company, Oracle, founded in 1977, sold the first commercial relational database and is now the world's leading database company and second-largest independent software company, with revenues of more than $10 billion, serving more than 145 countries.

Oracle databases are the de facto standard for large Internet sites, and Oracle advertisers are boastful but honest when they proclaim, "The Internet Runs on Oracle." Almost all big Internet sites run Oracle databases. Oracle's penetration of the database market runs deep and is not limited to dot-com implementations. Enterprise resource planning (ERP) application suites, data warehouses, and custom applications at many companies rely on Oracle. The demand for DBA resources remains higher than others during weak economic times.

This book is intended to help you on your exciting path toward becoming an Oracle9i Oracle Certified Associate (OCA), which is the first step on the path toward Oracle Certified Professional (OCP) and Oracle Certified Master (OCM) certification. Basic knowledge of Oracle SQL is an advantage when reading this book but is not mandatory. Using this book and a practice database, you can start learning Oracle and pass the IZ0-007 test: Introduction to Oracle9i: SQL.

Why Become an Oracle Certified Professional?

The number one reason to become an OCP is to gain more visibility and greater access to the industry's most challenging opportunities. Oracle certification is the best way to demonstrate your knowledge and skills in Oracle database systems. The certification tests are scenario-based, which is the most effective way to assess your hands-on expertise and critical problem-solving skills.

Certification is proof of your knowledge and shows that you have the skills required to support Oracle core products. The Oracle certification program can help a company to identify proven performers who have demonstrated their skills and who can support the company's investment in Oracle technology. It demonstrates that you have a solid understanding of your job role and the Oracle products used in that role.

OCPs are among the best paid in the IT industry. Salary surveys consistently show the OCP certification to yield higher salaries than other certifications, including Microsoft, Novell, and Cisco.

So, whether you are beginning a career, changing careers, securing your present position, or seeking to refine and promote your position, this book is for you!

Oracle Certifications

Oracle certifications follow a track that is oriented toward a job role. There are database administration, database operator, and developer tracks. Within each track, Oracle has a three-tiered certification program:

- The first tier is the Oracle Certified Associate (OCA). OCA certification typically requires you to complete two exams, the first via the Internet and the second in a proctored environment.
- The second tier is the Oracle Certified Professional (OCP), which builds upon and requires an OCA certification. The additional requirements for OCP certification are additional proctored exams.
- The third, and highest, tier is the Oracle Certified Master (OCM). OCM certification builds upon and requires OCP certification. To achieve OCM certification, you must attend two advanced Oracle Education classroom courses (from a specific list of qualifying courses) and complete a practicum exam.

The following material will address only the database administration track, because at the time of this writing, it was the only 9i track offered by Oracle. The other tracks have 8 and 8i certifications and will undoubtedly have 9i certifications. See the Oracle website at `http://www.oracle.com/education/certification` for the latest information.

Oracle9i Certified Database Associate

The role of the database administrator (DBA) has become a key to success in today's highly complex database systems. The best DBAs work behind the scenes, but are in the spotlight when critical issues arise. They plan, create, maintain, and ensure that the database is available for the business. They are always watching the database for performance issues and to prevent unscheduled downtime. The DBA's job requires broad understanding of the architecture of Oracle database and expertise in solving problems.

The Oracle9i Certified Database Associate is the entry-level certification for the database administration track and is required to advance toward the more senior certification tiers. This certification requires you to pass two exams that demonstrate your knowledge of Oracle basics:

- 1Z0-007: Introduction to Oracle9i: SQL
- 1Z0-031: Oracle9i Database: Fundamentals I

The 1Z0-007 exam, Introduction to Oracle9i: SQL, is offered on the Internet. The 1Z0-031 exam, Oracle9i Database: Fundamentals I, is offered at a Sylvan Prometric facility.

Oracle9i Certified Database Administrator

The OCP tier of the database administration track challenges you to demonstrate your continuing experience and knowledge of Oracle technologies. The Oracle9i Certified Database Administrator certification requires achievement of the Certified Database Associate tier, as well as passing the following two exams at a Sylvan Prometric facility:

- 1Z0-032: Oracle9i Database: Fundamentals II
- 1Z0-033: Oracle9i Database: Performance Tuning

Oracle9i Certified Master

The Oracle9i Certified Master is the highest level of certification that Oracle offers. To become a certified master, you must first achieve Certified Database Administrator status, then complete two advanced instructor-led classes at an Oracle education facility, and finally pass a hands-on exam at Oracle Education. The classes and practicum exam are offered only at an

Oracle education facility and may require travel. The advanced classes that will count toward your OCM requirement include the following:

- Oracle9i: Program with PL/SQL
- Oracle9i: Advanced PL/SQL
- Oracle9i: SQL Tuning Workshop
- Oracle9i: High Availability in an Internet Environment
- Oracle9i: Database: Implement Partitioning
- Oracle9i: Real Application Clusters Implementation
- Oracle9i: Data Warehouse Administration
- Oracle9i: Advanced Replication
- Oracle9i: Enterprise Manager

More Information

The most current information about Oracle certification can be found at `http://www.oracle.com/education/certification`. Follow the Certification link and choose the track that you are interested in. Read the Candidate Guide for the test objectives and test contents, and keep in mind that they can change at any time without notice.

OCA/OCP Study Guides

The Oracle9i database administration track certification consists of four tests: two for OCA level and two more for OCP level. Sybex offers several study guides to help you achieve these certifications:

- *OCA/OCP: Introduction to Oracle9i™ SQL Study Guide* (exam 1Z0-007: Introduction to Oracle9i: SQL)
- *OCA/OCP: Oracle9i™ DBA Fundamentals I Study Guide* (exam 1Z0-031: Oracle9i Database: Fundamentals I)
- *OCP: Oracle9i™ DBA Fundamentals II Study Guide* (exam 1Z0-032: Oracle9i Database: Fundamentals II)
- *OCP: Oracle9i™ DBA Performance Tuning Study Guide* (exam 1Z0-033: Oracle9i Database: Performance Tuning)

Additionally, these four books are offered in a boxed set: *OCP: Oracle9i™ DBA Certification Kit.*

Skills Required for DBA Certification

To pass the certification exams, you need to master the following skills:

- Write SQL SELECT statements that display data from either single or multiple tables.
- Restrict, sort, aggregate, and manipulate data using both single and group functions.
- Create and manage tables, views, constraints, synonyms, sequences, and indexes.
- Create users and roles to control user access and maintain security.
- Understand Oracle Server architecture (database and instance).
- Understand the physical and logical storage of the database, and be able to manage space allocation and growth.
- Manage data, including its storage, loading, and reorganization.
- Manage redo logs, automatic undo, and rollback segments.
- Use globalization features to choose a database character set and National Language Support (NLS) parameters.
- Configure Net8 on the server side and the client side.
- Use backup and recovery options.
- Archive redo log files and hot backups.
- Perform backup and recovery operations using Recovery Manager (RMAN).
- Use data dictionary views and set database parameters.
- Configure and use multithreaded server (MTS) and Connection Manager.
- Identify and tune database and SQL performance.
- Use the tuning/diagnostics tools STATSPACK, TKPROF, and EXPLAIN PLAN.
- Tune the size of data blocks, the shared pool, the buffer caches, and rollback segments.
- Diagnose contention for latches, locks, and rollback segments.

Tips for Taking the OCP Exam

Use the following tips to help you prepare for and pass each exam.

- Each OCP test contains about 60–80 questions to be completed in 90 minutes. Answer the questions you know first, so that you do not run out of time.
- Many questions on the exam have answer choices that at first glance look identical. Read the questions carefully. Do not just jump to conclusions. Make sure that you clearly understand exactly what each question asks.
- Most of the test questions are scenario-based. Some of the scenarios contain nonessential information and exhibits. You need to be able to identify what's important and what's not important.
- Do not leave any questions unanswered. There is no negative scoring. After selecting an answer, you can mark a difficult question or one that you're unsure of and come back to it later.
- When answering questions that you are not sure about, use a process of elimination to get rid of the obviously incorrect answers first. Doing this greatly improves your odds if you need to make an educated guess.
- If you're not sure of your answer, mark it for review and then look for other questions that may help you eliminate any incorrect answers. At the end of the test, you can go back and review the questions that you marked for review.

Where Do You Take the Exam?

You take the Introduction to Oracle9i: SQL exam (1Z0-007) via the Internet. To register for an online Oracle certification exam, you will need an Internet connection of at least 33Kbps, but a 56Kbps, LAN, or broadband connection is recommended. You will also need either Internet Explorer 5.0 (or above) or Netscape 4.*x* (Oracle does not recommend Netscape 5.*x* or 6.*x*). At the time of this writing, the online 1Z0-007 exam is $90. If you do not have a credit card to use for payment, you will need to contact Oracle to purchase a voucher. You can pay with a certification voucher, promotional code, or credit card.

You may take the other exams at any of the more than 800 Sylvan Prometric Authorized Testing Centers around the world. For the location of a testing center near you, call 1-800-891-3926. Outside the United States and Canada, contact your local Sylvan Prometric Registration Center. Usually, the tests can be taken in any order.

To register for a proctored Oracle Certified Professional exam at a Sylvan Prometric test center:

- Determine the number of the exam you want to take.
- Register with Sylvan Prometric online at `http://www.2test.com` or in North America, by calling 1-800-891-EXAM (800-891-3926). At this point, you will be asked to pay in advance for the exam. At the time of this writing, the exams are $125 each and must be taken within one year of payment.
- When you schedule the exam, you'll get instructions regarding all appointment and cancellation procedures, the ID requirements, and information about the testing-center location.

You can schedule exams up to six weeks in advance or as soon as one working day before the day you wish to take it. If something comes up and you need to cancel or reschedule your exam appointment, contact Sylvan Prometric at least 24 hours in advance.

What Does This Book Cover?

This book covers everything you need to pass the Introduction to Oracle9i: SQL exam. This exam is part of the Oracle9i Certified Database Associate certification tier in the database administration track. It teaches you the basics of Oracle and SQL. Each chapter begins with a list of exam objectives.

Chapter 1 Starts with the fundamentals of SQL and describes how to construct simple queries.

Chapter 2 Discusses SQL*Plus, Oracle's tool to interact with the database.

Chapter 3 Discusses the single-row functions available in Oracle, with details on how and where to use them.

Chapter 4 Explains data aggregations, Oracle's built-in group functions, and nesting of functions.

Chapter 5 Explains how data from multiple tables can be combined via joins and subqueries.

Chapter 6 Explores how to manipulate data—adding, combining, and removing data from tables. This chapter also covers how transaction control works.

Chapter 7 Discusses creating tables with the various datatypes and options available to store data.

Chapter 8 Describes how to create and manage views.

Chapter 9 Discusses database objects other than tables or views, including sequences, synonyms, and indexes.

Chapter 10 Covers security and user access, including user account maintenance and the different types of Oracle privileges.

Each chapter ends with Review Questions that are specifically designed to help you retain the knowledge presented. To really nail down your skills, read and answer each question carefully.

How to Use This Book

This book can provide a solid foundation for the serious effort of preparing for the OCA database administration exam track. To best benefit from this book, use the following study method:

1. Take the Assessment Test immediately following this introduction. (The answers are at the end of the test.) Carefully read over the explanations for any questions you get wrong, and note which chapters the material comes from. This information should help you plan your study strategy.

2. Study each chapter carefully, making sure that you fully understand the information and the test objectives listed at the beginning of each chapter. Pay extra close attention to any chapter related to questions you missed in the Assessment Test.

3. Complete all hands-on exercises in the chapter, referring to the chapter so that you understand the reason for each step you take. If you do not have an Oracle database available, be sure to study the examples carefully. Answer the Review Questions related to that chapter. (The answers appear at the end of each chapter, after the "Review Questions" section.)

4. Note the questions that confuse or trick you, and study those sections of the book again.

5. Before taking the exam, try your hand at the two bonus Practice Exams that are included on the CD that comes with this book. The questions on these exams appear only on the CD. This will give you a complete overview of what you can expect to see on the real test.

6. Remember to use the other products on the CD included with this book. The electronic flashcards and the EdgeTest exam preparation software have been specifically designed to help you study for and pass your exam. The electronic flashcards can be used on your Windows computer or on your Palm device.

To learn all the material covered in this book, you'll need to apply yourself regularly and with discipline. Try to set aside the same time period every day to study, and select a comfortable and quiet place to do so. If you work hard, you will be surprised at how quickly you learn this material. All the best!

What's on the CD?

We have worked hard to provide some really great tools to help you with your certification process. All of the following tools should be loaded on your workstation when you're studying for the test.

The EdgeTest for Oracle Certified DBA Preparation Software

Provided by EdgeTek Learning Systems, this test-preparation software prepares you to pass the Introduction to Oracle9i: SQL exam. In this test, you will find all of the questions from the book, plus two bonus Practice Exams that appear exclusively on the CD. You can take the Assessment Test, test yourself by chapter, take one or both of the Practice Exams, or take an exam randomly generated from all of the questions.

Electronic Flashcards for PC and Palm Devices

After you read the *OCA/OCP: Introduction to Oracle9i SQL Study Guide*, read the Review Questions at the end of each chapter, and study the Practice Exams included on the CD. But wait, there's more! Test yourself with the flashcards included on the CD. If you can get through these difficult questions and understand the answers, you'll know that you're ready for the exam.

The flashcards include 150 questions specifically written to hit you hard and make sure you are ready for the exam. Between the Review Questions, Practice Exams, and flashcards, you should be more than prepared for the exam.

OCA/OCP: Introduction to Oracle9i SQL Study Guide in PDF

Sybex offers this Oracle certification book on the CD so you can read the book on your PC or laptop. It is in Adobe Acrobat format. Acrobat Reader 5 is also included on the CD. This will be extremely helpful to readers who fly or commute on a bus or train and don't want to carry a book, as well as to readers who find it more comfortable reading from their computer.

How to Contact the Authors

You can reach Chip Dawes through D & D Technologies, Inc. (`www.ddtechnologies.com`)—a Chicago-based consultancy—or e-mail him at `chip@ddtechnologies.com`.

To contact Biju Thomas, you can e-mail him at `biju@bijoos.com` or visit his website for DBAs at `www.bijoos.com/oracle`.

Assessment Test

1. Which operator will be evaluated first in the following SELECT statement?

   ```
   SELECT (2+3*4/2-5) FROM dual;
   ```

   A. +

   B. *

   C. /

   D. -

2. Which line of the following code has an error?

   ```
   SELECT *
   FROM emp
   WHERE comm = NULL
   ORDER BY ename;
   ```

   A. SELECT *

   B. FROM emp

   C. WHERE comm = NULL

   D. There is no error in this statement.

3. Which two statements are true about NULL values?

   A. You cannot search for a NULL value in a column using the WHERE clause.

   B. If a NULL value is returned in the subquery or if NULL is included in the list when using a NOT IN operator, no rows will be returned.

   C. Only = and != operators can be used to search for NULL values in a column.

   D. In an ascending order sort, NULL values appear at the bottom of the result set.

   E. Concatenating a NULL value to a non-NULL string results in a NULL.

4. Which components are required to run iSQL*Plus from your PC? (Choose all that apply.)

   A. SQL*Plus installed on the PC

   B. Oracle Net on the PC

   C. HTTP Server

   D. iSQL*Plus Server

5. When you use the `DEFINE` *`variable`* command, what datatype is the variable?

   A. VARCHAR2

   B. CHAR

   C. LONG

   D. NUMBER

   E. None of the above; you must specify the datatype along with the variable.

6. Which function can return a non-`NULL` value if passed `NULL` arguments?

   A. `NULLIF`

   B. `LENGTH`

   C. `CONCAT`

   D. `INSTR`

   E. `TAN`

7. Using the following EMP table, you need to increase everyone's salary by 5 percent of their combined salary and bonus. Which of the following statements will achieve the desired results?

Column Name	emp_id	name	salary	bonus
Key Type	pk	pk		
NULLs/Unique	NN	NN	NN	
FK Table				
Datatype	VARCHAR2	VARCHAR2	NUMBER	NUMBER
Length	9	50	11,2	11,2

A. `UPDATE emp SET salary = (salary + bonus)*1.05;`

B. `UPDATE emp SET salary = salary*1.05 + bonus*1.05;`

C. `UPDATE emp SET salary = salary + (salary + bonus)*0.05;`

D. A, B, and C will achieve the desired results.

E. None of these statements will achieve the desired results.

8. The following statement will raise an exception on which line?

```
select dept_name, avg(all salary)
      ,count(*) "number of employees"
from emp , dept
where deptno = dept_no
  and count(*) > 5
group by dept_name
order by 2 desc;
```

A. `select dept_name, avg(all salary), count(*) "number of employees"`

B. `where deptno = dept_no`

C. `and count(*) > 5`

D. `group by dept_name`

E. `order by 2 desc;`

9. Your HR department wants to recognize the most senior employees in each department. You need to produce a report with the following requirements:

   - Display each department ID
   - For each department, show the earliest hire date
   - Show how many employees from each department were hired on the earliest hire date

   Will all three requirements be met with the following SQL statement?

```
select department_id
      ,min(hire_date)
      ,count(*)
   keep (dense_rank last order by hire_date asc)
from hr.employees
group by department_id;
```

A. The statement meets all three requirements.

B. The statement meets two of the three requirements.

C. The statement meets one of the three requirements.

D. The statement meets none of the three requirements.

E. The statement will raise an exception.

10. The DEPT table has the following data.

```
SQL> SELECT * FROM dept;

    DEPTNO DNAME          LOC
---------- -------------- ----------
        10 ACCOUNTING     NEW YORK
        20 RESEARCH       DALLAS
        30 SALES          CHICAGO
        40 OPERATIONS     BOSTON
```

Consider this INSERT statement:

```
INSERT INTO (SELECT * FROM dept WHERE deptno = 10)
VALUES (50, 'MARKETING', 'FORT WORTH');
```

Choose the best answer.

A. The INSERT statement is invalid; a valid table name is missing.

B. 50 is not a valid DEPTNO value, since the subquery limits DEPTNO to 10.

C. The statement will work without error.

D. A subquery and a VALUES clause cannot appear together.

11. At a minimum, how many join conditions should there be to avoid a Cartesian join if there are three tables in the FROM clause?

A. 1

B. 2

C. 3

D. There is no minimum.

12. Which two of the following queries is valid syntax that would return all rows from the EMPLOYEES and DEPARTMENTS tables, even if there are no corresponding/related rows in the other table.

A.
```
SELECT last_name, first_name, department_name
FROM   employees e FULL JOIN departments d
ON     e.department_id = d.department_id;
```

B.
```
SELECT last_name, first_name, department_name
FROM   employees e OUTER JOIN departments d
ON     e.department_id = d.department_id;
```

C.
```
SELECT e.last_name, e.first_name, d.department_name
FROM   employees e
LEFT OUTER JOIN departments d
ON     e.department_id = d.department_id
RIGHT OUTER JOIN employees f
ON     f.department_id = d.department_id;
```

D.
```
SELECT e.last_name, e.first_name, d.department_name
FROM   employees e
CROSS JOIN departments d
ON     e.department_id = d.department_id;
```

E.
```
SELECT last_name, first_name, department_name
FROM   employees
FULL OUTER JOIN departments USING (department_id);
```

13. Why does the following statement fail?

```
CREATE TABLE FRUITS&VEGETABLES
( NAME VARCHAR2 (40));
```

A. The table should have more than one column defined.

B. NAME is a reserved word, which cannot be used as a column name.

C. The table name is invalid.

D. Column length cannot exceed 30 characters.

14. Which datatype stores data outside the Oracle database?

A. UROWID

B. BFILE

C. BLOB

D. NCLOB

E. EXTERNAL

15. Which of the following statements are true? (Choose all that apply.)

A. Primary key constraints allow `NULL` values in the columns.

B. Unique key constraints allow `NULL` values in the columns.

C. Primary key constraints do not allow `NULL` values in columns.

D. A nonunique index cannot be used to enforce a primary key constraint.

16. Which operation cannot be performed using the `ALTER TABLE` statement?

A. Rename table

B. Rename column

C. Drop column

D. Drop `NOT NULL` constraint

17. INTERVAL datatypes store a period of time. Which components are included in the INTERVAL DAY TO SECOND column? (Choose all that apply.)

A. Years

B. Quarters

C. Months

D. Days

E. Hours

F. Minutes

G. Seconds

H. Fractional seconds

18. Which of the following statements are true? (Choose all that apply.)

A. The TRUNCATE statement is used to selectively remove rows from table.

B. The TRUNCATE statement is used to remove all rows from a table.

C. Rows removed using the TRUNCATE command cannot be undone (rolled back).

D. The TRUNCATE statement drops the constraints and triggers associated with the table.

E. The TRUNCATE statement invalidates all the constraints and triggers associated with the table.

19. Which data dictionary view holds information about the columns in a view?

A. USER_VIEWS

B. USER_VIEW_COLUMNS

C. USER_TAB_COLUMNS

D. USER_ALL_COLUMNS

20. The primary key of the STATE table is STATE_CD. The primary key of the CITY table is STATE_CD and CITY_CD. The STATE_CD column of the CITY table is the foreign key to the STATE table. There are no other constraints on these two tables. Consider the following view definition.

```
CREATE OR REPLACE VIEW state_city AS
SELECT a.state_cd, a.state_name, b.city_cd, b.city_name
FROM   state a, city b
WHERE  a.state_cd = b.state_cd;
```

Which of the following operations are permitted on the base tables of the view? (Choose all that apply.)

A. Insert a record into the CITY table

B. Insert a record into the STATE table

C. Update the STATE_CD column of the CITY table

D. Update the CITY_CD column of the CITY table

E. Update the CITY_NAME column of the CITY table

F. Update the STATE_NAME column of the STATE table

21. In Oracle9i, outer join syntax can be specified using the `LEFT JOIN` or `RIGHT JOIN` keywords or by using the (+) operator. Suppose that you have the two tables PRODUCTS and ORDERS. You need to get the ORDER# and PRODUCT# for all orders, even if there is no order placed for a particular product; that is, you want to get all of the rows from the PRODUCTS table. The PRODUCT# column is common to both tables. Which condition would return the desired result?

A. `WHERE PRODUCTS.PRODUCT# = ORDERS.PRODUCT#`

B. `WHERE PRODUCTS.PRODUCT#  (+) = ORDERS.PRODUCT#`

C. `WHERE PRODUCTS.PRODUCT# = ORDERS.PRODUCT# (+)`

D. `WHERE PRODUCTS.PRODUCT# (+) = ORDERS.PRODUCT# (+)`

22. Oracle9i supports the ISO SQL99 standard for specifying joins in queries. Which keywords are used to specify a Cartesian join using this syntax?

A. `NATURAL JOIN`

B. `CARTESIAN JOIN`

C. `OUTER JOIN`

D. `INNER JOIN`

E. `CROSS JOIN`

23. Outer joins in Oracle9i can be specified using the syntax `<table name> LEFT OUTER  JOIN <table name>`. Which keyword is optional?

A. `JOIN`

B. `OUTER`

C. `JOIN` and `OUTER`

D. None

24. The ORDERS table contains the following data:

```
select order_mode, sum(order_total)
from oe.orders
group by order_mode;

ORDER_MO SUM(ORDER_TOTAL)
-------- ----------------
direct          1903629.2
online          1764425.5
```

How much revenue will be inserted into the DIRECT_ORDERS table with the following SQL statement?

```
INSERT ALL
 WHEN order_mode='online' THEN
   INTO online_orders
    (customer_id, sales_rep_id, order_total)
    VALUES (customer_id, sales_rep_id, order_total)
 WHEN  order_mode ='direct' THEN
   INTO direct_orders
    (customer_id, sales_rep_id, order_total)
    VALUES (customer_id, sales_rep_id, order_total)
 WHEN  order_mode in ('online','direct') THEN
   INTO direct_orders
    (customer_id, sales_rep_id, order_total)
    VALUES (customer_id, sales_rep_id, order_total)
SELECT order_mode, customer_id, sales_rep_id,
    order_total
FROM orders;
```

A. 3668054.7

B. 1903629.2

C. 1764425.5

D. 5571683.9

25. With regard to the following SQL statements, which of the following options is most correct?

```
UPDATE emp
  SET salary = salary * 1.10
  WHERE class_code = 'A';
SAVEPOINT ClassA_FloorAdjusted;

UPDATE emp
  SET  salary = salary * 1.07
  WHERE class_code = 'B';
SAVEPOINT ClassB_FloorAdjusted;

UPDATE emp
  SET  salary = salary * 1.05
  WHERE class_code = 'C';
SAVEPOINT ClassC_FloorAdjusted;

ROLLBACK TO SAVEPOINT ClassB_FloorAdjusted;

UPDATE taxes
  SET max_tax = 76200*0.075
  WHERE tax_type = 'FICA';
SAVEPOINT MaxTax;

ROLLBACK to MaxTax;
ROLLBACK to ClassA_FloorAdjusted;

COMMIT;
```

A. No changes occur to the EMP table, but the TAXES table is changed.

B. Both the EMP and TAXES tables are changed.

C. Only EMP rows with CLASS_CODE equal to `'A'` are changed.

D. Only EMP rows with CLASS_CODES equal to `'C'` are changed.

E. No changes occur to either the EMP or the TAXES table.

26. You need to change employees in department 50 who have a job ID of 'ST_CLERK' to department 80 and to manager ID 145. Which option will best satisfy these requirements?

A.
```
update employees
set department_id = 80
and manager_id = 145
where department_id = 50
and job_id = 'ST_CLERK';
```

B.
```
update employees
set (department_id, manager_id) = (80, 145)
where department_id = 50
and job_id = 'ST_CLERK';
```

C.
```
update employees
set department_id = 80
   ,manager_id = 145
where department_id = 50
and job_id = 'ST_CLERK';
```

D. You need to use two UPDATE statements: one for DEPARTMENT_ID and one for MANAGER_ID.

27. The Marketing department has produced a master list of promotions for next month and placed it in table named NEW_PROMOTIONS. Some promotions are new and some have a new end date. You need to apply these promotions to the PROMOTIONS table using primary key PROMOTION_ID. Which statement best satisfies these requirements?

A.
```
update promotions p
set promo_end_date =
(select promo_end_date
from new_promotions np
where np.promo_id = p.promo_id);
```

B.
```
merge into promotions p using
(select promo_id, end_date
 from new_promotions) np
on (p.promo_id = np.promo_id)
when matched then update
set p.end_date = np.end_date
when not matched then insert
(select promo_id, end_date)
values (np.promo_id, np.end_date);
```

C.
```
upsert promotions p
with new_promotions np
on (p.promo_id = np.promo_id)
when matched then update
set p.end_date = np.end_date
when not matched then insert
(select promo_id, end_date)
values (np.promo_id, np.end_date);
```

D.
```
merge into promotions p using
(select promo_id, end_date
 from new_promotions) np
on (p.promo_id = np.promo_id)
if joined then update
set p.end_date = np.end_date
else insert
(select promo_id, end_date)
values (np.promo_id, np.end_date);
```

28. What order does Oracle use in resolving a table or view referenced in a SQL statement?

A. Table/view within user's schema, public synonym, private synonym

B. Table/view within user's schema, private synonym, public synonym

C. Public synonym, table/view within user's schema, private synonym

D. Private synonym, public synonym, table/view within user's schema

29. Which statement will assign the next number from the sequence EMP_SEQ to the variable EMP_KEY?

A. `emp_key := emp_seq.nextval;`

B. `emp_key := emp_seq.next_val;`

C. `emp_key := emp_seq.nextvalue;`

D. `emp_key := emp_seq.next_value;`

30. The table WKSYS.WK$CRAWLER_STAT has a B-tree index on the three columns WK$ITD, ID, and STAT_NAME. Which of the following statements could benefit from this index?

A.
```
insert into wk$crawler_stat
values (12,25,'timeout',NULL);
```

B.
```
delete from wh$crawler_stat where id = 25;
```

C.
```
select * from wk$crawler_stat
where wk$itd between 2 and 12;
```

D.
```
select * from wk$crawler_stat
where id = 25
  or stat_name like 'cache%';
```

31. Which of the following statements could use an index on the columns PRODUCT_ID and WAREHOUSE_ID of the OE.INVENTORIES table?

A.
```
select count(distinct warehouse_id)
from oe.inventories;
```

B.
```
select product_id, quantity_on_hand
from oe.inventories
where warehouse_id = 100;
```

C.
```
insert into oe.inventories values (5,100,32);
```

D. None of these statements could use the index

32. Which one of the following statements will succeed?

A.
```
grant create user, alter user to Katrina with admin
option;
```

B.
```
grant grant any privilege to Katrina with grant
option;
```

C.
```
grant create user, alter user to Katrina with grant
option;
```

D.
```
grant revoke any privilege to Katrina with admin
option;
```

33. What does the following statement do?

```
alter user effie identified by kerberos;
```

A. Creates user account effie

B. Changes the external authentication service for user effie

C. Makes effie a globally identified account

D. Changes user effie's password

34. Which of the following system privileges cannot be granted to a role?

A. `BECOME USER`

B. `UNLIMITED TABLESPACE`

C. `GRANT ANY ROLE`

D. `GRANT ANY PRIVILEGE`

35. User Rob granted `SELECT` on table OUTLN.OL$ to Chip `WITH GRANT OPTION`, and Chip has granted `SELECT` on OUTLN.OL$ to Ernie. Rob has also granted the DBA role to Chip `WITH ADMIN OPTION`, and Chip has granted DBA to Ernie. Chip leaves the department, and his account is dropped. Which privileges will Ernie still have if no other privileges are granted?

A. Both `SELECT` on table OUTLN.OL$ and DBA

B. Neither privilege

C. Only `SELECT` on table OUTLN.OL$

D. Only DBA

Answers to Assessment Test

1. B. In the arithmetic operators, unary operators are evaluated first, then multiplication and division, and finally addition and subtraction. The expression is evaluated from left to right. For more information about order of evaluation, see Chapter 1.

2. D. Although there is no error in this statement, the statement will not return the desired result. When a `NULL` is compared, you cannot use the = or != operators; you must use the `IS NULL` or `IS NOT NULL` operator. See Chapter 1 for more information about the comparison operators.

3. B, D. You can use the `IS NULL` or `IS NOT NULL` operator to search for `NULL`s or non-`NULL`s in a column. Since `NULL`s are sorted higher, they appear at the bottom of the result set in an ascending order sort. See Chapter 1 for more information about sorting `NULL` values.

4. C, D. iSQL*Plus architecture includes three layers. The client layer is the web browser. The middle layer has the HTTP Server, iSQL*Plus server, and Oracle Net. The third layer is the Oracle database. See Chapter 2 for more information.

5. B. Variables declared using the `DEFINE` command take the CHAR datatype. To assign a value to a variable, use `DEFINE` *`variable=value`*. See Chapter 2 for more information.

6. C. `CONCAT` will return a non-`NULL` if only one parameter is `NULL`. Both `CONCAT` parameters would need to be `NULL` for `CONCAT` to return `NULL`. The `NULLIF` function returns `NULL` if the two parameters are equal. The `LENGTH` of a `NULL` is `NULL`. `INSTR` will return `NULL` if `NULL` is passed in, and the tangent of a `NULL` is `NULL`. For more information about `NULL` values, see Chapter 3.

7. E. These statements don't account for possible `NULL` values in the BONUS column. For more information about `NULL` values, see Chapter 3.

8. C. Group functions cannot appear in the `WHERE` clause. To learn more about group functions, see Chapter 4.

9. B. The first two columns (lines 1 and 2) will meet the first two requirements, but the third column (lines 3 and 4) will report the number of employees with the most recent hire date. To report the number of employees with the oldest hire date, you need either `count(*) keep (dense_rank first order by hire_date asc)` or `count(*) keep (dense_rank last order by hire_date desc)`. See Chapter 4 for more information about group functions.

10. C. The statement will work without error. Option B would be correct if you used the `WITH CHECK OPTION` clause in the subquery. See Chapter 5 for more information about subqueries.

11. B. There should be at least *n*–1 join conditions when joining *n* tables to avoid a Cartesian join. To learn more about joins, see Chapter 5.

12. A, E. An outer join on both tables can be achieved using the `FULL OUTER JOIN` syntax. The join condition can be specified using the `ON` clause to specify the columns explicitly or using the `USING` clause to specify columns with common column names. Options B and D would result in errors. In option B, the join type is not specified; `OUTER` is an optional keyword. In option D, `CROSS JOIN` is used to get a Cartesian result, and Oracle9i does not expect a join condition. To learn more about joins, read Chapter 5.

13. C. Table and column names can have only letters, numbers, and three special characters: dollar sign ($), underscore (_), and pound sign (#). See Chapter 7 for more information about naming tables.

14. B. The BFILE datatype stores only the locator to an external file in the database; the actual data is stored as operating system files. BLOB, NCLOB, CLOB, and BFILE are the LOB datatypes in Oracle9i. EXTERNAL is not a valid datatype. See Chapter 7 for more information about datatypes.

15. B, C. Primary key and unique key constraints can be enforced using nonunique indexes. Unique keys allow `NULL` values in the columns, but a primary key does not. See Chapter 7 for more information about constraints.

16. B. You cannot rename a column in the table. To rename a column, you must re-create a table or create a view on the table with the new column name. See Chapter 7 for more information about modifying tables.

17. D, E, F, G, H. The INTERVAL DAY TO SECOND datatype is new to Oracle9i and is used to store an interval between two date/time components. See Chapter 7 for more information about Oracle9i datatypes.

18. B, C. You cannot specify a `WHERE` clause in the `TRUNCATE` statement; it removes all the rows in the table, releases the storage space (this is the default if you did not explicitly specify `KEEP STORAGE`), and does not drop or invalidate any of the dependent objects. See Chapter 6 for more information about the `TRUNCATE` statement.

19. C. USER_VIEWS shows the SQL used to create the view. The view columns are in the USER_TAB_COLUMNS view. The view USER_UPDATABLE_COLUMNS will show the columns of the view that can be updated. See Chapter 8 for more information about views.

20. D, E. In the join view, CITY is the key-preserved table. You can update the columns of the CITY table, except STATE_CD, because STATE_CD is not part of the view definition (the STATE_CD column in the view is from the STATE table). Since we did not include the STATE_CD column from the CITY table, no `INSERT` operations are permitted (STATE_CD is part of the primary key). If the view were defined as follows, all the columns of the CITY table would have been updatable, and new records could be inserted into the CITY table.

    ```
    CREATE OR REPLACE VIEW state_city AS
    SELECT b.state_cd, a.state_name, b.city_cd, b.city_name
    FROM   states a, cities b
    WHERE  a.state_cd = b.state_cd;
    ```

    See Chapter 8 for more information about views.

21. C. A (+) is specified after the column name of the table where there may not be a corresponding row. Since we want to get all rows from the PRODUCTS table, the outer-join operator is placed beside the column names of the ORDERS table. See Chapter 5 for more information about joins.

22. E. `CROSS JOIN` specifies a Cartesian join. A Cartesian join occurs when you do not have a common column to join two tables. All combinations of all rows from both tables will be retrieved. If Table A has *m* rows and Table B has *n* rows, a Cartesian join would retrieve $m \times n$ rows. See Chapter 5 for more information about Cartesian joins.

23. B. In specifying joins using SQL 1999 syntax, the `OUTER` and `INNER` keywords are optional. See Chapter 5 for more information about the ISO SQL99 syntax for joins.

24. D. The `ALL` clause tells Oracle to execute each and every `WHEN` clause it evaluates to `TRUE`. Two of the three `WHEN` clauses evaluate to `TRUE`. So, the DIRECT_ORDERS rows are inserted twice: in the second and third `WHEN` clause. Additionally, the ONLINE_ORDERS would be inserted in the third `WHEN` clause into the DIRECT_SALES table. To pass the certification exam, you must understand how to correctly interpret SQL to both identify problems and satisfy requirements. See Chapter 6 for more information about the `INSERT` statement.

25. C. Only CLASS_CODE `'A'` EMP rows are changed. The furthest we roll back is to the savepoint named ClassA_FloorAdjusted, so the only changes that are committed are those occurring before this savepoint (CLASS_CODE `'A'`) or after the rollback to savepoint (nothing). Chapter 6 discusses savepoints and rollbacks.

26. C. You can update multiple columns in a single `UPDATE` statement. The correct syntax to use when setting the columns to explicit values is to comma delimit each *`column = value`* clause. See Chapter 6 for more information on changing data with an `UPDATE` statement.

27. B. Option A will only update existing promotions, missing the new promotions. UPSERT appeared in marketing announcements of new Oracle9i features that are implemented via a MERGE statement. The correct syntax for the MERGE statement does not use an IF JOINED and ELSE construct; it uses a WHEN MATCHED and WHEN NOT MATCHED construct. See Chapter 6 for more information about modifying data with the MERGE statement.

28. B. Private synonyms override public synonyms, and tables or views owned by the user always resolve first. To learn more about synonyms, see Chapter 9.

29. A. This kind of question, which quizzes you on the precise syntax, really does appear on the exam. You'll need to know the correct spelling for sequence assignments. You can read about sequences in Chapter 9.

30. C. Indexes cannot improve the performance of INSERT statements. B-tree indexes can be used if a leading subset of columns is specified. A leading subset of columns for this index would need to include WK$ITD and optionally ID. Options B and D do not reference a leading subset of columns in the index. Option C is the only statement that references WK$ITD or a leading subset of indexed columns. You can read about indexes in Chapter 9.

31. A. The index contains all the information needed to satisfy the query in option A, and a full-index scan would be faster than a full-table scan. A leading subset of indexes columns is not specified in the WHERE clause of option B, and INSERT operations, as in option C, are slowed down by indexes. For more information on indexes, see Chapter 9.

32. A. The grant option cannot be used on system privileges, and `revoke any privilege` is not a valid privilege. For more information on privileges, see Chapter 10.

33. D. Option A would be possible in Oracle6, but the exam is on Oracle9i. The kerberos password is just there to obfuscate. Chapter 10 discusses authentication and user accounts.

34. B. UNLIMITED TABLESPACE is a special system privilege that must be granted to a user. BECOME USER is used for full database imports and comes standard as part of the IMP_FULL_DATABASE role. GRANT ANY ROLE and GRANT ANY PRIVILEGE have no restrictions on the grantee. Chapter 10 discusses system privileges and their restrictions.

35. D. Revocations of object privileges cascade, but system and role privilege revocations do not. The DBA role will remain after user Chip is dropped, but the object privilege SELECT on OUTLN.OL$ that Chip granted will be dropped when user Chip is dropped. For more information on database privileges, see Chapter 10.

Basic SQL SELECT Statements

INTRODUCTION TO ORACLE9i: SQL EXAM OBJECTIVES COVERED IN THIS CHAPTER:

✓ **Writing Basic SQL Select Statements**

- List the capabilities of SQL SELECT statements
- Execute a basic SELECT statement

✓ **Restricting and Sorting Data**

- Limit the rows retrieved by a query
- Sort the rows retrieved by a query

Exam objectives are subject to change at any time without prior notice and at Oracle's sole discretion. Please visit Oracle's Certification website (`http://www.oracle.com/education/certification/`) for the most current exam objectives listing.

The Oracle9i database provides many useful and powerful features. Many of the features are incorporated at the SQL level. SQL (pronounced "sequel") has been adopted by most relational database management systems (RDBMS). The American National Standards Institute (ANSI) has been refining standards for the SQL language for the past 20 years. Oracle, like many other companies, has taken the ANSI standard of SQL and extended it to include much additional functionality.

SQL is the basic language used to manipulate and retrieve data from the Oracle9i database. SQL is a nonprocedural language—it does not have programmatic constructs such as loop structures. PL/SQL is Oracle's procedural extension of SQL, and SQLJ allows embedded SQL operations in Java code. The scope of this test includes only SQL.

The SQL *SELECT* statement is used to query data from the database-storage structures, such as tables and views. In this chapter, you will learn how to write basic SQL statements to retrieve data from tables. You will also learn how to limit the information retrieved and to display the results in a specific order.

SQL Fundamentals

The basic structure of data storage in Oracle9i database is a table. A table consists of columns and its characteristics. Data is stored in the table as rows. Creating and maintaining tables are discussed in detail in Chapter 7, "Managing Tables and Constraints." To get started with SQL in this chapter, you will use the sample HR schema supplied with the Oracle9i database.

When you install Oracle software, choose the option to create a *seed database*. This database will have the sample schemas used in this book. The default IDs and password for the seed database are SYSTEM/MANAGER, SYS/CHANGE_ON_INSTALL. The account SYS is the Oracle dictionary owner, and SYSTEM is a DBA account. Initially, the sample schemas are locked. You need to connect to the database using SYSTEM, and then unlock the account using the `ALTER USER` statement. To unlock the HR schema, use `ALTER USER HR IDENTIFIED BY HRPASSWORD ACCOUNT UNLOCK;`. Now you can connect to the HR schema using the password HRPASSWORD.

SQL statements are like plain English but with specific syntax. SQL is a simple, yet powerful, language used to create, access, and manipulate data and structure in the database. SQL statements can be categorized as listed in Table 1.1.

TABLE 1.1 SQL Statement Categories

SQL Category	Description
Data Manipulation Language (DML)	Used to access, create, modify, or delete data in the existing structures of the database. DML statements include those to query information (`SELECT`), add new rows (`INSERT`), modify existing rows (`UPDATE`), delete existing rows (`DELETE`), perform a conditional update or insert operation (`MERGE`), see an execution plan of SQL (`EXPLAIN PLAN`), and lock a table to restrict access (`LOCK TABLE`).
Data Definition Language (DDL)	Used to define, alter, or drop database objects and their privileges. DDL statements include those to create, modify, drop, or rename objects (`CREATE`, `ALTER`, `DROP`, `RENAME`), remove all rows from a database object without dropping the structure (`TRUNCATE`), manage access privileges (`GRANT`, `REVOKE`), audit database use (`AUDIT`, `NOAUDIT`) and add a description about an object to the dictionary (`COMMENT`).

TABLE 1.1 SQL Statement Categories *(continued)*

SQL Category	Description
Transaction Control	Used to group a set of DML statements as a single transaction. Using these statements, you can save the changes (`COMMIT`) or discard the changes (`ROLLBACK`) made by DML statements. Also included in the transaction-control statements are statements to set a point or marker in the transaction for possible rollback (`SAVEPOINT`) and to define the properties for the transaction (`SET TRANSACTION`).
Session Control	Used to control the properties of a user session. (A *session* is the point from which you are connected to the database until you disconnect.) Session-control statements include those to control the session properties (`ALTER SESSION`) and to enable/disable roles (`SET ROLE`).
System Control	Used to manage the properties of the database. There is only one statement in this category (`ALTER SYSTEM`).

Table 1.1 provides an overview of all the statements that will be covered in this book. Do not worry if you do not understand certain terms, such as *role*, *session*, *privilege*, and so on. We will cover all the statements in the coming chapters with many examples. In this chapter, we will begin with writing simple statements to query the database (SELECT statements). But first, we need to review some SQL fundamentals.

Oracle Datatypes

When you create a table to store data in the database, you need to specify a datatype for all of the columns you define in the table. Oracle has many datatypes to suit application requirements. Oracle9i also supports ANSI and DB2 datatypes. The Oracle built-in datatypes can be broadly classified as shown in Table 1.2.

TABLE 1.2 Oracle Built-in Datatypes

Category	Datatypes
Character	CHAR, NCHAR, VARCHAR2, NVARCHAR2
Number	NUMBER
Long and raw	LONG, LONG RAW, RAW
Date and time	DATE, TIMESTAMP, TIMESTAMP WITH TIME ZONE, TIMESTAMP WITH LOCAL TIME ZONE, INTERVAL YEAR TO MONTH, INTERVAL DAY TO SECOND
Large object	CLOB, NCLOB, BCLOB, BFILE
Row ID	ROWID, UROWID

In this section, we will discuss only a few of the built-in datatypes to get started with SQL. All the datatypes and their usage are discussed in detail in Chapter 7.

CHAR(<*size*>)

The *CHAR* datatype is a fixed-length alphanumeric string, which has a maximum length in bytes. Data stored in CHAR columns is space-padded to fill the maximum length. Its size can range from a minimum of 1 byte to a maximum of 2000 bytes. The default size is 1.

When you create a column using the CHAR datatype, the database will ensure that all data placed in this column has the defined length. If the data is shorter than the defined length, it is space-padded on the right to the specified length. If the data is longer, an error is raised.

VARCHAR2(<*size*>)

The *VARCHAR2* datatype is a variable-length alphanumeric string, which has a maximum length in bytes. VARCHAR2 columns require only the amount of space needed to store the data and can store up to 4000 bytes. There is no default size for the VARCHAR2 datatype. An empty VARCHAR2(2000) column takes up as much room in the database as an empty VARCHAR2(2) column.

The default size of a CHAR datatype is 1. For a VARCHAR2 datatype, you must always specify the size.

The VARCHAR2 and CHAR datatypes have different comparison rules for trailing spaces. With the CHAR datatype, trailing spaces are ignored. With the VARCHAR2 datatype, trailing spaces are not ignored, and they sort higher than no trailing spaces. Here's an example:

CHAR datatype:	`'Yo' = 'Yo   '`
VARCHAR2 datatype:	`'Yo' < 'Yo   '`

NUMBER (<*p*>, <*s*>)

The *NUMBER* datatype stores numbers with a *precision* of *p* digits and a *scale* of *s* digits. The precision and scale values are optional. Numeric datatypes are used to store negative and positive integers, fixed-point numbers, and floating-point numbers. The precision can be between 1 and 38, and the scale has a range between –84 and 127. If the precision and scale are omitted, Oracle assumes the maximum of the range for both values.

You can have precision and scale digits in the integer part. The scale rounds the value after the decimal point to *s* digits. For example, if you define a column as NUMBER(5,2), the range of values you can store in this column is from –999.99 to 999.99; that is, 5–2=3 for the integer part, and the decimal part is rounded to two digits. Even if you do not include the decimal part for the value inserted, the maximum number you can store in a NUMBER(5,2) definition is 999.

Oracle will round numbers inserted into numeric columns with a scale smaller than the inserted number. For example, if a column were defined as NUMBER(4,2) and you specified a value of 12.125 to go into that column, the resulting number would be rounded to 12.13 before it was inserted into the column. If the value exceeds the precision, however, an Oracle error is returned. You cannot insert 123.1 into a column defined as NUMBER(4,2). Specifying the scale and precision does not force all inserted values to be a fixed length.

If the scale is negative, the number is rounded to the left of the decimal. Basically, a negative scale forces *s* number of zeros just to the left of the decimal.

If you specify a scale that is greater than the precision value, the precision defines the maximum number of digits to right of the decimal point after the zeros. For example, if a column is defined as NUMBER(3,5), the range of values you can store is from –0.00999 to 0.00999; that is, it requires two zeros (*s-p*) after the decimal point and rounds the decimal part to three digits (*p*) after zeros. Table 1.3 shows several examples of how numeric data is stored with various definitions.

TABLE 1.3 Precision and Scale Examples

Value	Datatype	Stored Value	Explanation
123.2564	NUMBER	123.2564	Range and precision are set to the maximum, so the datatype can store any value.
1234.9876	NUMBER(6,2)	1234.99	Since scale is only 2, the decimal part of the value is rounded to two digits.
12345.12345	NUMBER(6,2)	Error	The range of integer part is only from –9999 to 9999.
123456	NUMBER(6,2)	Error	Precision is larger than specified; range is only from –9999 to 9999.
1234.9876	NUMBER(6)	1235	Decimal part rounded to the next integer.
123456.1	NUMBER(6)	123456	Decimal part rounded.
12345.345	NUMBER(5,-2)	12300	Negative scale rounds the number <*s*> digits left to the decimal point. –2 rounds to hundreds.
1234567	NUMBER(5,-2)	1234600	Rounded to the nearest hundred.

TABLE 1.3 Precision and Scale Examples *(continued)*

Value	Datatype	Stored Value	Explanation
12345678	NUMBER(5,-2)	Error	Outside range; can have only five digits, excluding the two zeros representing hundreds, for a total of seven digits. (*s*-(-*p*)=*s*+*p*=5+2=7)
123456789	NUMBER(5,-4)	123460000	Rounded to nearest 10000.
1234567890	NUMBER(5,-4)	Error	Outside range; can have only five digits excluding the four trailing zeros.
12345.58	NUMBER(*, 1)	12345.6	Use of * in precision specifies the default limit (38).
0.1	NUMBER(4,5)	Error	Requires a zero after the decimal point (5–4=1)
0.01234567	NUMBER(4,5)	0.01235	Rounded to four digits after the decimal point and zero.
0.09999	NUMBER(4,5)	0.09999	Stored as it is; only four digits after the decimal point and zero.
0.099996	NUMBER(4,5)	Error	Rounding this value to four digits after the decimal and zero results in 0.1, which is outside the range.

DATE

The *DATE* datatype is used to store date and time information. This datatype can be converted to other forms for viewing, but it has a number of special functions and properties that make date manipulation and calculations simple. The time component of the DATE datatype has a resolution of one second—

no less. The DATE datatype occupies a storage space of seven bytes. The following information is contained within each DATE datatype:

- Century
- Year
- Month
- Day
- Hour
- Minute
- Second

Date values are inserted or updated in the database by converting either a numeric or character value into a DATE datatype using the function TO_DATE. Oracle defaults the format to display date as *DD-MON-YY*. This format shows that the default date must begin with a two-digit day, followed by a three-character abbreviation for the month, followed by a two-digit year. If you specify the date without including a time component, the time is defaulted to midnight, or 00:00:00 in military time. The *SYSDATE* function returns the current system date and time from the database server to which you're currently connected.

The default date format is specified using the initialization parameter NLS_DATE_FORMAT. The value of this parameter can be changed in the user's environment or in the user's session.

Operators and Literals

An *operator* is a manipulator that is applied to a data item in order to return a result. Special characters represent different operations in Oracle (+ represents addition, for example). Operators are commonly used in all programming environments, and you should already be familiar with the following operators, which may be classified into two types:

Unary operator *A unary operator* has only one operand. Examples are +2 and –5. They have the format *<operator><operand>*.

Binary operator A *binary operator* has two operands. Examples are 5+4 and 7*5. They have the format *<operand1><operator><operand2>*. You can insert spaces between the operand and operator to improve readability.

Arithmetic Operators

Arithmetic operators operate on numeric values. Table 1.4 shows the various arithmetic operators in Oracle and how to use them.

TABLE 1.4 Arithmetic Operators

Operator	Purpose	Example
+ -	Unary operators: Use to represent positive or negative data item. For positive items, the + is optional.	-234.44
+	Addition: Use to add two data items or expressions.	2+4
-	Subtraction: Use to find the difference between two data items or expressions.	20.4-2
*	Multiplication: Use to multiply two data items or expressions.	5*10
/	Division: Use to divide a data item or expression with another.	8.4/2

Do not use two hyphens (--) to represent double negation; use a space or parenthesis in between, as in -(-20). Two hyphens represent the beginning of a comment in SQL.

Concatenation Operator

The *concatenation operator* is used to concatenate or join two character (text) strings. The result of concatenation is another character string. Concatenating a zero-length string '' or a NULL with another string results in a string, not a NULL. Two vertical bars || are used as the concatenation operator.

Here are two examples:

- `'Oracle9i' || 'Database'` results in `'Oracle9iDatabase'`
- `'Oracle9i ' || 'Database'` results in `'Oracle9i Database'`

Set Operators

Set operators are used in compound queries—queries that combine the results of two queries. The number of columns selected in both queries must be the same. Table 1.5 lists the set operators and how to use them. Set operators are discussed in detail in Chapter 5, "Joins and Subqueries."

TABLE 1.5 Set Operators

Operator	Purpose
UNION	Returns all rows from either queries; no duplicate rows
UNION ALL	Returns all rows from either query, including duplicates
INTERSECT	Returns distinct rows that are returned by both queries
MINUS	Returns distinct rows that are returned by the first query but not returned by the second.

Operator Precedence

If multiple operators are used in the same expression, Oracle evaluates them in the *order of precedence* set in the database engine. Operators with higher precedence are evaluated before operators with lower precedence. Operators with the same precedence are evaluated from left to right. Table 1.6 lists the precedence.

TABLE 1.6 SQL Operator Precedence

Precedence	Operator	Purpose
1	- +	Unary operators, negation
2	* /	Multiplication, division
3	+ - ||	Addition, subtraction, concatenation

Using parentheses changes the order of precedence. The innermost parenthesis is evaluated first. In the expression 1+2*3, the result is 7, because 2*3 is evaluated first and the result is added to 1. In the expression (1+2)*3, 1+2 is evaluated first, and the result is multiplied by 3, giving 9.

Literals

Literals are values that represent a fixed value (constant). There are four types of literals:

- Text (or character)
- Integer
- Number
- Interval

You can use literals within many of the SQL functions, expressions, and conditions.

Text

The text literal must be enclosed in single quotation marks. Any character between the quotation marks is considered part of the text value. Oracle treats all text literals as though they were CHAR datatypes for comparison (blank padded). The maximum length of a text literal is 4000 bytes. Single quotation marks can be included in the literal text value by preceding it with another single quotation mark. Here are some examples of text literals:

- 'The Quick Brown Fox'
- 'That man''s suit is black'
- 'And I quote: "This will never do." '
- '12-SEP-2001'

Integer

Integer literals can be any number of numerals, excluding a decimal separator and up to 38 digits long. Here are two examples:

- 24
- –456

Number

Number literals can include scientific notation, as well as digits and the decimal separator. Here are some examples:

- 24
- –345.65
- 23E-10

Interval

Interval literals specify a period of time in terms of years and months or in terms of days and seconds. These literals correspond to the Oracle datatype INTERVAL YEAR TO MONTH and INTERVAL DAY TO SECOND. These datatypes will be discussed in more detail in Chapter 7.

Writing Simple Queries

A *query* is a request for information from the database tables. Simple queries are those that retrieve data from a single table. The basis of a query is the SELECT statement. Queries using multiple tables are discussed in later chapters.

Using the *SELECT* Statement

The SELECT statement is the most commonly used statement in SQL. It allows you to retrieve information already stored in the database. The statement begins with the keyword SELECT, followed by the column names whose data you want to query. You can either select information from all the columns (denoted by *) or name specific columns in the SELECT clause to retrieve data. The FROM clause provides the name of the table, view, or materialized view to use in the query. These objects are discussed in detail in later chapters. For simplicity, we will use tables for the rest of this chapter.

Let's use the JOBS table defined in the HR schema of the Oracle9i seed database created during installation. The JOBS table definition is provided in Table 1.7.

TABLE 1.7 JOBS Table Definition

Column Name	Datatype	length
JOB_ID	VARCHAR2	10
JOB_TITLE	VARCHAR2	30
MIN_SALARY	NUMBER	6,0
MAX_SALARY	NUMBER	6,0

The simple form of a SELECT statement to retrieve all the columns and rows from the JOBS table is as follows (only part of output result set is shown here):

```
SQL> SELECT * FROM jobs;

JOB_ID     JOB_TITLE                       MIN_SALARY MAX_SALARY
---------- ------------------------------- ---------- ----------
AD_PRES    President                            20000      40000
AD_VP      Administration Vice President        15000      30000
AD_ASST    Administration Assistant              3000       6000
FI_MGR     Finance Manager                       8200      16000
FI_ACCOUNT Accountant                            4200       9000
… … … … …
IT_PROG    Programmer                            4000      10000
MK_MAN     Marketing Manager                     9000      15000
MK_REP     Marketing Representative              4000       9000
HR_REP     Human Resources Representative        4000       9000
PR_REP     Public Relations Representative       4500      10500

19 rows selected.
SQL>
```

The keywords, column names, and table names are case insensitive. Only literals enclosed in single quotation marks are case sensitive in Oracle.

How do you list only the job title and minimum salary from this table? If you know the column names and the table name, writing the query is simple. Here, the column names are JOB_TITLE and MIN_SALARY, and the table name is JOBS. Execute the query by ending the query with a semicolon. In SQL*Plus, you can execute the query by entering a slash on a line by itself or by using the RUN command.

```
SQL> SELECT job_title, min_salary FROM jobs;

JOB_TITLE                           MIN_SALARY
----------------------------------- ----------
President                                20000
Administration Vice President            15000
Administration Assistant                  3000
Finance Manager                           8200
Accountant                                4200
Accounting Manager                        8200
Public Accountant                         4200
... ... ... ... ...
Programmer                                4000
Marketing Manager                         9000
Marketing Representative                  4000
Human Resources Representative            4000
Public Relations Representative           4500

19 rows selected.
SQL>
```

Notice that the numeric column (MIN_SALARY) is aligned to the right and the character column (JOB_TITLE) is aligned to the left. Does it seem that the column heading MIN_SALARY should be more meaningful? Well, you can provide a *column alias* to appear in the query results.

Column Alias Names

The column alias name is defined next to the column name with a space or by using the keyword AS. If you want a space in the column alias name, you must enclose it in double quotation marks. The case is preserved only when the alias name is enclosed in double quotation marks; otherwise, the display will be uppercase. The following example demonstrates using an alias name for the column heading in the previous query.

```
SQL> SELECT job_title AS Title,
  2  min_salary AS "Minimum Salary" FROM jobs
SQL> /

TITLE                               Minimum Salary
----------------------------------- --------------
President                                    20000
Administration Vice President                15000
Administration Assistant                      3000
Finance Manager                               8200
Accountant                                    4200
Accounting Manager                            8200
... ... ... ... ...
Programmer                                    4000
Marketing Manager                             9000
Marketing Representative                      4000
Human Resources Representative                4000
Public Relations Representative               4500

19 rows selected.
SQL>
```

In this listing, the column alias name Title appears in all capital letters because we did not enclose it in double quotation marks.

The asterisk (*) is used to select all columns in the table. This is very useful when you do not know the column names or when you are too lazy to type all of the column names.

Ensuring Uniqueness

The *DISTINCT* keyword (or UNIQUE keyword) following SELECT ensures that the resulting rows are unique. Uniqueness is verified against the complete row, not the first column. If you need to find the unique departments in the EMPLOYEES table, issue this query:

```
SQL> SELECT DISTINCT department_id FROM employees;

DEPARTMENT_ID
-------------
           10
           20
           30
           40
           50
           60
           70
           80
           90
          100
          110

12 rows selected.
SQL>
```

To demonstrate that uniqueness is enforced across the row, let's do one more query using the SELECT DISTINCT clause. Notice DEPARTMENT_ID repeating for each JOB_ID value.

```
SQL> SELECT DISTINCT department_id, job_id FROM employees;

DEPARTMENT_ID JOB_ID
------------- ----------
           10 AD_ASST
           20 MK_MAN
           20 MK_REP
           30 PU_CLERK
           30 PU_MAN
           40 HR_REP
           50 SH_CLERK
           50 ST_CLERK
           50 ST_MAN
```

```
… … … … …
            100 FI_ACCOUNT
            100 FI_MGR
            110 AC_ACCOUNT
            110 AC_MGR
                SA_REP

20 rows selected.
SQL>
```

SELECT * FROM TAB; shows all the tables and views in your schema.

The DUAL Table

The *DUAL table* is a dummy table available to all users in the database. It has one column and one row. The DUAL table is used to select system variables or to evaluate an expression. Here are a few examples:

```
SQL> SELECT SYSDATE, USER FROM dual;

SYSDATE   USER
--------- ------------------------------
18-SEP-02 HR

SQL> SELECT 'I''m ' || user || ' Today is ' || SYSDATE
  2  FROM dual;

'I''M'||USER||'TODAYIS'||SYSDATE
-----------------------------------------------------
I'm HR Today is 18-SEP-02
SQL>
```

SYSDATE and USER are built-in functions that provide information about the environment. These functions are discussed in Chapter 3, "Single-Row Functions."

Limiting Rows

A *WHERE* clause in the SELECT statement is used to limit the number of rows processed. Any logical conditions of the WHERE clause use the comparison operators. Rows are returned or operated upon where the data satisfies the logical condition(s) of the WHERE clause. You can use column names or expressions in the WHERE clause, but not column alias names. The WHERE clause follows the FROM clause in the SELECT statement.

How do you list the employees who work for department 90? The following example shows how to limit the query to only the records belonging to department 90 by using a WHERE clause.

```
SQL>SELECT first_name ||' '||last_name "Name",
  2          department_id
  3   FROM employees
  4   WHERE department_id =90;

Name                                       DEPARTMENT_ID
------------------------------------------ -------------
Steven King                                           90
Neena Kochhar                                         90
Lex De Haan                                           90
SQL>
```

You need not include the column names in the SELECT clause to use them in the WHERE clause.

Various operators available in Oracle9i can be used in the WHERE clause to limit the number of rows.

Comparison Operators

Comparison operators compare two values or expressions and give a Boolean result of TRUE, FALSE, or NULL. The comparison operators include those that test for equality, inequality, less than, greater than, and value comparisons.

= (Equality)

The = operator tests for equality. The test evaluates to TRUE if the values or results of an expression on both sides of the operator are equal.

```
SQL>SELECT first_name ||' '||last_name "Name",
  2         department_id
  3  FROM employees
  4  WHERE department_id =90;

Name                                         DEPARTMENT_ID
-------------------------------------------- -------------
Steven King                                             90
Neena Kochhar                                           90
Lex De Haan                                             90
SQL>
```

!=, <>, or ^= (Inequality)

You can use any one of these three operators to test for inequality. The test evaluates to TRUE if the values on both sides of the operator do not match. The operator <> works on all platforms, the use of other operators for inequality checking is not supported in all platforms.

```
SQL>SELECT first_name ||' '||last_name "Name",
  2         commission_pct
  3  FROM employees
  4  WHERE commission_pct !=.35;

Name                                         COMMISSION_PCT
-------------------------------------------- --------------
John Russell                                             .4
Karen Partners                                           .3
Alberto Errazuriz                                        .3
Gerald Cambrault                                         .3
… … … … … …
Jack Livingston                                          .2
Kimberely Grant                                         .15
Charles Johnson                                          .1

32 rows selected.
SQL>
```

< (Less Than)

The < operator evaluates to TRUE if the left side (expression or value) of the operator is less than the right side of the operator.

```
SQL>SELECT first_name ||' '||last_name "Name",
  2         commission_pct
  3  FROM employees
  4  WHERE commission_pct <.15;

Name                                      COMMISSION_PCT
----------------------------------------- --------------
Mattea Marvins                                        .1
David Lee                                             .1
Sundar Ande                                           .1
Amit Banda                                            .1
Sundita Kumar                                         .1
Charles Johnson                                       .1

6 rows selected.
SQL>
```

> (More Than)

The > operator evaluates to TRUE if the left side (expression or value) of the operator is greater than the right side of the operator.

```
SQL>SELECT first_name ||' '||last_name "Name",
  2         commission_pct
  3  FROM employees
  4  WHERE commission_pct >.35;

Name                                      COMMISSION_PCT
----------------------------------------- --------------
John Russell                                          .4
SQL>
```

<= (Less Than or Equal to)

The <= operator evaluates to TRUE if the left side (expression or value) of the operator is less than or equal to the right side of the operator.

```
SQL>SELECT first_name ||' '||last_name "Name",
  2        commission_pct
  3  FROM employees
  4  WHERE commission_pct <=.15;

Name                                          COMMISSION_PCT
--------------------------------------------- --------------
Oliver Tuvault                                           .15
Danielle Greene                                          .15
Mattea Marvins                                            .1
David Lee                                                 .1
Sundar Ande                                               .1
Amit Banda                                                .1
William Smith                                            .15
Elizabeth Bates                                          .15
Sundita Kumar                                             .1
Kimberely Grant                                          .15
Charles Johnson                                           .1

11 rows selected.
SQL>
```

>= (Greater Than or Equal to)

The >= operator evaluates to TRUE if the left side (expression or value) of the operator is greater than or equal to the right side of the operator.

```
SQL>SELECT first_name ||' '||last_name "Name",
  2        commission_pct
  3  FROM employees
  4  WHERE commission_pct >=.35;

Name                                          COMMISSION_PCT
--------------------------------------------- --------------
John Russell                                              .4
Janette King                                             .35
Patrick Sully                                            .35
Allan McEwen                                             .35
SQL>
```

ANY or *SOME*

The ANY or SOME operators are used to compare a value to each value in a list or subquery. The ANY and SOME operators always must be preceded by the comparison operators =, !=, <, >, <=, or >=.

```
SQL>SELECT first_name ||' '||last_name "Name",
  2         department_id
  3  FROM employees
  4  WHERE department_id <=ANY (10,15,20,25);

Name                                      DEPARTMENT_ID
----------------------------------------- -------------
Jennifer Whalen                                      10
Michael Hartstein                                    20
Pat Fay                                              20
SQL>
```

ALL

The ALL operator is used to compare a value to every value in a list or subquery. The ALL operator must always be preceded by the comparison operators =, !=, <, >, <=, or >=.

```
SQL>SELECT first_name ||' '||last_name "Name",
  2         department_id
  3  FROM employees
  4  WHERE department_id >=ALL (80,90,100);

Name                                      DEPARTMENT_ID
----------------------------------------- -------------
Nancy Greenberg                                     100
Daniel Faviet                                       100
John Chen                                           100
Ismael Sciarra                                      100
Jose Manuel Urman                                   100
Luis Popp                                           100
Shelley Higgins                                     110
William Gietz                                       110

8 rows selected.
SQL>
```

For all the comparison operators discussed, if one side of the operator is NULL, the result is NULL.

Logical Operators

Logical operators are used to combine the results of two comparison conditions to produce a single result or to reverse the result of a single comparison. NOT, AND, and OR are the logical operators.

NOT

The NOT operator is used to reverse the result. It evaluates to TRUE if the operand is FALSE, evaluates to FALSE if the operand is TRUE. NOT returns NULL if the operand is NULL.

```
SQL> SELECT first_name, department_id
  2  FROM   employees
  3* WHERE  not (department_id >= 30);

FIRST_NAME           DEPARTMENT_ID
-------------------- -------------
Jennifer                        10
Michael                         20
Pat                             20
SQL>
```

AND

The AND operator evaluates to TRUE if both operands are TRUE. It evaluates to FALSE if either operand is FALSE. Otherwise, it returns NULL.

```
SQL> SELECT first_name, salary
  2  FROM   employees
  3  WHERE  last_name = 'Smith'
  4* AND    salary    > 7500;

FIRST_NAME               SALARY
-------------------- ----------
Lindsey                    8000
SQL>
```

OR

The OR operator evaluates to TRUE if either operand is TRUE. It evaluates to FALSE if both operands are FALSE. Otherwise, it returns NULL.

```
SQL> SELECT first_name, last_name
  2  FROM   employees
  3  WHERE  first_name = 'Kelly'
  4* OR     last_name  = 'Smith';

FIRST_NAME           LAST_NAME
-------------------- -------------------------
Lindsey              Smith
William              Smith
Kelly                Chung
SQL>
```

Logical Operator Truth Tables

The following tables can be used as truth tables for the three logical operators.

AND Truth Table

AND	TRUE	FALSE	NULL
TRUE	TRUE	FALSE	NULL
FALSE	FALSE	FALSE	FALSE
NULL	NULL	FALSE	NULL

OR Truth Table

OR	TRUE	FALSE	NULL
TRUE	TRUE	TRUE	TRUE
FALSE	TRUE	FALSE	NULL
NULL	TRUE	NULL	NULL

NOT Truth Table

NOT	
TRUE	FALSE
FALSE	TRUE
NULL	NULL

Other Operators

In this section, we will discuss all the operators that can be used in the WHERE clause of the SQL statement that were not discussed earlier.

IN and *NOT IN*

The IN and NOT IN operators are used to test a membership condition. IN is equivalent to the =ANY operator, which evaluates to TRUE if the value exists in the list or the result set from a subquery. The NOT IN operator is equivalent to the !=ALL operator, which evaluates to TRUE if the value does not exist in the list or the result set from a subquery. The following examples demonstrate the use of these two operators.

```
SQL> SELECT first_name, last_name, department_id
  2  FROM   employees
  3  WHERE  department_id IN (10, 20, 90);

FIRST_NAME           LAST_NAME                 DEPARTMENT_ID
-------------------- ------------------------- ----------
Steven               King                              90
Neena                Kochhar                           90
Lex                  De Haan                           90
Jennifer             Whalen                            10
Michael              Hartstein                         20
Pat                  Fay                               20

6 rows selected.

SQL> SELECT first_name, last_name, department_id
  2  FROM   employees
  3  WHERE  department_id NOT IN
  4*        (10, 30, 40, 50, 60, 80, 90, 110, 100)
SQL> /
```

```
FIRST_NAME           LAST_NAME                 DEPARTMENT_ID
-------------------- ------------------------- -------------
Michael              Hartstein                            20
Pat                  Fay                                  20
Hermann              Baer                                 70
SQL>
```

When using the `NOT IN` operator, if any value in the list or the result returned from the subquery is `NULL`, the query returns no rows. For example, `last_name not in ('Smith', 'Thomas', NULL)` evaluates to `last_name != 'Smith' AND last_name != 'Thomas' AND last_name != NULL.` Any comparison on a `NULL` value results in `NULL`.

BETWEEN

The BETWEEN operator is used to test a range. BETWEEN A AND B evaluates to TRUE if the value is greater than or equal to *A* and less than or equal to *B*. If NOT is used, the result is the reverse. The following example lists all the employees whose salary is between $5,000 and $6,000.

```
SQL> SELECT first_name, last_name, salary
  2  FROM   employees
  3* WHERE  salary BETWEEN 5000 AND 6000;

FIRST_NAME           LAST_NAME                     SALARY
-------------------- ------------------------- ----------
Bruce                Ernst                           6000
Kevin                Mourgos                         5800
Pat                  Fay                             6000
SQL>
```

EXISTS

The EXISTS operator is always followed by a subquery in parentheses. (For more information on subqueries, refer to Chapter 5.) EXISTS evaluates to TRUE if the subquery returns at least one row. The following example lists the employees who work for Administration department.

```
SQL> SELECT last_name, first_name, department_id
     FROM   employees e
     WHERE  EXISTS (select 1 FROM departments d
                    WHERE  d.department_id = e.department_id
                    AND    d.department_name = 'Administration');

LAST_NAME                 FIRST_NAME           DEPARTMENT_ID
------------------------- -------------------- -------------
Whalen                    Jennifer                        10
SQL>
```

IS NULL and *IS NOT NULL*

To find the NULL values or NOT NULL values, you need to use the IS NULL operator. The = or != operator will not work with NULL values. IS NULL evaluates to TRUE if the value is NULL. IS NOT NULL evaluates to TRUE if the value is not NULL. To find the employees who do not have a department assigned, use this query:

```
SQL> SELECT last_name, department_id
     FROM   employees
     WHERE  department_id IS NULL;

LAST_NAME                 DEPARTMENT_ID
------------------------- -------------
Grant
SQL>
```

LIKE

Using the LIKE operator, you can perform pattern matching. The pattern-search character % is used to match any character and any number of characters. The pattern-search character _ is used to match any single character. If you are looking for the actual character % or _ in the pattern search, you can include an *escape character* in the search string and notify Oracle using the ESCAPE clause.

The following query searches for all employees whose first name begins with *Su* and last name does not begin with *S*.

```
SQL> SELECT first_name, last_name
  2  FROM   employees
  3  WHERE  first_name LIKE 'Su%'
  4* AND    last_name NOT LIKE 'S%';

FIRST_NAME           LAST_NAME
-------------------- -------------------------
Sundar               Ande
Sundita              Kumar
Susan                Mavris
SQL>
```

The following example looks for all JOB_ID values that begin with *AC_*. Since _ is a pattern-matching character, we must qualify it with an escape character. Oracle does not have a default escape character.

```
SQL> SELECT job_id, job_title
  2  FROM   jobs
  3  WHERE  job_id like 'AC\_%' ESCAPE '\';

JOB_ID     JOB_TITLE
---------- -----------------------------------
AC_MGR     Accounting Manager
AC_ACCOUNT Public Accountant
SQL>
```

Table 1.8 shows more examples of pattern matching.

TABLE 1.8 Pattern-Matching Examples

Pattern	Matches	Does Not Match
%SONI_1	SONIC1, ULTRASONI21	SONICS1, SONI315
_IME	TIME, LIME	IME, CRIME
\%SONI_1 ESCAPE '\'	%SONIC1, %SONI91	SONIC1, ULTRASONIC1
%ME_ _ _LE ESCAPE '\'	CRIME_FILE, TIME_POLE	CRIMESPILE, CRIME_ALE

Sorting Rows

The SELECT statement may include the ORDER BY clause to sort the resulting rows in a specific order based on the data in the columns. Without the ORDER BY clause, there is no guarantee that the rows will be returned in any specific order. If an ORDER BY clause is specified, by default, the rows are returned by ascending order of the columns specified. If you need to sort the rows in descending order, use the keyword DESC next to the column name. You may specify the keyword ASC to explicitly state to sort in ascending order, although it is the default. The ORDER BY clause follows the FROM clause and WHERE clause in the SELECT statement.

To retrieve all employee names of department 90 from the EMPLOYEES table ordered by last name, use this query:

```
SQL> SELECT first_name || ' ' || last_name "Employee Name"
  2  FROM   employees
  3  WHERE  department_id = 90
  4* ORDER BY last_name;

Employee Name
----------------------------------------------
Lex De Haan
Steven King
Neena Kochhar
SQL>
```

You can specify more than one column in the ORDER BY clause. In this case, the result set will be ordered by the first column in the ORDER BY clause, then the second, and so on. Columns or expressions not used in the SELECT clause can also be used in the ORDER BY clause. The following example shows the use of DESC and multiple columns in the ORDER BY clause.

```
SQL> SELECT first_name, hire_date, salary, manager_id mid
  2  FROM   employees
  3  WHERE  department_id IN (110,100)
  4* ORDER BY mid ASC, salary DESC, hire_date;
```

```
FIRST_NAME           HIRE_DATE     SALARY        MID
-------------------- --------- ---------- ----------
Shelley              07-JUN-94      12000        101
Nancy                17-AUG-94      12000        101
Daniel               16-AUG-94       9000        108
John                 28-SEP-97       8200        108
Jose Manuel          07-MAR-98       7800        108
Ismael               30-SEP-97       7700        108
Luis                 07-DEC-99       6900        108
William              07-JUN-94       8300        205

8 rows selected.
SQL>
```

You can use column alias names in the ORDER BY clause.

If the DISTINCT keyword is used in the SELECT clause, you can use only those columns listed in the SELECT clause in the ORDER BY clause. If you have used any operators on columns in the SELECT clause, the ORDER BY clause also should use them. Here is an example:

```
SQL> SELECT DISTINCT 'Region ' || region_id
  2  FROM   countries
  3  ORDER BY region_id;
ORDER BY region_id
         *
ERROR at line 3:
ORA-01791: not a SELECTed expression

SQL> SELECT DISTINCT 'Region ' || region_id
  2  FROM   countries
  3  ORDER BY 'Region ' || region_id;
```

```
'REGION'||REGION_ID
----------------------------------------------
Region 1
Region 2
Region 3
Region 4

SQL>
```

Not only can you use the column name or column alias to sort the result set of a query, you can also sort the results by specifying the position of the column in the SELECT clause. This is very useful if you have a lengthy expression in the SELECT clause and you need the results sorted on this value. The following example sorts the result set using positional values.

```
SQL> SELECT first_name, hire_date, salary, manager_id mid
  2  FROM   employees
  3  WHERE  department_id IN (110,100)
  4* ORDER BY 4, 2, 3;

FIRST_NAME           HIRE_DATE     SALARY        MID
-------------------- --------- ---------- ----------
Shelley              07-JUN-94      12000        101
Nancy                17-AUG-94      12000        101
Daniel               16-AUG-94       9000        108
John                 28-SEP-97       8200        108
Ismael               30-SEP-97       7700        108
Jose Manuel          07-MAR-98       7800        108
Luis                 07-DEC-99       6900        108
William              07-JUN-94       8300        205

8 rows selected.
SQL>
```

The ORDER BY clause cannot have more than 255 columns or expressions.

Sorting *NULLs*

By default, in an ascending order sort, the NULL values appear at the bottom of the result set; that is, NULLs are sorted higher. For descending order sorts, NULL values appear at the top of the result set—again, NULL values are sorted higher. The default behavior can be changed by using the NULLS FIRST or NULLS LAST keywords, along with the column names (or alias names or positions). The following examples demonstrate the use of NULLS FIRST in an ascending sort.

```
SQL> SELECT last_name, commission_pct
  2  FROM   employees
  3  WHERE  last_name LIKE 'R%'
  4* ORDER BY commission_pct ASC, last_name DESC;

LAST_NAME                  COMMISSION_PCT
------------------------- --------------
Russell                               .4
Rogers
Raphaely
Rajs

SQL> SELECT last_name, commission_pct
  2  FROM   employees
  3  WHERE  last_name LIKE 'R%'
  4* ORDER BY commission_pct ASC NULLS FIRST, last_name
DESC;

LAST_NAME                  COMMISSION_PCT
------------------------- --------------
Rogers
Raphaely
Rajs
Russell                               .4
SQL>
```

Why Do We Limit and Sort Rows?

The power of an RDBMS and SQL lies in getting exactly what we want from the database. The sample tables we considered under the HR schema are small, so even if you get all the information from the table, you can still find the specific data that you're seeking. But what if you have a huge transaction table, with millions of rows?

You know how easy it is to look through a catalog in the library to find a particular book, or to search through an alphabetical listing to find your name. When querying a large table, make sure you know what you want.

The `WHERE` clause lets you query for exactly what you're looking for. The `ORDER BY` clause lets you sort rows. The following steps can be used as an approach to query data from single table.

1. Know the columns of the table. You may issue the `DESCRIBE` command to get the column names and datatype. Understand which column has what information.
2. Pick the column names you are interested in including in the query. Use these columns in the `SELECT` clause.
3. Identify the column or columns where you can limit the rows or the columns that can show you only the rows of interest. Use these columns in the `WHERE` clause of the query, and supply the values as well as the appropriate operator.
4. If the query returns more than few rows, you may be interested in having them sorted in a particular order. Specify the column names and the sorting order in the `ORDER BY` clause of the query.

Let's consider a table named PURCHASE_ORDERS. First, use the `DESCRIBE` command to list the columns.

```
SQL> DESCRIBE purchase_orders
```

```
Name                 Null?    Type
-------------------- -------- --------------
ORDER#               NOT NULL NUMBER (16)
ORDER_DT             NOT NULL DATE
CUSTOMER#            NOT NULL VARCHAR2 (12)
BACK_ORDER                    CHAR (1)
ORD_STATUS                    CHAR (1)
TOTAL_AMT            NOT NULL NUMBER (18,4)
SALES_TAX                     NUMBER (12,2)
```

The objective of the query is to find the completed orders that do not have any sales tax. You want to see the order number and total amount of the order. The corresponding columns that appear in the SELECT clause are ORDER# and TOTAL_AMT. Since you're interested in only the rows with no sales tax in the completed orders, the columns to appear in the WHERE clause are SALES_TAX (checking for zero sales tax) and ORD_STATUS (checking for completeness of order, status code C). Since the query returns multiple rows, you want to order them by the order number. Notice that the SALES_TAX column can be NULL, so you want to make sure that you get all rows that have a sales tax amount of zero or NULL.

```
SELECT order#, total_amt
FROM   purchase_orders
WHERE  ord_status = 'C'
AND    (sales_tax IS NULL
OR      sales_tax = 0)
ORDER BY order#;
```

An alternative is to use the NVL function to deal with the NULL values. This function is discussed in Chapter 3.

Using Expressions

An *expression* is a combination of one or more values, operators, and SQL functions that result in a value. The result of an expression generally assumes the datatype of its components. The simple expression 5+6 evaluates to 11 and assumes a datatype of NUMBER. Expressions can appear in the following clauses:

- The SELECT clause of queries
- The WHERE clause, ORDER BY clause, and HAVING clause
- The VALUES clause of the INSERT statement
- The SET clause of the UPDATE statement

We will review the syntax of using these statements in later chapters.

You can include parentheses to group and evaluate expressions, and then apply the result to the rest of the expression. When parentheses are used, the expression in the innermost parentheses is evaluated first. Here is an example of a compound expression: ((2*4)/(3+1))*10. The result of 2*4 is divided by the result of 3+1. Then the result from the division operation is multiplied by 10.

The *CASE* Expression

The *CASE* expression is new to Oracle9i and can be used to derive the IF…THEN…ELSE logic in SQL. Here is the syntax of the simple CASE expression:

```
CASE <expression>
WHEN <compare value> THEN <return value> … … …
[ELSE <return value>]
END
```

The CASE expression begins with the keyword CASE and ends with the keyword END. The ELSE clause is optional, the WHEN clause can be repeated for 128 times. The following query displays a description for the REGION_ID column based on the value.

```
SQL> SELECT country_name, region_id,
            CASE region_id WHEN 1 THEN 'Europe'
                           WHEN 2 THEN 'America'
                           WHEN 3 THEN 'Asia'
                           ELSE 'Other' END Continent
     FROM   countries
     WHERE  country_name LIKE 'I%';
```

```
COUNTRY_NAME         REGION_ID CONTINE
-------------------- ---------- -------
Israel                        4 Other
India                         3 Asia
Italy                         1 Europe
SQL>
```

The other form of the CASE expression is the searched CASE, where the values are derived based on a condition. This version has the following syntax:

```
CASE
WHEN <condition> THEN <return value> … … …
[ELSE <return value>]
END
```

The following example categorizes the salary as Low, Medium, and High using a searched CASE expression.

```
SQL> SELECT first_name, department_id, salary,
            CASE WHEN salary < 6000 THEN 'Low'
                 WHEN salary < 10000 THEN 'Medium'
                WHEN salary >= 10000 THEN 'High' END Category
     FROM   employees
     WHERE department_id <= 30
     ORDER BY first_name;

FIRST_NAME           DEPARTMENT_ID     SALARY CATEGO
-------------------- ------------- ---------- ------
Alexander                       30       3100 Low
Den                             30      11000 High
Guy                             30       2600 Low
Jennifer                        10       4400 Low
Karen                           30       2500 Low
Michael                         20      13000 High
Pat                             20       6000 Medium
Shelli                          30       2900 Low
Sigal                           30       2800 Low

9 rows selected.
SQL>
```

Summary

Data in the Oracle database is managed and accessed using SQL. A SELECT statement is used to query data from a table or view. You can limit the rows selected by using a WHERE clause and order the retrieved data using the ORDER BY clause.

In this chapter, we reviewed fundamentals of SQL, including datatypes and operators. The CHAR and VARCHAR2 datatypes are used to store alphanumeric information. The NUMBER datatype is used to store any numeric value. Date values can be stored using the DATE datatype. Oracle has a wide range of operators: arithmetic, concatenation, set, comparison, membership, logical, pattern matching, range, and existence and NULL checking.

The CASE expression is new to Oracle9i. It is used to bring conditional logic to SQL.

Exam Essentials

Understand the operators. Know the various operators that can be used in queries. The parentheses around an expression change the precedence of the operators.

Know how to execute a SQL statement. You can execute a SQL statement by ending the statement with a semicolon, and in SQL*Plus, by having the / on a line by itself or by using the RUN command.

Understand the WHERE clause. The WHERE clause specifies a condition to limit the number or rows returned. You cannot use column alias names in this clause.

Understand the ORDER BY clause. The ORDER BY clause is used to sort the result set from a query. You can specify ascending order or descending order for the sort. Ascending order is the default.

Know the order of clauses in the SELECT statement. The SELECT statement must have a FROM clause. The WHERE clause, if it exists, should follow the FROM clause and precede the ORDER BY clause.

Know the use of the DUAL table. The DUAL table is a dummy table in Oracle with one column and one row. This table is commonly used to get the values of system variables such as SYSDATE or USER.

Know the characters used for pattern matching. The % character is used to match zero or more characters. The _ character is used to match one, and only one, character. The SQL operator used with pattern-matching character is LIKE.

Key Terms

Before you take the exam, be certain you are familiar with the following terms:

- unary operator
- arithmetic operators
- binary operators
- CASE
- CHAR
- column alias
- comparison operators
- concatenation operator
- DATE
- DISTINCT
- DUAL table
- escape character
- expression
- literals
- logical operators
- NUMBER
- operator
- order of precedence
- precision
- query
- scale
- seed database
- SELECT
- set operators
- SYSDATE
- VARCHAR2
- WHERE

Commands Used in This Chapter

The following table summarizes the commands used in this chapter.

Command	Purpose
`SELECT * FROM <table name>`	Used to query all the columns and all rows of the table
`SELECT <column>, <columns>... FROM <table name>`	Used to query selected columns and all rows from the table
`SELECT <column>... FROM <table name> WHERE <column> = <value>...`	Used to query selected columns and to restrict rows that satisfy <*value*> for the <*column*>
`SELECT <column>, <columns>... FROM <table name> WHERE <column> = <value>... ORDER BY <column>...`	Used to query selected columns and restrict rows with result set sorted

Review Questions

1. You issue the following query:

```
SELECT salary "Employee Salary"
FROM employees;
```

How will the column heading appear in the result?

A. EMPLOYEE SALARY

B. EMPLOYEE_SALARY

C. Employee Salary

D. employee_salary

2. The EMP table is defined as follows:

EMP Table		
Column	**Datatype**	**Length**
EMPNO	NUMBER	4
ENAME	VARCHAR2	30
SALARY	NUMBER	14,2
COMM	NUMBER	10,2
DEPTNO	NUMBER	2

You perform the following two queries:

```
1. SELECT empno enumber,  ename
   FROM emp ORDER BY 1;
2. SELECT empno,  ename
   FROM emp ORDER BY  empno ASC;
```

Which of the following is true?

A. Statements 1 and 2 will produce the same result.

B. Statement 1 will execute; statement 2 will return an error.

C. Statement 2 will execute; statement 1 will return an error.

D. Statements 1 and 2 will execute but produce different results.

3. You issue the following SELECT statement on the EMP table shown in question 2.

```
SELECT (200+((salary*0.1)/2)) FROM emp;
```

What will happen to the result if all of the parentheses are removed?

A. No difference, because the answer will always be NULL.

B. No difference, because the result will be the same.

C. The result will be higher.

D. The result will be lower.

4. In the following SELECT statement, which component is a literal? (Choose all that apply.)

```
SELECT 'Employee Name: ' || ename
FROM emp where deptno = 10;
```

A. 10

B. ename

C. Employee Name:

D. ||

5. When you try to save 34567.2255 into a column defined as NUMBER(7,2) what value is actually saved?

A. 34567.00

B. 34567.23

C. 34567.22

D. 3456.22

6. What is the default display length of the DATE datatype column?

A. 8

B. 9

C. 19

D. 6

7. What will happen if you query the EMP table shown in question 2 with the following?

```
SELECT empno, DISTINCT ename, salary FROM emp;
```

A. EMPNO, unique values of ENAME and then SALARY are displayed.

B. EMPNO, unique values of the two columns, ENAME and SALARY, are displayed.

C. `DISTINCT` is not a valid keyword in SQL.

D. No values will be displayed because the statement will return an error.

8. Which clause in a query limits the rows selected?

A. `ORDER BY`

B. `WHERE`

C. `SELECT`

D. `FROM`

9. The following listing shows the records of the EMP table.

```
EMPNO ENAME          SALARY      COMM    DEPTNO
--------- ---------- --------- --------- ---------
     7369 SMITH           800                  20
     7499 ALLEN          1600       300        30
     7521 WARD           1250       500        30
     7566 JONES          2975                  20
     7654 MARTIN         1250      1400        30
     7698 BLAKE          2850                  30
     7782 CLARK          2450     24500        10
     7788 SCOTT          3000                  20
     7839 KING           5000     50000        10
     7844 TURNER         1500         0        30
     7876 ADAMS          1100                  20
     7900 JAMES           950                  30
     7902 FORD           3000                  20
     7934 MILLER         1300     13000        10
```

When you issue the following query, which value will be displayed in the first row?

```
SELECT empno
FROM emp
WHERE deptno = 10
ORDER BY ename DESC;
```

A. MILLER

B. 7934

C. 7876

D. No rows will be returned because ename cannot be used in the ORDER BY clause.

10. Refer to the listing of records in the EMP table in question 9. How many rows will the following query return?

```
SELECT * FROM emp WHERE ename BETWEEN 'A' AND 'C'
```

A. 4

B. 2

C. A character column cannot be used in the BETWEEN operator.

D. 3

11. Refer to the EMP table in question 2. When you issue the following query, which line has an error?

```
SELECT empno "Enumber", ename "EmpName"
FROM emp
WHERE deptno = 10
AND  "Enumber" = 7782
ORDER BY "Enumber";
```

A. 1

B. 5

C. 4

D. No error; the statement will finish successfully.

12. You issue the following query:

```
SELECT empno, ename
FROM emp
WHERE empno = 7782 OR empno = 7876;
```

Which other operator can replace the OR condition in the WHERE clause?

A. IN

B. BETWEEN .. AND ..

C. LIKE

D. <=

E. >=

13. The following are clauses of the SELECT statement:

1. WHERE
2. FROM
3. ORDER BY

In which order should they appear in a query?

A. 1, 3, 2

B. 2, 1, 3

C. 2, 3, 1

D. The order of these clauses does not matter.

14. Which statement searches for PRODUCT_ID values that begin with DI_ from the ORDERS table?

A. `SELECT * FROM ORDERS`
`WHERE PRODUCT_ID = 'DI%';`

B. `SELECT * FROM ORDERS`
`WHERE PRODUCT_ID LIKE 'DI_' ESCAPE '\';`

C. `SELECT * FROM ORDERS`
`WHERE PRODUCT_ID LIKE 'DI\_%' ESCAPE '\';`

D. `SELECT * FROM ORDERS`
`WHERE PRODUCT_ID LIKE 'DI\_' ESCAPE '\';`

E. `SELECT * FROM ORDERS`
`WHERE PRODUCT_ID LIKE 'DI_%' ESCAPE '\';`

15. COUNTRY_NAME and REGION_ID are valid column names in the COUNTRIES table. Which one of the following statements will execute without an error?

A.
```
SELECT country_name, region_id,
CASE region_id = 1 THEN 'Europe',
     region_id = 2 THEN 'America',
     region_id = 3 THEN 'Asia',
     ELSE 'Other' END Continent
FROM   countries;
```

B.
```
SELECT country_name, region_id,
CASE (region_id WHEN 1 THEN 'Europe',
                WHEN 2 THEN 'America',
                WHEN 3 THEN 'Asia',
                ELSE 'Other') Continent
FROM   countries;
```

C.
```
SELECT country_name, region_id,
CASE region_id WHEN 1 THEN 'Europe'
               WHEN 2 THEN 'America'
               WHEN 3 THEN 'Asia'
               ELSE 'Other' END Continent
FROM   countries;
```

D.
```
SELECT country_name, region_id,
CASE region_id WHEN 1 THEN 'Europe'
               WHEN 2 THEN 'America'
               WHEN 3 THEN 'Asia'
               ELSE 'Other' Continent
FROM   countries;
```

16. Which special character is used to query all the columns from the table without listing each column by name?

    A. %

    B. &

    C. @

    D. *

17. The EMPLOYEE table has the following data:

```
EMP_NAME   HIRE_DATE     SALARY
---------- --------- ----------
SMITH      17-DEC-90        800
ALLEN      20-FEB-91       1600
WARD       22-FEB-91       1250
JONES      02-APR-91       5975
WARDEN     28-SEP-91       1250
BLAKE      01-MAY-91       2850
```

What will be the value in the first row of the result set when the following query is executed?

```
SELECT hire_date FROM employee
ORDER BY salary, emp_name;
```

A. 02-APR-91

B. 17-DEC-90

C. 28-SEP-91

D. The query is invalid, because you cannot have a column in the ORDER BY clause that is not part of the SELECT clause.

18. Which SQL statement will query the EMPLOYEES table for FIRST_NAME, LAST_NAME, and SALARY of all employees in DEPARTMENT_ID 40 in the alphabetical order of last name?

A.
```
SELECT first_name last_name salary
FROM   employees
ORDER BY last_name
WHERE  department_id = 40;
```

B.
```
SELECT first_name, last_name, salary
FROM   employees
ORDER BY last_name ASC
WHERE  department_id = 40;
```

C.
```
SELECT first_name last_name salary
FROM  employees
WHERE  department_id = 40
ORDER BY last_name ASC;
```

D.
```
SELECT first_name, last_name, salary
FROM   employees
WHERE  department_id = 40
ORDER BY last_name;
```

E.
```
SELECT first_name, last_name, salary
FROM   TABLE employees
WHERE  department_id IS 40
ORDER BY last_name ASC;
```

19. When doing pattern matching using the `LIKE` operator, which character is used as the default escape character by Oracle?

A. |

B. /

C. \

D. There is no default escape character in Oracle9i.

20. Column alias names cannot be used in which clause?

A. `SELECT` clause

B. `WHERE` clause

C. `ORDER BY` clause

D. None of the above

Answers to Review Questions

1. C. Column alias names enclosed in quotation marks will appear as typed. Spaces and mixed case appear in the column alias name only when the alias is enclosed in double quotation marks.

2. A. Statements 1 and 2 will produce the same result. You can use the column name, column alias, or column position in the `ORDER BY` clause. The default sort order is ascending. For a descending sort, you must explicitly specify that order with the `DESC` keyword.

3. B. In the arithmetic evaluation, multiplication and division have precedence over addition and subtraction. Even if you do not include the parentheses, `salary*0.1` will be evaluated first. The result is then divided by 2, and its result is added to 200.

4. A, C. Character literals in the SQL statement are enclosed in single quotation marks. Literals are concatenated using `||`. Employee Name: is a character literal, and 10 is a numeric literal.

5. B. Since the numeric column is defined with precision 7 and scale 2, you can have five digits in the integer part and two digits after the decimal point. The digits after the decimal are rounded.

6. B. The default display format of the DATE column is *DD-MON-YY*, whose length is 9. This is U.S. specific and will be different as user settings vary.

7. D. `DISTINCT` is used to display a unique result row, and it should follow immediately after the keyword `SELECT`. Uniqueness is identified across the row, not a single column.

8. B. The `WHERE` clause is used to limit the rows returned from a query. The `WHERE` clause condition is evaluated, and rows are returned only if the result is `TRUE`. The `ORDER BY` clause is used to display the result in certain order.

9. B. There are three records belonging to DEPTNO 10: EMPNO 7934 (MILLER), 7839 (KING), and 7782 (CLARK). When you sort their names by descending order, MILLER is the first row to display. You can use alias names and columns that are not in the SELECT clause in the ORDER BY clause.

10. D. Here, a character column is compared against a string using the BETWEEN operator, which is equivalent to ename >= 'A' AND ename <= 'C'. The name CLARK will not be included in this query, because 'CLARK' is > 'C'.

11. C. Column alias names cannot be used in the WHERE clause. They can be used in the ORDER BY clause.

12. A. The IN operator can be used. You can write the WHERE clause as **WHERE empno IN** (7782, 7876);

13. B. The FROM clause appears after the SELECT statement, followed by WHERE and ORDER BY clauses. The FROM clause specifies the table names, the WHERE clause limits the result set, and the ORDER BY clause sorts the result.

14. C. Since _ is a special pattern-matching character, you need to include the ESCAPE clause in LIKE. The % character matches any number of characters including 0, and _ matches a single character.

15. C. A CASE expression begins with the keyword CASE and ends with keyword END.

16. D. An asterisk (*) is used to denote all columns in a table.

17. B. The default sorting order for numeric column is ascending. The columns are sorted first by salary and then by name, so the row with the lowest salary is displayed first. It is perfectly valid to use a column in the ORDER BY clause that is not part of the SELECT clause.

18. D. In the `SELECT` clause, the column names should be separated by commas. An alias name may be provided for each column with a space or using the keyword `AS`. The `FROM` clause should appear after the `SELECT` clause. The `WHERE` clause appears after the `FROM` clause. The `ORDER BY` clause comes after the `WHERE` clause.

19. D. There is no default escape character in Oracle9i. If your search includes pattern-matching characters such as _ or %, define an escape character using the `ESCAPE` keyword in the `LIKE` operator.

20. B. Column alias names cannot be used in the `WHERE` clause of the SQL statement. In the `ORDER BY` clause, you can use the column name or alias name, or indicate the column by its position in the `SELECT` clause.

SQL*Plus Overview

INTRODUCTION TO ORACLE9i: SQL EXAM OBJECTIVES COVERED IN THIS CHAPTER:

✓ **Writing Basic SQL Select Statements**

- Differentiate between SQL statements and iSQL*Plus commands

✓ **Producing Readable Output with iSQL*Plus**

- Produce queries that require a substitution variable
- Produce more readable output
- Create and execute script files

Exam objectives are subject to change at any time without prior notice and at Oracle's sole discretion. Please visit Oracle's Certification website (`http://www.oracle.com/education/certification/`) for the most current exam objectives listing.

SQL*Plus, widely used by DBAs and developers to interact with the database, is a powerful tool from Oracle. Using SQL*Plus, you can execute all SQL statements and PL/SQL programs, format results from queries, and administer the database. iSQL*Plus is the web interface for SQL*Plus (available on the Windows platform only, as of this release).

SQL*Plus is packaged with the Oracle software and can be installed using the client software installation routine on any machine. This tool is automatically installed when you install the server software.

In this chapter, we will discuss the capabilities of SQL*Plus and its usage. Since SQL*Plus commands are a superset of iSQL*Plus commands, we will address the tool as SQL*Plus throughout this chapter.

SQL*Plus Fundamentals

When you start SQL*Plus on Windows, it prompts you for the *username*, *password*, and *host string*, as shown in Figure 2.1. The host, or connect, string is the database alias name. If you omit the connect string, SQL*Plus tries to connect you to the local database defined in the `ORACLE_SID` variable.

FIGURE 2.1 SQL*Plus logon screen

Log On

User Name: hr

Password: **

Host String: SQL9i

OK Cancel

Connecting to SQL*Plus

Once you are in SQL*Plus, you can connect to another database or change your connection by using the CONNECT command, with this syntax:

```
CONNECT <username>/<password>@<connectstring>
```

The slash separates the username and password. The connect string following @ is the database alias name. If you omit the password, you will be prompted to enter it. You may omit the connect string to connect to a local database.

For DOS and Unix platforms, SQL*Plus comes in character mode. You can invoke and connect to SQL*Plus using the sqlplus command, with this syntax:

```
sqlplus username/password@connectstring
```

If you invoke the tool with just sqlplus, you will be prompted for username and password. If you invoke SQL*Plus with a username, you will be prompted for a password. Figure 2.2 shows an example of invoking SQL*Plus from Unix.

Use the DISCONNECT command to disconnect your session from the database. To connect again, use the CONNECT command.

```
SQL> DISCONNECT
Disconnected from Oracle9i Enterprise Edition Release
9.0.1.1.1 -
   Production
With the Partitioning option
JServer Release 9.0.1.1.1 - Production
SQL> SELECT * FROM tab;
SP2-0640: Not connected
SQL> CONNECT hr/hr@sql9i
Connected.
SQL>
```

sqlplus -help displays a help screen to show the various options available with starting SQL*Plus.

To exit from SQL*Plus, use the EXIT command. On platforms where a return code is used, you can provide a return code while exiting. You may also use the QUIT command to complete the session. EXIT and QUIT are synonymous.

FIGURE 2.2 SQL*Plus on Unix

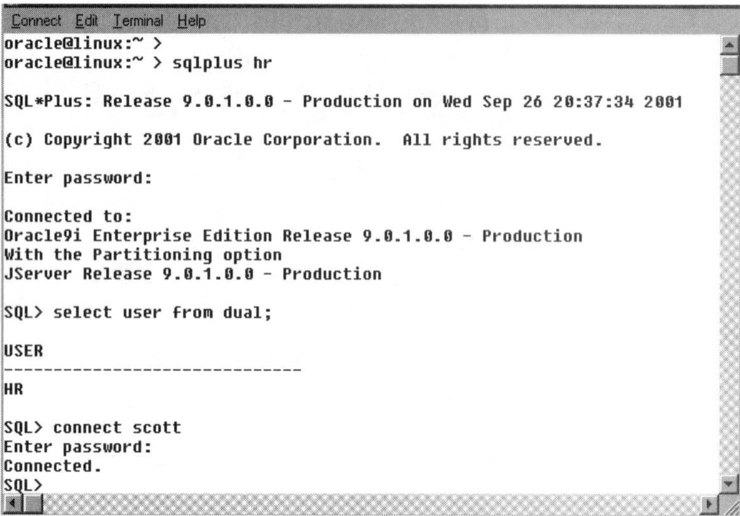

Connect Edit Terminal Help
oracle@linux:~ >
oracle@linux:~ > sqlplus hr
SQL*Plus: Release 9.0.1.0.0 - Production on Wed Sep 26 20:37:34 2001
(c) Copyright 2001 Oracle Corporation. All rights reserved.
Enter password:
Connected to:
Oracle9i Enterprise Edition Release 9.0.1.0.0 - Production
With the Partitioning option
JServer Release 9.0.1.0.0 - Production
SQL> select user from dual;
USER

HR
SQL> connect scott
Enter password:
Connected.
SQL>

As noted in Chapter 1, "Basic SQL SELECT Statements", you should choose to create a seed database when you install Oracle software, so that you have access to the sample schemas used in this book. The default IDs and password for the seed database are SYSTEM/MANAGER, SYS/CHANGE_ON_INSTALL. Also, you will need to unlock the account for the sample schemas using the ALTER USER statement. To unlock the HR schema, use ALTER USER HR IDENTIFIED BY HRPASSWORD ACCOUNT UNLOCK;.

To change the password, you can use the PASSWORD command. The password will not be echoed to the screen. The username argument is optional. If it is not included, the command changes the current user's password. To change another user's password, you must have the ALTER USER privilege.

```
SQL> PASSWORD scott
Changing password for SCOTT
New password: *****
Retype new password: *****
Password changed
SQL>
```

```
SQL> SHOW USER
USER is "SYSTEM"
SQL> PASSWORD
Changing password for SYSTEM
Old password: *******
New password: *******
Retype new password: *******
Password changed
SQL>
```

Using SQL*Plus

Once you are connected to SQL*Plus, you get the SQL> prompt. This is the default prompt, which can be changed using the SET SQLPROMPT command. Type the command you wish to execute at this prompt. With SQL*Plus, you can enter, edit, and execute SQL statements, perform database administration, and execute statements interactively by accepting user input. You can also format query results and perform calculations.

Entering SQL Statements

A SQL statement can spread across multiple lines, and the commands are case insensitive. The previously executed SQL statement will always be available in the *SQL buffer*. The buffer can be edited or saved to a file. You can terminate a SQL statement in any of the following ways:

- End with a semicolon (;). The statement is completed and executed.
- Enter a slash (/) on a new line by itself. The statement in the buffer is executed.
- Enter a blank line. The statement is saved in the buffer.

The RUN command can be used instead of a slash to execute a statement in the buffer. The SQL prompt returns when the statement has completed execution. You can enter your next command at the prompt.

Only SQL statements and PL/SQL blocks are stored in the SQL buffer; SQL*Plus commands are not stored in the buffer.

Entering SQL*Plus Commands

SQL*Plus has its own commands to perform specific tasks on the database, as well as to format the query results. Unlike SQL statements, which are terminated with a semicolon or a blank line, SQL*Plus commands are entered on a single line. Pressing Enter executes the SQL*Plus command.

If you wish to continue a SQL*Plus command onto the next line, you must end the current line with a hyphen (-), which indicates command continuation. This is in contrast to SQL statements, which can be continued to the next line without a continuation operator. For example, the following SQL statement gives an error, because SQL*Plus treats the minus operator (-) as a continuation character.

```
SQL> SELECT 800 -
> 400 FROM dual;
SELECT 800  400 FROM dual
            *
ERROR at line 1:
ORA-00923: FROM keyword not found where expected
SQL>
```

You need to put the minus operator in the next line for the query to succeed:

```
SQL> SELECT 800
  2  - 400 FROM dual;

   800-400
----------
       400
SQL>
```

Use Ctrl+C to cancel a command in SQL*Plus. For example, if you need to cancel a query on a large table, press Ctrl+C (press and hold down the Ctrl key and C key together) to cancel the execution. An operating system setting can map another key combination for this purpose.

Getting Information with the *DESCRIBE* Command

The DESCRIBE command is used to get information on the database objects. Using DESCRIBE on a table or view shows the columns, its datatypes, and whether or not each column can be NULL. Using DESCRIBE on a stored program such as procedure or function shows the parameters that need to be passed in/out, its datatype, and if there is a default value. You can abbreviate this command to the first four characters or more— DESC, DESCR, and DESCRIB are valid.

If you're connected to the HR schema, and need to see the tables and views in this schema, use the following query:

```
SQL> SELECT * FROM tab;

TNAME                          TABTYPE  CLUSTERID
------------------------------ ------- ----------
COUNTRIES                      TABLE
DEPARTMENTS                    TABLE
EMPLOYEES                      TABLE
EMP_DETAILS_VIEW               VIEW
JOBS                           TABLE
JOB_HISTORY                    TABLE
LOCATIONS                      TABLE
REGIONS                        TABLE

8 rows selected.
SQL>
```

The following example uses the DESCRIBE command on a table and on a procedure.

```
SQL> DESC countries

 Name                            Null?    Type
 ------------------------------- -------- ------------
 COUNTRY_ID                      NOT NULL CHAR(2)
 COUNTRY_NAME                             VARCHAR2(40)
 REGION_ID                                NUMBER
```

```
SQL> DESCRIB Add_Job_History
PROCEDURE Add_Job_History
 Argument Name          Type                In/Out Default?
 ---------------------- ------------------- ------ --------
 P_EMP_ID               NUMBER(6)           IN
 P_START_DATE           DATE                IN
 P_END_DATE             DATE                IN
 P_JOB_ID               VARCHAR2(10)        IN
 P_DEPARTMENT_ID        NUMBER(4)           IN
SQL>
```

Editing the SQL Buffer

The most recent SQL statement executed or entered is stored in the SQL buffer of SQL*Plus. You can run the command in this buffer again by simply typing a slash or using the RUN command.

SQL*Plus provides a set of commands to edit the buffer. Suppose that you want to add another column or add an ORDER BY condition to the statement in the buffer. You do not need to type the entire SQL statement again. Instead, just edit the existing statement in the buffer.

One way to edit the SQL*Plus buffer is to use the EDIT command to write the buffer to an operating system file named afiedt.buf (this is the default filename, which can be changed), and then use a system editor to make changes.

You can use your favorite text editor by defining it in SQL*Plus. For example, to make Notepad your favorite editor, just issue the command DEFINE _EDITOR = NOTEPAD. You need to provide the entire path if the program is not available in the search path.

Another way to edit the buffer is to use the SQL*Plus editing commands. You can make changes, delete lines, add text, and list the buffer contents using the commands described in the following sections. Most editing commands operate on the current line. You can change the current line simply by typing the line number. All commands can be abbreviated except DEL (which is already abbreviated).

LIST

The LIST command lists the contents of the buffer. The asterisk indicates the current line. The abbreviated command for LIST is L.

```
SQL> L
  1  SELECT empno, ename
  2* FROM emp
SQL> LIST LAST
  2* FROM emp
SQL>
```

The command `LIST m n` displays lines from *m* through *n*. If you substitute * for *m* or *n*, it implies the current line. The command `LIST LAST` displays the last line.

APPEND

The `APPEND text` command adds text to the end of line. The abbreviated command is `A`.

```
SQL> A  WHERE empno <> 7926
  2* FROM emp WHERE empno <> 7926
SQL>
```

CHANGE

The `CHANGE /old/new` command changes an old entry to a new entry. The abbreviated command is `C`. If you omit *new*, *old* will be deleted.

```
SQL> C /<>/=
  2* FROM emp WHERE empno = 7926
SQL> C /7926
  2* FROM emp WHERE empno =
SQL>
```

INPUT

The `INPUT text` command adds a line of text. Its abbreviation is `I`. If *text* is omitted, you can add as many lines you wish.

```
SQL> I
  3  7777 AND
  4  empno = 4354
  5
SQL> I ORDER BY 1
SQL> L
  1  SELECT empno, ename
  2  FROM emp WHERE empno =
```

```
  3  7777 AND
  4  empno = 4354
  5* ORDER BY 1
SQL>
```

DEL

The DEL command used alone or with * deletes the current line. The DEL *m n* command deletes lines from *m* through *n*. If you substitute * for *m* or *n*, it implies the current line. The command DEL LAST deletes the last line.

```
SQL> 3
  3* 7777 AND
SQL> DEL
SQL> L
  1  SELECT empno, ename
  2  FROM emp WHERE empno =
  3  empno = 4354
  4* ORDER BY 1
SQL> DEL 3 *
SQL> L
  1  SELECT empno, ename
  2* FROM emp WHERE empno =
SQL>
```

CLEAR BUFFER

The CLEAR BUFFER command (abbreviated CL BUFF) clears the buffer. This deletes all lines from the buffer.

```
SQL> L
  1  SELECT empno, ename
  2* FROM emp WHERE empno =
SQL> CL BUFF
buffer cleared
SQL> L
No lines in SQL buffer.
SQL>
```

Using Script Files

SQL*Plus provides commands to save the SQL buffer to a file, as well as to run SQL statements from a file. SQL statements saved in a file are called a *script file*.

You can work with script files as follows:

- To save the SQL buffer to an operating system file, use the command `SAVE` *`filename`*. If you do not provide an extension, the saved file will have an extension of `.sql`.
- By default, the `SAVE` command will not overwrite an existing file. If you wish to overwrite an existing file, you need to use the keyword `REPLACE`.
- To add the buffer to the end of an existing file, use the `SAVE` *`filename`* `APPEND` command.
- You can edit the saved file using the `EDIT` *`filename`* command.
- You can bring the contents of a script file to the SQL buffer using the `GET` *`filename`* command.
- If you wish to run a script file, use the command `START` *`filename`*. You can also run a script file using *`@filename`*.
- An *`@@filename`* used inside a script file looks for the filename in the directory where the parent script file is saved and executes it.

The following steps will familiarize you with the script file commands, as well as the other topics we have covered so far:

1. Enter the following SQL. The third line is a blank line, so that the SQL is saved in the buffer.

```
SQL> SELECT employee_id, first_name, last_name
  2  FROM   employees
  3
SQL>
```

2. List the SQL buffer.

```
SQL> L
  1  SELECT employee_id, first_name, last_name
  2* FROM   employees
SQL>
```

3. Save the buffer to a file named `myfile`. The default extension will be `.sql`.

```
SQL> SAVE myfile
Created file MYFILE.sql
SQL>
```

4. Choose to edit the file.

```
SQL> EDIT myfile
SQL>
```

5. Add `WHERE EMPLOYEE_ID = 106` as the third line to the SQL statement.

6. List the buffer.

```
SQL> LIST
  1  SELECT employee_id, first_name, last_name
  2* FROM   employees
SQL>
```

7. The buffer listed is still the old buffer. The edited changes are not reflected because we edited the file `MYFILE`, which is not yet loaded to the buffer.

8. Bring the file contents to the buffer.

```
SQL> GET myfile
  1  SELECT employee_id, first_name, last_name
  2  FROM   employees
  3* WHERE employee_id = 106
SQL>
```

9. List the buffer to verify its contents.

```
SQL> LI
  1  SELECT employee_id, first_name, last_name
  2  FROM   employees
  3* WHERE employee_id = 106
SQL>
```

10. Change the employee number from 106 to 110.

```
SQL> C/106/110
  3* WHERE employee_id = 110
SQL>
```

11. Save the buffer again to the same file.

```
SQL> SAVE myfile
SP2-0540: File "MYFILE.sql" already exists.
Use "SAVE filename[.ext] REPLACE".
SQL>
```

12. An error was returned, because SAVE will not overwrite the file by default.

13. Save the file using the REPLACE keyword.

```
SQL> SAVE myfile REPLACE
Wrote file MYFILE.sql
SQL>
```

14. Execute the file.

```
SQL> START myfile

EMPLOYEE_ID FIRST_NAME           LAST_NAME
----------- -------------------- ---------
        110 John                 Chen
SQL>
```

15. Change the employee number from 110 to 106 and append this SQL to the file, then execute it using @.

```
SQL> C/110/106
  3* WHERE employee_id = 106
SQL> SAVE myfile APPEND
Appended file to MYFILE.sql
SQL> @MYFILE
EMPLOYEE_ID FIRST_NAME           LAST_NAME
----------- -------------------- ---------
        110 John                 Chen

EMPLOYEE_ID FIRST_NAME           LAST_NAME
----------- -------------------- ---------
        106 Valli                Pataballa
SQL>
```

Saving Query Results to a File

You can use the SPOOL *filename* command to save the query results to a file. By default, the SPOOL command creates an .lst file extension.

SPOOL OFF stops writing the output to the file. SPOOL OUT stops the writing of output and sends the output file to the printer.

Adding Comments to a Script File

Having comments in the script file improves the readability and understanding of the code. You can enter comments in SQL*Plus using the REMARKS (abbreviated REM) command. Lines in the script file beginning with the keyword REM are comments and are not executed. You can also enter a comment between /* and */.

While executing a script file with comments, the remarks entered using the REMARKS command are not displayed on the screen, but the comments within /* and */ are displayed on the screen with prefix DOC> when there is more than one line between /* and */. SET DOCUMENT OFF turns this off.

Customizing the SQL*Plus Environment

SQL*Plus has a set of *environment variables* that control the way that SQL*Plus displays data and assigns special characters. The SHOW ALL command lists the current environment.

If you are using SQL*Plus for Windows, you can set the environment by choosing Options from the menu bar and then selecting the Environment option.

Using the *SET* Command

You can customize the environment by using the SET command to change the values of environment variables. The syntax is as follows:

```
SET variable value
```

Table 2.1 lists the variables that are commonly adjusted with the SET commands. Most of the variables can be abbreviated (COM for COMPATIBILITY, for example). Use the SHOW *variable* command to see the current value of the variable from the environment setting.

TABLE 2.1 Common Environment Variables Used with the *SET* Command

Variable Name and Allowed Value	Purpose
ARRAY[SIZE] {15|*n*}	Sets the number of rows—called a batch—that SQL*Plus will fetch from the database at one time
AUTO[COMMIT] {OFF|ON|IMM[EDIATE]|*n*}	Controls when Oracle commits pending changes to the database
AUTOT[RACE] {OFF|ON|TRACE[ONLY]} [EXP[LAIN]] [STAT[ISTICS]]	Displays a report on the execution of successful SQL DML statements
COLSEP {_|*text*}	Sets the text to be printed between selected columns
DEF[INE] {'&'|*c*|OFF|ON}	Sets the character used to prefix substitution variables to *c*
ECHO {OFF|ON}	Controls whether the START command lists each command in a script file as the command is executed
EDITF[ILE] *filename*[.ext]	Sets the default filename for the EDIT command
EMB[EDDED] {OFF|ON}	Controls where each report begins on the page
ESC[APE] {\\|*c*|OFF|ON}	Defines the character you enter as the escape character
FEED[BACK] {6|*n*|OFF|ON}	Displays the number of records returned by a query when a query selects at least *n* records
FLAGGER {OFF|ENTRY|INTERMED[IATE]|FULL}	Checks to make sure that SQL statements conform to the ANSI/ISO SQL92 standard

TABLE 2.1 Common Environment Variables Used with the *SET* Command *(continued)*

Variable Name and Allowed Value	Purpose
`FLU[SH] {OFF|ON}`	Controls when output is sent to the user's display device
`HEA[DING] {OFF|ON}`	Controls printing of column headings in reports
`HEADS[EP] {||c|OFF|ON}`	Defines the character you enter as the heading separator character
`LIN[ESIZE] {80|n}`	Sets the total number of characters that SQL*Plus displays on one line before beginning a new line
`LONG {80|n}`	Sets the maximum width (in bytes) for displaying LONG, CLOB, and NCLOB values; and for copying LONG values
`LONGC[HUNKSIZE] {80|n}`	Sets the size (in bytes) of the increments in which SQL*Plus retrieves a LONG, CLOB, or NCLOB value
`NEWP[AGE] {1|n|NONE}`	Sets the number of blank lines to be printed from the top of each page to the top title
`NULL` *text*	Sets the text that represents a null value in the result of a SQL SELECT command
`NUMF[ORMAT]` *format*	Sets the default format for displaying numbers
`NUM[WIDTH] {10|n}`	Sets the default width for displaying numbers
`PAGES[IZE] {24|n}`	Sets the number of lines in each page

TABLE 2.1 Common Environment Variables Used with the *SET* Command *(continued)*

<table>
<tr><th>Variable Name and Allowed Value</th><th>Purpose</th></tr>
<tr><td>PAU[SE] {OFF|ON|text}</td><td>Allows you to control scrolling of your terminal when running reports</td></tr>
<tr><td>SERVEROUT[PUT] {OFF|ON} [SIZE n] [FOR[MAT] {WRA[PPED]| WOR[D_WRAPPED]|TRU[NCATED]}]</td><td>Controls whether to display the output (that is, DBMS_OUTPUT.PUT_LINE) of stored procedures in SQL*Plus</td></tr>
<tr><td>SHOW[MODE] {OFF|ON}</td><td>Controls whether SQL*Plus lists the old and new settings of a SQL*Plus system variable when you change the setting with SET</td></tr>
<tr><td>SQLBL[ANKLINES] {ON|OFF}</td><td>Controls whether SQL*Plus allows blank lines within a SQL command</td></tr>
<tr><td>SQLC[ASE] {MIX[ED]|LO[WER]|UP[PER]}</td><td>Converts the case of SQL commands just prior to execution</td></tr>
<tr><td>SQLCO[NTINUE] {> |text}</td><td>Sets the character sequence SQL*Plus displays as a prompt after you continue a SQL*Plus command on an additional line using a hyphen (–)</td></tr>
<tr><td>SQLN[UMBER] {OFF|ON}</td><td>Sets the prompt for the second and subsequent lines of a SQL statement</td></tr>
<tr><td>SQLPRE[FIX] {#|c}</td><td>Sets the SQL*Plus prefix character, which you use with a SQL*Plus command on a separate line, to execute the command immediately, without affecting the SQL statement you are entering</td></tr>
<tr><td>SQLP[ROMPT] {SQL>|text}</td><td>Sets the SQL*Plus command prompt</td></tr>
<tr><td>SQLT[ERMINATOR] {;|c|OFF|ON}</td><td>Sets the character used to end and execute SQL statements to c</td></tr>
</table>

TABLE 2.1 Common Environment Variables Used with the *SET* Command *(continued)*

Variable Name and Allowed Value	Purpose
`SUF[FIX] {SQL|text}`	Sets the default file extension that SQL*Plus uses in commands that refer to command files
`TERM[OUT] {OFF|ON}`	Controls the display of output generated by commands executed from a command file
`TI[ME] {OFF|ON}`	Controls whether the current time will appear before each command prompt
`TIMI[NG] {OFF|ON}`	Controls whether timing statistics are displayed on each SQL command run
`TRIM[OUT] {OFF|ON}`	Controls whether blanks are removed at the end of each displayed line
`TRIMS[POOL] {ON|OFF}`	Controls whether blanks are removed at the end of each spooled line
`UND[ERLINE] {-|c|ON|OFF}`	Sets the character used to underline column headings in SQL*Plus reports to *c*
`VER[IFY] {OFF|ON}`	Controls whether SQL*Plus lists the text of a SQL statement before and after SQL*Plus replaces substitution variables with values
`WRA[P] {OFF|ON}`	Controls whether SQL*Plus truncates the display of a selected row if it is too long for the current line width

More than one variable can be set using a single SET command (or SHOW command). For example, you might issue the following commands:

```
SET TIME ON
SET PAGESIZE 24
SET LINESIZE 80
```

However, it's easier to specify all three variables in one SET command:

```
SET TIME ON PAGESIZE 24 LINESIZE 80
```

You may review all the available SET commands using the HELP SET command in SQL*Plus. The HELP command provides help on all the SQL*Plus commands.

Using the *SHOW* Command

The SHOW command is used to display the value of a SQL*Plus environment variable. All the variables available for use with the SET command (see Table 2.1) can also be used with the SHOW command to see their current value. For example, this query shows the current value of the PAGESIZE and LINESIZE variables:

```
SQL> SHOW LINESIZE PAGESIZE
linesize 80
pagesize 14
SQL>
```

SHOW ALL lists the values of all variables.

The SHOW command can also display values of other variables, such as the current username and Oracle release. Table 2.2 lists the additional options that can be used with the SHOW command.

TABLE 2.2 Additional *SHOW* Command Options

Option	Purpose
BTITLE	Displays the current value of BTITLE
ERRORS	Displays the most recent errors encountered in compiling a view or PL/SQL program unit
PARAMETERS <*parameter name*>	Displays the value of a database initialization parameter

TABLE 2.2 Additional *SHOW* Command Options *(continued)*

Option	Purpose
RELEASE	Displays the current Oracle database release number
REPFOOTER	Displays the current value of REPFOOTER
REPHEADER	Displays the current value of REPHEADER
SGA	Displays the current size of the System Global Area
SQLCODE	Displays the return code of the most recent SQL statement
TTITLE	Displays the current value of TTITLE
USER	Displays the username connected to the database

The following example demonstrates a few of the SHOW commands.

```
SQL> SHOW SGA

Total System Global Area  118255568 bytes
Fixed Size                   282576 bytes
Variable Size              83886080 bytes
Database Buffers           33554432 bytes
Redo Buffers                 532480 bytes
SQL>

SQL> SHOW USER
USER is "SCOTT"
SQL>

SQL> SHOW SQLCODE
sqlcode 0
SQL>

SQL> SELECT * FROM notable;
SELECT * FROM notable
              *
```

```
ERROR at line 1:
ORA-00942: table or view does not exist
SQL>
SQL> SHOW SQLCODE
sqlcode 942
SQL>
```

Real World Scenario

What If *HELP* Is Not Available?

By default, the seed database you create during installation of the software comes with HELP. However, sometimes when you seek HELP, SQL*Plus will display this message:

```
No HELP available!
```

Don't worry, you can load the help table and start using the HELP command.

If for some reason, HELP is not available, first log in to SQL*Plus using the SYSTEM ID on the server:

```
sqlplus system/manager
```

Next, run the script `hlpbld.sql`, found under the `sqlplus/admin/help` directory of your Oracle installation. The following example assumes `C:\Oracle\Ora90` as the Oracle installation directory.

```
@C:\Oracle\Ora90\sqlplus\admin\help\hlpbld.sql helpus.sql
```

Saving the Environment

You can save the current SQL*Plus environment using the command STORE SET *filename*. SQL*Plus creates a `.sql` file. You may run this file at any time to set up your customized environment.

Wouldn't it be nice to have the environment set the way you like it when you log in to SQL*Plus? Well, there is a way to do this. Create a `login.sql` file in the current directory of your SQL*Plus executable or in the search path of Oracle. This file will be executed when you log in to SQL*Plus. For example, to display the name and username when connected and display the current time at the prompt, create a `login.sql` file using the following lines:

```
SET PAGES 0 FEEDBACK OFF
PROMPT Welcome to SQL*Plus!
```

```
SELECT
 'You are connected to ' || GLOBAL_NAME || ' as ' || USER
FROM GLOBAL_NAME;
SET TIME ON PAGESIZE 24 LINESIZE 80 HEADING ON FEEDBACK ON
```

Figure 2.3 shows the SQL*Plus window setup immediately after login.

FIGURE 2.3 A SQL*Plus window

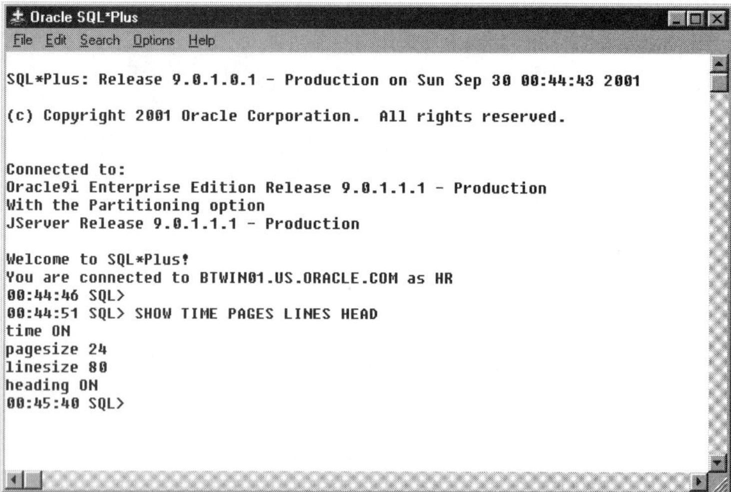

You may GET the contents of a script file with SQL*Plus commands to the SQL buffer, but trying to run the SQL*Plus commands from the buffer produces error. Use the @ or START command to run your script files.

Producing More Readable Output

Often, the results returned from SQL*Plus wrap to the next line or do not have the proper formatting. You can use simple SQL*Plus formatting commands to produce more readable output and better-looking reports. In this section, you will learn how to do the following:

- Set page and line sizes
- Define the width for a column

- Format column headings
- Display meaningful headings
- Format numeric and date datatype values
- Wrap character columns
- Suppress duplicate values
- Add a title and footer

Imagine that you have been asked to produce a report of all employees in department 50 with information on the employee ID, name, job ID, salary, and manager ID from the EMPLOYEES table of the HR schema. You issue the following query and get output similar to that shown in Figure 2.4.

```
SQL> SELECT employee_id, first_name || ' ' ||
  2         last_name emp_name, job_id, salary, manager_id
  3  FROM   employees
  4* WHERE  department_id = 50;
```

FIGURE 2.4 Query output

```
Oracle SQL*Plus
File Edit Search Options Help
EMPLOYEE_ID EMP_NAME                                       JOB_ID         SALARY
----------- ---------------------------------------------- ---------- ----------
MANAGER_ID
----------
        120 Matthew Weiss                                  ST_MAN           8000
       100

        121 Adam Fripp                                     ST_MAN           8200
       100

        122 Payam Kaufling                                 ST_MAN           7900
       100


EMPLOYEE_ID EMP_NAME                                       JOB_ID         SALARY
----------- ---------------------------------------------- ---------- ----------
MANAGER_ID
----------
        123 Shanta Vollman                                 ST_MAN           6500
       100

        124 Kevin Mourgos                                  ST_MAN           5800
       100

        125 Julia Nayer                                    ST_CLERK         3200
       120
```

Obviously, this output is not in a pretty format. You certainly would not want to present this listing as a report. Let's format this listing to make it more visually appealing.

Setting Page and Line Sizes

First, check the settings, using the SHOW command to find the values of the PAGESIZE and LINESIZE environment variables:

```
SQL> SHOW PAGESIZE LINESIZE
pagesize 14
linesize 80
SQL>
```

Let's adjust these settings to format a page size of 54 lines and a line length of 55 using the SET command. We'll also turn off the "45 rows selected" feedback.

```
SQL> SET PAGESIZE 55 LINESIZE 54
SQL> SET FEEDBACK OFF
```

Formatting Columns

You can use the COLUMN command to format column headings and display column data. To display a different heading for the EMP_NAME column, you can use this syntax:

```
COLUMN oldname HEADING "newname"
```

You can change the column display width using the FORMAT command. In our sample output, you see a lot of spaces after the employee name. Let's reduce the column display width for the name column and change the column heading used for the display:

```
SQL> COLUMN emp_name HEADING "Employee Name" FORMAT A20
```

Now we have many columns, but not enough space to display a whole row in one line. Let's make the display of the heading in two lines using the default head separator (HEADSEP) character, which is |:

```
COLUMN employee_id HEADING "Emp|ID" FORMAT 0999
```

To format the data display in the SALARY column, use the FORMAT command with the money format:

```
COLUMN salary FORMAT "$9,999.99"
```

The format models used with data are explained in detail in Chapter 3, "Single-Row Functions."

If you format a character column with an insufficient width, the data wraps to the next line, you can change the wrapping behavior using the option WRAPPED (default), WORD_WRAPPED, or TRUNCATED in the COLUMN command. You can also specify column justification using the JUSTIFY value option. Justification values available are RIGHT, LEFT, CENTER. For example, if you want to format the COMMENTS column to have a display width of 30, word-wrapped, and right-justified, with the column heading Comments, use the following command:

```
SQL> COLUMN comments HEADING "Comments" WORD_WRAPPED -
> JUSTIFY RIGHT FORMAT A30
SQL>
```

To display the current settings for a column, use the COLUMN command and column name without any options:

```
SQL> COLUMN comments
COLUMN   COMMENTS ON
HEADING  'Comments'
FORMAT   A30
JUSTIFY right word_wrap
SQL>
```

To copy the characteristics of a column to another column, use the LIKE option. In the report we are formatting, let's copy the characteristics of the EMPLOYEE_ID column to the MANAGER_ID column and give it a different heading:

```
SQL> COLUMN manager_id LIKE employee_id HEADING "Mgr|Id"
SQL>
```

Suppressing Duplicate Values

You can suppress the display of duplicate column values using the BREAK ON *column_name* command. The BREAK command has options to skip lines, pages, and so on, along with the NODUPLICATE option. Let's sort our report listing in the order of JOB_ID and group each JOB_ID together to prepare for using the BREAK ON command. Here is our query:

```
SQL> SELECT job_id, employee_id, first_name || ' ' ||
  2         last_name emp_name, salary, manager_id
  3  FROM   employees
  4  WHERE  department_id = 50
  5* ORDER BY job_id, emp_name;
```

To introduce breaks on the JOB_ID column and suppress the display of duplicate JOB_ID values, use the following command:

```
SQL> BREAK ON job_id SKIP 2 NODUPLICATES
```

Adding Headers and Footers

SQL*Plus provides commands for adding a header and footer to the report, as well as headers and footers to each page. The TTITLE and BTITLE commands insert page headers and footers, respectively. The REPHEADER and REPFOOTER commands add a report title and footer, respectively.

You can specify the following formatting specifications for headers and footers:

- COL <*n*> begins the header/footer at column <*n*>.
- SKIP <*n*> skips <*n*> lines.
- TAB <*n*> inserts <*n*> tab characters.
- BOLD displays the header/footer in bold.
- LEFT aligns the header/footer to the left of the page.
- RIGHT aligns the header/footer to the right of the page.
- CENTER aligns the header/footer to the center of the page.

You can display a page heading using the TTITLE command. The heading will be repeated for each page of the report. The page size is determined by the PAGESIZE variable. If the TTITLE command is followed by just the text in quotation marks, the current date and page number are displayed a line above the title text. Here is an example:

```
SQL> TTITLE "Current Date and Time"
SQL> SELECT SYSTIMESTAMP FROM dual;

Tue Nov 27                                    page    1
                Current Date and Time
SYSTIMESTAMP
-------------------------------------------------------
27-NOV-01 07.54.18.000000 PM -08:00
SQL>
```

If you add more formatting information to the TTITLE command, the page number and date display above the title are turned off. Here is an example:

```
SQL> TTITLE CENTER "Current Date and Time"
SQL> SELECT SYSTIMESTAMP FROM dual;

                    Current Date and Time
SYSTIMESTAMP
----------------------------------------------------
27-NOV-01 07.57.06.000000 PM -08:00
SQL>
```

The BTITLE command is used to set up a page footer (bottom title) for every page of the report. BTITLE works in a manner similar to the TTILE command. Here is an example that inserts the page number in the right corner of each page:

```
SQL> BTITLE RIGHT "PAGE " SQL.PNO.
```

The REPHEADER command adds a title to the report. This title will appear below the TTITLE and only on the first page. Here is an example:

```
SQL> REPHEADER "This is the report header"
```

Similarly, REPFOOTER is used to display a report footer at the end of the report, like this:

```
SQL> REPFOOTER "This is the report footer"
```

Using the title or footer command by itself will display the current setting of these variables. Alternatively, you can use the SHOW command to display the header and footer settings.

```
SQL> TTITLE
ttitle ON and is the following 30 characters:
CENTER "Current Date and Time"

SQL> BTITLE
btitle ON and is the following 21 characters:
RIGHT "PAGE " SQL.PNO
SQL> REPFOOTER
repfooter ON and is the following 27 characters:
"This is the report footer"
SQL> REPHEADER
repheader ON and is the following 27 characters:
```

```
"This is the report header"
SQL>

SQL> SHOW TTITLE BTITLE REPFOOTER REPHEADER
ttitle ON and is the following 30 characters:
CENTER "Current Date and Time"
btitle ON and is the following 21 characters:
RIGHT "PAGE " SQL.PNO
repfooter ON and is the following 27 characters:
"This is the report footer"
repheader ON and is the following 27 characters:
"This is the report header"
SQL>
```

Here is an example of a three-line page title. The first line is aligned to the center, the second line starts at column 10, and the third line is aligned to the right. The title begins after three blank lines and leaves two blank lines after. Notice that the command is continued to the next lines using the continuation character.

```
SQL> TTITLE SKIP 3 -
> CENTER "First line of title aligned center" -
> SKIP 1 COL 10 "Second line begins at col 10" SKIP 1 -
> RIGHT "Third line aligned right" SKIP 3
SQL> LIST
  1* SELECT SYSTIMESTAMP FROM dual
SQL> /


              First line of title aligned center
         Second line begins at col 10
                                Third line aligned right


SYSTIMESTAMP
-------------------------------------------------------
27-NOV-01 08.38.42.000001 PM -08:00
SQL>
```

This example adds a report title with a page number:

```
SQL> TTITLE CENTER "Employee Information" SKIP 1 -
>       CENTER ==================== -
>       SKIP 1 LEFT "Dept 50" -
>       RIGHT 'PAGE: ' SQL.PNO SKIP 2
```

Clearing Formatting

To clear the customizations on a column, use the CLEAR option. To turn off the column characteristics, use the OFF option. To turn column characteristics on, use the ON option. Here are some examples:

```
SQL> COLUMN COMMENTS OFF
SQL> COLUMN COMMENTS ON
SQL> COLUMN COMMENTS CLEAR
SQL> COLUMN COMMENTS
SP2-0046: COLUMN 'COMMENTS' not defined
SQL>
```

The CLEAR command can be used to clear the formatting applied to columns, clear the breaks and computations, clear the screen, or clear the SQL buffer. Here are some examples:

```
SQL> CLEAR BREAKS
breaks cleared
SQL> CLEAR COLUMNS
columns cleared
SQL> CLEAR BUFFER
buffer cleared
SQL> CLEAR COMPUTES
computes cleared
SQL> CLEAR SCREEN
```

The following commands will turn off the display of headers and footers.

```
SQL> TTITLE OFF
SQL> BTITLE OFF
SQL> REPHEADER OFF
SQL> REPFOOTER OFF
```

Using a Script File to Create a Report

Now you have a pretty report. You have entered all these formatting commands to produce your report. What about the next time? You can save the formatting and query in a script file and just run the file to produce the report whenever you want to. Here is the script listing:

```
REM MYFIRSTREP.SQL
REM TO PRACTICE REPORT FORMATTING
REM CREATE ON 09-30-2001
REM
SET PAGES 55 LINES 54 TRIMS ON
SET FEEDBACK OFF ECHO OFF DOCUMENT OFF
SET UNDERLINE =
/*
   This is an example of multiple-line comments.
   Following lines are column-formatting commands.
*/
COLUMN employee_id HEADING "Empl|Id" FORMAT 0999
COLUMN emp_name HEADING "Employee Name" FORMAT A20
COLUMN job_id HEADING "Position"
COLUMN manager_id LIKE employee_id HEADING "Mgr|Id"
COLUMN salary FORMAT "$9,999" HEADING "Salary"
/*
   Save the output to a file. Provide a heading.
*/
SPOOL EMPINFO.LST
TTITLE CENTER "Employee Information" SKIP 1 -
       CENTER ==================== SKIP 1 LEFT "Dept 50" -
      RIGHT 'PAGE: ' SQL.PNO SKIP 2
REM
REM Suppress duplicate JOB_ID values
REM
BREAK ON job_id SKIP 2 NODUPLICATES
--
-- Two hyphens can also be used to specify a comment.
-- The query
SELECT job_id, employee_id, first_name || ' ' ||
       last_name emp_name, salary, manager_id
```

```
FROM   employees
WHERE  department_id = 50
ORDER BY job_id, emp_name
/
REM Clear customizations
REM
CLEAR COLUMNS
CLEAR BREAKS
TTITLE OFF
SET FEEDBACK ON DOCUMENT ON
```

Executing the script produces the EMPINFO.LST file, with the following output:

```
                 Employee Information
                 ====================
Dept 50                                PAGE:         1

            Empl                                  Mgr
Position      Id Employee Name         Salary    Id
========== ===== ==================== ======= =====
SH_CLERK    0196 Alana Walsh           $3,100  0124
            0185 Alexis Bull           $4,100  0121
            0187 Anthony Cabrio        $3,000  0121
            0193 Britney Everett       $3,900  0123
            0198 Donald OConnell       $2,600  0124
            0199 Douglas Grant         $2,600  0124
            0183 Girard Geoni          $2,800  0120
… … …
            0128 Steven Markle         $2,200  0120
            0132 TJ Olson              $2,100  0121
            0141 Trenna Rajs           $3,500  0124


ST_MAN      0121 Adam Fripp            $8,200  0100
            0124 Kevin Mourgos         $5,800  0100
            0120 Matthew Weiss         $8,000  0100
            0122 Payam Kaufling        $7,900  0100
            0123 Shanta Vollman        $6,500  0100
```

Performing Summary Operations

COMPUTE is a SQL*Plus command to perform any summary operation on the grouped columns. Normally, BREAK and COMPUTE appear together in the script files. The summary operations available with COMPUTE are SUM, MINIMUM, MAXIMUM, AVG, STD, VARIANCE, COUNT, and NUMBER. The LABEL clause in the COMPUTE command provides a label for the summary result. Here is an example to calculate the total salary for each department's employees (we limit the rows to only the employees whose name begin with *S*):

```
SQL> BREAK ON department_id
SQL> COMPUTE SUM LABEL "Dept Total" OF salary -
> ON department_id
SQL> SELECT department_id, first_name, salary
  2  FROM   employees
  3  WHERE  first_name like 'S%'
  4* ORDER BY department_id, first_name
SQL> /

DEPARTMENT_ID FIRST_NAME               SALARY
------------- -------------------- ----------
           30 Shelli                     2900
              Sigal                      2800
*************                      ----------
Dept Total                               5700
           40 Susan                      6500
*************                      ----------
Dept Total                               6500
           50 Samuel                     3200
              Sarah                      4000
              Shanta                     6500
              Stephen                    3200
              Steven                     2200
*************                      ----------
Dept Total                              19100
```

Edit the `myfirstrep.sql` file and add the following line after the BREAK command:

```
COMPUTE AVG LABEL "Avg Salary" OF salary ON job_id
```

Real World Scenario

Develop a Weekly Report to Monitor the New Objects Created in the Database

The application manager wants to know the modules that are migrated to production every week. He wants to know the schema, object name, type of object, and date created for all objects created in the past week. As the DBA of the production database, Ann must prepare the report and e-mail it to the manager. Since this report is to be generated every week, she wants to create a script and schedule it to run every Monday morning.

Ann knows the information her manager is looking for is available in the DBA view named DBA_OBJECTS. (You need the SELECT ANY TABLE, SELECT_CATALOG_ROLE, or DBA privilege to query this view; you may connect to the database as SYSTEM/MANAGER.) Let's help Ann create the script.

```
SQL> DESCRIBE dba_objects
 Name                           Null?    Type
 ------------------------------ -------- -------------
 OWNER                                   VARCHAR2(30)
 OBJECT_NAME                             VARCHAR2(128)
 SUBOBJECT_NAME                          VARCHAR2(30)
 OBJECT_ID                               NUMBER
 DATA_OBJECT_ID                          NUMBER
 OBJECT_TYPE                             VARCHAR2(18)
 CREATED                                 DATE
 LAST_DDL_TIME                           DATE
 TIMESTAMP                               VARCHAR2(19)
 STATUS                                  VARCHAR2(7)
 TEMPORARY                               VARCHAR2(1)
```

```
GENERATED                                    VARCHAR2(1)

SECONDARY                                    VARCHAR2(1)

SQL>
```

The columns needed for the report are OWNER, OBJECT_TYPE, OBJECT_NAME, CREATED, and STATUS. These are the columns included in the SELECT clause. Of course, the FROM clause will specify DBA_OBJECTS. The SYSDATE function returns the current date and time, so we need to find all the objects that are created after SYSDATE-7. This goes in the WHERE clause. Using the ORDER BY clause, we'll order the results by the object type and name.

The query is ready, so let's think about the formatting needed. Since Ann wants the report to be able to print on an A4 sheet, the width of the report should not exceed 72 characters per line and 68 lines per page. That's SET LINESIZE 72 PAGESIZE 68. We need to apply formatting to each column in the report to minimize the blank spaces between columns and to have one row of results in one line. We will store the report in the directory /dba/reports.

```
REM SCRIPT TO REPORT OBJECTS CREATED IN THE PAST WEEK

REM

REM Created on 02-OCT-2002 by Ann Alexander

REM

SET PAGES 68 LINES 72

SET FEEDBACK OFF

SPOOL /dba/reports/NEWOBJ.LST

TTITLE "OBJECTS CREATED IN THE DATABASE DURING PAST WEEK"

COL OBJECT_TYPE FORMAT A12

COL NAME        FORMAT A30

SELECT object_type, owner ||'.'|| object_name as name,

       TO_CHAR(created, 'mm-dd-yyyy hh24:mi:ss')

       "CREATED ON", status
```

```
FROM   dba_objects
WHERE  created >= (SYSDATE - 7)
ORDER BY object_type, name;
SPOOL OFF
TTITLE OFF
CLEAR COLUMNS
SET FEEDBACK ON
```

The output of the report is similar to the sample below, which is saved to /dba/reports/NEWOBJ.LST.

```
SQL> @ANNS_REP


Sun Nov 04                                       page    1
   OBJECTS CREATED IN THE DATABASE DURING PAST WEEK


OBJECT_TYPE  NAME           CREATED ON           STATUS
------------ ------------   -------------------  -------
VIEW         HR.EMP_COMM    10-28-2002 19:43:53  VALID
SQL>
```

Accepting Values at Runtime

To create an interactive SQL statement, you can define variables in the SQL statement. This allows the user to supply values at runtime, further enhancing the ability to reuse your scripts. SQL*Plus lets you define variables in your scripts. An ampersand (&), followed by a variable name, prompts for and accepts values at runtime. For example, the following SELECT statement queries the DEPARTMENTS table based on the department number supplied at runtime.

```
SQL> SELECT department_name
  2  FROM   departments
```

```
  3  WHERE   department_id = &dept
  4  /
Enter value for dept: 10
old   3: WHERE   DEPARTMENT_ID = &dept
new   3: WHERE   DEPARTMENT_ID = 10

DEPARTMENT_NAME
---------------
Administration

1 row selected.
SQL>
```

Using Substitution Variables

Suppose that you have defined DEPT as a variable in your script, but you want to avoid the prompt for the value at runtime. SQL*Plus prompts you for a value only when the variable is undefined. You can define a *substitution variable* in SQL*Plus using the `DEFINE` command to provide a value. The variable will always have the CHAR datatype associated with it. Here is an example of defining a substitution variable:

```
SQL> DEFINE DEPT = 20
SQL> DEFINE DEPT
DEFINE DEPT            = "20" (CHAR)
SQL> LIST
  1  SELECT department_name
  2  FROM    departments
  3* WHERE   department_id = &DEPT
SQL> /
old   3: WHERE   DEPARTMENT_ID = &DEPT
new   3: WHERE   DEPARTMENT_ID = 20

DEPARTMENT_NAME
---------------
Marketing

1 row selected.
SQL>
```

Using the DEFINE command without any arguments shows the defined variables.

A . (dot) is used to append characters immediately after the substitution variable. The dot separates the variable name and the literal that follows immediately. If you need a dot to be part of the literal, provide two dots continuously. For example, the following query appends _REP to the user input when seeking a value from the JOBS table.

```
SQL> SELECT job_id, job_title FROM jobs
  2* WHERE  job_id = '&JOB._REP'
SQL> /
Enter value for job: MK
old   2: WHERE  JOB_ID = '&JOB._REP'
new   2: WHERE  JOB_ID = 'MK_REP'

JOB_ID     JOB_TITLE
---------- -----------------------
MK_REP     Marketing Representative

1 row selected.
SQL>
```

The old line with the variable and the new line with the substitution are displayed. You can turn off this display by using the command SET VERIFY OFF.

Saving a Variable for a Session

Consider the following SQL, saved to a file named ex01.sql. When you execute this script file, you will be prompted for COL1 and COL2 values multiple times:

```
SQL> SELECT &COL1, &COL2
  2  FROM   &TABLE
  3  WHERE  &COL1 = '&VAL'
  4  ORDER BY &COL2
  5
SQL> SAVE ex01
Created file ex01.sql
```

```
SQL> @ex01
Enter value for col1: FIRST_NAME
Enter value for col2: LAST_NAME
old   1: SELECT &COL1, &COL2
new   1: SELECT FIRST_NAME, LAST_NAME
Enter value for table: EMPLOYEES
old   2: FROM   &TABLE
new   2: FROM   EMPLOYEES
Enter value for col1: FIRST_NAME
Enter value for val: John
old   3: WHERE  &COL1 = '&VAL'
new   3: WHERE  FIRST_NAME = 'John'
Enter value for col2: LAST_NAME
old   4: ORDER BY &COL2
new   4: ORDER BY LAST_NAME

FIRST_NAME           LAST_NAME
-------------------- ---------
John                 Chen
John                 Russell
John                 Seo

3 rows selected.
SQL>
```

When using substitution variables for character or date values, make sure that you enclose the variables in single quotes, otherwise the user has to enclose them in quotes at runtime. If not enclosed in single quotes, Oracle considers any non-numeric value as a column name.

The user can enter different or wrong values for each prompt. To avoid multiple prompts, use the && (double ampersand), where the variable is saved for the session.

To clear a defined variable you can use the UNDEFINE command. Let's edit the ex01.sql file to make it look like this:

```
SELECT &&COL1, &&COL2
FROM   &TABLE
```

```
WHERE  &COL1 = '&VAL'
ORDER BY &COL2
/
UNDEFINE COL1 COL2
```

Using Positional Notation for Variables

Instead of variable names, you can use positional notation, where each variable is identified by &1, &2, and so on. The values are assigned to the variables by position. Do this by putting an ampersand (&), followed by a numeral, in place of a variable name. Consider the following query:

```
SQL> SELECT department_name, department_id
  2  FROM   departments
  3  WHERE  &1 = &2;
Enter value for 1: DEPARTMENT_ID
Enter value for 2: 10
old   3: WHERE  &1 = &2
new   3: WHERE  DEPARTMENT_ID = 10

DEPARTMENT_NAME                DEPARTMENT_ID
------------------------------ -------------
Administration                            10

1 row selected.
SQL>
```

If you save the SQL as a script file, you can submit the substitution variable values while invoking the script (as command-line arguments). Each time you run this command file, START replaces each &1 in the file with the first value (called an *argument*) after START *filename*, then replaces each &2 with the second value, and so forth. Here is an example of saving and executing the previous query:

```
SQL> SAVE ex02
Created file ex02.sql
SQL> SET VERIFY OFF
SQL> @ex02 department_id 20
```

```
DEPARTMENT_NAME                DEPARTMENT_ID
------------------------------ -------------
Marketing                                 20

1 row selected.
SQL>
```

Although we did not specify two ampersands for positional substitution variables, SQL*Plus keeps the values of these variables for the session (since we passed the values as parameters to a script file). Next time you run any script with positional substitution variables, Oracle uses these values to execute the script.

Using the *ACCEPT* Command

SQL*Plus provides the ACCEPT command to accept values from the user. This command is a useful way to provide the user with a prompt and to get user input. Also, the ACCEPT command lets you define the datatype of the variable. The PROMPT option lets you display text to the user. You can hide the user input by specifying the HIDE option, this is especially useful for accepting passwords.

To see some examples of using the ACCEPT command, we'll create a script file named ex03.sql, and then run it in SQL*Plus.

```
REM SCRIPT TO DEMONSTRATE ACCEPT and PROMPT
ACCEPT PWD CHAR PROMPT 'Enter your password:' HIDE
PROMPT
PROMPT This query displays the Employee ID and Name for
PROMPT the employees in the department you supply
PROMPT ================================================
ACCEPT DEPTNUMB NUMBER PROMPT "Enter Department Number: "
SET VERIFY OFF
SELECT employee_id, last_name
FROM   employees
WHERE  department_id = &DEPTNUMB
ORDER BY last_name;
SET VERIFY ON

SQL> @ex03
Enter your password:**
```

```
This query displays the Employee ID and Name for
the employees in the department you supply
================================================
Enter Department Number: 10

EMPLOYEE_ID LAST_NAME
----------- -------------------------
        200 Whalen

1 row selected.
SQL>
```

Using iSQL*Plus

*iSQL*Plus* is the web interface of SQL*Plus. You do not need to install the client software on your PC—all you need is a browser to connect to a database. Then you can start using iSQL*Plus. Here, we will cover the iSQL*Plus architecture and interface.

iSQL*Plus Architecture

iSQL*Plus architecture has three components:

Database layer You must have a valid username in the Oracle database. The database layer consists of the Oracle9i database and *Oracle Net.* (SQL*Plus has this layer.)

Middle layer The middle layer consists of the Oracle HTTP server (Apache) and *iSQL*Plus server*. The middle layer can be on the same server where the database resides. The connection identifier you enter on the login screen should be defined in the `tnsnames.ora` file on this layer. (SQL*Plus does not have this layer.)

Client layer The client layer is a user interface running on the web browser. You need to know the URL of the HTTP server (`http://hostname.domain/isqlplus`). (SQL*Plus needs the SQL*Plus executable, which may be on the client PC or with the database layer.)

Working with iSQL*Plus

Figure 2.5 shows the iSQL*Plus login screen. Click the Help icon to open the iSQL*Plus user guide in a separate window. Enter the username, password, and connection identifier. Then click Log In to connect to the database. If you have DBA privileges, you can connect to the database as SYSDBA or SYSOPER.

FIGURE 2.5 The iSQL*Plus login screen

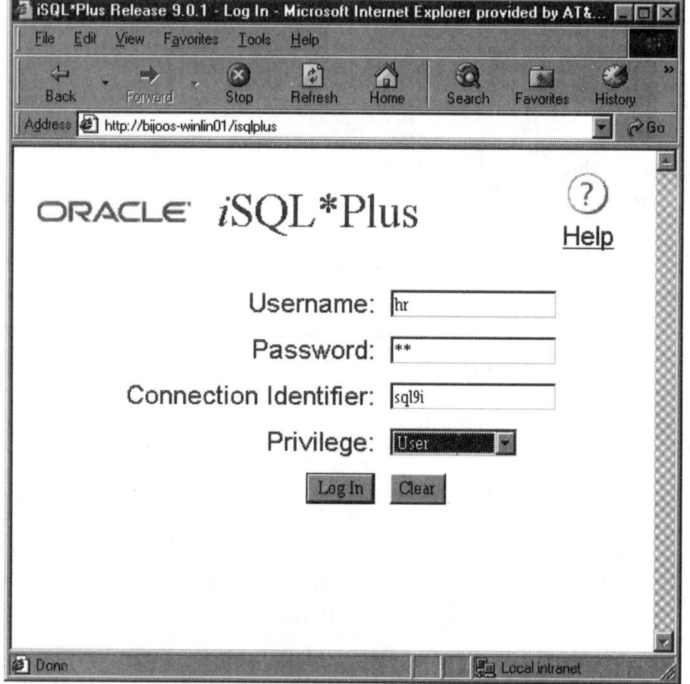

Figure 2.6 shows the iSQL*Plus work screen. The Password icon lets you change your password. To log out of the iSQL*Plus session, click the Logout icon. For the Script Location option, specify the script to load into the work area. You can browse the folders using the Browse button and load the script to the work area using the Load Script button. The window under "Enter Statements" is the work area. Enter your SQL statements here, and execute them by clicking the Execute button. The output can be displayed on this work screen, displayed in a separate window, or sent to a file.

FIGURE 2.6 The iSQL*Plus work screen

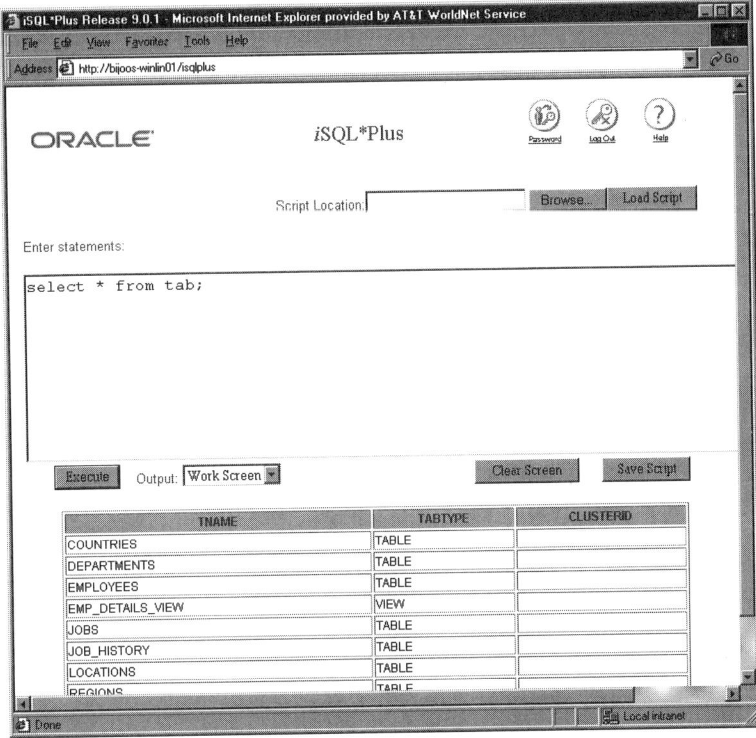

Ending a SQL statement with ; or entering a / in a new line will not execute statements in the iSQL*Plus work area. You must click the Execute button to execute the statements in the window. If you have multiple iSQL*Plus commands or SQL statements, make sure you terminate each iSQL*Plus command with a semicolon.

To see how this works, enter the following SQL in the iSQL*Plus work area:

```
SELECT department_name, department_id
FROM   departments
WHERE  department_id = &deptid
```

Now, click the Execute button. A screen will pop up to accept values for the substitution variable, as shown in Figure 2.7. When you click the Submit for Execution button, the result will be displayed.

FIGURE 2.7 Accepting values in iSQL*Plus

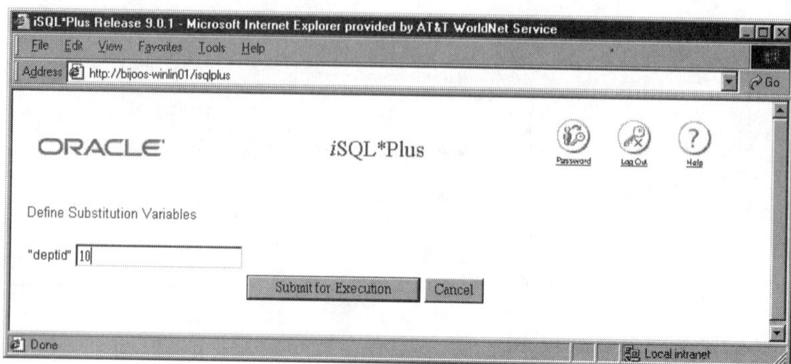

iSQL*Plus Restrictions

Since iSQL*Plus is web-based, certain commands have not been implemented (at least, at the time this book was published). The version of iSQL*Plus used for this book is 9.0.1.1. None of the SQL buffer-editing commands are implemented in iSQL*Plus. Following are the SQL*Plus commands that are not available in iSQL*Plus:

ACCEPT	CLEAR SCREEN	EXIT
GET	HOST	PASSWORD
PAUSE	SAVE	SPOOL
STORE	WHENEVER OSERROR EXIT	WHENEVER SQLERROR EXIT

The following SET commands are also not available in iSQL*Plus:

COLSEP	EDITFILE	FLUSH
NEWPAGE	PAUSE	SHIFTINOUT
SQLBLANKLINES	SQLCONTINUE	SQLNUMBER
SQLPREFIX	SQLPROMPT	SUFFIX
TAB	TERMOUT	TIME
TRIMOUT	TRIMSPOOL	

Summary

SQL*Plus is Oracle's native tool to interact with the database. SQL*Plus supports all SQL statements and has its own formatting and enhancement commands. In Oracle9i, SQL*Plus includes commands to support database administration. Using this tool, you can produce interactive SQL statements and formatted reports.

SQL*Plus has its own buffer where SQL statements are buffered. You can edit the buffer using SQL*Plus editing commands. The `DESCRIBE` command is used to get information on a table, view, function, or procedure.

Multiple SQL and SQL*Plus commands can be stored in a file and can be executed as a unit. Such files are called script files. The `SET` command is used to set various environment settings in SQL*Plus. The `COLUMN` command is used to define the characteristics of columns used in a SQL query.

You can define variables in SQL*Plus. Variables can be used in the SQL statements also. Values will be accepted as user input when the SQL is executed. Defined variables in SQL*Plus always have CHAR datatype.

iSQL*Plus is the web interface to SQL*Plus. iSQL*Plus consists of three layers: the client layer (web browser), the middle layer (Oracle HTTP server and iSQL*Plus server), and the database layer (Oracle database and Oracle Net). Certain SQL*Plus commands are not available in iSQL*Plus.

Exam Essentials

Understand the SQL statements and SQL*Plus commands. SQL*Plus is a tool to interact with the Oracle database using SQL statements. SQL*Plus has its own commands to format query results and perform database administrative tasks.

Know the system variables used to set up the environment. Practice using the various `SET` commands. The `SHOW ALL` command lists all the values for the environment variables.

Learn the formatting commands. Query results can be formatted using `COLUMN`, `BREAK`, `TTITLE`, `BTITLE`, `REPHEADER`, `REPFOOTER`, and `SET` commands.

Know the commands used to edit the SQL buffer. The SQL buffer in SQL*Plus stores SQL statements. SQL*Plus commands such as LIST, CHANGE, DEL, INPUT, and APPEND are available to edit the buffer contents.

Know how to create and execute script files. You can create a script file from the buffer, add commands to the file, and execute the script file. Understand the difference between @ and @@, as well as & and &&.

Know the architecture of iSQL*Plus. Understand the components of iSQL*Plus and which layer each component fits into.

Key Terms

Before you take the exam, make sure you're familiar with the following terms:

environment variables	password
host string	script file
iSQL*Plus	SQL buffer
iSQL*Plus server	substitution variable
Oracle Net	username

Commands Used in This Chapter

The following table summarizes the SQL*Plus commands discussed in this chapter. For more information about each command, including its syntax, issue HELP *<command name>* from the SQL*Plus prompt. HELP INDEX provides the list of all SQL*Plus commands, including the ones used for database administration.

Command	Purpose
@	Runs the SQL*Plus statements in the specified script or command file.

Command	Purpose
@@	Runs the specified command file. This command is similar to the @ command, useful for running nested command files because it looks for the specified command file in the same path as the command file from which it was called.
/	Executes the SQL command from the SQL buffer.
ACCEPT	Reads a line of input and stores it in a variable.
APPEND	Adds text to the end of the current line in the SQL buffer.
BREAK	Specifies where and how to make format changes to a report.
BTITLE	Similar to TTITLE, but provides a title at the bottom of each page.
CHANGE	Changes the first occurrence of the specified text on the current line of the SQL buffer.
CLEAR	Erases the current format settings for columns, breaks, computes, etc.
COLUMN	Defines display attributes for a column.
COMPUTE	Defines and prints summary lines.
CONNECT	Connects a given username to Oracle.
DEFINE	Defines a user variable and assigns it a CHAR value.
DEL	Deletes one or more lines of the SQL buffer.
DESCRIBE	Lists the column definitions for a table, view, or synonym, or the specifications for a function or procedure.
DISCONNECT	Commits pending changes to the database and logs the current user out of Oracle, but does not exit SQL*Plus.
EDIT	Edits the SQL buffer or a file.
EXIT	Disconnects from Oracle and terminates SQL*Plus.
GET	Loads text from a command file to the SQL buffer.
HELP	Gets help on a SQL*Plus command.

Command	Purpose
INPUT	Adds one or more lines of text after the current line in the SQL buffer.
LIST	Lists one or more lines of the SQL buffer.
PASSWORD	Allows you to change a password without echoing the password.
PAUSE	Displays the specified text, then waits for the user to press Return after displaying a page of query results.
PROMPT	Displays the specified message or a blank line on the screen.
QUIT	Similar to EXIT.
REMARK	Specifies single-line comments.
REPFOOTER	Provides a report footer, appearing once for each report.
REPHEADER	Provides a report header, appearing once for each report.
RUN	Executes the SQL command currently in the SQL buffer.
SAVE	Saves the contents of the SQL buffer in an operating system file.
SET	Sets a system variable to alter the SQL*Plus environment settings.
SHOW	Shows the value of a SQL*Plus system variable or the current SQL*Plus environment.
SPOOL	Stores query results in an operating system file.
START	Runs the SQL*Plus statements in the specified command file.
STORE	Saves attributes of the current SQL*Plus environment in a command file.
TTITLE	Places and formats a title at the top of each report page.
UNDEFINE	Deletes one or more user variables that are defined.

Review Questions

1. What is wrong with the following statements submitted in SQL*Plus?

```
DEFINE V_DEPTNO = 20
SELECT LAST_NAME, SALARY
FROM    EMPLOYEES
WHERE DEPARTMENT_ID = V_DeptNo;
```

   A. Nothing is wrong. The query lists the employee name and salary of the employees who belong to department 20.

   B. The DEFINE statement declaration is wrong.

   C. The substitution variable is not preceded with the & character.

   D. The substitution variable in the WHERE clause should be V_DEPTNO instead of V_DeptNo.

2. Which command in SQL*Plus is used to save the query output to a file?

   A. PRINT

   B. SAVE

   C. REPLACE

   D. SPOOL

3. How would you execute a SQL statement in the SQL buffer of SQL*Plus? (Choose all that apply.)

   A. Enter a slash (/).

   B. Enter an ampersand (&).

   C. Enter a semicolon (;).

   D. Press Ctrl+D (^D).

4. You issue the SQL*Plus command `SPOOL ON`. Which task is accomplished?

   A. The next screen output from the SQL*Plus session is saved into a file named `afiedt.buf`.

   B. The next screen output from the SQL*Plus session is saved into a file named `ON.lst`.

   C. The next screen output from the SQL*Plus session is sent to the printer.

   D. Nothing happens; a filename is missing from the command.

5. Which SQL*Plus command always overwrites a file?

   A. `SPOOL`

   B. `RUN`

   C. `REPLACE`

   D. `SAVE`

6. Which SQL*Plus command is used to display a title on every page of the report?

   A. `TOPTITLE`

   B. `TITLE`

   C. `TTITLE`

   D. `REPTITLE`

7. Choose two commands that are not valid in iSQL*Plus.

   A. `PASSWORD`

   B. `TTITLE`

   C. `CONNECT`

   D. `EXIT`

8. Which character is used to indicate that the command is continued on the next line in SQL*Plus?

   A. -

   B. /

   C. \

   D. >

9. You have the following SQL in the SQL buffer of SQL*Plus:

```
SELECT EMPLOYEE_ID, LAST_NAME
FROM   EMPLOYEES
WHERE  LAST_NAME = FIRST_NAME
ORDER BY LAST_NAME
```

   You perform the following SQL*Plus commands on the buffer:

```
3
c/NAME/NAMES/
```

   Which SQL command will be in the buffer?

   A.
```
SELECT EMPLOYEE_ID, LAST_NAMES
FROM   EMPLOYEES
WHERE  LAST_NAMES = FIRST_NAMES
ORDER BY LAST_NAMES
```

   B.
```
SELECT EMPLOYEE_ID, LAST_NAME
FROM   EMPLOYEES
WHERE  LAST_NAMES = FIRST_NAME
ORDER BY LAST_NAME
```

   C.
```
SELECT EMPLOYEE_ID, LAST_NAME
FROM   EMPLOYEES
WHERE  LAST_NAMES = FIRST_NAMES
ORDER BY LAST_NAME
```

   D.
```
SELECT EMPLOYEE_ID, LAST_NAME
FROM   EMPLOYEES
WHERE  LAST_NAME = FIRST_NAME
ORDER BY LAST_NAME
```

10. Which of the following is the correct syntax to define a variable?

   A. DEFINE *variable=value*

   B. DEFINE *variable datatype := value*

   C. DEFINE &*variable*

   D. DEFINE *variable value*

   E. None of the above

11. Which SET option turns off the display of the old and new SQL statement line when variables are used?

   A. ECHO OFF

   B. HEADING OFF

   C. VERIFY OFF

   D. FEEDBACK OFF

   E. DEFINE OFF

12. Which of the following is not a valid option with the SAVE command?

   A. CREATE

   B. REPLACE

   C. APPEND

   D. INSERT

13. You execute the following lines of code in SQL*Plus:

```
SQL> SELECT department_id, first_name, salary
  2  FROM   employees
  3  WHERE  first_name LIKE 'S%'
  4  ORDER BY department_id, first_name
  5
SQL> COLUMN department_id FORMAT A20
SQL> C/department_id/employee_id
```

Which of the following best describes the code?

A. The department_id in the COLUMN command is replaced with employee_id.

B. The department_id in the COLUMN command is cleared (deleted).

C. The department_id in the fourth line of the SELECT statement is replaced with employee_id.

D. All the department_id occurrences in the SELECT statement are replaced with employee_id.

14. Which of the following is not a valid method for including comments?

A. Prefix comments with --.

B. Begin comment line with REMARK.

C. Begin comment line with #.

D. Include comments between /* and */.

15. Consider the following SQL:

```
SELECT department_id, last_name, salary
FROM   employees
ORDER BY department_id, last_name
```

Which SQL*Plus command(s) will display the total salary for each department and suppress listing of duplicate department IDs?

A. COMPUTE SUM OF SALARY ON DEPARTMENT_ID
BREAK ON DEPARTMENT_ID

B. BREAK ON DEPARTMENT_ID NODUPLICATES
COMPUTE SUM ON SALARY FOR DEPARTMENT_ID

C. BREAK ON DEPARTMENT_ID NODUPLICATES -
SUM ON SALARY

D. None of the above. SQL*Plus cannot be used to total column values.

16. When using iSQL*Plus, how do you write the query results to a file?

    A. Use the SPOOL command to specify an output filename.

    B. Use the Output drop-down button and select File.

    C. Perform option A *and* B.

    D. Perform either option A *or* B.

17. What will happen when you click the Execute button with the following SQL in iSQL*Plus?

```
SELECT employee_id, last_name, first_name
FROM   employees
WHERE  department_id = &deptid
```

    A. Nothing will happen, because the statement is missing a ;.

    B. An error is produced, because substitution variables are not allowed in iSQL*Plus.

    C. A new window will be opened to accept the value for DEPTID.

    D. The cursor moves to the string input area to accept value for DEPTID.

18. Which two statements regarding substitution variables are true?

    A. &*variable* is defined by SQL*Plus, and its value will be available for the duration of the session.

    B. &&*variable* is defined by SQL*Plus, and its value will be available for the duration of the session.

    C. &*n* (where *n* is a any integer) variables are defined by SQL*Plus when values are passed in as arguments to the script, and their values will be available for the duration of the session.

    D. &&*variable* is defined by SQL*Plus, and its value will be available only for every reference to that variable in the current SQL.

19. The contents of the script file MYSQL.sql are as follows:

```
SET PAGES 55 LINES 80 FEEDBACK OFF
SELECT last_name, first_name
FROM   employees
WHERE  employee_id = &empid;
```

What will happen when you issue the START MYSQL 101 command?

A. 101 will be substituted for the variable EMPID.

B. You will be prompted to enter a value for EMPID.

C. An error will be returned because EMPID is not preceded by &&.

20. The EMP table is defined with the following columns:

```
EMPID        NUMBER (5)
ENAME        VARCHAR2 (30)
JOB_TITLE    VARCHAR2 (30)
```

You execute the following SQL, and supply a value as shown.

```
SQL> SELECT * FROM EMP
  2  WHERE  ENAME = &name;
Enter value for name: John
```

What will be the result?

A. All the column values from the EMP table are displayed for the record with ENAME as John.

B. An error is returned, because John is a character literal and must be enclosed in quotation marks.

C. An error is returned, because Name is a reserved word in SQL*Plus, so it cannot be used as a variable.

D. The input value John will be converted to uppercase, and values from the EMP table are displayed for the record with ENAME as JOHN.

Answers to Review Questions

1. C. The query will return an error, because the substitution variable is used without an ampersand (&) character. In this query, Oracle treats `V_DEPTNO` as another column name from the table and returns an error. Substitution variables are not case sensitive.

2. D. The `SPOOL` command is used to save the query results to a file. Issue `SPOOL` ***`filename`*** before the query and `SPOOL OFF` after the query to save the contents. The `SAVE` command is used to save the SQL statement in the buffer.

3. A. You can execute a statement in the SQL buffer using the slash. A semicolon will just display the buffer again (similar to the `LIST` command).

4. B. The `SPOOL` command is used to save the SQL*Plus session output in a file. The `SPOOL` command expects a filename or the keywords `OUT` or `OFF`. `SPOOL OFF` will turn off spooling; `SPOOL OUT` will turn off spooling and send the output file contents to a printer. If an extension is not specified for the filename, a default extension of `.lst` is added.

5. A. The `SPOOL` command always creates a new file; it will not append to an existing file. The `SAVE` command will give an error if the file exists. To overwrite an existing file, you need to specify the `REPLACE` option with `SAVE`. `REPLACE` is not a valid command.

6. C. `TTITLE` is used to specify a title at the top of every page. A report title at the beginning of the report can be specified using the `REPHEADER` command.

7. A, D. Certain SQL*Plus commands are not available in iSQL*Plus. Most of the unavailable commands are not implemented because they are not relevant on a web interface. Some commands are not implemented because they are not secure on the web server.

8. A. The continuation character in SQL*Plus is `-`. You do not need to use a continuation character for SQL statements, but you need one for the SQL*Plus commands. This is because SQL*Plus commands do not need to be terminated with `;` or `/`, whereas SQL statements have a terminator.

9. B. The first SQL*Plus command, `3`, makes the third line on the buffer as the current line. The next command, `c`, changes the first occurrence of NAME to NAMES.

10. A. To define a variable, you use the syntax `DEFINE` *`variable`*`=`*`value`*. The variable will always be the CHAR datatype. To list the value of a variable, use `DEFINE` *`variable`*.

11. C. `SET VERIFY OFF` will turn off the old and new line display when variables are used. `SET ECHO OFF` turns off the display of SQL statements when running scripts. `SET HEADING OFF` turns off the display of column headings. `SET FEEDBACK OFF` turns off the feedback after executing each SQL statement. `SET DEFINE OFF` turns off scanning for substitution variables in the SQL.

12. D. The `SAVE` command is used to write the SQL buffer to a file. `CREATE` is the default behavior; the file should not exist for this option to work. `REPLACE` overwrites the file. `APPEND` adds the buffer to the end of the file if the file exists. The same options are also valid for the `STORE SET` command, which is used to save the `SET` environment to a file.

13. C. `C` is the abbreviation for `CHANGE`, which is a SQL buffer-editing command. Only SQL statements are saved in the buffer; SQL*Plus commands are not saved. Since the `SELECT` statement was the last SQL statement, the cursor stayed in the last line of that statement. Therefore, the `CHANGE` command was applied on the line beginning with the `ORDER BY` clause.

14. C. Comments increase the readability of scripts. Comments using `--` or `/* */` can be included anywhere in the SQL, but `REMARK` should be on a line of its own. SQL*Plus ignores the rest of the line for `REMARK` and `--` comments.

15. A. You need both the `BREAK` and `COMPUTE` commands to group values and perform an operation (like sum or average). `NODUPLICATES` is the default behavior for the `BREAK` command. You can optionally include a `LABEL` clause in the `COMPUTE` command to replace the default column heading.

16. B. The `SPOOL` command is disabled in iSQL*Plus. You need to select the File option from the Output drop-down list and specify a filename. Similarly, the Load Script button can be used as the `GET` command, and the Clear Screen button can be used as the `CLEAR SCREEN` command.

17. C. When substitution variables are used in iSQL*Plus, a new window will open to get the values for all variables before executing the SQL.

18. B, C. When a variable is preceded by double ampersands, SQL*Plus defines that variable. Similarly, when you pass values to a script using the `START` *`script_name arguments`*, SQL*Plus defines those variables. Once a variable is defined, its value will be available for the duration of the session or until you use `UNDEFINE` *`variable`*.

19. B. You can pass values of substitution variables as parameters to a script only when the substitution variables are defined as positional variables (&1, &2, and so on).

20. B. The `WHERE` clause of the query will become `WHERE ENAME = John`. Oracle will look for a column named John in the EMP table and return an error. The character literal must be enclosed in quotation marks. The `WHERE` clause should be written as `WHERE ENAME = '&NAME'`.

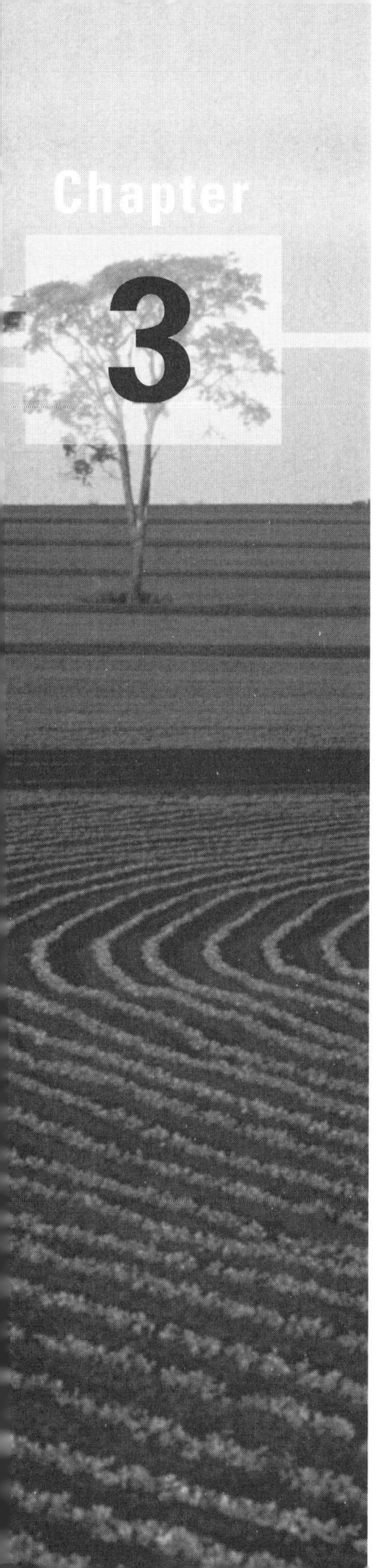

Single-Row Functions

INTRODUCTION TO ORACLE9i: SQL EXAM OBJECTIVES COVERED IN THIS CHAPTER:

✓ **Single-Row Functions**

- Describe various types of functions available in SQL
- Use character, number, and date functions in SELECT statements
- Use conversion functions

Exam objectives are subject to change at any time without prior notice and at Oracle's sole discretion. Please visit Oracle's Certification website (`http://www.oracle.com/education/certification/`) for the most current exam objectives listing.

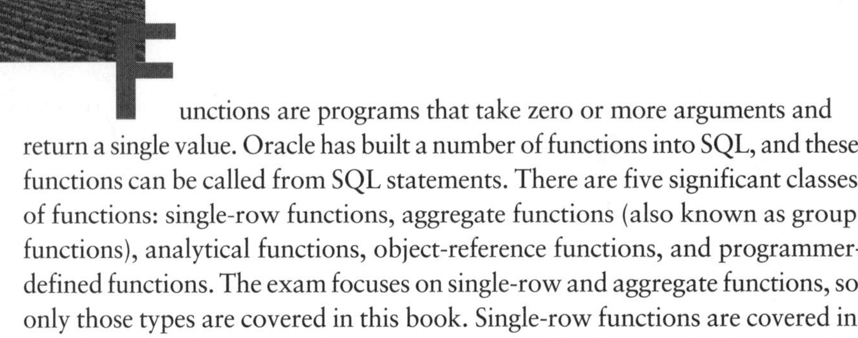

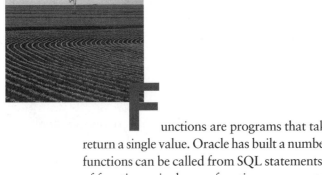

Functions are programs that take zero or more arguments and return a single value. Oracle has built a number of functions into SQL, and these functions can be called from SQL statements. There are five significant classes of functions: single-row functions, aggregate functions (also known as group functions), analytical functions, object-reference functions, and programmer-defined functions. The exam focuses on single-row and aggregate functions, so only those types are covered in this book. Single-row functions are covered in this chapter, and aggregate functions are covered in Chapter 4, "Aggregating Data And Group Functions."

Single-row functions operate on expressions derived from columns or literals, and they are executed once for each row retrieved. In this chapter, we will cover which single-row functions are available, the rules for how to use them, and what to expect on the exam about single-row functions.

Single-Row Function Fundamentals

There are many types of *single-row* functions built into SQL. These include character, numeric, date, conversion, and miscellaneous single-row functions, as well as programmer-written stored functions.

All single-row functions can be incorporated into SQL (and PL/SQL). These single-row functions can be used in the SELECT, WHERE, and ORDER BY clauses of SELECT statements. For example, the following query includes the TO_CHAR, UPPER, and SOUNDEX single-row functions:

```
SELECT ename, TO_CHAR(hiredate,'Day, DD-Mon-YYYY')
FROM emp
WHERE UPPER(ename) LIKE 'AL%'
ORDER BY SOUNDEX(ename)
```

Single-row functions also can appear in other types of statements, such as the SET clause of an UPDATE statement, the VALUES clause of an INSERT statement, and the WHERE clause of a DELETE statement. The certification exam tends to focus on the use of functions in SELECT statements, so we will use examples of SELECT statements in this chapter.

Single-row functions cannot be used in the HAVING clause of SQL statements. Only group functions can appear in the HAVING clause (as discussed in Chapter 4).

The built-in functions presented in this chapter are grouped by topic (character functions, date functions, and so on) and within each topic in alphabetical order. The only exceptions are the first two functions, NVL() and NVL2(), which appear first, due to their importance.

Functions can be nested, so that the output from one function is used as input to another. Nested functions can include single-row functions nested within group functions or group functions nested within either single-row functions or other group functions. See Chapter 4 for details on nesting functions.

NULLs and Single-Row Functions

One area in which beginners frequently have difficulty and where even veterans sometimes stumble is the treatment of *NULLs*. You can expect at least one question on the exam to address the use of NULLs, and it probably won't look like a question on the use of NULLs.

NULL values represent unknown data or a lack of data. Any arithmetic operation on a NULL results in a NULL. This NULL-in/NULL-out model is followed for most functions, as well. Only the functions CONCAT, DECODE, DUMP, NVL, NVL2, and REPLACE can return non-NULL values when called with a NULL argument.

NULL Value Functions

Of the functions that work with NULL values, the NVL and NVL2 (for NullVaLue) functions are most important, as they directly deal with the problem of NULLs.

NULL Value (*NVL*)

NVL takes two arguments, NVL(*x1*, *x2*), where *x1* and *x2* are expressions. The NVL function returns *x2* if *x1* is NULL. If *x1* is not NULL, then *x1* is returned.

For example, suppose that we need to calculate total compensation in our sample EMP table, which contains SALARY and BONUS columns. What happens if we simply add SALARY and BONUS?

```
SELECT first_name, last_name, salary, bonus
      ,salary + bonus total_comp
FROM  employees;

FIRST_NAME  LAST_NAME  SALARY  BONUS  TOTAL_COMP
----------  ---------  ------  -----  ----------
Joe         Ellison      3000    400        3400
Aparna      Sridharan    3500
Jose        Cortez       3000   1200        4200
```

You see that Aparna, who did not draw a bonus, shows up with no total compensation. This is because 3500+NULL=NULL, which is not our desired result. If a row has NULL in the BONUS column, the result will be NULL.

We can use the NVL function to substitute a zero in place of any NULL we encounter, like this:

```
SELECT first_name, last_name, salary, bonus
      ,salary + NVL(bonus,0) total_comp
FROM  employees;

FIRST_NAME  LAST_NAME  SALARY  BONUS  TOTAL_COMP
----------  ---------  ------  -----  ----------
Joe         Ellison      3000    400        3400
Aparna      Sridharan    3500               3500
Jose        Cortez       3000   1200        4200
```

We can see that the NVL function allowed us to calculate Aparna's compensation as 3500+0=3500, which is correct.

NULL Value 2 (*NVL2*)

The function NVL2 is a variation of NVL. NVL2 takes three arguments, NVL2(*x1*, *x2*, *x3*), where *x1*, *x2*, and *x3* are expressions. NVL2 returns *x3* if *x1* is NULL, and *x2* if *x1* is not NULL. This function is new to 9i.

For the example presented in the previous section, we could also use the NVL2 function and write the code a bit differently:

```
SELECT first_name, last_name, salary, bonus
      ,NVL2(bonus,salary + bonus,salary) total_comp
FROM  employees;

FIRST_NAME  LAST_NAME  SALARY  BONUS       TOTAL_COMP
----------  ---------  ------  ----------  ----------
Joe         Ellison      3000         400        3400
Aparna      Sridharan    3500                    3500
Jose        Cortez       3000        1200        4200
```

Using the NVL2 function, if BONUS is not NULL, then SALARY+BONUS is returned. If BONUS is NULL, then only SALARY is returned.

The NVL function allows you to perform some value substitution for NULLs. The NVL2 function, on the other hand, allows you to implement an IF…THEN…ELSE construct based on the nullity of data. Both are useful tools to deal with NULL values.

Be prepared for a possible exam question that tests your knowledge of when to use an NVL function in a calculation. Such a question probably won't mention NVL, and may not look like it is testing your knowledge of NULLs.

Using Single-Row Character Functions

Single-row character functions operate on character data. Most have one or more character arguments, and most return character values.

Character Function Overview

Table 3.1 summarizes the single-row character functions. We will cover each of these functions in the "Character Function Descriptions" section.

TABLE 3.1 Character Function Summary

Function	Description
ASCII	Returns the ASCII decimal equivalent of a character
CHR	Returns the character given the decimal equivalent
CONCAT	Concatenates two strings; same as the operator ||
INITCAP	Returns the string with the first letter of each word in uppercase
INSTR	Finds the numeric starting position of a string within a string
INSTRB	Same as INSTR, but counts bytes instead of characters
LENGTH	Returns the length of a string in characters
LENGTHB	Returns the length of a string in bytes
LOWER	Converts a string to all lowercase
LPAD	Left-fills a string to a set length using a specified character
LTRIM	Strips leading characters from a string
RPAD	Right-fills a string to a set length using a specified character
RTRIM	Strips trailing characters from a string
REPLACE	Performs substring search and replace
SUBSTR	Returns a section of the specified string, specified by numeric character positions
SUBSTRB	Returns a section of the specified string, specified by numeric byte positions

TABLE 3.1 Character Function Summary *(continued)*

Function	Description
SOUNDEX	Returns a phonetic representation of a string
TRANSLATE	Performs character search and replace
TRIM	Strips leading, trailing, or both leading and trailing characters from a string
UPPER	Converts a string to all uppercase

Character Function Descriptions

The character functions are arranged in alphabetical order, with descriptions and examples of each one.

ASCII

ASCII(<*c1*>) takes a single argument, where *c1* is a character string. This function returns the ASCII decimal equivalent of the first character in *c1*. See also CHR() for the inverse operation.

```
SELECT ASCII('A') Big_A, ASCII('z') Little_Z FROM dual;

     BIG_A   LITTLE_Z
---------- ----------
        65        122
```

CHR

CHR(<*i*>[USING NCHAR_CS]) takes a single argument, where *i* is an integer. This function returns the character equivalent of the decimal (binary) representation of the character. If the optional USING NCHAR_CS is included, the character from the national character set is returned. The default behavior is to return the character from the database character set.

```
SELECT CHR(65), CHR(122), CHR(223) FROM dual;

CHAR65 CHAR122 CHAR233
------ ------- -------
A      z       ß
```

CONCAT

CONCAT(<*c1*>,<*c2*>) takes two arguments, where *c1* and *c2* are both character strings. This function returns *c2* appended to *c1*. If *c1* is NULL, then *c2* is returned. If *c2* is NULL, then *c1* is returned. If both *c1* and *c2* are NULL, then NULL is returned. CONCAT returns the same results as using the concatenation operator: *c1*||*c2*.

```
SELECT CONCAT('Peter ','Mackovicky') username FROM dual;

USERNAME
----------------
Peter Mackovicky
```

INITCAP

INITCAP(<*c1*>) takes a single argument, where *c1* is a character string. This function returns *c1* with the first character of each word in uppercase and all others in lowercase. Words are delimited by white space, control characters, and punctuation symbols.

```
SELECT INITCAP('the three musketeers') book_title
FROM dual;

BOOK_TITLE
--------------------
The Three Musketeers
```

INSTR

INSTR(<*c1*>,<*c2*>[,<*i*>[,<*j*>]]) takes four arguments, where *c1* and *c2* are character strings, and *i* and *j* are integers. This function returns the numeric character position in *c1* where the *j* th occurrence of *c2* is found. The search begins at the *i* th character position in *c1*. INSTR returns a 0 when the requested string is not found. If *i* is negative, the search is performed backwards, from right to left, but the position is still counted from left to right. Both *i* and *j* default to 1.

```
SELECT INSTR('Mississippi', 'i',3,3) test1
      ,INSTR('Mississippi', 'i',1,3) test1
      ,INSTR('Mississippi', 'i',-2,3) test3
FROM dual;
```

```
     TEST1      TEST1      TEST3
---------- ---------- ----------
        11          8          2
```

Real World Scenario

How Do You Parse Data Using SQL?

The INSTR function is used to parse text strings. It is frequently used in conjunction with the SUBSTR function to extract a substring from an unknown starting point in the text string. If you want to extract the second field in a pipe-delimited list, you can use INSTR to find the second and third occurrence of the pipe character, then the SUBSTR function to extract the text in between these two positions.

```
SELECT text_string

FROM unparsed

WHERE key=2;


TEXT_STRING

------------

Jan|Feb|Mar
```

In the example above, you can see that the second field begins with character 5 and extends for three characters. The INSTR function can be used to determine these positions. The first pipe character (|) found in TEXT_STRING, using a search that begins at character position 1 of TEXT_STRING, is found at character position 4, as shown by INSTR(text_string,'|',1,1). The second pipe can be found at character position 8 using INSTR(text_string,'|',1,2). Therefore, the second field begins one character after the first pipe and ends one character before the third pipe. You can generalize this starting character position as INSTR(text_string,'|',1,1)+1. You can generalize the length of the second field as INSTR(text_string,'|',1,2)-INSTR(text_string,'|',1,1)-1.

```
SELECT SUBSTR(text_string
       ,INSTR(text_string,'|',1,1)+1
       ,INSTR(text_string,'|',1,2)
       -INSTR(text_string,'|',1,1)-1)  Field2
FROM unparsed
WHERE key=2;

FIELD2
------
Feb
```

So, let's use this generalized formula on a number of text strings of varying length.

```
SELECT text_string
      ,SUBSTR(text_string
         ,INSTR(text_string,'|',1,1)+1
         ,INSTR(text_string,'|',1,2)
         -INSTR(text_string,'|',1,1)-1)  Field2
FROM unparsed
WHERE key<=5;

TEXT_STRING             FIELD2
----------------------- -------
Sunday|Monday|Tuesday   Monday
Jan|Feb|Mar             Feb
a|b|c                   b
```

one|two|three	two
First|Second|Third	Second

If you are just getting started with SQL, don't let this complex example intimidate you. Review the SUBSTR and INSTR functions, as well as the section on nesting functions in Chapter 4, then come back and step through it slowly.

INSTRB

INSTRB(<*c1*>,<*c2*>[,<*i*>[,<*j*>]]) is the same as INSTR(), except it returns bytes instead of characters. For single-byte character sets, INSTRB() is equivalent to INSTR().

LENGTH

LENGTH(<*c*>) takes a single argument, where *c* is a character string. This function returns the numeric length in characters of *c*. If *c* is NULL, a NULL is returned.

```
SELECT LENGTH('The Three Musketeers') title_length
FROM dual;

TITLE_LENGTH
------------
          20
```

LENGTHB

LENGTHB(<*c*>) is the same as LENGTH(), except it returns bytes instead of characters. For single-byte character sets, LENGTHB() is equivalent to LENGTH().

LOWER

LOWER(<*c*>) takes a single argument, where *c* is a character string. This function returns the character string *c* with all characters in lowercase. It frequently appears in WHERE clauses. See also UPPER for the inverse operation.

```
SELECT colorname, LOWER(colorname)
FROM itemdetail
WHERE LOWER(colorname) LIKE '%white%';
```

```
COLORNAME       LOWER(COLORNAME)
--------------- ----------------
Winterwhite     winterwhite
White           white
Off White       off white
```

LPAD

LPAD(<*c1*>,<*i*> [, <*c2*>]) takes three arguments, where *c1* and *c2* are character strings and *i* is an integer. This function returns the character string *c1* expanded in length to *i* characters, using *c2* to fill in space as needed on the left side of *c1*. If *c1* is more than *i* characters, it is truncated to *i* characters. *c2* defaults to a single space. See also RPAD.

```
SELECT LPAD(answer,7,'.') dot_padded
      ,LPAD(answer,7, ' ') space_padded
      ,answer unpadded
FROM questions;

DOT_PAD SPACE_P UNPADDED
------- ------- ----------
....Yes     Yes Yes
.....No      No No
..Maybe   Maybe Maybe
```

LTRIM

LTRIM(<*c1*>,[, <*c2*>]) takes two arguments, where *c1* and *c2* are character strings. This function returns *c1* without any leading characters that appear in *c2*. If no *c2* characters are leading characters in *c1*, then *c1* is returned unchanged. *c2* defaults to a single space. See also RTRIM.

```
SELECT LTRIM('Mississippi','Mis') test1
      ,LTRIM('Rpadded          ') test2
      ,LTRIM('          Lpadded') test3
      ,LTRIM('     Lpadded', 'Z') test4
FROM dual;

TES TEST2             TEST3   TEST4
--- ----------------- ------- ------------
ppi Rpadded           Lpadded      Lpadded
```

In the example above, all occurrences of the trimmed characters *M*, *i*, or *s* are trimmed from the input string *Mississippi*, beginning on the left (with *M*) and continuing until the first character that is not an *M*, *i*, or *s* is encountered. Note that the trailing *i* is not trimmed; only the leading characters are removed. In TEST4, there is no occurrence of *Z*, so the input string is returned unchanged.

RPAD

RPAD(<*c1*>,<*i*>[, <*c2*>]) takes two arguments, where *c1* and *c2* are character strings and *i* is an integer. This function returns the character string *c1* expanded in length to *i* characters, using *c2* to fill in space as needed on the right side of *c1*. If *c1* is more than *i* characters, it is truncated to *i* characters. *c2* defaults to a single space. See also LPAD.

```
SELECT RPAD(table_name,38,'.') table_name
      ,num_rows
FROM user_tables;

TABLE_NAME                             NUM_ROWS
-------------------------------------- --------
TEMP_ERRORS...........................        9
CUSTOMERS.............................  367,296
```

RTRIM

RTRIM(<*c1*>,<*c2*>) takes two arguments, where *c1* and *c2* are character strings. This function returns *c1* without any trailing characters that appear in *c2*. If no *c2* characters are trailing characters in *c1*, then *c1* is returned unchanged. *c2* defaults to a single space. See also LTRIM.

```
SELECT RTRIM('Mississippi','ip') test1
      ,RTRIM('Rpadded          ') test2
      ,RTRIM('Rpadded    ', 'Z') test3
      ,RTRIM('          Lpadded') test4
FROM dual;

TEST1   TEST2   TEST3       TEST4
------- ------- ----------- ----------------
Mississ Rpadded Rpadded              Lpadded
```

REPLACE

REPLACE(<*c1*>, <*c2*> [,<*c3*>]) takes three arguments, where *c1*, *c2*, and *c3* are character strings. This function returns *c1* with all occurrences of *c2* replaced with *c3*. *c3* defaults to NULL. If *c3* is NULL, all occurrences of *c2* are removed. If *c2* is NULL, then *c1* is returned unchanged. If *c1* is NULL, then NULL is returned.

```
SELECT REPLACE('uptown','up','down') FROM dual;

REPLACE(
--------
downtown
```

This function can come in handy when you need to do some dynamic substitutions. For example, suppose that you have a number of indexes that were created in the _DATA tablespace instead of in the _INDX tablespace.

```
SELECT index_name, tablespace_name
FROM user_indexes
WHERE tablespace_name like '%DATA%';

INDEX_NAME        TABLESPACE_NAME
----------------- ----------------
PK_DEPT           HR_DATA
PK_PO_MASTER      PO_DATA
```

You can generate the DDL to rebuild these misplaced indexes in the correct location. In this scenario, you know your tablespace naming convention has an INDX tablespace for every DATA tablespace. You use the REPLACE function to generate the new tablespace name, replacing the *DATA* with *INDX*. So the HR index is rebuilt in the HR_INDX tablespace, and the PO index is rebuilt in the PO_INDX tablespace.

```
SELECT 'ALTER INDEX '||index_name||
                    ' rebuild tablespace '||
REPLACE(tablespace_name,'DATA','INDX')||';' DDL
FROM user_indexes
WHERE tablespace_name LIKE '%DATA%';
```

```
DDL
----------------------------------------------------
ALTER INDEX PK_DEPT rebuild tablespace HR_INDX;
ALTER INDEX PK_PO_MASTER rebuild tablespace PO_INDX;
```

SUBSTR

SUBSTR(<*c1*>, <*x*> [, <*y*>]) takes three arguments, where *c1* is a character string and both *x* and *y* are integers. This function returns the portion of *c1* that is *y* characters long, beginning at position *x*. If *x* is negative, the position is counted backwards (that is, right to left). This function returns NULL if *y* is 0 or negative. *y* defaults to the remainder of string *c1*.

```
SELECT SUBSTR('The Three Musketeers',1,3) Part1
      ,SUBSTR('The Three Musketeers',5,5) Part2
      ,SUBSTR('The Three Musketeers',11) Part3
      ,SUBSTR('The Three Musketeers',-10) Part3a
FROM dual;

PAR PART2 PART3      PART3A
--- ----- ---------- ----------
The Three Musketeers Musketeers
```

Real World Scenario

How Can I Really Use SUBSTR?

A handy DBA use for SUBSTR is to count the average number of rows per data block in a table. Knowing the average number of rows per block will let you estimate disk space for that table.

A DBA frequently needs to estimate the disk space that a certain table will require. If you have a sample of a thousand or so rows of real data, you can load it, measure it, and accurately estimate the amount of disk space that will be required for the full data load. For example, if you know that an average of 100 rows fit in each 4KB data block, it becomes easy to estimate disk space for 1,000,000 rows as 1,000,000 rows / 100 rows per data block * 4KB per data block, which yields 40,000KB.

To count rows per data block, you need to use ROWIDs. ROWIDs have the format *OOOOOOFFFBBBBBBRRR*, where the *O*s represent the OID (object ID), the *F*s represent the relative file number, the *B*s the block number, and the *R*s the row number within the block. You can count rows grouped on the *O*, *F*, and *B* parts of the ROWID (see Chapter 4 for more information on aggregate functions and grouping) to get the number of rows in each data block. This becomes the inline view or FROM subquery below (see Chapter 5, "Joins and Subqueries," for more information on subqueries). The main query then reports the minimum number of rows in a data block, the maximum number of rows in a data block, the average number of rows per data block, and the sum of all the rows in the table. (Note that if your table has chained rows, this technique will not properly count those chained blocks.)

```
SELECT MIN(cnt), MAX(cnt), AVG(cnt), SUM(cnt)
FROM (SELECT COUNT(*) cnt
      FROM customer_orders
      GROUP BY SUBSTR(ROWID,1,15));

  MIN(CNT)   MAX(CNT)   AVG(CNT)   SUM(CNT)
---------- ---------- ---------- ----------
        60        332 202.145213    1446349
```

This is a complex example using an inline view and grouping functions together with a single-row function. If you're just starting out with SQL, read the rest of the book, then come back and check out this ROWID example again.

SUBSTRB

SUBSTRB(<*c1*>,<*i*>[, <*j*>]) takes three arguments, where *c1* is a character string and both *i* and *j* are integers. This function is the same as SUBSTR, except *i* and *j* are counted in bytes instead of characters. For single-byte character sets, they are equivalent.

SOUNDEX

SOUNDEX(<*c1*>) takes a single argument, where *c1* is a character string. This function returns the soundex phonetic representation of *c1*. The SOUNDEX function is usually used to locate names that sound alike.

```
SELECT SOUNDEX('Dawes') Dawes
      ,SOUNDEX('Daws') Daws
      ,SOUNDEX('Dawson') Dawson
FROM dual;

DAWES DAWS DAWSON
----- ---- ------
D200  D200 D250
```

TRANSLATE

TRANSLATE(<*c1*>, <*c2*> ,<*c3*>) takes three arguments, where *c1*, *c2*, and *c3* are character strings. This function returns *c1* with all occurrences of characters in *c2* replaced with the positionally corresponding characters in *c3*. A NULL is returned if any of *c1*, *c2*, or *c3* is NULL. If *c3* has fewer characters than *c2*, the unmatched characters in *c2* are removed from *c1*. If *c2* has fewer characters than *c3*, the unmatched characters in *c3* are ignored.

```
SELECT TRANSLATE('fumble','uf','aR') test1
      ,TRANSLATE('When in the course','en','?~') test2
      ,TRANSLATE('mISSISSIppI','Mis','mIS') test3
FROM dual;

TEST1  TEST2              TEST3
------ ------------------ -----------
Ramble Wh?~ i~ th? cours? MISSISSIppI
```

TRIM

TRIM([[<*c1*>] <*c2*> FROM] <*c3*>) can take three arguments, where *c2* and *c3* are character strings. If present, *c1* can be one of the following literals: LEADING, TRAILING, or BOTH. This function returns *c3* with all *c1* (leading, trailing, or both) occurrences of characters in *c2* removed. A NULL is returned if any of *c1*, *c2*, or *c3* is NULL. *c1* defaults to BOTH. *c2* defaults to a space character. (This function was introduced in Oracle8i.)

```
SELECT TRIM('   fully padded   ') test1
      ,TRIM('   left padded') test2
      ,TRIM('right padded   ') test3
FROM dual;

TEST1        TEST2       TEST3
------------ ----------- ------------
fully padded left padded right padded
```

UPPER

UPPER(<*c*>) takes a single argument, where *c* is a character string. This function returns the character string *c* with all characters in uppercase. UPPER frequently appears in WHERE clauses. See also LOWER.

You can use a function in the WHERE clause for a different purpose than you would in the SELECT clause of a SQL statement. For example, if you wanted to report on the name, job, and hire date for all employees whose names begin with *Kin*, such as 'King', 'KING' or 'king', you would use the UPPER function in the WHERE clause to perform this case-insensitive search. The unmodified column ENAME that appears in the SELECT clause will ensure that the name will be reported in whatever format it exists in the table, whether it is uppercase, lowercase, or mixed case.

```
SELECT ename, job, hiredate
FROM emp
WHERE UPPER(ename) LIKE 'KIN%';

ENAME      JOB       HIREDATE
---------- --------- --------------------
King       President 17-Nov-1981 00:00:00


SELECT ename, UPPER(ename)
FROM emp;
```

```
ENAME      UPPER(ENAME)
---------- ----------
Smith      SMITH
Allen      ALLEN
Ward       WARD
Jones      JONES
```

Using Single-Row Numeric Functions

Single-row numeric functions operate on numeric data and perform some kind of mathematical or arithmetic manipulation. All have numeric arguments and return numeric values. The trigonometric functions all operate on radians, not degrees. Oracle does not provide a built-in conversion function to convert radians to or from degrees.

Numeric Function Overview

Table 3.2 summarizes the single-row numeric functions. We will cover each of these functions in the "Numeric Function Descriptions" section.

TABLE 3.2 Numeric Function Summary

Function	Description
ABS	Returns the absolute value
ACOS	Returns the arc cosine
ASIN	Returns the arc sine
ATAN	Returns the arc tangent
ATAN2	Returns the arc tangent; takes two inputs
BITAND	Returns the result of a bitwise AND on two inputs

TABLE 3.2 Numeric Function Summary *(continued)*

Function	Description
CEIL	Returns the next higher integer
COS	Returns the cosine
COSH	Returns the hyperbolic cosine
EXP	Returns the base of natural logarithms raised to a power
FLOOR	Returns the next smaller integer
LN	Returns the natural logarithm
LOG	Returns the logarithm
MOD	Returns the modulo (remainder) of a division operation
POWER	Returns a number raised to an arbitrary power
ROUND	Rounds a number
SIGN	Returns an indicator of sign: negative, positive, or zero
SIN	Returns the sine
SINH	Returns the hyperbolic sine
SQRT	Returns the square root of a number
TAN	Returns the tangent
TANH	Returns the hyperbolic tangent
TRUNC	Truncates a number

Numeric Function Descriptions

The numeric functions are arranged in alphabetical order, with descriptions and examples of each one.

ABS

ABS(<*n*>) takes a single argument, where *n* is a number. This function returns the absolute value of *n*.

```
SELECT ABS(-52) negative
      ,ABS(52)  positive
FROM dual;

  NEGATIVE   POSITIVE
---------- ----------
        52         52
```

ACOS

ACOS(<*n*>) takes a single argument, where *n* is a number between –1 and 1. This function returns the arc cosine of *n* expressed in radians, accurate to 30 digits of precision.

```
SELECT ACOS(-1) pi
      ,ACOS(1) zero
FROM dual;

        PI       ZERO
---------- ----------
3.14159265          0
```

ASIN

ASIN(<*n*>) takes a single argument, where *n* is a number between –1 and 1. This function returns the arc sine of *n* expressed in radians, accurate to 30 digits of precision.

```
SELECT ASIN(1) high
      ,ASIN(0) middle
      ,ASIN(-1) low
FROM dual;

      HIGH     MIDDLE        LOW
---------- ---------- ----------
1.57079633          0 -1.5707963
```

ATAN

ATAN(<*n*>) takes a single argument, where *n* is a number. This function returns the arc tangent of *n* expressed in radians, accurate to 30 digits of precision.

```
SELECT ATAN(9E99) high
      ,ATAN(0) middle
      ,ATAN(-9E99) low
FROM dual;

      HIGH     MIDDLE        LOW
---------- ---------- ----------
1.57079633          0 -1.5707963
```

ATAN2

ATAN2(<*n1*>, <*n2*>) takes two arguments, where *n1* and *n2* are numbers. This function returns the arc tangent of *n1* and *n2* expressed in radians, accurate to 30 digits of precision. ATAN2(*n1*,*n2*) is equivalent to ATAN(*n1*/*n2*).

```
SELECT ATAN2(9E99,1) high
      ,ATAN2(0,3.1415) middle
      ,ATAN2(-9E99,1) low
FROM dual;

      HIGH     MIDDLE        LOW
---------- ---------- ----------
1.57079633          0 -1.5707963
```

BITAND

BITAND(<*n1*>,< *n2*>) takes two arguments, where *n1* and *n2* are positive integers or zero. This function performs a bitwise AND operation on the two input values and returns the results, also an integer. It is used to examine bit fields. A number of data dictionary tables have numeric bit fields, and the data dictionary views use the BITAND function to show the data. For example, USER_COL_COMMENTS is defined as follows:

```
SELECT o.name table_name, c.name column_name
      , co.comment$ comment
```

```
FROM sys.obj$ o
    ,sys.col$ c
    ,sys.com$ co
WHERE o.owner# = userenv('SCHEMAID')
  AND o.type# in (2, 4)
  AND o.obj# = c.obj#
  AND c.obj# = co.obj#(+)
  AND c.intcol# = co.col#(+)
  AND BITAND(c.property, 32) = 0 /* not hidden column */;
```

CEIL

CEIL(<*n*>) takes a single argument, where *n* is a number. This function returns the smallest integer that is greater than or equal to *n*. CEIL rounds up to a whole number. See also FLOOR.

```
SELECT CEIL(9.8)
      ,CEIL(-32.85)
      ,CEIL(0)
      ,CEIL(5)
FROM dual;

CEIL(9.8) CEIL(-32.85)    CEIL(0)    CEIL(5)
---------- ------------ ---------- ----------
        10          -32          0          5
```

COS

COS(<*n*>) takes a single argument, where *n* is a number in radians. This function returns the cosine of *n*, accurate to 36 digits of precision.

```
SELECT COS(-3.14159)
FROM dual;

COS(-3.14159)
-------------
           -1
```

COSH

COSH(<*n*>) takes a single argument, where *n* is a number. This function returns the hyperbolic cosine of *n*, accurate to 36 digits of precision.

```
SELECT COSH(1.4)
FROM dual;

 COSH(1.4)
----------
2.15089847
```

EXP

EXP(<*n*>) takes a single argument, where *n* is a number. This function returns *e* (the base of natural logarithms) raised to the nth power, accurate to 36 digits of precision.

```
SELECT EXP(1) "e" FROM dual;

         e
----------
2.71828183
```

FLOOR

FLOOR(<*n*>) takes a single argument, where *n* is a number. This function returns the largest integer that is less than or equal to *n*. FLOOR rounds down to a whole number. See also CEIL.

```
SELECT FLOOR(9.8)
      ,FLOOR(-32.85)
      ,FLOOR(137)
FROM dual;

FLOOR(9.8) FLOOR(-32.85) FLOOR(137)
---------- ------------- ----------
         9           -33        137
```

LN

`LN(<n>)` takes a single argument, where *n* is a number greater than 0. This function returns the natural logarithm of *n*, accurate to 36 digits of precision.

```
SELECT LN(2.7) FROM dual;

   LN(2.7)
----------
.993251773
```

LOG

`LOG(<n1>, <n2>)` takes two arguments, where *n1* and *n2* are numbers. This function returns the logarithm base *n1* of *n2*, accurate to 36 digits of precision.

```
SELECT LOG(8,64)
      ,LOG(3,27)
      ,LOG(2,1024)
      ,LOG(2,8)
FROM dual;

LOG(8,64)  LOG(3,27) LOG(2,1024)   LOG(2,8)
---------- ---------- ----------- ----------
         2          3          10          3
```

MOD

`MOD(<n1>, <n2>)` takes two arguments, where *n1* and *n2* are numbers. This function returns *n1* modulo *n2*, or the remainder of *n1* divided by *n2*. If *n1* is negative, the result is negative. The sign of *n2* has no effect on the result. This behavior differs from the mathematical definition of the modulus operation.

```
SELECT MOD(14,5)
      ,MOD(8,2.5)
      ,MOD(-64,7)
FROM dual;

 MOD(14,5) MOD(8,2.5) MOD(-64,7)
---------- ---------- ----------
         4         .5         -1
```

POWER

POWER(<*n1*>, <*n2*>) takes two arguments, where *n1* and *n2* are numbers. This function returns *n1* to the *n2*th power.

```
SELECT POWER(2,10)
      ,POWER(3,3)
      ,POWER(5,3)
      ,POWER(2,-3)
FROM dual;

POWER(2,10) POWER(3,3) POWER(5,3) POWER(2,-3)
----------- ---------- ---------- -----------
       1024         27        125        .125
```

ROUND

ROUND(<*n1*>, <*n2*>) takes two arguments, where *n1* is a number and *n2* is an integer. This function returns *n1* rounded to *n2* digits of precision to the right of the decimal. If *n2* is negative, *n1* is rounded to left of the decimal. This function is similar to TRUNC.

```
SELECT ROUND(12345,-2) test1
      ,ROUND(12345.54321,2) test2
FROM dual;

     TEST1      TEST2
---------- ----------
     12300   12345.54
```

SIGN

SIGN(<*n*>) takes a single argument, where *n* is a number. This function returns –1 if *n* is negative, 1 if *n* is positive, and 0 if *n* is 0.

```
SELECT SIGN(-2.3)
      ,SIGN(0)
      ,SIGN(47)
FROM dual;

SIGN(-2.3)    SIGN(0)   SIGN(47)
---------- ---------- ----------
        -1          0          1
```

SIN

SIN(<*n*>) takes a single argument, where *n* is a number in radians. This function returns the sine of *n*, accurate to 36 digits of precision.

```
SELECT SIN(1.57079) FROM dual;

SIN(1.57079)
------------
           1
```

SINH

SINH(<*n*>) takes a single argument, where *n* is a number. This function returns the hyperbolic sine of *n*, accurate to 36 digits of precision.

SQRT

SQRT(<*n*>) takes a single argument, where *n* is a number. This function returns the square root of *n*.

```
SELECT SQRT(64)
      ,SQRT(49)
      ,SQRT(5)
FROM dual;

  SQRT(64)   SQRT(49)    SQRT(5)
---------- ---------- ----------
         8          7 2.23606798
```

TAN

TAN(<*n*>) takes a single argument, where *n* is a number in radians. This function returns the tangent of *n*, accurate to 36 digits of precision.

```
SELECT TAN(1.57079633/2) "45_degrees" FROM dual;

45_Degrees
----------
         1
```

TANH

TANH(<*n*>) takes a single argument, where *n* is a number. This function returns the hyperbolic tangent of *n*, accurate to 36 digits of precision.

```
SELECT TANH( ACOS(-1) ) hyp_tan_of_pi FROM dual;

HYP_TAN_OF_PI
-------------
   .996272076
```

TRUNC

TRUNC(<*n1*>, <*n2*>) takes two arguments, where *n1* is a number and *n2* is an integer. This function returns *n1* truncated to *n2* digits of precision to the right of the decimal. If *n2* is negative, *n1* is truncated to left of the decimal. See also ROUND.

```
SELECT TRUNC(123.456,2) pos
      ,TRUNC(123.456,-1) neg
FROM dual;

       POS        NEG
---------- ----------
    123.45        120
```

Using Single-Row Date Functions

Single-row date functions operate on DATE datatypes. Most have one or more date arguments, and most return a date value. Date data is stored internally as numbers. The whole number portion is the number of days since January 1, 4712 B.C., and the decimal portion is the fraction of a day (for example, 0.5=12 hours).

Date Format Conversion

National Language Support (NLS) parameters and arguments allow you to internationalize your Oracle database system. NLS internationalizations include date representations, character sets, alphabets, and alphabetical ordering.

Oracle will implicitly or automatically convert its numeric date data to and from character data using the format model specified with NLS_DATE_FORMAT. You can change this date format model for each session with the ALTER SESSION SET NLS_DATE_FORMAT command. Here's an example:

```
ALTER SESSION SET NLS_DATE_FORMAT='DD-Mon-YYYY
HH24:MI:SS';
```

This ALTER SESSION command will set the implicit conversion mechanism to display date data in the format specified, such as 12-Dec-2002 15:45:32. This conversion works both ways. If the character string '30-Nov-2002 20:30:00' were inserted, updated, or assigned to a date column or variable, the correct date would be entered.

If the format model were 'DD/MM/YY' or 'MM/DD/YY', there could be some ambiguity in the conversion of some dates, such as 12 April 2000 (04/12/00 or 12/04/00). To avoid problems with implicit conversions, Oracle provides four explicit date/character conversion functions: TO_DATE, TO_CHAR, TO_DSINTERVAL, and TO_YMINTERVAL. These explicit conversion functions are covered in the "Using Single-Row Conversion Functions" section later in this chapter.

Date Function Overview

Table 3.3 summarizes the single-row date functions. We will cover each of these functions in the "Date Function Descriptions" section.

TABLE 3.3 Date Function Summary

Function	Description
ADD_MONTHS	Adds a number of months to a date
CURRENT_DATE	Returns the current date
CURRENT_TIMESTAMP	Returns the current date and time in a TIMESTAMP datatype
DBTIMEZONE	Returns the database's time zone
EXTRACT	Returns a component of a date/time expression
FROM_TZ	Returns a timestamp with time zone for a given timestamp

TABLE 3.3 Date Function Summary *(continued)*

Function	Description
LAST_DAY	Returns the last day of a month
LOCALTIMESTAMP	Returns the current date and time in the session time zone
MONTHS_BETWEEN	Returns the number of months between two dates
NEW_TIME	Returns the date/time in a different time zone
NEXT_DAY	Returns the next day of a week following a given date
ROUND	Rounds a date/time
SESSIONTIMEZONE	Returns the time zone for the current session
SYS_EXTRACT_UTC	Returns the UTC (GMT) for a timestamp with a time zone
SYSDATE	Returns the current date/time
SYSTIMESTAMP	Returns the current timestamp
TRUNC	Truncates a date to a given granularity
TZ_OFFSET	Returns the offset from UTC for a time zone name

Date Function Descriptions

The date functions are arranged in alphabetical order, with descriptions and examples of each one.

ADD_MONTHS

`ADD_MONTHS(<d>, <i>)` takes two arguments, where *d* is a date and *i* is an integer. This function returns the date *d* plus *i* months. If *i* is a decimal number, the database will implicitly convert it to an integer by truncating the decimal portion (for example, 3.9 becomes 3).

```
SELECT SYSDATE
      ,ADD_MONTHS(SYSDATE,3)  plus_3
      ,ADD_MONTHS(SYSDATE,-2) minus_2
FROM dual;

SYSDATE     PLUS_3      MINUS_2
----------- ----------- -----------
30-Nov-2002 28-Feb-2003 30-Sep-2002
```

CURRENT_DATE

CURRENT_DATE takes no arguments and returns the current date in the Gregorian calendar for the session's time zone. This function is new to Oracle9i.

```
SELECT SYSDATE
      ,CURRENT_DATE
      ,SESSIONTIMEZONE
FROM dual;

SYSDATE   CURRENT_D SESSIONTIMEZONE
--------- --------- ---------------
23-SEP-01 23-SEP-01 -05:00
```

CURRENT_TIMESTAMP

CURRENT_TIMESTAMP([<*p*>]) returns the current date and time in the session's time zone to *p* digits of precision. *p* can be an integer 0 through 9 and defaults to 6. This function is new to Oracle9i. See also LOCALTIMESTAMP.

```
SELECT CURRENT_TIMESTAMP FROM dual;

CURRENT_TIMESTAMP
-----------------------------------
23-SEP-01 07.05.25.705085 PM -05:00

SELECT SYSDATE
      ,CURRENT_TIMESTAMP
      ,SESSIONTIMEZONE
FROM dual;
```

```
SYSDATE   CURRENT_TIMESTAMP                   SESSIONTIMEZONE
--------- ----------------------------------- ---------------
23-SEP-01 23-SEP-01 07.07.58.810545 PM -05:00 -05:00
```

DBTIMEZONE

DBTIMEZONE returns the database's time zone, as set by the latest CREATE DATABASE or ALTER DATABASE SET TIME_ZONE statement. Note that after changing the database time zone with the ALTER DATABASE statement, the instance must be bounced (restarted) for the change to take effect. The time zone is a character string specifying the hours and minutes offset from UTC (Coordinated Universal Time, also known as GMT, or Greenwich Mean Time) or a time zone region name. The valid time zone region names can be found in the TZNAME column of the view V$TIMEZONE_NAMES. This function is new to Oracle9i.

```
ALTER DATABASE SET TIME_ZONE='-06:00';

Database altered.

SHUTDOWN
STARTUP

SELECT DBTIMEZONE FROM dual;

DBTIME
------
-06:00

ALTER DATABASE SET TIME_ZONE='US/Central';

Database altered.

SHUTDOWN
STARTUP

SELECT DBTIMEZONE FROM dual;
```

```
DBTIMEZONE
-----------
US/Central
```

EXTRACT

EXTRACT(<*c*> FROM <*dt*>) extracts and returns the specified component *c* of date/time or interval expression *dt*. The valid components are YEAR, MONTH, DAY, HOUR, MINUTE, SECOND, TIMEZONE_HOUR, TIMEZONE_MINUTE, TIMEZONE_REGION, and TIMEZONE_ABBR. The specified component must exist in the expression. So, to extract a TIMEZONE_HOUR, the date/time expression must be a TIMESTAMP WITH TIME ZONE datatype. This function is new to Oracle9i.

```
SELECT SYSDATE
      ,EXTRACT(YEAR FROM SYSDATE ) YEAR
      ,EXTRACT(MONTH FROM SYSTIMESTAMP) MONTH
      ,EXTRACT(TIMEZONE_HOUR FROM SYSTIMESTAMP) TZH
FROM dual;

SYSDATE                    YEAR      MONTH        TZH
-------------------- ---------- ---------- ----------
24-SEP-2002 05:04:26       2002          9         -5
```

FROM_TZ

FROM_TZ(<*ts*>,<*tz*>) returns a timestamp with time zone for the timestamp *ts* using time zone value *tz*. The character string *tz* specifies the hours and minutes offset from UTC or is a time zone region name. The valid time zone region names can be found in the TZNAME column of the view V$TIMEZONE_NAMES. This function is new to Oracle9i.

```
SELECT LOCALTIMESTAMP ts1
      ,FROM_TZ(LOCALTIMESTAMP,'-07:00') ts2
FROM dual;

TS1                          TS2
---------------------------- ----------------------------------
24-SEP-01 04.57.23.793802 AM 24-SEP-01 04.57.23.793802 AM -07:00
```

LAST_DAY

LAST_DAY(<*d*>) takes a single argument, where *d* is a date. This function returns the last day of the month for the date *d*.

```
SELECT SYSDATE
      ,LAST_DAY(SYSDATE)   END_OF_MONTH
      ,LAST_DAY(SYSDATE)+1 NEXT_MONTH
FROM dual;

SYSDATE     END_OF_MONTH NEXT_MONTH
----------- ------------ -----------
09-SEP-2002 30-SEP-2002  01-OCT-2002
```

LOCALTIMESTAMP

LOCALTIMESTAMP([<*p*>]) returns the current date and time in the session's time zone to *p* digits of precision. *p* can be 0 to 9 and defaults to 6. This function is similar to CURRENT_TIMESTAMP. The difference is that the return datatype for CURRENT_TIMESTAMP is TIMESTAMP WITH TIME ZONE, whereas the return datatype for LOCALTIMESTAMP is just TIMESTAMP. This function is new to Oracle9i.

```
SELECT CURRENT_TIMESTAMP
      ,LOCALTIMESTAMP
FROM dual;

CURRENT_TIMESTAMP                   LOCALTIMESTAMP
----------------------------------- ----------------------------
24-SEP-02 05.09.38.096944 AM -05:00 24-SEP-02 05.09.38.096944 AM
```

MONTHS_BETWEEN

MONTHS_BETWEEN(<*d1*>, <*d2*>) takes two arguments, where *d1* and *d2* are both dates. This function returns the number of months that *d2* is later than *d1*. A whole number is returned if *d1* and *d2* are the same day of the month or if both dates are the last day of a month.

```
SELECT MONTHS_BETWEEN('19-Dec-2002','19-Mar-2003') test1
      ,MONTHS_BETWEEN('19-Dec-2002','19-Mar-2002') test2
FROM dual
```

```
     TEST1      TEST2
---------- ----------
        -3          9
```

NEW_TIME

NEW_TIME(<*d*>, <*tz1*>, <*tz2*>) takes three arguments, where *d* is a date and both *tz1* and *tz2* are one of the time zone constants (shown in Table 3.4). This function returns the date in time zone *tz2* for date *d* in time zone *tz1*. To get UTC (GMT) use the SYS_EXTRACT_UTC function.

```
SELECT SYSDATE Chicago
      ,NEW_TIME(SYSDATE,'CDT','PDT') Los_Angeles
FROM dual;

CHICAGO              LOS_ANGELES
-------------------- --------------------
23-Nov-2002 10:00:00 23-Nov-2002 08:00:00
```

TABLE 3.4 Time Zone Constants

Code	Time Zone
GMT	Greenwich Mean Time
NST	Newfoundland Standard Time
AST	Atlantic Standard Time
ADT	Atlantic Daylight Time
BST	Bering Standard Time
BDT	Bering Daylight Time
CST	Central Standard Time
CDT	Central Daylight Time
EST	Eastern Standard Time

TABLE 3.4 Time Zone Constants *(continued)*

Code	Time Zone
EDT	Eastern Daylight Time
MST	Mountain Standard Time
MDT	Mountain Daylight Time
PST	Pacific Standard Time
PDT	Pacific Daylight Time
YST	Yukon Standard Time
YDT	Yukon Daylight Time
HST	Hawaii-Alaska Standard Time
HDT	Hawaii-Alaska Daylight Time

NEXT_DAY

NEXT_DAY(<*d*>, <*dow*>) takes two arguments, where *d* is a date and *dow* is a text string containing the full or abbreviated day of the week in the session's language. This function returns the next *dow* following *d*. The time portion of the return date is the same as the time portion of *d*.

```
SELECT NEXT_DAY('01-Jan-2000','Monday')     "1st Monday"
      ,NEXT_DAY('01-Nov-2004','Tuesday')+7 "2nd Tuesday"
FROM dual;

1st Monday  2nd Tuesday
----------- -----------
03-Jan-2000 09-Nov-2004
```

ROUND

ROUND(<*d*> [, <*fmt*>]) takes two arguments, where *d* is a date and *fmt* is a character string containing a date-format string. This function returns *d* rounded to the granularity specified in *fmt*.

```
SELECT SYSDATE,ROUND(SYSDATE,'HH24') FROM dual;

SYSDATE              ROUND(SYSDATE,'HH24'
-------------------- --------------------
24-Nov-1999 09:23:56 24-Nov-1999 09:00:00
```

SESSIONTIMEZONE

SESSIONTIMEZONE takes no arguments and returns the database's time zone offset as per the last ALTER SESSION statement. SESSIONTIMEZONE will default to DBTIMEZONE if it is not changed with an ALTER SESSION statement. This function is new to Oracle9i.

```
SELECT DBTIMEZONE
      ,SESSIONTIMEZONE
FROM dual;

DBTIMEZONE  SESSIONTIMEZONE
----------- ---------------
US/Central  -05:00
```

SYS_EXTRACT_UTC

SYS_EXTRACT_UTC(<*ts*>) takes a single argument, where *ts* is a TIMESTAMP WITH TIME ZONE. This function returns the UTC (GMT) time for the timestamp *ts*. This function is new to Oracle9i.

```
SELECT CURRENT_TIMESTAMP local
      ,SYS_EXTRACT_UTC(CURRENT_TIMESTAMP) GMT
FROM dual;

LOCAL                               GMT
----------------------------------- ----------------------------
24-SEP-01 05.24.46.313662 AM -05:00 24-SEP-01 10.24.46.313662 AM
```

SYSTIMESTAMP

SYSTIMESTAMP takes no arguments and returns a TIMESTAMP WITH TIME ZONE for the current database date and time. The fractional second is returned with six digits of precision. This function is new to Oracle9i.

```
SELECT SYSTIMESTAMP
      ,SYSDATE
```

```
FROM dual;

SYSTIMESTAMP                        SYSDATE
----------------------------------- --------------------
24-SEP-01 05.25.46.644150 AM -05:00 24-SEP-2002 05:25:46
```

SYSDATE

SYSDATE takes no arguments and returns the current date and time to the second.

```
SELECT SYSDATE FROM dual;

SYSDATE
--------------------
24-Nov-2002 09:26:01
```

SYSDATE is one of the most commonly used Oracle functions. There's a good chance you'll see it on the exam.

TRUNC

TRUNC(<*d*> [, <*fmt*>]) takes two arguments, where *d* is a date and *fmt* is a character string containing a date-format string. This function returns *d* truncated to the granularity specified in *fmt*.

```
SELECT TRUNC(last_analyzed,'HH')
FROM user_tables
WHERE table_name='TEST_CASE';

TRUNC(LAST_ANALYZED,
--------------------
28-Mar-2002 11:00:00
```

TZ_OFFSET

TZ_OFFSET(<*tz*>) takes a single argument, where *tz* is a time zone offset or time zone name. This function returns the numeric time zone offset for a textual time zone name. The valid time zone names can be obtained from the TZNAME column in the V$TIMEZONE_NAMES view. This function is new to Oracle9i.

```
SELECT TZ_OFFSET(DBTIMEZONE) CHICAGO
      ,TZ_OFFSET('US/Eastern') NEW_YORK
      ,TZ_OFFSET('Europe/London') LONDON
      ,TZ_OFFSET('Asia/Singapore') SINGAPORE
FROM dual;

CHICAGO NEW_YORK LONDON  SINGAPORE
------- -------- ------- ---------
-05:00  -04:00   +01:00  +08:00
```

Using Single-Row Conversion Functions

Single-row conversion functions operate on multiple datatypes. The TO_CHAR and TO_NUMBER functions have a significant number of formatting codes that can be used to display date and number data in a wide assortment of representations. The exam may include a question that tests your recollection of some of the nuances of these formatting codes. General usage in a professional setting would afford you the opportunity to look them up in a reference. In the test setting, you must recall them.

Conversion Function Overview

Table 3.5 summarizes the single-row conversion functions. We will cover each of these functions in the "Conversion Function Descriptions" section.

TABLE 3.5 Conversion Function Summary

Function	Description
ASCIISTR	Converts characters to ASCII
BIN_TO_NUM	Converts a string of bits to a number
CAST	Converts datatypes
CHARTOROWID	Casts a character to ROWID datatype
COMPOSE	Converts to Unicode

TABLE 3.5 Conversion Function Summary *(continued)*

Function	Description
CONVERT	Converts from one character set to another
DECOMPOSE	Decomposes a Unicode string
HEXTORAW	Casts a hexadecimal to a raw
NUMTODSINTERVAL	Converts a number to an interval day to second
NUMTOYMINTERVAL	Converts a number to an interval year to month
RAWTOHEX	Casts a raw to a hexadecimal
ROWIDTOCHAR	Casts a ROWID to a character
TO_CHAR	Converts and formats a date into a string
TO_DATE	Converts a string to a date, specifying the format
TO_DSINTERVAL	Converts a string to an interval day to second
TO_MULTIBYTE	Converts a single-byte character to its corresponding multibyte equivalent
TO_NUMBER	Casts a numeric string to a number, specifying the format
TO_SINGLE_BYTE	Converts a multibyte character to its corresponding single-byte equivalent
TO_YMINTERVAL	Converts a string to an interval year to month
UNISTR	Converts UCS2 Unicode

Conversion Function Descriptions

The conversion functions are arranged in alphabetical order, with descriptions and examples of each one.

ASCIISTR

ASCIISTR(<*c1*>) takes a single argument, where *c1* is a character string. This function returns the ASCII equivalent of all the characters in *c1*. This function leaves ASCII characters unchanged, but non-ASCII characters are returned in an ASCII representation. This function is new to Oracle9i.

```
SELECT ASCIISTR('cañon')
      ,ASCIISTR('faβ')
FROM dual;

ASCIISTR( ASCIIST
--------- -------
ca\00F1on fa\00DF
```

BIN_TO_NUM

BIN_TO_NUM(<*b*>) takes a single argument, where *b* is a comma-delimited list of bits. This function returns the numeric representation of all the bit-field set *b*. It essentially converts a base 2 number into a base 10 number. Bit fields are the most efficient structure to store simple yes/no and true/false data. Numerous bit fields can be combined into a single numeric column. The use of bit fields departs from a normalized relational model, since one column represents more than one value, but this encoding can enhance performance and/or reduce disk-space usage. This function is new to Oracle9i. See also BITAND.

To understand the number returned from the BIN_TO_NUM function, recall from base 2 (binary) counting, that the rightmost digit counts the ones, the next counts the twos, the next counts the fours, then eights, and so on. Thus, the number 13 is represented in binary as 1101. There are 1 one, 0 twos, 1 four, and 1 eight, which add up to 13 in base 10.

```
SELECT BIN_TO_NUM(1,1,0,1) bitfield1
      ,BIN_TO_NUM(0,0,0,1) bitfield2
      ,BIN_TO_NUM(1,1) bitfield3
FROM dual;
```

```
BITFIELD1  BITFIELD2  BITFIELD3
---------- ---------- ----------
        13          1          3
```

CAST

CAST(<*c*> AS <*t*>) takes two arguments, where *c* is an expression, subquery, or MULTISET clause and *t* is a datatype. This function converts the expression *c* into datatype *t*. The *CAST* function is most frequently used to convert data into programmer-defined datatypes, but it can also be used to convert data to built-in datatypes. No translation is performed; only the datatype is converted. Table 3.6 shows the datatypes that can be converted using CAST. This function is new to Oracle9i.

TABLE 3.6 CAST Datatype Conversions

Convert from / to	CHAR, VARCHAR2	NCHAR, NVARCHAR2	DATETIME, INTERVAL	NUMBER	RAW	ROWID, UROWID
CHAR, VARCHAR2	Yes	No	Yes	Yes	Yes	Yes
NCHAR, NVARCHAR2	No	Yes	Yes	Yes	Yes	Yes
DATETIME, INTERVAL	Yes	No	Yes	No	No	No
NUMBER	Yes	No	No	Yes	No	No
RAW	Yes	No	No	No	Yes	No
ROWID, UROWID	Yes	No	No	No	No	Yes

```
SELECT CAST(SYSDATE AS VARCHAR2(24)) NOW
FROM dual;

NOW
------------------------
24-SEP-2002 06:10:33
```

CHARTOROWID

CHARTOROWID(<c>) takes a single argument, where c is a character string. This function returns c as a *ROWID* datatype. No translation is performed; only the datatype is converted.

```
SELECT test_id
FROM test_case
WHERE rowid = CHARTOROWID('AAAAoSAACAAAALiAAA');
```

COMPOSE

COMPOSE(<c>) takes a single argument, where *c* is a character string. This function returns c as a *Unicode* string in its fully normalized form, in the same character set as c. The COMPOSE and DECOMPOSE functions support Unicode 3.0 and are new to Oracle9i. The Unicode 3.0 standard allows you to combine, or *compose*, a valid character from a base character and a modifier.

For example, you can create the Spanish *ñ* character by combining a lowercase *n* with a tilde modifier. The Unicode character 0x006E (shown in hex) is a lowercase *n*, and 0x0303 (also in hex) is a modifier that places a tilde above the preceding character. In the following example, the result of this COMPOSE operation is stored in a table called MY_TEST. Also stored in this table is a character composed of a lowercase *w* together with the tilde modifier. This modified *w* does not appear in any known character set, but with Unicode and the COMPOSE function, we can create it.

```
CREATE TABLE my_test
(test_char  NVARCHAR2(8)
);

INSERT INTO my_test
   SELECT COMPOSE(UNISTR('\006E') || UNISTR('\0303')
          ) test_char
   FROM dual;

INSERT INTO my_test
   SELECT COMPOSE('w' || UNISTR('\0303')) test_char
   FROM dual;
```

We can confirm what was stored in the table through the use of the DECOMPOSE and DUMP functions. (See the sections on DECOMPOSE and DUMP later in this chapter.)

```
SELECT RAWTOHEX(DECOMPOSE(test_char)) decomp
      ,DUMP(test_char,1016) dump
FROM my_test

DECOMP     DUMP
---------- ----------------------------------------
006E0303   Typ=1 Len=2 CharacterSet=AL16UTF16: 0,f1
00770303   Typ=1 Len=4 CharacterSet=AL16UTF16: 0,77,3,3
```

We can see that the composed *ñ* character is stored in its native form as hex 0x00F1, while the nonexistent *w* with tilde character is stored as its composed parts. Support for Unicode allows globalization of a database.

CONVERT

CONVERT(<*c*>, <*dset*> [,<*sset*>]) takes three arguments, where *c* is a character string and *dset* and *sset* are character set names. This function returns the character string *c* converted from the source character set *sset* to the destination character set *dset*. No translation is performed. If the character does not exist in both character sets, the replacement character for the character set is used. *sset* defaults to the database character set.

DECOMPOSE

DECOMPOSE(<*c*>) takes a single argument, where *c* is a character string. This function returns *c* as a Unicode string after canonical decomposition in the same character set as *c*. The COMPOSE and DECOMPOSE functions support Unicode 3.0 and are new to Oracle9i. See the example in the section on COMPOSE.

HEXTORAW

HEXTORAW(<*x*>) takes a single argument, where *x* is a hexadecimal string. This function returns the hexadecimal string *x* converted to a RAW datatype. There is no translation performed; only the datatype is changed.

```
INSERT INTO printers(printer_nbr, manufacturer, model,
        init_string)
VALUES (12,'HP','LaserJet',HEXTORAW('1B45'));
```

NUMTODSINTERVAL

NUMTODSINTERVAL(<*x*> , <*c*>) takes two arguments, where *x* is a number and *c* is a character string denoting the units for *x*. This function converts the number *x* into an INTERVAL DAY TO SECOND datatype. Valid units are 'DAY', 'HOUR', 'MINUTE', and 'SECOND'. *c* can be uppercase, lowercase, or mixed case. This function is new to Oracle9i.

```
SELECT SYSDATE
      ,SYSDATE+NUMTODSINTERVAL(2,'HOUR') "2 hours later"
      ,SYSDATE+NUMTODSINTERVAL(30,'MINUTE') "30 minutes later"
FROM dual;

SYSDATE              2 hours later        30 minutes later
-------------------- -------------------- --------------------
24-SEP-2002 06:27:03 24-SEP-2002 08:27:03 24-SEP-2002 06:57:03
```

NUMTOYMINTERVAL

NUMTOYMINTERVAL(<*x*> , <*c*>) takes two arguments, where *x* is a number and *c* is a character string denoting the units for *x*. This function converts the number *x* into an INTERVAL YEAR TO MONTH datatype. Valid units are 'YEAR' and 'MONTH'. *c* can be uppercase, lowercase, or mixed case. This function is new to Oracle9i.

```
SELECT SYSDATE
      ,SYSDATE+NUMTOYMINTERVAL(2,'YEAR') "2 years later"
      ,SYSDATE+NUMTOYMINTERVAL(6,'MONTH') "6 months later"
FROM dual;

SYSDATE              2 years later        6 months later
-------------------- -------------------- --------------------
24-SEP-2001 06:24:22 24-SEP-2003 06:24:22 24-MAR-2002 06:24:22
```

RAWTOHEX

RAWTOHEX(<*x*>) takes a single argument, where *x* is a raw string. This function returns the raw string *x* converted to hexadecimal. There is no translation performed; only the datatype is changed.

```
SELECT RAWTOHEX(init_string)
FROM printers
```

```
WHERE model='LaserJet' AND  manufacturer='HP';

RAWTOHEX(INIT_STRING)
----------------------
1B45
```

ROWIDTOCHAR

ROWIDTOCHAR(<*x*>) takes a single argument, where *x* is a character string in the format of a ROWID. This function returns the character string *x* converted from a ROWID. There is no translation performed; only the datatype is changed.

```
SELECT ROWIDTOCHAR(rowid) FROM test_case
WHERE rownum = 1;

ROWIDTOCHAR(ROWID)
------------------
AAAAoSAACAAAALiAAA
```

TO_CHAR

TO_CHAR(<*x*> [,<*fmt* >[,<*nlsparm*>]]) takes three arguments, where *x* is either a date or a number, *fmt* is a format string specifying the format that *x* will appear in, and *nlsparm* specifies language or location formatting conventions. This function returns *x* converted into a character string.

Date Conversion

If *x* is a date, *fmt* is a date format code (see Table 3.7) and *nlsparm* is an NLS_DATE_LANGUAGE specification, if included. Note that the spelled-out numbers always appear in English, while the day or month may appear in the NLS language.

```
SELECT TO_CHAR(SYSDATE,'Day Ddspth,Month YYYY'
              ,'NLS_DATE_LANGUAGE=German') Today_Heute
FROM dual;

TODAY_HEUTE
----------------------------------------
Samstag    Twenty-Seventh,November  2002
```

```
SELECT TO_CHAR(SYSDATE
              ,'"On the "Ddspth" day of "Month, YYYY')
FROM dual;

TO_CHAR(SYSDATE,'"ONTHE"DDSPTH"DAYOF"MONTH,Y
--------------------------------------------
On the Twenty-Seventh day of November , 2002
```

TABLE 3.7 Date Format Codes

Date Code	Format Code Description	Example
AD or BC	Epoch indicator	'YYYY AD' = 2002 AD
A.D. or B.C.	Epoch indicator with periods	'YYYY A.D.' = 2002 A.D.
AM or PM	Meridian indicator	'HH12AM' = 09AM
A.M. or P.M.	Meridian indicator with periods	'HH A.M.'= 09 A.M.
DY	Day of week abbreviated	Mon, Tue, Fri
DAY	Day of week spelled out	Monday, Tuesday, Friday
D	Day of week (1–7)	1,2,3,4,5,6,7
DD	Day of month (1–31)	1,2,3,4...31
DDD	Day of year (1–366)	1,2,3,4...366
FF	Fractional seconds	.34127
J	Julian day (days since 4712BC)	2451514, 2451515, 2451516
W	Week of the month (1–5)	1,2,3,4,5
WW, IW	Week of the year, ISO week of the year	1,2,3,4...53
MM	Two-digit month	01,02,03...12

TABLE 3.7 Date Format Codes *(continued)*

Date Code	Format Code Description	Example
MON	Month name abbreviated	Jan, Feb, Mar...Dec
MONTH	Month name spelled out	January, February...December
Q	Quarter	1, 2, 3, 4
RM	Roman numeral month (I–XII)	I,II,III,IV,V...XII
YYYY, YYY, YY, Y	Four-digit year; last 3, 2, 1 digits in the year	1999, 999, 99, 9 2000, 000, 00, 0
YEAR	Year spelled out	Two thousand two
SYYYY	If BC, year is shown as negative	-1250
RR	Used for data input with only two digits for the year	See description following table
HH, HH12	Hour of the half-day (1–12)	1,2,3...12
HH24	Hour of the day (0–23)	0,1,2...23
MI	Minutes of the hour (0–59)	0,1,2...59
SS	Seconds of the minute (0–59)	0,1,2...59
SSSSS	Seconds of the day (0–86399)	0,1,2...86399
TZD	Time zone daylight savings; must correspond to TZR	CST
TZH	Time zone hour, together with TZM is time zone offset	07
TZM	Time zone minute, together with TZH is time zone offset	00

TABLE 3.7 Date Format Codes *(continued)*

Date Code	Format Code Description	Example
TZR	Time zone region	US/Central, Mexico/BajaNorte
, . / - ; :	Punctuation	Literal display
'text'	Quoted text	Literal display

The RR code is used for data input with only two digits for the year. It is intended to deal with two-digit years before and after 2000. It rounds the century based on the current year and the two-digit year, entered as follows:

- If the current year is >= 50 and the two-digit year is <50, the century is rounded up to the next century.
- If the current year is >= 50 and the two-digit year is >= 50, the century is unchanged.
- If the current year is < 50 and the two-digit year is < 50 the century is unchanged.
- If the current year is < 50 and the two-digit year is >=50, the century is rounded down to the previous century.

So, if the current year is 2003 (<50) and the two-digit year is entered as 62 (>=50), the year is interpreted as 1962.

For any of the numeric codes, the ordinal and/or spelled-out representation can be displayed with the modifier codes `th` (for ordinal) and `sp` (for spelled out). Here is an example:

```
SELECT SYSDATE
      ,TO_CHAR(SYSDATE,'Mmspth') Month
      ,TO_CHAR(SYSDATE,'DDth') Day
      ,TO_CHAR(SYSDATE,'Yyyysp') Year
FROM dual;

SYSDATE     MONTH    DAY  YEAR
----------- -------- ---- -------------------------------------
01-DEC-1999 Twelfth  01ST One Thousand Nine Hundred Ninety-Nine
```

For any of the spelled-out words or ordinals, case follows the pattern of the first two characters in the code. If the first two characters are uppercase, the spelled-out words are all uppercase. If the first two characters are lowercase, the spelled-out words are all lowercase. If the first two characters are uppercase then lowercase, the spelled-out words have the first letter in uppercase and the remaining characters in lowercase.

```
SELECT TO_CHAR(SYSDATE,'MONTH') upperCase
      ,TO_CHAR(SYSDATE,'Month') mixedCase
      ,TO_CHAR(SYSDATE,'month') lowerCase
FROM dual;

UPPERCASE MIXEDCASE LOWERCASE
--------- --------- ---------
DECEMBER  December  december
```

Number Conversion

If `x` is a number, *`fmt`* is a numeric format code (see Table 3.8).

```
SELECT TO_CHAR(123456,'9.99EEEE')
      ,TO_CHAR(123456,'9.9EEEE')
FROM dual;

TO_CHAR(12 TO_CHAR(1
---------- ---------
  1.23E+05   1.2E+05
```

`nlsparm` can include `NLS_NUMERIC_CHARACTERS` for specifying decimal and grouping symbols (format symbols `D` and `G`, respectively), `NLS_CURRENCY` for specifying the currency symbol (format symbol `L`), and `NLS_ISO_CURRENCY` for specifying the ISO international currency symbol (format symbol `C`). The `NLS_CURRENCY` symbol and the `NLS_ISO_CURRENCY` mnemonic are frequently different. For example, the `NLS_CURRENCY` symbol for U.S. dollars is $, but this symbol is not uniquely American, so the ISO symbol for U.S. dollars is `USD`.

```
SELECT TO_CHAR(-1234.56,'C099G999D99MI'
                ,'NLS_NUMERIC_CHARACTERS='',.''
                  NLS_CURRENCY=''DM''
                  NLS_ISO_CURRENCY=''GERMANY''
                 ') Balance
FROM dual;
```

```
BALANCE
--------------
DEM001.234,56-
```

TABLE 3.8 Numeric Format Codes

Numeric Code	Format Code Description	Example
9	Numeric digits with leading space if positive and a leading – (minus) if negative.	9999.9 = 1234.5 9999.9 = -1234.5 9999.9 = .3
0	Leading and/or trailing zeros.	0009.90 = 0012.30
,	Comma, for use as a group separator. It cannot appear after a period or decimal code.	9,999.9 = 1,234.5
G	Local group separator, could be comma (,) or period (.).	9G999D9 = 1,234.5 9G999D9 = 1.234,5
.	Period, for use as the decimal character. It cannot appear more than once or to the left of a group separator.	9,999.9 = 1,234.5
D	Local decimal character, could be comma (,) or period (.).	9G999D9 = 1,234.5 9G999D9 = 1.234,5
$	Dollar-sign currency symbol.	$999 = $123
L	Local currency symbol.	L999 = $123 L999 = Euro123
FM	No leading or trailing blanks.	FM99.99 = .1
EEEE	Scientific notation.	9.9EEEE = 1.2E+05
MI	Negative as a trailing minus.	999MI = 137-
PR	Negative in angle brackets (< >).	999PR = <137>
S	Negative as a leading minus.	S999 = -137

TABLE 3.8 Numeric Format Codes *(continued)*

Numeric Code	Format Code Description	Example
RN	Uppercase Roman numeral.	RN = XXIV
rn	Lowercase Roman numeral.	rn = xxiv
X	Hexadecimal	XX = FC

TO_DATE

TO_DATE(<*c*> [,<*fmt*> [,<*nlsparm*>]]) takes three arguments, where *c* is a character string, *fmt* is a format string specifying the format that *c* appears in (see Table 3.7), and *nlsparm* specifies language or location formatting conventions. This function returns *c* converted into the DATE datatype.

```
INSERT INTO demo (demo_key, date_col)
VALUES (1,TO_DATE('04-Oct-1957','DD-Mon-YYYY') );
```

TO_DSINTERVAL

TO_DSINTERVAL(<*c*> [,<*nlsparm*>]) takes two arguments, where *c* is a character string and *nlsparm* specifies the decimal and group separator characters. This function returns *c* converted into an INTERVAL DAY TO SECOND datatype. This function is new to Oracle9i.

```
SELECT SYSDATE
      ,SYSDATE+TO_DSINTERVAL('007 12:00:00') "+7½ days"
      ,SYSDATE+TO_DSINTERVAL('030 00:00:00') "+30 days"
FROM dual;

SYSDATE              +7½ days             +30 days
-------------------- -------------------- --------------------
24-SEP-2002 06:58:28 01-OCT-2002 18:58:28 24-OCT-2002 06:58:28
```

TO_MULTI_BYTE

TO_MULTI_BYTE(<*c*>) takes a single argument, where *c* is a character string. This function returns a character string containing *c* with all single-byte characters converted to their multibyte counterparts. This function is useful only in databases using character sets with both single-byte and multibyte characters. See also TO_SINGLE_BYTE.

TO_NUMBER

TO_NUMBER(<*c*> [,<*fmt*> [,<*nlsparm*>]]) takes three arguments, where *c* is a character string, *fmt* is a format string specifying the format that *c* appears in, and *nlsparm* specifies language or location formatting conventions. This function returns the numeric value represented by *c*.

TO_SINGLE_BYTE

TO_SINGLE_BYTE(<*c*>) takes a single argument, where *c* is a character string. This function returns a character string containing *c* with all multibyte characters converted to their single-byte counterparts. This function is useful only in databases using character sets with both single-byte and multibyte characters. See also TO_MULTI_BYTE.

TO_YMINTERVAL

TO_YMINTERVAL(<*c*>) takes a single argument, where *c* is a character string. This function returns *c* converted into an INTERVAL YEAR TO MONTH datatype. This function is new to Oracle9i.

```
SELECT SYSDATE
      ,SYSDATE+TO_YMINTERVAL('01-03') "+15 months"
      ,SYSDATE-TO_YMINTERVAL('00-03') "- 3 months"
FROM dual;

SYSDATE              +15 months           - 3 months
-------------------- -------------------- --------------------
24-SEP-2001 06:54:41 24-DEC-2002 06:54:41 24-JUN-2001 06:54:41
```

UNISTR

UNISTR(<*c*>) takes a single argument, where *c* is a character string. This function returns *c* in Unicode in the database Unicode character set. Include UCS2 characters by prepending a backslash (\) to the character's numeric code. Include the backslash character by specifying two backslashes (\\). This function is new to Oracle9i.

```
SELECT UNISTR('\00A3')
      ,UNISTR('\00F1')
      ,UNISTR('ca\00F1on')
```

```
FROM dual;

UN UN UNISTR('CA
-- -- ----------
 £  ñ  c a ñ o n
```

Using Other Single-Row Functions

This is the catchall category to include all the single-row functions that don't fit into the other categories. Some are incredibly useful, like DECODE; others are rather esoteric, like DUMP or VSIZE.

Miscellaneous Function Overview

Table 3.9 summarizes the single-row miscellaneous functions. We will cover each of these functions in the "Miscellaneous Function Descriptions" section.

TABLE 3.9 Miscellaneous Function Summary

Function	Description
BFILENAME	Returns a BFILE locator for the specified file and directory
COALESCE	Returns the first non-NULL in a list
DECODE	Inline case statement (an IF...THEN...ELSE function)
DUMP	Returns a raw substring in the specified encoding (octal/hex/character/decimal).
EMPTY_BLOB	Returns an empty BLOB locator
EMPTY_CLOB	Returns an empty CLOB locator
GREATEST	Sorts the arguments and returns the largest
LEAST	Sorts the arguments and returns the smallest
NULLIF	Returns NULL if two expressions are equal

TABLE 3.9 Miscellaneous Function Summary *(continued)*

Function	Description
SYS_CONNECT_BY_PATH	Returns root-to-node values in a CONNECT BY query
SYS_CONTEXT	Returns various session attributes, such as IP address, terminal, and current user
UID	Returns the numeric user ID for the current session
USER	Returns the username for the current session
USERENV	Deprecated in favor of SYS_CONTEXT
VSIZE	Returns the internal size in bytes for an expression

Miscellaneous Function Descriptions

The miscellaneous functions are arranged in alphabetical order, with descriptions and examples of each one.

BFILENAME

BFILENAME(<*dir*>, <*file*>) takes two arguments, where *dir* is a directory and *file* is a filename. This function returns an empty BFILE locator. This function is used to initialize a BFILE variable or BFILE column in a table. When used, the BFILE is instantiated. Neither *dir* nor *file* needs to exist at the time BFILENAME is called, but both must exist when the locator is used.

```
DECLARE
   BFILE_LOC  BFILE;
BEGIN
   BFILE_LOC := BFILENAME('C:\DATA\','Foo.dat');
...
```

COALESCE

COALESCE(<*exp_list*>) takes one argument, where *exp_list* is a list of expressions. This function returns the first non-NULL value in the list *exp_list*. If all expressions in *exp_list* are NULL, then NULL is returned. Each expression in *exp_list* should be the same datatype. This function is new to Oracle9i and is very useful, without being as cryptic as DECODE can sometimes be.

```
SELECT COALESCE(NULL,'Oracle','24') string_type
      ,COALESCE(3,14,COS(0)) nbr_type
      ,COALESCE(SYS_CONTEXT('USERENV','BG_JOB_ID')
               ,SYS_CONTEXT('USERENV','FG_JOB_ID')
               ) test3
FROM dual;

STRING   NBR_TYPE TEST3
------ ---------- ------
Oracle          3 0
```

DECODE

`DECODE(<x> ,<m1>, <r1> [,<m2> ,<r2>...] [, <d>])` can use multiple arguments. `x` is an expression. *m1* is a matching expression to compare with *x*. If *m1* is equivalent to *x*, then *r1* is returned; otherwise, additional matching expressions (*m2*, *m3*, *m4*, and so on) are compared, if they are included, and the corresponding result (*r2*, *r3*, *r4*, and so on) is returned. If no match is found and the default expression *d* is included, then *d* is returned. This function acts like a case statement in C, Pascal, or Ada. `DECODE` is a very powerful tool that can make SQL very efficient—or very dense and nonintuitive. Let's look at some examples to help clarify its use.

In the following example, we query the V$SESSION table to see who is executing which command in the database. The COMMAND column displays a numeric code for each command, but we want to report a textual description for a few important commands. We use `DECODE` in the fourth column to examine the contents of V$SESSION.COMMAND. If the COMMAND is 0, then we display *None*; if it is 2, we display *Insert*, and so on. If the command is not in our list, we display the default, *Other*.

```
SELECT sid ,serial# ,username
      ,DECODE(command
       ,0,'None'
       ,2,'Insert'
       ,3,'Select'
       ,6,'Update'
       ,7,'Delete'
       ,8,'Drop'
       ,'Other') cmd
```

```
FROM v$session
WHERE type <> 'BACKGROUND';

       SID    SERIAL# USERNAME       CMD
---------- ---------- -------------- -------
         7        147                None
         8        147                None
         9         24 CHIPD          Other
        11          4 CHIPD          Select
```

DECODE does not have to return a value; it can return NULL. The following example returns NULL if GRANTABLE does not equal 'YES'. There is no default specified in the arguments.

```
SELECT owner, table_name, grantor, grantee
      ,DECODE(grantable,'YES','With Grant Option')
FROM user_tab_privs
WHERE privilege = 'SELECT';

OWNER TABLE_NAME      GRANTOR  GRANTEE  DECODE(GRANTABLE,
----- --------------- -------- -------- -----------------
CHIPD ZIP_STATE_CITY  CHIPD    SCOTT    With Grant Option
SYS   V_$INSTANCE     SYS      CHIPD
SYS   DBA_DATA_FILES  SYS      CHIPD
```

See the examples in "Nesting Functions" section in Chapter 4 for more advanced uses of DECODE.

DUMP

DUMP(<*x*> [,<*fmt*> [,<*n1*> [,<*n2*>]]]) can take four arguments, where *x* is an expression. *fmt* is a format specification for octal (1008), decimal (1010), hexadecimal (1016), or single characters (1017). *n1* is the starting byte offset within *x*, and *n2* is the length in bytes to dump. This function returns a character string containing the datatype of *x* in numeric notation (for example, 2=number, 12=date), the length in bytes of *x*, and the internal representation of *x*. This function is mainly used for troubleshooting data problems.

```
SELECT global_name
      ,DUMP(global_name,1017,8,5) dump_string
FROM global_name;

GLOBAL_NAME  DUMP_STRING
------------ --------------------------------------------
ORACLE.WORLD Typ=1 Len=12 CharacterSet=WE8ISO8859P1: W,O,R,L,D
```

See the section on "Oracle Internal Datatypes" in the *OCI Programmer's Guide* for a complete listing of the numeric notation for datatypes.

EMPTY_BLOB

EMPTY_BLOB() takes no arguments. This function returns an empty BLOB locator. This function is used to initialize a BLOB variable or BLOB column in a table. When used, the BLOB is instantiated but not populated.

```
INSERT INTO bclob (pk,clob_col,blob_col)
VALUES (43, EMPTY_CLOB(), EMPTY_BLOB() );
```

EMPTY_CLOB

EMPTY_CLOB() takes no arguments. This function returns an empty CLOB locator. This function is used to initialize a CLOB variable or CLOB column in a table. When used, the CLOB is instantiated but not populated. (See the previous section for an example.)

GREATEST

GREATEST(<*exp_list*>) takes one argument, where *exp_list* is a list of expressions. This function returns the expression that sorts highest in the datatype of the first expression. If the first expression is any of the character datatypes, a VARCHAR2 is returned, and the comparison rules for VARCHAR are used for character literal strings. A NULL in the expression list results in a NULL being returned.

```
SELECT GREATEST('19','24',9) string FROM dual;

STRING
-------
9
```

The comparison rules used by GREATEST and LEAST on character literals order trailing spaces higher than no spaces. This behavior follows the non-padded comparison rules of the VARCHAR datatype. Note the ordering of the leading and trailing spaces: trailing spaces are greatest and leading spaces least.

```
SELECT GREATEST(' Yes','Yes','Yes ')
        ,LEAST(' Yes','Yes','Yes ')
FROM dual;

GREA LEAST
---- -----
Yes   Yes
```

To remember the comparison rules for trailing and leading space in character literals, think, "Leading equals least."

LEAST

LEAST(<*exp_list*>) takes one argument, where *exp_list* is a list of expressions. This function returns the expression that sorts lowest in the datatype of the first expression. If the first expression is any of the character datatypes, a VARCHAR2 is returned.

```
SELECT LEAST(SYSDATE,'15-MAR-2002','17-JUN-2002') oldest
FROM dual;

OLDEST
-----------
27-NOV-2001

SELECT ename, sal, LEAST(sal, 3000) FROM emp;

ENAME             SAL LEAST(SAL,3000)
---------- ---------- ---------------
SMITH             800             800
ALLEN            1600            1600
KING             5000            3000
```

NULLIF

NULLIF(<*x1*> , <*x2*>) takes two arguments, where *x1* and *x2* are expressions. This function returns NULL if *x1* equals *x2*; otherwise it returns *x1*. If *x1* is NULL, NULLIF returns NULL. This function is new to Oracle9i.

To facilitate visualizing a NULL, the following example has the NULL indicator set to ?. So a ? in the query results that follow represents a NULL.

```
SELECT ename
      ,mgr
      ,comm
      ,NULLIF(comm,0) test1
      ,NULLIF(0,comm) test2
      ,NULLIF(mgr,comm) test3
FROM scott.emp
WHERE empno IN (7844,7839,7654,7369);

ENAME       MGR  COMM TEST1 TEST2 TEST3
---------- ---- ---- ----- ----- -----
SMITH      7902    ?     ?     0  7902
MARTIN     7698 1400  1400     0  7698
KING          ?    ?     ?     0     ?
TURNER     7698    0     ?     ?  7698
```

SYS_CONNECT_BY_PATH

SYS_CONNECT_BY_PATH(<*x*> , <*c*>) takes two arguments, where *x* is a column and *c* is a single character. This function works only with hierarchical queries—queries that use the CONNECT BY clause. It returns the path of column *x*, delimited by character *c*, from root to node for each row returned by the CONNECT BY condition. This function is new to Oracle9i.

```
SELECT ename
      ,SYS_CONNECT_BY_PATH(ename, '|') Reporting_Chain
FROM scott.emp
START WITH ename = 'KING'
CONNECT BY PRIOR empno = mgr
```

```
ENAME      REPORTING_CHAIN
---------- ------------------------
KING       |KING
JONES      |KING|JONES
SCOTT      |KING|JONES|SCOTT
ADAMS      |KING|JONES|SCOTT|ADAMS
FORD       |KING|JONES|FORD
SMITH      |KING|JONES|FORD|SMITH
BLAKE      |KING|BLAKE
ALLEN      |KING|BLAKE|ALLEN
WARD       |KING|BLAKE|WARD
MARTIN     |KING|BLAKE|MARTIN
TURNER     |KING|BLAKE|TURNER
JAMES      |KING|BLAKE|JAMES
CLARK      |KING|CLARK
MILLER     |KING|CLARK|MILLER
```

SYS_CONTEXT

SYS_CONTEXT(<*n*> , <*p*> [, <*length*>]) can take three arguments, where *n* is a namespace, *p* is a parameter associated with namespace *n*, and *length* is the length of the return value, in bytes. *length* defaults to 256. The built-in namespace USERENV contains information on the current session (see Table 3.10). This function is new to Oracle9i and supersedes the USERENV function, which has been deprecated.

The SYS_CONTEXT function retrieves session information. Therefore, it cannot work with real application clusters or parallel queries.

```
SELECT SYS_CONTEXT('USERENV','IP_ADDRESS')
FROM dual;

SYS_CONTEXT('USERENV','IP_ADDRESS')
-------------------------------------
192.168.1.100
```

Table 3.10 lists the parameters available in the USERENV namespace for the SYS_CONTEXT function.

TABLE 3.10 Parameters in the USERENV Namespace

Parameter	Description
AUDITED_CURSORID	Returns the cursor ID of the SQL that triggered the auditing.
AUTHENTICATION_DATA	Returns the data used to authenticate a login user.
AUTHENTICATION_TYPE	Returns the method used to authenticate a user. The return value can be DATABASE for database-authenticated accounts, OS for externally identified accounts, NETWORK for globally identified accounts, or PROXY for OCI proxy authentication.
BG_JOB_ID	Returns the job ID (i.e., DBA_JOBS) if the session was created by a background process. Returns NULL if the session is a foreground session. See also FG_JOB_ID.
CLIENT_IDENTIFIER	Returns the client session identifier in the global context. It can be set with the DBMS_SESSION built-in package.
CLIENT_INFO	Returns the 64 bytes of user session information stored by DBMS_APPLICATION_INFO.
CURRENT_SCHEMA	Returns the current schema as set by ALTER SESSION SET CURRENT_SCHEMA or, by default, the login schema / ID.
CURRENT_SCHEMAID	Returns the numeric ID for CURRENT_SCHEMA.
CURRENT_SQL	Returns the SQL that triggered Fine-Grained Auditing (use only within scope inside the event handler for Fine-Grained Auditing).
CURRENT_USER	Returns the current username. This is the same functionality as the USER function.

TABLE 3.10 Parameters in the USERENV Namespace *(continued)*

Parameter	Description
CURRENT_USERID	Returns the numeric current user ID. This is the same functionality as the UID function.
DB_DOMAIN	Returns the contents of the DB_DOMAIN init.ora parameter.
DB_NAME	Returns the contents of the DB_NAME init.ora parameter.
ENTRYID	Returns the auditing entry identifier (only available if the init.ora parameter AUDIT_TRAIL is set to TRUE).
EXTERNAL_NAME	Returns the operating system name of the database user for local connections.
FG_JOB_ID	Returns the job ID of the current session if a foreground process created it. Returns NULL if the session is a background session. See also BG_JOB_ID.
GLOBAL_CONTEXT_MEMORY	Returns the number in the SGA by the globally access context.
HOST	Returns the hostname of the machine where the client connected from. This is not the same terminal in V$SESSION.
INSTANCE	Returns the instance number for the instance the session is connected to. This is always 1, unless you are running Oracle Parallel Server.
IP_ADDRESS	Returns the IP address of the machine where the client connected from. If the session is not established via TCP/IP and Net8, it returns NULL.
ISDBA	Returns TRUE if the user connected AS SYSDBA.
LANG	Returns the ISO abbreviation for the language name.

TABLE 3.10 Parameters in the USERENV Namespace *(continued)*

Parameter	Description
LANGUAGE	Returns a character string containing the language and territory used by the session and the database character set in the form *language_territory.characterset.*
NETWORK_PROTOCOL	Returns the network protocol being used as specified in the PROTOCOL= section of the connect string or `tnsnames.ora` definition.
NLS_CALENDAR	Returns the calendar for the current session.
NLS_CURRENCY	Returns the currency for the current session.
NLS_DATE_FORMAT	Returns the date format for the current session.
NLS_SORT	Returns the binary or linguistic sort basis.
NLS_TERRITORY	Returns the territory for the current session.
OS_USER	Returns the operating system username for the current session.
PROXY_USER	Returns the name of the database user who opened the current session for the session user.
PROXY_USERID	Returns the numeric ID for the database user who opened the current session for the session user.
SESSION_USER	Returns the database username for the current session.
SESSION_USERID	Returns the numeric database user ID for the current session.
SESSIONID	Returns the auditing session identifier AUDSID. This parameter is out of scope for distributed queries.

TABLE 3.10 Parameters in the USERENV Namespace *(continued)*

Parameter	Description
TERMINAL	Returns the terminal identifier for the current session. This is the same as the terminal in V$SESSION.

UID

UID takes no parameters and returns the integer user ID for the current user. The user ID uniquely identifies each user in a database and can be selected from the DBA_USERS view.

```
SELECT username, account_status
FROM dba_users
WHERE user_id=UID;

USERNAME                ACCOUNT_STATUS
----------------------- ---------------
CHIPD                   OPEN

INSERT INTO audit_table (who,when,what)
VALUES (UID, SYSDATE, audit_action);
```

USER

USER takes no parameters and returns a character string containing the username for the current user.

```
SELECT USER, UID
FROM dual;

USER                          UID
-------------------- ----------
CHIPD                          26
```

USERENV

USERENV(<*opt*>) takes a single argument, where *opt* is one of the following options:

- ISDBA returns TRUE if the SYSDBA role is enabled in the current session.
- SESSIONID returns the AUDSID auditing session identifier.
- ENTRYID returns the auditing entry identifier if auditing is enabled for the instance (the init.ora parameter AUDIT_TRAIL is set to TRUE).
- INSTANCE returns the instance identifier that the session is connected to. This option is useful only if you are running the Oracle Parallel Server and have multiple instances.
- LANGUAGE returns the language, territory, and database character set. The delimiters are an underscore (_) between language and territory, and a period (.) between the territory and character set.
- LANG returns the ISO abbreviation of the session's language.
- TERMINAL returns a VARCHAR2 string containing information on operating system identifier for your current session's terminal. The option can appear in uppercase, lowercase, or mixed case.

The USERENV function has been deprecated in release Oracle9i. See the SYS_CONTEXT function.

```
SELECT USERENV('ISDBA')
FROM dual;

USEREN
------
FALSE
```

VSIZE

VSIZE(<*x*>) takes a single argument, where *x* is an expression. This function returns the size in bytes of the internal representation of the *x*.

```
SELECT VSIZE(user), user
FROM dual;

VSIZE(USER) USER
----------- -------
          5 CHIPD
```

Summary

This chapter introduced single-row functions. You learned that single-row functions return a value for each row as it is retrieved from the table.

Single-row functions can be used in the SELECT, WHERE, and ORDER BY clauses of SELECT statements. We covered the rich assortment of functions available in each datatype and some functions that work on any datatype.

Exam Essentials

Understand where single-row functions can be used. Single-row functions can be used in the SELECT, WHERE, and ORDER BY clauses of SELECT statements. Single-row functions cannot appear in a HAVING clause.

Know the effects that NULL values can have on arithmetic and other functions. Any arithmetic operation on a NULL results in a NULL. This is true of most functions as well. Use the NVL and NVL2 functions to deal with NULLs.

Know how date arithmetic works. When adding or subtracting numeric values from a DATE datatype, whole numbers represent days. Also, the new date/time intervals INTERVAL YEAR TO MONTH and INTERVAL DAY TO SECOND can be added or subtracted from date/time datatypes. You need to know how to interpret and create expressions that add or subtract intervals to or from dates.

Know the datatypes for the various date/time functions. Oracle introduced many new date/time functions to support the new date/time datatypes. You need to know the return datatypes for these functions. SYSDATE and CURRENT_DATE return a DATE datatype. CURRENT_TIMESTAMP and SYSTIMESTAMP return a TIMESTAMP WITH TIME ZONE datatype. LOCALTIMESTAMP returns a TIMESTAMP datatype.

Know the format models for converting dates to/from character strings. In practice, you can simply look up format codes in a reference. For the exam, you must have them memorized.

Understand the use of the DECODE function. DECODE acts like a case statement in C, Pascal, or Ada. Learn how this function works and how to use it.

Key Terms

Before you take the exam, make sure you're familiar with the following terms:

- National Language Support (NLS)
- NULL
- ROWID
- single-row functions
- Unicode

Review Questions

1. You want to display each project's start date as the day, week, number, and year. Which statement will give output like the following?

   `Tuesday  Week 23, 2002`

   A. `Select proj_id, to_char(start_date, 'DOW  Week WOY YYYY') from projects`

   B. `Select proj_id, to_char(start_date,'Day'||' Week'||' WOY, YYYY') from projects;`

   C. `Select proj_id, to_char(start_date,'Day" Week" WW, YYYY') from projects;`

   D. `Select proj_id, to_char(start_date,'Day Week# , YYYY') from projects;`

   E. You can't calculate week numbers with Oracle.

2. What will the following statement return?

   ```
   SELECT last_name, first_name, start_date
   FROM employees
   WHERE hire_date < TRUNC(SYSDATE) - 5;
   ```

   A. Employees hired within the past 5 years

   B. Employees hired within the past 5 days

   C. Employees hired more than 5 years ago

   D. Employees hired more than 5 days ago

3. Which assertion about the following statements is most true?

```
SELECT name, region_code||phone_number
FROM customers;
SELECT name, CONCAT(region_code,phone_number)
FROM customers;
```

A. If the REGION_CODE is NULL, the first statement will not include that customer's PHONE_NUMBER.

B. If the REGION_CODE is NULL, the second statement will not include that customer's PHONE_NUMBER.

C. Both statements will return the same data.

D. The second statement will raise an exception if the REGION_CODE is NULL for any customer.

4. Which single-row function could you use to return a specific portion of a character string?

A. INSTR

B. SUBSTR

C. LPAD

D. LEAST

5. The Sales department is simplifying the pricing policy for all products. All surcharges are being incorporated into the base price for all products in the consumer division (code C), and the new base price is increasing by the lesser of 0.5 percent of the old base price or 10 percent of the old surcharge. Using the PRODUCT table described below, you need to implement this change.

Column Name	sku	name	division	base_price	surcharge
Key Type	pk				
NULLs/Unique	NN	NN	NN	NN	
FK Table					
Datatype	NUMBER	VARCHAR2	VARCHAR2	NUMBER	NUMBER
Length	16	16	4	11,2	11,2

Which of the following statements will achieve the desired results?

A.
```
UPDATE product SET
 base_price = base_price + surcharge +
       LEAST(base_price * 0.005
            ,surcharge * 0.1)
,surcharge = NULL
WHERE division='C'
```

B.
```
UPDATE product SET
 base_price = base_price + NVL(surcharge,0) +
       LEAST(base_price * 0.005
            ,surcharge * 0.1)
,surcharge = NULL
WHERE division='C'
```

C.
```
UPDATE product SET
base_price = base_price + NVL(surcharge,0) +
  COALESCE(LEAST(base_price*0.005
                ,surcharge * 0.1)
          ,base_price * 0.005)
,surcharge = NULL
WHERE division='C'
```

D. A, B, and C will all achieve the desired results.

E. None of these statements will achieve the desired results.

6. Which function(s) accept arguments of any datatype? (Choose all that apply.)

A. SUBSTR

B. NVL

C. ROUND

D. DECODE

E. SIGN

7. What will be returned by `SIGN(ABS(NVL(-32,0)))`?

   A. 1

   B. 32

   C. –1

   D. 0

   E. `NULL`

8. One of your database users asked you to provide a command that will show her the `NLS_DATE_FORMAT` that is currently set in her session. Which command would you recommend?

   A. `SELECT SYS_CONTEXT('USERENV', 'NLS_DATE_FORMAT') FROM dual;`

   B. `SELECT SYS_CONTEXT('NLS_DATE_FORMAT') FROM dual;`

   C. `SELECT SYS_CONTEXT('NLS_DATE_FORMAT','USERENV') FROM dual;`

   D. `SELECT NLS_DATE_FORMAT FROM dual;`

9. Which two functions could you use to strip leading characters from a character string?

   A. `LTRIM`

   B. `SUBSTR`

   C. `RTRIM`

   D. `INSTR`

   E. `MOD`

10. You have been asked to randomly assign 25 percent of the employees to a new training program. Employee numbers are assigned as consecutive numbers to the employees. Which statement below will print the employee number and name of every fourth employee?

A.
```
SELECT MOD(empno, 4), ename
FROM employees
WHERE MOD(empno,4) = 0;
```

B.
```
SELECT empno, ename
FROM employees
WHERE MOD(empno, 4) = .25;
```

C.
```
SELECT MOD(empno, 4) ename
FROM employees
WHERE MOD(empno, 4) = 0;
```

D.
```
SELECT empno, ename
FROM employees
WHERE MOD(empno, 4) = 0;
```

11. Which function will convert the ASCII code 97 to its equivalent letter *a*?

A. `ASC(97)`

B. `ASCIISTR(97)`

C. `ASCII(97)`

D. `CHR(97)`

12. Which date components does the `CURRENT_TIMESTAMP` function display?

A. Session date, session time, and session time zone offset

B. Session date and session time

C. Session date and session time zone offset

D. Session time zone offset

13. Using the SALESPERSON_REVENUE table described below, which statements will properly display the TOTAL_REVENUE (CAR_SALES + WARRANTY_SALES) of each salesperson?

Column Name	salesperson_id	car_sales	warranty_sales
Key Type	pk		
NULLs/Unique	NN	NN	
FK Table			
Datatype	NUMBER	NUMBER	NUMBER
Length	11,2	11,2	11,2

A.
```
SELECT salesperson_id,car_sales,warranty_sales
      ,car_sales + warranty_sales total_sales
FROM salesperson_revenue;
```

B.
```
SELECT salesperson_id,car_sales,warranty_sales
      ,car_sales + NVL2(warranty_sales,0) total_sales
FROM salesperson_revenue;
```

C.
```
SELECT salesperson_id,car_sales,warranty_sales
      ,NVL2(warranty_sales, car_sales
      + warranty_sales, car_sales) total_sales
FROM salesperson_revenue;
```

D.
```
SELECT salesperson_id,car_sales,warranty_sales
     ,car_sales + COALESCE(car_sales, warranty_sales,
car_sales
      + warranty_sales) total_sales
FROM salesperson_revenue;
```

14. Which function could be used to return the IP address for the machine where the client session connected from?

A. COOKIE

B. NETINFO

C. SYS_CONTEXT

D. SYS_CONNECT_BY_PATH

15. In Oracle, what do trigonometric functions operate on?

    A. Degrees

    B. Radians

    C. Gradients

    D. The default is radians, but degrees or gradients can be specified.

16. What will the following SQL statement return?

    ```
    SELECT COALESCE(NULL,'Oracle ','Certified') FROM dual;
    ```

    A. `NULL`

    B. Oracle

    C. Certified

    D. Oracle Certified

17. Which expression will always return the date one year later than the current date?

    A. `SYSDATE + 365`

    B. `SYSDATE + TO_YMINTERVAL('01-00')`

    C. `CURRENT_DATE + 1`

    D. `NEW_TIME(CURRENT_DATE,1,'YEAR')`

18. Which function will return a TIMESTAMP WITH TIME ZONE datatype?

    A. `CURRENT_TIMESTAMP`

    B. `LOCALTIMESTAMP`

    C. `CURRENT_DATE`

    D. `SYSDATE`

19. Which statement would change all occurrences of the string `'IBM'` to the string `'SUN'` in the DESCRIPTION column of the VENDOR table?

A. `SELECT TRANSLATE(description, 'IBM', 'SUN') FROM vendor`

B. `SELECT CONVERT(description, 'IBM', 'SUN') FROM vendor`

C. `SELECT EXTRACT(description, 'IBM', 'SUN') FROM vendor`

D. `SELECT REPLACE(description, 'IBM', 'SUN') FROM vendor`

20. Which function implements IF..THEN...ELSE logic?

A. `INITCAP()`

B. `REPLACE()`

C. `DECODE()`

D. `IFELSE()`

Answers to Review Questions

1. C. Double quotation marks must surround literal strings like `" Week"`.

2. D. The TRUNC function removes the time portion of a date by default, and whole numbers added to or subtracted from dates represent days added or subtracted from that date. `TRUNC(SYSDATE) -5` means five days ago at midnight.

3. C. Both statements are equivalent.

4. B. `INSTR` returns a number. `LPAD` adds to a character string. `LEAST` does not change an input string.

5. C. Statements A and B do not account for `NULL` surcharges correctly and will set the base price to `NULL` where the surcharge is `NULL`. In statement C, the `LEAST` function will return a `NULL` if surcharge is `NULL`, in which case the BASE_PRICE * 0.005 would be added.

6. B, D. `ROUND` does not accept character arguments. `SUBSTR` accepts only character arguments. `SIGN` accepts only numeric arguments.

7. A. The functions are evaluated from the innermost to outermost, as follows:

   ```
   SIGN(ABS(NVL(-32,0))) = SIGN(ABS(-32)) = SIGN(32) = 1
   ```

8. A. The syntax for the `SYS_CONTEXT` function requires that the first argument be the namespace and the second argument be the parameter. There is no pseudo-column `NLS_DATE_FORMAT`, so it cannot be selected from DUAL.

9. A, B. `RTRIM` removes trailing (not leading) characters. The others return numbers.

10. D. `MOD` returns the number remainder after division. Answers A and C don't return the employee number, and `MOD(empno,4)` won't return a decimal.

11. D. The `CHR` function converts an ASCII code to a letter. `ASCII` does the inverse, converting a letter into its ASCII code. `ASCIISTR` converts a string to its ASCII equivalent. There is no `ASC` function.

12. A. The CURRENT_TIMESTAMP function returns the session date, session time, and session time zone offset.

13. C. Option A will result in NULL TOTAL_SALES for rows where there are NULL WARRANTY_SALES. Option B is not the correct syntax for NVL2, because it requires three arguments. With option C, if WARRANTY_SALES is NULL, then CAR_SALES is returned; otherwise, CAR_SALES+WARRANTY_SALES is returned. The COALESCE function returns the first non-NULL argument and could be used to obtain the desired results, but the first argument here is CAR_SALES, which is not NULL, and therefore COALESCE will always return CAR_SALES.

14. C. The COOKIE and NETINFO functions do not exist. The SYS_CONTEXT function returns session information, and one of the parameters in the USERENV namespace is IP_ADDRESS, which returns the IP address for the machine where the client connected from. The SYS_CONNECT_BY_PATH function is used for CONNECT BY (hierarchical) queries.

15. B. Oracle trigonometric functions operate only on radians.

16. B. The COALESCE function returns the first non-NULL parameter, which is the character string 'Oracle '.

17. B. Option A will not work if there is a Feb 29 (leap year) in the next 365 days. Option B will always add one year to the present date. Option C will return the date one day later. NEW_TIME is used to return the date/time in a different time zone.

18. A. LOCALTIMESTAMP does not return the time zone. CURRENT_DATE and SYSDATE return neither fractional seconds nor a time zone.

19. D. CONVERT is used to change from one character set to another. EXTRACT works on date/time datatypes. TRANSLATE changes all occurrences of each character with a positionally corresponding character, so 'I like IBM' would become 'S like SUN'.

20. C. The INITCAP function capitalizes the first letter in each word. The REPLACE function performs search-and-replace string operations. There is no IFELSE function. The DECODE function is the one that implements IF...THEN...ELSE logic.

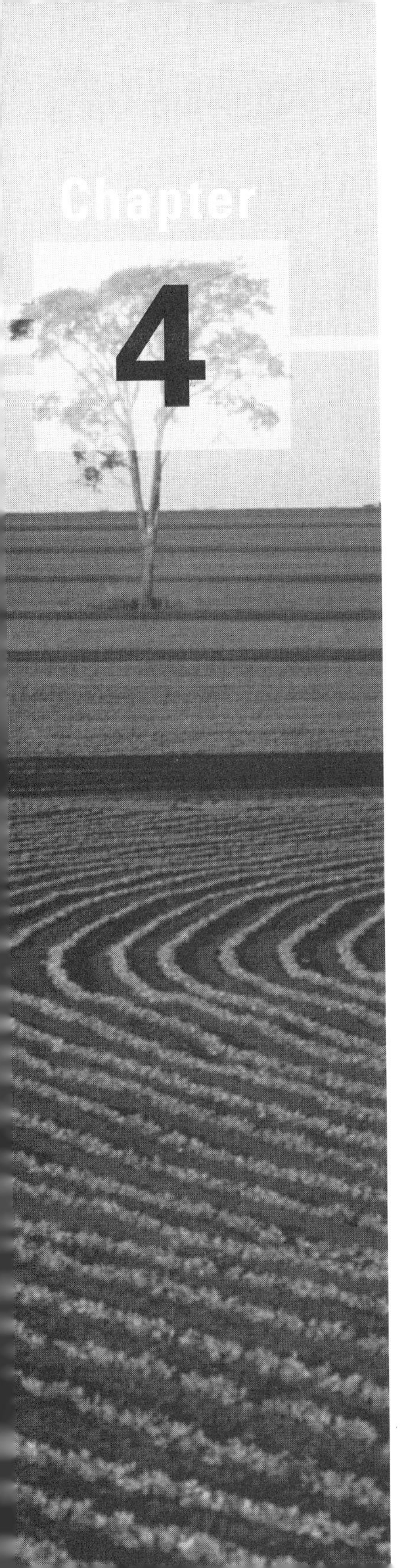

Aggregating Data And Group Functions

INTRODUCTION TO ORACLE9i: SQL EXAM OBJECTIVES COVERED IN THIS CHAPTER:

✓ **Aggregating Data using Group Functions**

- Identify the available group functions
- Use group functions
- Group data using the GROUP BY clause
- Include or exclude grouped rows by using the HAVING clause

Exam objectives are subject to change at any time without prior notice and at Oracle's sole discretion. Please visit Oracle's Certification website (`http://www.oracle.com/education/certification/`) for the most current exam objectives listing.

As explained in the previous chapter, functions are programs that take zero or more arguments and return a single value. The exam focuses on two types of functions: single-row and aggregate (group) functions. Single-row functions were covered in Chapter 3, "Single-Row Functions." Group functions are covered in this chapter.

Group functions differ from single-row functions in how they are evaluated. Single-row functions are evaluated once for each row retrieved. Group functions are evaluated on groups of one or more rows at a time.

In this chapter, you will learn which group functions are available in SQL, the rules for how to use them, and what to expect on the exam about aggregating data and group functions. Lastly, we will explore nesting function calls together. SQL allows you to nest group functions within calls to single-row functions, as well as nest single-row functions within calls to group functions. The exam usually has at least one question on nesting functions.

Group Function Fundamentals

Group functions are sometimes called *aggregate functions* and return a value based on a number of inputs. The exact number of inputs is not determined until the query is executed and all rows are fetched. This differs from single-row functions, in which the number of inputs is known at parse time—before the query is executed. Because of this difference, group functions have slightly different requirements and behavior than single-row functions.

Group functions do not process `NULL` values and do not return a `NULL` value, even when `NULL`s are the only values evaluated. For example, a `COUNT` or `SUM` of `NULL` values will result in 0.

Most of the group functions can be applied either to ALL values or to only the DISTINCT values for the specified expression. When ALL is specified, all non-NULL values are applied to the group function. When DISTINCT is specified, only one of each non-NULL value is applied to the function.

To better understand the difference of ALL versus DISTINCT, let's look at the SCOTT.EMP table—specifically, at salaries of the employees in department 20:

```
SELECT empno,sal
FROM scott.emp
WHERE deptno=20
ORDER BY sal;

     EMPNO        SAL
---------- ----------
      7369        800
      7876       1100
      7566       2975
      7788       3000
      7902       3000
```

If we average *all* of the values, we get (800+1100+2975+3000+3000)/5, or 2175. If, on the other hand, we average only the *distinct* values, we don't include the second 3000, and get (800+1100+2975+3000)/4, or 1968.75.

The DISTINCT keyword is often used with the COUNT function.

```
SELECT AVG(sal) avg
      ,AVG(ALL sal) avg_all
      ,AVG(DISTINCT sal) avg_dist
      ,COUNT(sal) cnt
      ,COUNT(DISTINCT sal) cnt_dist
      ,SUM(sal) sum_all
      ,SUM(DISTINCT sal) sum_dist
FROM scott.emp
WHERE deptno = 20

  AVG AVG_ALL AVG_DIST COUNT COUNT_DIST SUM_ALL SUM_DIST
----- ------- -------- ----- ---------- ------- --------
 2175    2175  1968.75     5          4   10875     7875
```

Using Group Functions

As with single-row functions, Oracle offers a rich variety of multiple-row functions. These functions can appear in the SELECT or HAVING clauses of SELECT statements. When used in the SELECT clause, they usually require a GROUP BY clause, as well. If no GROUP BY clause is specified, the default grouping is for the entire result set. Group functions cannot appear in the WHERE clause of a SELECT statement.

Unlike with single-row functions, you cannot use programmer-written functions on grouped data.

Group Function Overview

Table 4.1 summarizes the available group functions. We will cover each of these functions in the "Group Function Descriptions" section.

TABLE 4.1 Group Function Summary

Function	Description
AVG	Returns the statistical mean
CORR	Returns the coefficient of correlation of number pairs
COUNT	Returns the number of non-NULL rows
COVAR_POP	Returns the population covariance of number pairs
COVAR_SAMP	Returns the sample covariance of number pairs
CUME_DIST	Returns the cumulative distribution of values within groupings
DENSE_RANK	Returns the ranking of rows within an ordered group, without skipping ranks on ties

TABLE 4.1 Group Function Summary *(continued)*

Function	Description
FIRST	Modifies other aggregate functions to return expressions based on ordering of the second column expression
GROUP_ID	Returns a group identifier used to uniquely identify duplicate groups
GROUPING	Returns 0 for nonsummary rows or 1 for summary rows
KEEP	Modifies other aggregate functions to return the first or last value in a grouping
LAST	Modifies other aggregate functions to return expressions based on ordering of the secondary column expression
MAX	Returns the largest value
MIN	Returns the smallest value
PERCENT_RANK	Returns the percentile ranking of the specified value
PERCENTILE_CONT	Returns the interpolated value that would fall in the specified percentile position using a continuous model
PERCENTILE_DISC	Returns the interpolated value that would fall in the specified percentile position using a discrete model
RANK	Returns the ranking of rows within an ordered group, skipping ranks when ties occur
REGR_AVGX	Returns average x value in non-NULL (y,x) pairs
REGR_AVGY	Returns average y value in non-NULL (y,x) pairs
REGR_COUNT	Returns number of non-NULL (y,x) pairs
REGR_INTERCEPT	Returns the linear regression y intercept

TABLE 4.1 Group Function Summary *(continued)*

Function	Description
REGR_R2	Returns the linear regression coefficient of determination
REGR_SLOPE	Returns the linear regression slope
REGR_SXX	Returns the sum of the squares of the independent variable expression
REGR_SXY	Returns the sum of the products of the independent variable expression and the dependent variable expression
REGR_SYY	Returns the sum of the squares of the dependent variable expression
STDDEV	Returns the standard deviation
STDDEV_POP	Returns the population standard deviation
STDDEV_SAMP	Returns the sample standard deviation
SUM	Adds all values and returns the result
VAR_POP	Returns the population variance
VAR_SAMP	Returns the sample variance
VARIANCE	Returns the sample variance or 1 for sample size 1

Group Function Descriptions

The group functions are arranged in alphabetical order, with descriptions and examples of each one.

AVG

This function has the syntax AVG([{DISTINCT | ALL}] <*n*>), where *n* is a numeric expression. The AVG function returns the mean of the expression *n*. If neither DISTINCT nor ALL is specified in the function call, the default is ALL.

```
SELECT job_id, AVG(salary)
FROM hr.employees
WHERE job_id like 'AC%'
GROUP BY job_id;

JOB_ID     AVG(SALARY)
---------- -----------
AC_ACCOUNT        8300
AC_MGR           12000
```

CORR

CORR(<*y*> , <*x*>) takes two arguments, where *y* and *x* are numeric expressions representing the dependent and independent variables, respectively. This function returns the coefficient of correlation of a set of number pairs.

The coefficient of correlation is a measure of strength of the relationship between the two numbers. CORR can return a NULL. The coefficient of correlation is calculated from those *x*, *y* pairs that are both not NULL using the formula COVAR_POP(*y*,*x*) / (STDDEV_POP(*y*) * STDDEV_POP(*x*)).

```
SELECT CORR(list_price,min_price) correlation
      ,COVAR_POP(list_price,min_price) covariance
      ,STDDEV_POP(list_price) stddev_popy
      ,STDDEV_POP(min_price) stddev_popx
FROM oe.product_information
WHERE list_price IS NOT NULL
 AND  min_price IS NOT NULL;

CORRELATION   COVARIANCE STDDEV_POPY STDDEV_POPX
----------- ------------ ----------- -----------
  .99947495   206065.903  496.712198  415.077696
```

COUNT

This function has the syntax COUNT({* | [DISTINCT | ALL] <*x*>}), where *x* is an expression. The COUNT function returns the number of rows in the query. If an expression is given and neither DISTINCT nor ALL is specified, the default is ALL. The asterisk (*) is a special quantity—it counts all rows in the result set, regardless of NULLs.

In the example that follows, we count the number of rows in the HR.EMPLOYEES table (the number of employees), the number of departments that have employees in them (DEPT_COUNT), and the number of employees that have a department (NON_NULL_DEPT_COUNT). We can see from the results that one employee is not assigned to a department, and the other 106 are assigned to one of 11 departments.

```
SELECT COUNT(*) emp_count
      ,COUNT(DISTINCT department_id) dept_count
      ,COUNT(ALL department_id) non_null_dept_count
FROM hr.employees;

EMP_COUNT  DEPT_COUNT  NON_NULL_DEPT_COUNT
---------- ----------  -------------------
       107         11                  106
```

This next example looks at the number of employees drawing a commission, as well as the distinct number of commissions drawn. We see that 35 out of 107 employees draw a commission, and there are seven different commission levels in use.

```
SELECT COUNT(*)
      ,COUNT(commission_pct) comm_count
      ,COUNT(DISTINCT commission_pct) distinct_comm
FROM hr.employees;

  COUNT(*) COMM_COUNT DISTINCT_COMM
---------- ---------- -------------
       107         35             7
```

COVAR_POP

`COVAR_POP(<y> , <x>)` takes two arguments, where *y* and *x* are numeric expressions. This function returns the population covariance of a set of number pairs, which can be `NULL`.

The covariance is a measure of how two sets of data vary in the same way. The population covariance is calculated from those *y*, *x* pairs that are both not `NULL` using the formula `(SUM(y*x) - SUM(y) * SUM(x) / COUNT(x)) / COUNT(x)`.

```
SELECT category_id
      ,COVAR_POP(list_price,min_price) population
      ,COVAR_SAMP(list_price,min_price) sample
FROM oe.product_information
GROUP BY category_id;

CATEGORY_ID POPULATION     SAMPLE
----------- ---------- ----------
         11    92805.0    98992.0
         12    26472.3    29781.4
         13    25142.1    26465.4
         14    17983.0    18800.4
         15     7650.8     8160.9
         16      431.4      479.3
         17     5466.1     5739.5
         19   417343.9   426038.6
         21       21.5       25.1
         22       45.0       67.5
         24   109428.3   114639.2
         25    27670.3    31623.1
         29     3446.8     3574.4
         31  1424679.2  1709615.0
         32     4575.1     4815.9
         33      945.0     1134.0
         39     1035.1     1086.9
```

COVAR_SAMP

COVAR_SAMP(<*y*> , <*x*>) takes two arguments, where *y* and *x* are numeric expressions representing the dependent and independent variables, respectively. This function returns the sample covariance of a set of number pairs, which can be NULL.

The covariance is a measure of how two sets of data vary in the same way. The sample covariance is calculated from those *x*, *y* pairs that are both not NULL using the formula (SUM(*y***x*) - SUM(*y*) * SUM(*x*) / COUNT(*x*)) / (COUNT(*x*)-1).

```
SELECT SUM(list_price*min_price) sum_xy
      ,SUM(list_price) sum_y
      ,SUM(min_price) sum_x
      ,REGR_COUNT(list_price,min_price) count_x
      ,COVAR_SAMP(list_price,min_price) COVARIANCE
FROM oe.product_information;

    SUM_XY      SUM_Y      SUM_X    COUNT_X COVARIANCE
---------- ---------- ---------- ---------- ----------
  73803559      71407      60280        285     206791
```

CUME_DIST

This function has the syntax:

CUME_DIST(<*val_list*>) WITHIN GROUP (ORDER BY *col_list* [ASC|DESC] [NULLS {first|last}])

where *val_list* is a comma-delimited list of expressions that evaluate to numeric constant values, and *col_list* is the comma-delimited list of column expressions. CUME_DIST returns the cumulative distribution of a value in *val_list* within a distribution in *col_list*.

The cumulative distribution is a measure of ranking within the ordered group and will be in the range 0< CUME_DIST <= 1. See also PERCENT_RANK.

```
SELECT department_id
      ,COUNT(*) emp_count
      ,AVG(salary) mean
      ,PERCENTILE_CONT(0.5) WITHIN GROUP
           (ORDER BY salary DESC) Median
      ,PERCENT_RANK(10000) WITHIN GROUP
           (ORDER BY salary DESC)*100 Pct_Rank_10K
```

```
      ,CUME_DIST(10000) WITHIN GROUP
           (ORDER BY salary DESC) Cume_Dist_10K
FROM hr.employees
GROUP BY department_id;
```

```
DEPARTMENT_ID EMP_COUNT  MEAN   MEDIAN PCT_RANK_10K CUME_DIST_10K
------------- ---------- ----   ------ ------------ -------------
           10          1  4400    4400       .00000      0.500000
           20          2  9500    9500     50.00000      0.666667
           30          6  4150    2850     16.66667      0.285714
           40          1  6500    6500       .00000      0.500000
           50         45  3476    3100       .00000      0.021739
           60          5  5760    4800       .00000      0.166667
           70          1 10000   10000       .00000      1.000000
           80         34  8956    8900     23.52941      0.342857
           90          3 19333   17000    100.00000      1.000000
          100          6  8600    8000     16.66667      0.285714
          110          2 10150   10150     50.00000      0.666667
NULL                   1  7000    7000       .00000      0.500000
```

DENSE_RANK

This function has the syntax:

```
DENSE_RANK(<val_list>) WITHIN GROUP (ORDER BY col_list
[ASC|DESC] [NULLS {first|last}])
```

where *val_list* is a comma-delimited list of numeric constant expressions (expressions that evaluate to numeric constant values), and *col_list* is the comma-delimited list of column expressions. DENSE_RANK returns the row's rank within an ordered group. When there are ties, ranks are not skipped. For example, if there are three items tied for first, then second, and third will not be skipped. See also RANK.

```
SELECT department_id
      ,COUNT(*) emp_count
      ,AVG(salary) mean
      ,DENSE_RANK(10000) WITHIN GROUP
           (ORDER BY salary DESC) dense_rank_10K
FROM hr.employees
GROUP BY department_id;
```

```
DEPARTMENT_ID  EMP_COUNT   MEAN DENSE_RANK_10K
------------- ---------- ------ --------------
           10          1   4400              1
           20          2   9500              2
           30          6   4150              2
           40          1   6500              1
           50         45   3476              1
           60          5   5760              1
           70          1  10000              1
           80         34   8956              7
           90          3  19333              3
          100          6   8600              2
          110          2  10150              2
NULL                   1   7000              1
```

To understand this ranking, let's look closer at department 80. We see that 10,000 is the seventh highest salary in department 80. Even though there are eight employees that make more than 10000. The duplicates are not counted for ranking purposes.

```
SELECT salary, COUNT(*)
FROM hr.employees
WHERE department_id=80
 AND  salary > 9000
GROUP BY salary
ORDER BY salary DESC;

    SALARY   COUNT(*)
---------- ----------
     14000          1
     13500          1
     12000          1
     11500          1
     11000          2
     10500          2
     10000          3
      9600          1
      9500          3
```

FIRST

See KEEP.

GROUP_ID

GROUP_ID( ) takes no arguments and requires a GROUP BY clause. GROUP_ID returns a numeric identifier that can be used to uniquely identify duplicate groups. For *i* duplicate groups, GROUP_ID will return values 0 through i-*1*.

GROUPING

GROUPING(*x*) takes a single argument, where *x* is an expression in the GROUP BY clause of the query. The GROUPING function is applicable only for queries that have a GROUP BY clause and a ROLLUP or CUBE clause. The ROLLUP and CUBE clauses create summary rows (sometimes called *superaggregates*) containing NULL in the grouped expressions. The GROUPING function returns a 1 for these summary rows and a 0 for the nonsummary rows, and it is used to distinguish the summary rows from the nonsummary rows.

This function becomes significant when the data values being aggregated may contain NULL values, such as the MARITAL_STATUS column of the SH.CUSTOMERS table in the following example.

```
SELECT cust_gender gender
      ,cust_marital_status marital_status
      ,GROUPING(cust_gender) gender_superagg
      ,GROUPING(cust_marital_status) marital_superagg
      ,COUNT(*)
FROM sh.customers
GROUP BY CUBE(cust_marital_status,cust_gender);
```

```
                                     GENDER    MARITAL
GENDER MARITAL_STATUS   COUNT(*)   SUPERAGG   SUPERAGG
------ -------------- ---------- ---------- ----------
F      married              4701          0          0
M      married              9328          0          0
NULL   married             14029          1          0
F      single               5898          0          0
M      single              12868          0          0
NULL   single              18766          1          0
```

```
F       NULL                    5716          0         0
F       NULL                   16315          0         1
M       NULL                   11489          0         0
M       NULL                   33685          0         1
NULL    NULL                   17205          1         0
NULL    NULL                   50000          1         1
```

In these results, the 0s for MARITAL_SUPERAGG show regular rows, and the 1s show superaggregates.

KEEP

The KEEP function has the syntax:

```
agg_function KEEP(DENSE_RANK {FIRST|LAST}
ORDER BY col_list [ASC|DESC] [NULLS {first|last}]))
```

where *agg_function* is an aggregate function, and *col_list* is a list of columns to be ordered for the grouping.

This function is sometimes referred to as either the FIRST or the LAST function, and it is actually a modifier for one of the other group functions, such as COUNT or MIN. The KEEP function returns the first or last row of a sorted group. It is used to avoid the need for a self-join, looking for the MIN or MAX.

```
SELECT department_id
      ,MIN(hire_date) earliest
      ,MAX(hire_date) latest
      ,COUNT(salary) KEEP
           (DENSE_RANK FIRST ORDER BY hire_date) FIRST
      ,COUNT(salary) KEEP
           (DENSE_RANK LAST ORDER BY hire_date) LAST
FROM hr.employees
GROUP BY department_id;

DEPARTMENT_ID EARLIEST    LATEST          FIRST    LAST
------------- ----------- -----------   -------  ------
           10 17-Sep-1987 17-Sep-1987         1       1
           20 17-Feb-1996 17-Aug-1997         1       1
           30 07-Dec-1994 10-Aug-1999         1       1
           40 07-Jun-1994 07-Jun-1994         1       1
```

```
 50 01-May-1995 08-Mar-2000          1          1
 60 03-Jan-1990 07-Feb-1999          1          1
 70 07-Jun-1994 07-Jun-1994          1          1
 80 30-Jan-1996 21-Apr-2000          1          2
 90 17-Jun-1987 13-Jan-1993          1          1
100 16-Aug-1994 07-Dec-1999          1          1
110 07-Jun-1994 07-Jun-1994          2          2
    24-May-1999 24-May-1999          1          1
```

We can see from the query above that department 80's earliest and latest anniversary dates are 30-Jan-1996 and 21-Apr-2000. The FIRST and LAST columns show us that there was one employee hired on the earliest anniversary date (30-Jan-1996) and two hired on the latest anniversary date (21-Apr-2000). Likewise, we can see that department 110 has two employees hired on the earliest anniversary date (07-Jun-1994) and two on the latest anniversary date (07-Jun-1994). If we look at the detailed data below, this becomes more clear.

```
SELECT department_id,hire_date
FROM hr.employees
WHERE department_id IN (80,110)
ORDER BY 1,2;

DEPARTMENT_ID HIRE_DATE
------------- -----------
           80 30-Jan-1996
           80 04-Mar-1996
           80 24-Jan-2000
           80 29-Jan-2000
... some rows deleted for brevity
           80 23-Feb-2000
           80 24-Mar-2000
           80 21-Apr-2000
           80 21-Apr-2000
          110 07-Jun-1994
          110 07-Jun-1994
```

LAST

See KEEP.

MAX

This function has the syntax MAX([{DISTINCT | ALL}] <*x*>), where *x* is an expression. This function returns the highest value in the expression *x*.

- If the expression *x* is a date/time datatype, it returns a DATE. For dates, the maximum is the latest date.
- If the expression *x* is a numeric datatype, it returns a NUMBER. For numbers, the maximum is the largest number.
- If the expression is a character datatype, it returns a VARCHAR2. For character strings, the maximum is the one that sorts highest based on the database character set.

Although the inclusion of either DISTINCT or ALL is syntactically acceptable, their use does not affect the calculation of a MAX; the largest distinct value is the same as the largest of all values.

```
SELECT MAX(hire_date)
      ,MAX(salary)
      ,MAX(last_name)
FROM hr.employees;

MAX(HIRE_DA MAX(SALARY) MAX(LAST_NAME)
----------- ----------- --------------
21-APR-2000       24000 Zlotkey
```

MIN

This function has the syntax MIN([{DISTINCT | ALL}] <*x*>), where *x* is an expression. This function returns the lowest value in the expression *x*.

- If the expression *x* is a date/time datatype, it returns a DATE. For dates, the minimum is the earliest date.
- If the expression *x* is a numeric datatype, it returns a NUMBER. For numbers, the minimum is the smallest number.
- If the expression is a character datatype, it returns a VARCHAR2. For character strings, the minimum is the one that sorts lowest based on the database character set.

Although the inclusion of either DISTINCT or ALL is syntactically acceptable, their use does not affect the calculation of a MIN: the smallest distinct value is the same as the smallest value.

```
SELECT MIN(hire_date)
      ,MIN(salary)
      ,MIN(last_name)
FROM hr.employees;

MIN(HIRE_DA MIN(SALARY) MIN(LAST_NAME)
----------- ----------- --------------
17-JUN-1987        2100 Abel
```

PERCENT_RANK

The PERCENT_RANK function has the syntax:

```
PERCENT_RANK(<val_list>) WITHIN GROUP (ORDER BY col_list
[ASC|DESC] [NULLS {first|last}])
```

where *val_list* is a comma-delimited list of expressions that evaluate to numeric constant values, and *col_list* is the comma-delimited list of column expressions. PERCENT_RANK returns the percent ranking of a value in *val_list* within a distribution in *col_list*. The percent rank *x* will be in the range 0<= *x* <= 1.

The main difference between PERCENT_RANK and CUME_DIST is that PERCENT_RANK will always return a 0 for the first row in any set, while the CUME_DIST function cannot return a 0. We can use the PERCENT_RANK and CUME_DIST functions to examine the rankings of employees with a salary over 10,000 in the HR.EMPLOYEES table. Notice the different results for departments 40 and 70.

```
SELECT DEPARTMENT_ID
      ,COUNT(*) emp_count
      ,AVG(salary) mean
      ,PERCENTILE_CONT(0.5) WITHIN GROUP
          (ORDER BY salary DESC) median
      ,PERCENT_RANK(10000) WITHIN GROUP
          (ORDER BY salary DESC)*100 pct_rank_10K
      ,CUME_DIST(10000) WITHIN GROUP
          (ORDER BY salary DESC)*100 cume_dist_10K
```

```
FROM hr.employees
GROUP BY department_id;

DEPARTMENT_ID EMP_COUNT  MEAN MEDIAN PCT_RANK_10K CUME_DIST_10K
------------- ---------  ---- ------ ------------ -------------
           10         1  4400   4400            0            50
           20         2  9500   9500           50            67
           30         6  4150   2850           17            29
           40         1  6500   6500            0            50
           50        45  3476   3100            0             2
           60         5  5760   4800            0            17
           70         1 10000  10000            0           100
           80        34  8956   8900           24            34
           90         3 19333  17000          100           100
          100         6  8600   8000           17            29
          110         2 10150  10150           50            67
NULL                  1  7000   7000            0            50
```

PERCENTILE_CONT

PERCENTILE_CONT has the syntax:

```
PERCENTILE_CONT(<x>) WITHIN GROUP (ORDER BY col_list
[ASC|DESC])
```

where x is a percentile value in the range 0<x<1, and *col_list* is the sort specification. PERCENTILE_CONT returns the interpolated value that would fall in percentile position x within the sorted group *col_list*.

This function assumes a continuous distribution and is most useful for obtaining the median value of an ordered group. The median value is defined to be the midpoint in a group of ordered numbers—half of the values are above the median, and half of the values are below the median.

The median together with the mean or average are the two most common measures of central tendency used to analyze data. See the AVG function for more information on calculating the mean.

For our example, we will use the SCOTT.EMP table, ordered by department number.

```
SELECT ename ,deptno ,sal
FROM scott.emp
ORDER BY deptno ,sal;

ENAME          DEPTNO        SAL
---------- ---------- ----------
MILLER             10       1300
CLARK              10       2450
KING               10       5000
SMITH              20        800
ADAMS              20       1100
JONES              20       2975
SCOTT              20       3000
FORD               20       3000
JAMES              30        950
WARD               30       1250
MARTIN             30       1250
TURNER             30       1500
ALLEN              30       1600
BLAKE              30       2850
```

We can see that for department 10, there are three SAL values: 1300, 2450, and 5000. The median would be 2450, because there is one value above this number and one value below this number. The median for department 30 is not so straightforward, since there are six values and the middle value is actually between the two data points 1250 and 1500. To get the median for department 30, we need to interpolate the midpoint. There are two common techniques used to interpolate this median value: one technique uses a continuous model and one uses a discrete model. In the continuous model, the midpoint is assumed to be the value halfway between the 1250 and 1500, which is 1375. Using the discrete model, the median must be an actual data point and, depending on whether the data is ordered ascending or descending, the median would be 1250 or 1500.

```
SELECT deptno
      ,PERCENTILE_CONT(0.5) WITHIN GROUP
           (ORDER BY sal DESC) "CONTINUOUS"
      ,PERCENTILE_DISC(0.5) WITHIN GROUP
           (ORDER BY sal DESC) "DISCRETE DESC"
      ,PERCENTILE_DISC(0.5) WITHIN GROUP
           (ORDER BY sal ASC) "DISCRETE ASC"
      ,AVG(sal) mean
FROM scott.emp
GROUP BY deptno;

    DEPTNO CONTINUOUS DISCRETE DESC DISCRETE ASC   MEAN
---------- ---------- ------------- ------------ ------
        10       2450          2450         2450   2917
        20       2975          2975         2975   2175
        30       1375          1500         1250   1567
```

PERCENTILE_DISC

PERCENTILE_DISC has the syntax:

```
PERCENTILE_DISC(<x>) WITHIN GROUP (ORDER BY col_list
[ASC|DESC])
```

where *x* is a percentile value in the range 0<*x*<1 and *col_list* is the sort specification. PERCENTILE_DISC returns the smallest cumulative distribution value from the *col_list* set that is greater than or equal to value *x*.

This function assumes a discrete distribution. Sometimes, data cannot be averaged in a meaningful way. Date data, for example, cannot be averaged, but you can calculate the median date in a group of dates. For example, to calculate the median hire date for employees in each department, we could run the following query:

```
SELECT department_id
      ,COUNT(*) emp_count
      ,MIN(HIRE_DATE) first
      ,MAX(HIRE_DATE) last
      ,PERCENTILE_DISC(0.5) WITHIN GROUP
           (ORDER BY HIRE_DATE) median
FROM hr.employees
GROUP BY department_id;
```

```
DEPARTMENT_ID  EMP_COUNT FIRST     LAST      MEDIAN
------------- ---------- --------- --------- ---------
           10          1 17-SEP-87 17-SEP-87 17-SEP-87
           20          2 17-FEB-96 17-AUG-97 17-FEB-96
           30          6 07-DEC-94 10-AUG-99 24-JUL-97
           40          1 07-JUN-94 07-JUN-94 07-JUN-94
           50         45 01-MAY-95 08-MAR-00 15-MAR-98
           60          5 03-JAN-90 07-FEB-99 25-JUN-97
           70          1 07-JUN-94 07-JUN-94 07-JUN-94
           80         34 30-JAN-96 21-APR-00 23-MAR-98
           90          3 17-JUN-87 13-JAN-93 21-SEP-89
          100          6 16-AUG-94 07-DEC-99 28-SEP-97
          110          2 07-JUN-94 07-JUN-94 07-JUN-94
                       1 24-MAY-99 24-MAY-99 24-MAY-99
```

RANK

RANK has the syntax:

```
RANK(<val_list>) WITHIN GROUP (ORDER BY col_list
[ASC|DESC] [NULLS {first|last}])
```

where *val_list* is a comma-delimited list of numeric constant expressions (expressions that evaluate to numeric constant values), and *col_list* is the comma-delimited list of column expressions. RANK returns the row's rank within an ordered group.

When there are ties, ranks of equal value are assigned equal rank, and the number of tied rows is skipped before the next rank is assigned. For example, if there are three items tied for first, the second and third items will be skipped, and the next will be fourth.

```
SELECT department_id
      ,COUNT(*) emp_count
      ,AVG(salary) mean
      ,RANK(10000) WITHIN GROUP
           (ORDER BY salary DESC) dense_rank_10K
FROM hr.employees
GROUP BY department_id;
```

```
DEPARTMENT_ID  EMP_COUNT   MEAN DENSE_RANK_10K
------------- ---------- ------ --------------
           10          1   4400              1
           20          2   9500              2
           30          6   4150              2
           40          1   6500              1
           50         45   3476              1
           60          5   5760              1
           70          1  10000              1
           80         34   8956              9
           90          3  19333              4
          100          6   8600              2
          110          2  10150              2
                       1   7000              1
```

To understand this ranking, let's look closer at department 80. We see that 10,000 is the seventh highest salary in department 80. But since there are eight employees who make more than 10,000, the rank of 10,000 is 9. The duplicates are counted for ranking purposes.

```
SELECT salary, COUNT(*)
FROM hr.employees
WHERE department_id=80
 AND  salary > 9000
GROUP BY salary
ORDER BY salary DESC;

    SALARY   COUNT(*)
---------- ----------
     14000          1
     13500          1
     12000          1
     11500          1
     11000          2
     10500          2
     10000          3
      9600          1
      9500          3
```

REGR_AVGX

REGR_AVGX(<*y*>,<*x*>) takes two arguments, where *y* and *x* are numeric expressions representing the dependent and independent variables, respectively. This linear-regression function returns the numeric average *x* value after eliminating NULL *x*,*y* pairs. REGR_AVGX first removes *y*,*x* pairs that have a NULL in either *y* or *x*, then computes AVG(*x*). REGR_AVGX can return NULL.

```
SELECT REGR_AVGX(losal,hisal) avgx
      ,REGR_AVGY(losal,hisal) avgy
      ,REGR_COUNT(losal,hisal) r_count
      ,REGR_INTERCEPT(losal,hisal) intercept
      ,REGR_R2(losal,hisal) fit
      ,REGR_SLOPE(losal,hisal) slope
FROM scott.salgrade;

AVGX   AVGY    R_COUNT INTERCEPT  FIT       SLOPE
------ ------  ------- ---------- --------- ----------
3519.8 1660.8        5 878.085277 .864454268 .222374772
```

REGR_AVGY

REGR_AVGY(<*y*>,<*x*>) takes two arguments, where *y* and *x* are numeric expressions representing the dependent and independent variables, respectively. This linear-regression function returns the numeric average *y* value after eliminating NULL *x*,*y* pairs.

REGR_AVGY first removes *y*,*x* pairs that have a NULL in either *y* or *x*, then computes AVG(*y*). REGR_AVGY can return NULL. See the description of REGR_AVGX for an example.

REGR_COUNT

REGR_COUNT(<*y*>,<*x*>) takes two arguments, where *y* and *x* are numeric expressions representing the dependent and independent variables, respectively. This linear-regression function returns the number of non-NULL *x*,*y* pairs.

REGR_COUNT first removes *y*,*x* pairs that have a NULL in either *y* or *x*, then counts the remaining number of pairs. REGR_COUNT can return a 0, but not a NULL. See the description of REGR_AVGX for an example.

REGR_INTERCEPT

REGR_INTERCEPT(<*y*>,<*x*>) takes two arguments, where *y* and *x* are numeric expressions representing the dependent and independent variables, respectively. This function returns the numeric *y* intercept of the linear-regression line.

REGR_INTERCEPT first removes *y*,*x* pairs that have a NULL in either *y* or *x*, then computes the *y* intercept. REGR_INTERCEPT can return NULL. When the data are fitted to a line, the formula $y = A + Bx$ can be used to represent the data, where *A* is the intercept and *B* is the slope. See the description of REGR_AVGX for an example.

REGR_R2

REGR_R2(<*y*>,<*x*>) takes two arguments, where *y* and *x* are numeric expressions representing the dependent and independent variables, respectively. This function returns the numeric coefficient of determination, or R^2, which can be in the range $0 < R^2 <= 1$ or NULL.

This coefficient is a measure of how well the data fits the line, with 1 being a direct linear relationship. See the description of REGR_AVGX for an example.

REGR_SLOPE

REGR_SLOPE(<*y*>,<*x*>) takes two arguments, where *y* and *x* are numeric expressions representing the dependent and independent variables, respectively. This linear-regression function returns the numeric slope of the line of non-NULL *x*,*y* pairs using the least-squares fit.

REGR_SLOPE first removes *y*,*x* pairs that have a NULL in either *y* or *x*, then computes the slope of the line that best runs through the *y*,*x* data points. See the description of REGR_AVGX for an example.

REGR_SXX

REGR_SXX(<*y*>,<*x*>) takes two arguments, where *y* and *x* are numeric expressions representing the dependent and independent variables, respectively. This function returns the sum of the squares of *x*, which can be NULL.

The sum of the squares of *x* is used together with the REGR_R2, REGR_SXY, and REGR_SYY functions to validate the fitness of a model. REGR_SXX is calculated as:

```
REGR_COUNT(y,x) * VAR_POP(x)
```

or

```
SUM(x*x) - SUM(x)*SUM(x)/REGR_COUNT(y,x)
```

Here is an example:

```
SELECT REGR_COUNT(losal,hisal) r_count
      ,VAR_POP(hisal) var_pop
      ,COVAR_POP(losal,hisal) covar_pop
      ,REGR_SXX(losal,hisal) SXX
      ,REGR_SXY(losal,hisal) SXY
      ,REGR_SYY(losal,hisal) SYY
FROM scott.salgrade;

R_COUNT    VAR_POP  COVAR_POP        SXX        SXY        SYY
------- ---------- ---------- ---------- ---------- ----------
      5 10887008.2 2420995.96 54435040.8 12104979.8  3113920.8
```

REGR_SXY(<y>,<x>)

REGR_SXY(<*y*>,<*x*>) takes two arguments, where *y* and *x* are numeric expressions representing the dependent and independent variables, respectively. This function returns the sum of the products of *y* and *x*, which can be NULL. This product is used together with the REGR_R2, REGR_SXX, and REGR_SYY functions to validate the fitness of a model. REGR_SXY is calculated as:

REGR_COUNT(*y*,*x*) * COVAR_POP(*y*,*x*)

or

SUM(*y***x*) - (SUM(*y*)*SUM(*x*)/REGR_COUNT(*y*,*x*))

See the description of REGR_SXX for an example.

REGR_SYY

REGR_SYY(<*y*>,<*x*>) takes two arguments, where *y* and *x* are numeric expressions representing the dependent and independent variables, respectively. This function returns the sum of the squares of *y*, which can be NULL.

The sum of the squares of *y* is used together with the REGR_R2, REGR_SXX, and REGR_SXY functions to validate the fitness of a model. REGR_SYY is calculated as:

REGR_COUNT(*y*,*x*) * VAR_POP(*y*)

or

SUM(*y***y*) - SUM(*y*)*SUM(*y*)/REGR_COUNT(*y*,*x*)

See the description of REGR_SXX for an example.

STDDEV

This function has the syntax STDDEV([{DISTINCT | ALL}] <*x*>), where *x* is a numeric expression. The STDDEV function returns the numeric standard deviation of the expression *x*.

The standard deviation is calculated as the square root of the variance. STDDEV is very similar to the STDDEV_SAMP function, except STDDEV will return 0 when there is only one row of input, while STDDEV_SAMP will return NULL.

To analyze the central tendency of data, you can look for the mean or median, discussed earlier in this chapter. To analyze the opposite or the measure of dispersion in the data, Oracle offers standard deviation and variance.

```
SELECT department_id
      ,PERCENTILE_CONT(0.5) WITHIN GROUP
            (ORDER BY salary DESC) median
      ,AVG(salary) mean
      ,VARIANCE(salary)
      ,STDDEV(salary)
FROM hr.employees
GROUP BY department_id;

DEPARTMENT_ID  MEDIAN       MEAN VARIANCE(SALARY) STDDEV(SALARY)
------------- ------- ---------- ---------------- --------------
           10    4400       4400                0              0
           20    9500       9500         24500000     4949.74747
           30    2850       4150         11307000     3362.58829
           40    6500       6500                0              0
           50    3100 3475.55556       2214161.62     1488.00592
           60    4800       5760          3708000     1925.61678
           70   10000      10000                0              0
           80    8900 8955.88235       4135873.44      2033.6847
           90   17000 19333.3333       16333333.3     4041.45188
          100    8000       8600          3244000     1801.11077
          110   10150      10150          6845000     2616.29509
NULL             7000       7000                0              0
```

STDDEV_POP

STDDEV_POP(<*x*>) takes a single argument, where *x* is a numeric expression. This function returns the numeric population standard deviation of the expression *x*. The population standard deviation is calculated as the square root of the population variance VAR_POP.

```
SELECT department_id
      ,STDDEV(salary)
      ,STDDEV_POP(salary)
      ,STDDEV_SAMP(salary)
FROM hr.employees
GROUP BY department_id;

DEPARTMENT_ID STDDEV(SALARY) STDDEV_POP(SALARY) STDDEV_SAMP(SALARY)
------------- -------------- ------------------ -------------------
           10              0                  0 NULL
           20     4949.74747               3500          4949.74747
           30     3362.58829          3069.6091          3362.58829
           40              0                  0 NULL
           50     1488.00592         1471.37963          1488.00592
           60     1925.61678         1722.32401          1925.61678
           70              0                  0 NULL
           80      2033.6847         2003.55437           2033.6847
           90     4041.45188         3299.83165          4041.45188
          100     1801.11077         1644.18166          1801.11077
          110     2616.29509               1850          2616.29509
NULL                       0                  0 NULL
```

STDDEV_SAMP

STDDEV_SAMP(<*x*>) takes a single argument, where *x* is a numeric expression. This function returns the numeric sample standard deviation of the expression *x*.

The sample standard deviation is calculated as the square root of the sample variance VAR_SAMP. See the description of STDDEV_POP for an example.

SUM

This function has the syntax SUM([{DISTINCT | ALL}] <*x*>), where *x* is a numeric expression. This function returns the sum of the expression *x*.

```
SELECT SUM(blocks)
FROM user_tables;

SUM(BLOCKS)
-----------
      12265
```

VAR_POP

VAR_POP(<*x*>) takes a single argument, where *x* is a numeric expression. This function returns the numeric population variance of *x*. The population variance is calculated with the formula (SUM(*x***x*) – SUM(*x*) * SUM(*x*) / COUNT(*x*)) / COUNT(*x*).

```
SELECT department_id
      ,VARIANCE(salary)
      ,VAR_POP(salary)
      ,VAR_SAMP(salary)
FROM hr.employees
GROUP BY department_id;

DEPARTMENT_ID VARIANCE(SALARY) VAR_POP(SALARY) VAR_SAMP(SALARY)
------------- ---------------- --------------- ----------------
           10                0               0 NULL
           20         24500000        12250000         24500000
           30         11307000         9422500         11307000
           40                0               0 NULL
           50       2214161.62      2164958.02       2214161.62
           60          3708000         2966400          3708000
           70                0               0 NULL
           80       4135873.44       4014230.1       4135873.44
           90       16333333.3      10888888.9       16333333.3
          100          3244000      2703333.33          3244000
          110          6845000         3422500          6845000
NULL                         0               0 NULL
```

VAR_SAMP

VAR_SAMP(<*x*>) takes a single argument, where x is a numeric expression. This function returns the numeric sample variance of x.

The sample variance is calculated with the formula (SUM(*x***x*) - SUM(*x*) * SUM(*x*) / COUNT(*x*)) / (COUNT(*x*)-1).

See the description of VAR_POP for an example.

VARIANCE

This function has the syntax VARIANCE([{DISTINCT | ALL}] <*x*>), where x is a numeric expression. This function returns the variance of the expression x. It differs slightly from the VAR_SAMP function.

When the number of expressions (COUNT(*x*)) = 1, VARIANCE returns a 0, whereas VAR_SAMP returns a NULL. When (COUNT(*x*)) = 0, they both return a NULL.

```
SELECT department_id
       ,COUNT(*)
       ,VARIANCE(salary)
       ,VAR_POP(salary)
       ,VAR_SAMP(salary)
FROM hr.employees
GROUP BY department_id;

DEPARTMENT_ID VARIANCE(SALARY) VAR_POP(SALARY) VAR_SAMP(SALARY)
------------- ---------------- --------------- ----------------
           10                0               0 NULL
           20         24500000        12250000         24500000
           30         11307000         9422500         11307000
           40                0               0 NULL
           50       2214161.62      2164958.02       2214161.62
           60          3708000         2966400          3708000
           70                0               0 NULL
           80       4135873.44       4014230.1       4135873.44
           90       16333333.3      10888888.9       16333333.3
          100          3244000      2703333.33          3244000
          110          6845000         3422500          6845000
NULL                         0               0 NULL
```

Grouping Data with *GROUP BY*

As the name implies, group functions work on data that is grouped. We tell the database how to group or categorize the data with a GROUP BY clause. Whenever we use a group function in the SELECT clause of a SELECT statement, we must place all nongrouping/nonconstant columns in the GROUP BY clause. If no GROUP BY clause is specified (only group functions and constants appear in the SELECT clause), the default grouping becomes the entire result set. When the query executes and the data is fetched, it is grouped based on the GROUP BY clause, and the group function is applied.

```
SELECT cust_state_province, count(*) customer_count
FROM sh.customers
GROUP BY cust_state_province;

CUST_STATE_PROVINCE  CUSTOMER_COUNT
-------------------- --------------
AK                              119
AL                              172
AR                              466
Aichi                           148
Alicante                        438
Almeria                          81
Alsace                          197
Andhra Pradesh                  272
Aquitaine                       150
```

In this example, we categorize (group) the data by state, and apply the group function (COUNT). It returns the number of rows (in our case, customers) for each state in the CUSTOMERS table. If we want to order the results by the number of customers, our ORDER BY clause can contain either the column number or the grouping function.

```
SELECT cust_state_province, count(*) customer_count
FROM sh.customers
GROUP BY cust_state_province
ORDER BY COUNT(*) DESC;
```

or

```
SELECT cust_state_province, count(*) customer_count
FROM sh.customers
```

```
GROUP BY cust_state_province
ORDER BY 2 DESC;

CUST_STATE_PROVINCE  CUSTOMER_COUNT
-------------------- --------------
CA                             2597
Baden-Wuerttemberg             2307
Nordrhein-Westfalen            2260
Noord-Brabant                  2131
FL                             1907
Bayern                         1829
```

 **Real World Scenario**

Finding How Many Rows Fit in a Data Block

Sometimes, you don't need to group the data in the same way that you report it. If you are interested in how many grouped rows resulted or in the average number of rows for a particular grouping, you can GROUP BY an expression that does not appear in the SELECT list. For example, if we want to know how our sample data loaded into a table, in order to size that table, we will need to know how many rows, on average, fit into a data block. We get this meta-data by counting rows that are grouped on the data block portion of the ROWID—the first 15 characters. Then we take the average of the resulting counts.

```
SELECT AVG(row_count), MAX(row_count), MIN(row_count)

FROM (SELECT COUNT(*) row_count

      FROM zip_codes

      GROUP BY SUBSTR(rowid,1,15));


AVG(ROW_COUNT) MAX(ROW_COUNT) MIN(ROW_COUNT)

-------------- -------------- --------------

    30.7509418             44              6
```

> The subquery in the FROM clause returns one count for each data block. We'll cover subqueries in more detail in Chapter 5, "Joins and Subqueries," but we treat this subquery as if it were a view. Here, we see that we average about 31 rows per data block. It's then a simple extrapolation to approximate how many data blocks we will need to load an arbitrary number of rows.

Limiting Grouped Data with *HAVING*

Group functions cannot be used in the WHERE clause. For example, if we want to query the total sales per month and channel that are not PROMO_ID 9999, and return only those month/channel combinations with over $2,000,000 in gross sales, we would have trouble with the following query:

```
SELECT t.fiscal_month_desc ,s.channel_id
       ,SUM(s.quantity_sold)
       ,SUM(s.amount_sold)
FROM sh.times t
    ,sh.sales s
WHERE t.time_id = s.time_id
 AND  s.promo_id <> 9999
 AND  SUM(S.amount_sold) > 2000000
GROUP BY t.fiscal_month_desc, s.channel_id;
```

The database doesn't know what the SUM is when extracting the rows from the table—remember that the grouping is done after all rows have been fetched. We get an exception when we try to use SUM in the WHERE clause. The correct way to get the requested information is to instruct the database to group all the rows, then limit the output of those grouped rows. We do this with the HAVING clause:

```
SELECT t.fiscal_month_desc ,s.channel_id
       ,SUM(s.quantity_sold)
       ,SUM(s.amount_sold)
FROM sh.times t
    ,sh.sales s
WHERE t.time_id = s.time_id
 AND  s.promo_id <> 9999
GROUP BY t.fiscal_month_desc, s.channel_id
HAVING SUM(S.amount_sold) > 2000000;
```

As you can see in the previous query, a SQL statement can have both a WHERE clause and a HAVING clause. WHERE filters data before grouping; HAVING filters data after grouping.

You might encounter an exam question that tests whether you will incorrectly put a group function in the WHERE clause.

Creating Superaggregates with *CUBE* and *ROLLUP*

The CUBE and ROLLUP modifiers to the GROUP BY clause allow you to create aggregations of aggregates, or superaggregates. These superaggregates or summary rows are included with the result set in a way similar to using the COMPUTE statement on control breaks in SQL*Plus; that is, they are included in the data and contain NULL values in the aggregated columns. ROLLUP creates hierarchical aggregates. CUBE creates aggregates for all combinations of columns specified. Key advantages of CUBE and ROLLUP are that they will allow more robust aggregations than COMPUTE and they work with any SQL-enabled tool.

These superaggregations can be visualized with a simple example using the SH.CUSTOMERS tables. This table has a NOT NULL column CUST_GENDER, which contains either "F" or "M". The CUST_MARITAL_STATUS column contains one of three values: "married", "single", or NULL. Counting the number of customers without using CUBE or ROLLUP, we get:

```
SELECT CUST_GENDER gender
       ,NVL(cust_marital_status,'unknown') marital_status
       ,COUNT(*)
FROM sh.customers
GROUP BY cust_gender,NVL(cust_marital_status,'unknown');

GENDER MARITAL_STATUS   COUNT(*)
------ -------------- ----------
F      married              4701
F      single               5898
F      unknown              5716
M      married              9328
M      single              12868
M      unknown             11489
```

But suppose we want subtotals for each gender—a count of all female customers regardless of marital status and a count of all male customers regardless of marital status. We could use the ROLLUP modifier to roll up the CUST_MARITAL_STATUS column, leaving subtotals on the grouped column CUST_GENDER:

```
SELECT CUST_GENDER gender
      ,NVL(cust_marital_status,'unknown') marital_status
      ,COUNT(*)
FROM sh.customers
GROUP BY cust_gender
     ,ROLLUP(NVL(cust_marital_status,'unknown'));

GENDER MARITAL_STATUS   COUNT(*)
------ -------------- ----------
F      married              4701
F      single               5898
F      unknown              5716
F                          16315  (subtotal)
M      married              9328
M      single              12868
M      unknown             11489
M                          33685  (subtotal)
```

Now, if we want to add an aggregation for all genders as well, we put the CUST_GENDER column into the ROLLUP modifier, as follows:

```
SELECT CUST_GENDER gender
      ,NVL(cust_marital_status,'unknown') marital_status
      ,COUNT(*)
FROM sh.customers
GROUP BY ROLLUP
      (cust_gender,NVL(cust_marital_status,'unknown'));

GENDER MARITAL_STATUS   COUNT(*)
------ -------------- ----------
F      married              4701
F      single               5898
F      unknown              5716
```

```
F                              16315 (subtotal)
M      married                  9328
M      single                  12868
M      unknown                 11489
M                              33685 (subtotal)
                               50000 (grand total)
```

The order of the columns in the ROLLUP modifier is significant, because this order determines where Oracle produces subtotals. ROLLUP creates hierarchical aggregations, so the order of the expressions in the ROLLUP clause is significant. The ordering follows the same conventions used in the GROUP BY clause—most general to most specific. When we reverse the order in our example, we get different subtotals.

```
SELECT CUST_GENDER gender
      ,NVL(cust_marital_status,'unknown') marital_status
      ,COUNT(*)
FROM sh.customers
GROUP BY ROLLUP
      (NVL(cust_marital_status,'unknown'),cust_gender);

GENDER MARITAL_STATUS         COUNT(*)
------ -------------------- ----------
F      married                    4701
M      married                    9328
       married                   14029 (subtotal)
F      single                     5898
M      single                    12868
       single                    18766 (subtotal)
F      unknown                    5716
M      unknown                   11489
       unknown                   17205 (subtotal)
                                 50000 (grand total)
```

Suppose we want all of these subtotals, both by CUST_GENDER and by CUST_MARITAL_STATUS. This requirement calls for the CUBE modifier, which will produce all possible aggregations, not just those in the hierarchy of columns specified.

```
SELECT CUST_GENDER gender
      ,NVL(cust_marital_status,'unknown') marital_status
      ,COUNT(*)
FROM sh.customers
GROUP BY CUBE
      (cust_gender,NVL(cust_marital_status,'unknown'));

GENDER MARITAL_STATUS         COUNT(*)
------ -------------------- ----------
F      married                    4701
F      single                     5898
F      unknown                    5716
F                                16315 (subtotal)
M      married                    9328
M      single                    12868
M      unknown                   11489
M                                33685 (subtotal)
       married                   14029 (subtotal)
       single                    18766 (subtotal)
       unknown                   17205 (subtotal)
                                 50000 (grand total)
```

The number of aggregations created by the CUBE modifier is the number of distinct combinations of data values in all of the columns that appear in the CUBE clause. CUBE creates aggregations for all combinations of columns, so unlike ROLLUP, the order of expressions in a CUBE is not significant.

Nesting Functions

Functions can be *nested* so that the output from one function is used as input to another. Operators have an inherent precedence of execution such as * before +, but function precedence is based on position only. Functions are evaluated innermost to outermost and left to right. This nesting technique is common with some functions, such as DECODE (covered in Chapter 3), where it can be used to implement limited IF...THEN...ELSE logic within a SQL statement.

For example, the V$SYSSTAT view contains one row for each of three interesting sort statistics. If you want to report all three statistics on a single line, you can use DECODE combined with SUM to filter out data in the SELECT clause. This filtering operation is usually done in the WHERE or HAVING clause, but if you want all three statistics on one line, you can issue this command:

```
SELECT SUM (DECODE
         (name,'sorts (memory)',value,0)) in_memory
       ,SUM (DECODE
         (name,'sorts (disk)',  value,0)) on_disk
       ,SUM (DECODE
         (name,'sorts (rows)',  value,0)) rows_sorted
FROM v$sysstat;

IN_MEMORY ON_DISK ROWS_SORTED
--------- ------- -----------
      728      12      326714
```

What happens in the previous statement is a single pass through the V$SYSSTAT table. The presummary result set would have the same number of rows as V$SYSSTAT (232, for instance). Of these 232 rows, all rows and columns have zeros, except for one row in each column that has the data of interest (see Table 4.2). The summation operation then adds all the zeros to your interesting data and gives you the results you want.

TABLE 4.2 Presummarized Result Set

in_memory	on_disk	rows_sorted
0	0	0
0	12	0
0	0	0
0	0	326714
728	0	0
0	0	0

Another example of nesting DECODE and a group function is this example, using MAX and nested DECODE functions:

```
SELECT owner ,table_name ,grantor ,grantee
,MAX(DECODE(privilege,'SELECT'
    ,DECODE(grantable,'YES','g','Y'),' '))SEL
,MAX(DECODE(privilege,'INSERT'
    ,DECODE(grantable,'YES','g','Y'),' '))INS
,MAX(DECODE(privilege,'UPDATE'
    ,DECODE(grantable,'YES','g','Y'),' '))UPD
,MAX(DECODE(privilege,'DELETE'
    ,DECODE(grantable,'YES','g','Y'),' '))DEL
FROM dba_tab_privs
WHERE table_name = UPPER('&TableName')
GROUP BY owner, table_name, grantor, grantee
ORDER BY grantee, table_name;

OWNER  TABLE_NAME      GRANTOR  GRANTEE  S I U D
------ --------------- -------- -------- - - - -
CHIPD  ZIP_STATE_CITY  CHIPD    SCOTT    g Y Y
```

In this example, we want to report select, insert, update, and delete privileges on a table, with a single table per line instead of a single privilege per line. This statement will report a g if the privilege was granted with the grant option, a Y if the privilege was granted without the grant option, and a space if the privilege was not granted. This example takes advantage of the ordinal progression from space to *Y* to *g*: `' '< 'Y'< 'g'`.

Nested functions can include single-row functions nested within group functions, as you've just seen, or group functions nested within either single-row functions or other group functions. For example, suppose that you need to report on the departments in the EMP table, showing either the number of jobs or the number of managers, whichever is greater. You would enter the following:

```
SELECT deptno, GREATEST(COUNT(DISTINCT job)
       ,COUNT(DISTINCT mgr)) cnt
       ,COUNT(DISTINCT job) jobs
       ,COUNT(DISTINCT mgr) mgrs
FROM emp
```

```
GROUP BY deptno;

    DEPTNO        CNT       JOBS       MGRS
---------- ---------- ---------- ----------
        10          4          4          2
        20          4          3          4
        30          3          3          2
```

You can also nest group functions within group functions. To report the maximum number of jobs in a single department, you would query:

```
SELECT MAX(COUNT(DISTINCT job))
FROM emp
GROUP BY deptno;

MAX(COUNT(DISTINCTJOB))
-----------------------
                      4
```

Summary

Group functions can be used in the SELECT, HAVING, and ORDER BY clauses of SELECT statements. Most group functions can be applied to all data values or only to the distinct data values. Except for COUNT(*), group functions ignore NULLS. Programmer-written functions cannot be used as group functions.

Exam Essentials

Understand the usage of DISTINCT in group functions. When DISTINCT is specified, only one of each non-NULL value is applied to the function. To apply all non-NULL values, the keyword ALL should be used.

Know where group functions can be used. Group functions can be used in SELECT, ORDER BY, and HAVING clauses. They cannot be used in WHERE clauses.

Know how MIN and MAX sort date and character data. Older dates evaluate closer to lower values, while newer dates evaluate to higher values. Character data, even if it contains numbers, is sorted according to the `NLS_SORT` specification.

Understand the difference between RANK and DENSE_RANK. `RANK` skips rankings when ties occur. `DENSE_RANK` does not skip rankings.

Know which expressions in a SELECT list must appear in a GROUP BY clause. If any grouping is performed, all nongroup function expressions and nonconstant expressions must appear in the `GROUP BY` clause.

Know the difference between CUBE and ROLLUP. `CUBE` will generate more superaggregate rows than `ROLLUP`. `CUBE` will generate all possible superaggregates, while `ROLLUP` generates them only according to the hierarchy specified.

Know the order of precedence for evaluating nested functions. You may need to evaluate an expression containing nested functions. Make sure you understand the left to right order of precedence used to evaluate these expressions.

Key Terms

Before you take the exam, make sure you're familiar with the following terms:

aggregate functions

superaggregate

Review Questions

1. Which function should be used to assign rankings to rows, giving duplicate ranking for ties, and not skip any ranks after ties?

   A. DENSE_RANK

   B. SPARSE_RANK

   C. RANK

   D. ROWNUM

2. Which statement will generate the most rows?

   A. select ORDER_MODE,SALES_REP_ID, sum(ORDER_TOTAL)
   from oe.orders
   group by ROLLUP (ORDER_MODE,SALES_REP_ID);

   B. select ORDER_MODE,SALES_REP_ID, sum(ORDER_TOTAL)
   from oe.orders
   group by CUBE (ORDER_MODE,SALES_REP_ID);

   C. select ORDER_MODE,SALES_REP_ID, sum(ORDER_TOTAL)
   from oe.orders
   group by ORDER_MODE,SALES_REP_ID;

   D. They will all generate the same number of rows.

3. Based on the output below, which GROUP BY clause was used?

```
DEPARTMENT_ID YEAR   COUNT(*)
------------- ---- ----------
           30 1999          1
           30               1
           50 1999          9
           50 2000          4
           50              13
           60 1999          1
           60               1
           80 1999          5
           80 2000          7
           80              12
          100 1999          1
          100               1
              1999          1
                            1
                           29
```

   A. GROUP BY CUBE(department_id,to_char(hire_date,'YYYY'))

   B. GROUP BY department_id,to_char(hire_date,'YYYY')

   C. GROUP BY ROLLUP(department_id,to_char(hire_date,'YYYY'))

   D. GROUP BY department_id,ROLLUP(,to_char(hire_date,'YYYY'))

4. Which of the following group functions can return a NULL when there is one row in the aggregation?

   A. MIN

   B. MAX

   C. VARIANCE

   D. VAR_SAMP

5. Which of the functions below requires a GROUP BY clause in the SQL statement?

   A. CUBE

   B. GROUPING

   C. GROUP_ID

   D. All of thc above

   E. None of the above

6. Which of the following functions is not an Oracle group function?

   A. REGR_SXY

   B. CORR

   C. SKEW

   D. COVAR_POP

   E. All of the above functions are valid.

7. What is the GROUPING function used for?

   A. The GROUPING function is identical to the GROUP BY function, but executes faster.

   B. The GROUPING function is used to eliminate NULL values prior to aggregation.

   C. The GROUPING function identifies superaggregate rows.

   D. The GROUPING function is deprecated in Oracle 9i and should not be used.

8. How will the results of the following two statements differ?

```
Statement 1:
SELECT MAX(longitude), MAX(latitude)
FROM zip_state_city;

Statement 2:
SELECT MAX(longitude), MAX(latitude)
FROM zip_state_city
GROUP BY state;
```

   A. Statement 1 will fail because it is missing a GROUP BY clause.

   B. Statement 2 will return one row, and statement 1 may return more than one row.

   C. Statement 2 will display a longitude and latitude for each ZIP_STATE_CITY.

   D. Statement 1 will display two values, and statement 2 will display two values for each state.

9. Which group functions would you use to compute the mean and median values for a set of data?

   A. MEAN and MEDIAN

   B. AVG and PERCENTILE_CONT

   C. MEAN and PERCENTILE_DISC

   D. AVG and MEDIAN

10. Using the SALES table described below you need to report the following:

- Gross, net, and earned revenue
- For the second and third quarters of 1999
- For sales in the states Illinois, California, and Texas (codes IL, CA, and TX)

Column Name	state_code	sales_date	gross	net	earned
Key Type	pk	pk			
NULLs/Unique	NN	NN	NN	NN	NN
FK Table					
Datatype	VARCHAR2	DATE	NUMBER	NUMBER	NUMBER
Length	2		11,2	11,2	11,2

Will all the requirements be met with the following SQL statement?

```
SELECT state_code, SUM(ALL gross), SUM(net),
SUM(earned)
FROM sales_detail
WHERE TRUNC(sales_date,'Q') BETWEEN
                 TO_DATE('01-Apr-1999','DD-Mon-YYYY')
             AND TO_DATE('01-Sep-1999','DD-Mon-YYYY')
 AND  state_code IN ('IL','CA','TX')
GROUP BY state_code;
```

A. The statement meets all three requirements.

B. The statement meets two of the three requirements.

C. The statement meets one of the three requirements.

D. The statement meets none of the three requirements.

E. The statement will raise an exception.

11. Which assertion about the following queries is true?

```
SELECT COUNT(DISTINCT mgr), MAX(DISTINCT salary)
FROM emp;
SELECT COUNT(ALL mgr), MAX(ALL salary)
FROM emp;
```

A. They will always return the same numbers in columns 1 and 2.

B. They may return different numbers in column 1 but will always return the same number in column 2.

C. They may return different numbers in column 1 and may return different numbers in column 2.

D. They will always return the same number in column 1 but may return different numbers in column 2.

12. Which line in the following statement will raise an exception?

```
1  SELECT department_id ,COUNT(*)
2         ,VAR_POP(DISTINCT salary)
3         ,VAR_POP(salary)
4  FROM hr.employees
5 GROUP BY department_id;
```

A. Line 1

B. Line 2

C. Line 3

D. Line 5

E. There is no error.

13. What will the following SQL statement return?

```
select min(cust_income_level)
  keep (dense_rank last order by cust_credit_limit)
from sh.customers;
```

A. The smallest CUST_INCOME_LEVEL in the CUSTOMERS table

B. The smallest CUST_INCOME_LEVEL and the highest CUST_CREDIT_LIMIT in the CUSTOMERS table

C. The minimum CUST_INCOME_LEVEL for the maximum CUST_CREDIT_LIMIT

D. The missing comma will raise a syntax error.

14. How will the results of the following two statements differ?

```
Statement 1:
SELECT COUNT(*), SUM(salary)
FROM hr.employees;

Statement 2:
SELECT COUNT(salary), SUM(salary)
FROM hr.employees;
```

A. Statement 1 will return one row, and statement 2 may return more than one row.

B. Both statements will fail because they are missing a GROUP BY clause.

C. Both statements will return the same results.

D. Statement 2 may return a smaller COUNT value than statement 1.

15. How will the results of the following two statements differ?

```
Statement 1:
SELECT COUNT(cust_gender)
FROM sh.customers;

Statement 2:
SELECT regr_count(cust_marital_status,cust_gender)
FROM sh.customers;
```

A. Statement 2 may return a smaller COUNT value than statement 1.

B. Both statements will return the same results.

C. Statement 1 will return one row, and statement 2 may return more than one row.

D. Both statements will fail because they are missing a GROUP BY clause.

16. Which of the following is not a group function?

    A. AVG()

    B. COUNT()

    C. LEAST()

    D. STDDEV()

    E. CORR()

17. Why does the following SELECT statement fail?

```
SELECT colorname Colour, MAX(cost)
FROM itemdetail
WHERE UPPER(colorname) LIKE '%WHITE%'
GROUP BY colour
HAVING COUNT(*) > 20;
```

    A. A GROUP BY clause cannot contain a column alias.

    B. The condition COUNT(*) > 20 should be in the WHERE clause.

    C. The GROUP BY clause must contain the group functions used in the SELECT list.

    D. The HAVING clause can contain only the group functions used in the SELECT list.

18. What will the following SQL statement return?

```
select max(prod_pack_size)
from sh.products
where min(prod_weight_class) = 5;
```

    A. An exception will be raised.

    B. The largest PROD_PACK_SIZE for rows containing PROD_WEIGHT_CLASS of 5 or higher

    C. The largest PROD_PACK_SIZE for rows containing PROD_WEIGHT_CLASS of 5

    D. The largest PROD_PACK_SIZE in the SH.PRODUCTS table

19. Why will the following query raise an exception?

```
select dept_no, avg(distinct salary)
      ,count(job) job_count
from emp
where mgr like 'J%'
  or  abs(salary) > 10
having count(job) > 5
order by 2 desc;
```

A. The HAVING clause cannot contain a group function.

B. The GROUP BY clause is missing.

C. ABS() is not an Oracle function.

D. The query will not raise an exception.

20. What will the GRP column in the following SQL return?

```
select sales_rep_id,sum(order_total)
      ,grouping(sales_rep_id) grp
from oe.orders
group by cube(sales_rep_id)
```

A. The query will raise an exception.

B. The GRP column will be a cumulative count of SALES_REP_ID.

C. The GRP column will be a cumulative sum of ORDER_TOTAL, grouped by SALES_REP_ID.

D. The GRP column will be a superaggregate identifier.

Answers to Review Questions

1. A. Both the RANK and DENSE_RANK functions will assign the same rankings to duplicate values, but the RANK function will skip rank values when it encounters duplicate values. The SPARSE_RANK function does not exist. The ROWNUM pseudo-column, if used in a view, can provide rankings, but would not give equal ranking to duplicate values or skip any rankings.

2. B. The CUBE modifier in the GROUP BY clause generates aggregates for all possible group combinations in the CUBE modifier, producing subtotals for each order mode, each sales rep ID, and a grand total. The ROLLUP modifier produces only subtotals for each order mode and a grand total. A GROUP BY without a CUBE or ROLLUP modifier does not produce any subtotals. If you try it with the Oracle sample schema, you will see that the CUBE option return 24 rows, the ROLL option return 14 rows, and the plain GROUP BY option return 11 rows.

3. C. Since there is no subtotal for year 1999 or 2000, the CUBE modifier could not have been used. Since there are subtotals for the departments, a ROLLUP modifier had to be used. Option D would not have generated the last row in the report, which provides a grand total across all department/year combinations.

4. D. MIN and MAX always return a numeric value. The only difference between the VARIANCE and VAR_SAMP functions is that the VAR_SAMP function will return a NULL if there is only one row in the aggregation, whereas VARIANCE will return a 0.

5. D. All of the above functions require a GROUP BY function to be used.

6. C. There is no SKEW function in Oracle9i.

7. C. A GROUP BY clause together, with a CUBE or ROLLUP operator, is required for the GROUPING function. The GROUPING function was new to 8.1.6 and is still an important aggregate function that identifies superaggregate rows.

8. D. Option B has the statement numbers transposed. This one was intended to be a trick question. You should read all the answers carefully; the exam may have trick questions like this one.

9. B. There is no MEAN or MEDIAN function. To obtain these values, use the AVG function to obtain mean and either PERCENTILE_CONT or PERCENTILE_DISC to obtain the median.

10. A. All requirements are met. The gross, net, and earned revenue requirements are satisfied with the SELECT clause. The second and third quarter sales requirement is satisfied with the first predicate of the WHERE clause—the sales date will be truncated to the first day of a quarter, thus 01-Apr-1999 or 01-Jul-1999 for the required quarters (which are both between 01-Apr-1999 and 01-Sep-1999). The state codes requirement is satisfied by the second predicate in the WHERE clause. This question is intentionally misleading, but so are some exam questions (and, unfortunately, some of the code in some shops).

11. B. The first column in the first query is counting the distinct MGR values in the table. The first column in the second query is counting all MGR values in the table. If a manager appears twice, the first query will count her one time, but the second will count her twice. Both the first query and the second query are selecting the maximum salary value in the table.

12. B. The DISTINCT option is not valid for the VAR_POP function.

13. C. There is no missing comma; the SELECT list contains a single expression. The KEEP or LAST function is a modifier for another group function. In this case, the MIN function is modified to return the minimum CUST_INCOME_LEVEL for those rows having the LAST, or highest, CUST_CREDIT_LIMIT.

14. D. The COUNT(*) will count all rows in the table. The COUNT(salary) will count only the number salary values that appear in the table. If there are any rows with a NULL salary, statement 2 will not count them.

15. A. The `COUNT(cust_gender)` will count all rows in the table where CUST_GENDER is not `NULL`. The `REGR_COUNT(cust_marital_status, cust_gender)` will count all rows in the table where CUST_MARITAL_STATUS and CUST_GENDER are both not `NULL`.

16. C. `LEAST` is a single-row function.

17. A. A `GROUP BY` clause must contain the column or expressions on which to perform the grouping operation. It cannot use column aliasing.

18. A. You cannot place a group function in the `WHERE` clause.

19. B. There is at least one column in the `SELECT` list that is not a constant or group function, so a `GROUP BY` clause is mandatory.

20. D. The `GROUPING` function returns a 0 for ordinary rows and a 1 for superaggregate rows.

Joins and Subqueries

INTRODUCTION TO ORACLE9i: SQL EXAM OBJECTIVES COVERED IN THIS CHAPTER:

✓ **Displaying Data from Multiple Tables**

- Write SELECT statements to access data from more than one table using equality and nonequality joins
- View data that generally does not meet a join condition by using outer joins
- Join a table to itself using a self-join

✓ **Subqueries**

- Describe the types of problems that subqueries can solve
- Define subqueries
- List the types of subqueries
- Write single-row and multiple-row subqueries

Exam objectives are subject to change at any time without prior notice and at Oracle's sole discretion. Please visit Oracle's Certification website (`http://www.oracle.com/education/certification/`) for the most current exam objectives listing.

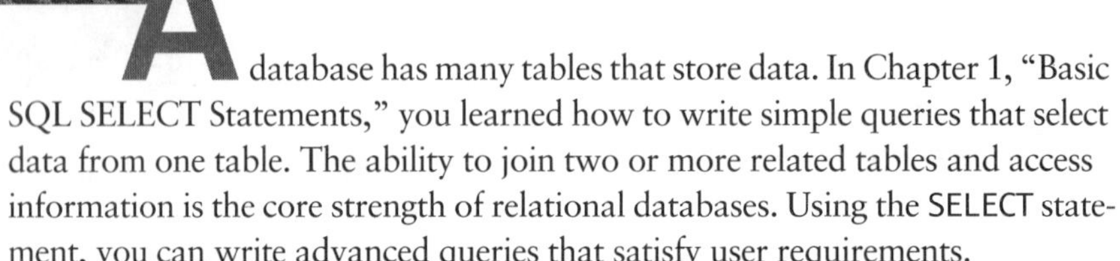

A database has many tables that store data. In Chapter 1, "Basic SQL SELECT Statements," you learned how to write simple queries that select data from one table. The ability to join two or more related tables and access information is the core strength of relational databases. Using the SELECT statement, you can write advanced queries that satisfy user requirements.

This chapter focuses on querying data from more than one table using table joins and subqueries. Oracle9i has enhanced the capabilities of joins by conforming to the ANSI/ISO SQL1999 standard. You'll need to understand how the various types of joins and subqueries work, as well as the proper syntax, for the exam.

Multiple-Table Queries

In RDBMS, related data can be stored in multiple tables. You use the power of SQL to relate the information and query data. A SELECT statement has a mandatory SELECT clause and FROM clause. The SELECT clause can have a list of columns, expressions, functions, and so on. The FROM clause tells you in which table(s) to look for the required information. So far, you have seen only one table in the FROM clause; in this chapter, you will learn how to retrieve data from more than one table.

A *join* is a query that combines rows from two or more tables or views. Oracle performs a join whenever multiple tables appear in the query's FROM clause. The query's SELECT clause can have the columns or expressions from any or all of these tables.

In order to query data from more than one table, you need to identify common columns that relate the two tables. In the WHERE clause, you define the relationship between the tables listed in the FROM clause using comparison operators. The relationship can be specified using a JOIN clause instead of the WHERE clause. The JOIN clause is new to Oracle9i, added to conform to the ISO/ANSI SQL1999 standard. Throughout this section, you'll see examples of queries using the Oracle syntax as well as the ISO/ANSI SQL1999 standard. A query from multiple tables without a relationship or common column is known as Cartesian join or cross join and is discussed later in this chapter.

If multiple tables have the same column names, the duplicate column names should be qualified in the queries with their table name or table alias. Exceptions to this rule are discussed later in this chapter in the section, "Using ANSI Syntax."

Simple Joins

The most common operator used to relate two tables is the equality operator (=). If you relate two tables using an equality operator, it is an *equality join*, also known as an *equijoin*. This type of join combines rows from two tables that have equivalent values for the specified columns. A simple join is also known as an *inner join*, because it returns only the rows that satisfy the join condition.

For example, let's consider a simple join between the DEPARTMENTS and LOCATIONS tables of the HR schema. The common column in these tables is LOCATION_ID. We will query these tables to get the location ID, city name, and department names in that city.

```
SELECT locations.location_id, city, department_name
FROM   locations, departments
WHERE  locations.location_id = departments.location_id;
```

Here, we are retrieving data from two tables—two columns from the LOCATIONS table and one column from the DEPARTMENTS table. These two tables are joined in the `WHERE` clause using an equality operator on the LOCATION_ID column. It is not necessary for the column names in both tables to have the same name to have a join. Notice that the LOCATION_ID column is qualified with its table name for every occurrence. Qualifying column names avoids ambiguity and increases the readablility of the query. If the same column name belongs to more than one table each column name must be qualified (except when using SQL ANSI syntax).

To execute a join of three or more tables, Oracle takes these steps:

1. Oracle joins two of the tables based on the join conditions, comparing their columns.
2. Oracle joins the result to another table, based on join conditions.
3. Oracle continues this process until all tables are joined into the result.

Complex Joins

Apart from specifying the join condition in the WHERE clause, you may also have another condition to limit the rows retrieved. Such joins are known as *complex joins*. For example, if you are interested only in the departments that are outside the United States, use this query:

```
SQL> SELECT locations.location_id, city, department_name
  2  FROM   locations, departments
  3  WHERE locations.location_id = departments.location_id
  4* AND    country_id != 'US';

LOCATION_ID CITY                 DEPARTMENT_NAME
----------- -------------------- -----------------
       1800 Toronto              Marketing
       2400 London               Human Resources
       2700 Munich               Public Relations
       2500 Oxford               Sales
SQL>
```

Using Table Aliases

Like columns, tables can also have alias names. Specify the *table alias name* next to the table, separated with a space. The query in the previous section can be rewritten using alias names, as follows:

```
SELECT l.location_id, city, department_name
FROM   locations l, departments d
WHERE  l.location_id = d.location_id
AND    country_id != 'US';
```

Table aliases increase the readability of the query. They also can be used to shorten long table names with shorter alias names.

When tables (or views or materialized views) are specified in the FROM clause, Oracle looks for the object in the schema (or user) connected to the database. If the table belongs to another schema, you must qualify it with the schema name. (You may avoid this by using synonyms, which are discussed in Chapter 9, "Other Database Objects.") You can use the schema owner to qualify a table; you can use the table name or table name and schema owner to qualify a column. Here is an example:

```
SELECT locations.location_id, hr.locations.city,
       department_name
```

```
FROM   hr.locations, hr.departments
WHERE  locations.location_id = departments.location_id;
```

You can qualify a column name with its schema and table only when the table name is qualified with the schema. In the previous SQL, we qualified the column CITY with the schema HR. This is possible only if you qualify the LOCATIONS table with the schema. The following SQL will produce an error.

```
SQL>SELECT locations.location_id,hr.locations.city,
  2        department_name
  3   FROM locations,hr.departments
  4   WHERE locations.location_id =departments.location_id;

SELECT locations.location_id,hr.locations.city
                                        *
ERROR at line 1:
ORA-00904:invalid column name
SQL>
```

When table alias names are used, you must qualify the column names with the alias name only; qualifying the columns with the table name will produce an error, as in this example:

```
SQL> SELECT locations.location_id, city, department_name
  2  FROM   locations l, hr.departments d
  3* WHERE  locations.location_id = d.location_id
SQL> /
WHERE  locations.location_id = d.location_id
                *
ERROR at line 3:
ORA-00904: invalid column name
SQL>
```

The correct syntax is to replace `locations.location_id` with `l.location_id` in the `SELECT` and `WHERE` clauses.

Using ANSI Syntax

The difference between traditional Oracle join syntax and the ANSI/ISO SQL1999 syntax is that in ANSI, the join type is specified explicitly in the

FROM clause. Using the ANSI syntax is clearer and is recommended over the traditional Oracle syntax. Simple joins can have the following forms:

```
<table name> NATURAL [INNER] JOIN <table name>

<table name> [INNER] JOIN <table name> USING (<columns>)

<table name> [INNER] JOIN <table name> ON <condition>
```

The following sections discuss each of the syntax forms in detail. In all three syntaxes, the keyword INNER is optional and is the default.

NATURAL JOIN

The NATURAL keyword indicates a *natural join*, where the join is based on all columns with same name in both tables. In this type of join, you should not qualify the column names with the table name or table alias name. Let's go back to our example of querying the DEPARTMENTS and LOCATIONS table using the LOCATION_ID as the join column. The new Oracle syntax is:

```
SELECT location_id, city, department_name
FROM   locations NATURAL JOIN departments;
```

The common column in these two tables is LOCATION_ID, and that column is used to join the tables. When specifying NATURAL JOIN, the columns with the same name in both tables should also have same datatype. The following query will return the same results.

```
SELECT location_id, city, department_name
FROM   departments NATURAL JOIN locations;
```

Notice that, even though the LOCATION_ID column is in both tables, we did not qualify this column in the SELECT clause. You cannot qualify the column names when using the NATURAL JOIN clause. The following query will result in an error.

```
SQL> SELECT l.location_id, city, department_name
  2* FROM   departments NATURAL JOIN locations l;
SELECT l.location_id, city, department_name
       *
ERROR at line 1:
ORA-25155: column used in NATURAL join cannot have
qualifier
SQL>
```

If you use SELECT *, common columns are listed only once in the result set. The following example demonstrates this. The common column in COUNTRIES table and REGIONS table is the REGION_ID.

```
SQL> DESCRIBE regions
 Name                    Null?    Type
 ----------------------- -------- ------------
 REGION_ID               NOT NULL NUMBER
 REGION_NAME                      VARCHAR2(25)

SQL> DESCRIBE countries
 Name                    Null?    Type
 ----------------------- -------- ------------
 COUNTRY_ID              NOT NULL CHAR(2)
 COUNTRY_NAME                     VARCHAR2(40)
 REGION_ID                        NUMBER

SQL> SELECT *
  2  FROM   regions NATURAL JOIN countries;

 REGION_ID REGION_NAME      CO COUNTRY_NAME
---------- ---------------- -- ------------------
         1 Europe           UK United Kingdom
         1 Europe           NL Netherlands
         1 Europe           IT Testing Update
         1 Europe           FR France
```

Here is another example, which joins three tables:

```
SELECT region_name, country_name, city
FROM   regions
NATURAL JOIN countries
NATURAL JOIN locations;
```

The same query written in traditional Oracle syntax is:

```
SELECT region_name, country_name, city
FROM   regions, countries, locations
WHERE  regions.region_id = countries.region_id
AND    countries.country_id = locations.country_id;
```

JOIN ... USING

If there are many columns that have the same names in the tables you are joining and they do not have the same datatype, or you want to specify the columns that should be considered for an equijoin, you can use the `JOIN ... USING` syntax. The `USING` clause specifies the column names that should be used to join the tables. The column names should not be qualified with a table name or table alias. Here is an example:

```
SELECT location_id, city, department_name
FROM   locations JOIN departments USING (location_id);
```

Let's consider this syntax with joining more than two tables.

```
SELECT region_name, country_name, city
FROM   regions
JOIN   countries USING (region_id)
JOIN   locations USING (country_id);
```

Here, the REGIONS table is joined with the COUNTRIES table using the REGION_ID column, and its result is joined with the LOCATIONS table using the COUNTRY_ID column.

The following query will result in an error because there is no common column between REGIONS and LOCATIONS tables.

```
SQL> SELECT region_name, country_name, city
  2  FROM   regions
  3  JOIN   locations USING (country_id)
  4  JOIN   countries USING (region_id);

JOIN   locations USING (country_id)
                               *
ERROR at line 3:
ORA-00904: invalid column name
SQL>
```

You may add a `WHERE` clause to limit the number of rows and an `ORDER BY` clause to sort the rows retrieved along with any type of join operation.

```
SELECT region_name, country_name, city
FROM   regions
JOIN   countries USING (region_id)
JOIN   locations USING (country_id)
WHERE  country_id = 'US'
ORDER BY 1;
```

Remember that you cannot use alias or table names to qualify the column names used in the join operation anywhere in the query when using the `NATURAL JOIN` or `JOIN USING` syntax.

JOIN … ON

When you do not have common column names between tables to make a join or if you want to specify arbitrary join conditions, you may use the `JOIN ON` syntax. This syntax specifically defines the join condition using the column names. You may qualify column names with a table name or alias name. If the column name is common to multiple tables involved in the query, those column names must be qualified.

Using the `JOIN ON` syntax over the traditional join method separates the table joins from the other conditions. Since this syntax explicitly states the join condition, it is easier to read and understand. Here is the three-table example we used in the previous section, written using the `JOIN ON` syntax:

```
SELECT region_name, country_name, city
FROM   regions r
JOIN   countries c ON r.region_id = c.region_id
JOIN   locations l ON c.country_id = l.country_id
WHERE  country_id = 'US';
```

Multi-Table Joins

A *multi-table join* is a join of more than two tables. In the ANSI syntax, joins are performed from left to right. The first join condition can reference columns from only the first and second tables; the second join condition can reference columns from the first, second, and third tables; and so on. Consider the following example:

```
SELECT first_name, department_name, city
FROM   employees e
JOIN   departments d
ON (e.department_id = d.department_id)
JOIN   locations l
ON (d.location_id = l.location_id);
```

The first join to be performed is EMPLOYEES and DEPARTMENTS. The first join condition can reference columns in EMPLOYEES and

DEPARTMENTS, but cannot reference columns in LOCATIONS. The second join condition can reference columns from all three tables.

How Do You Specify Join Conditions When You Have More Than One Column to Join?

Consider the sample tables and data shown here.

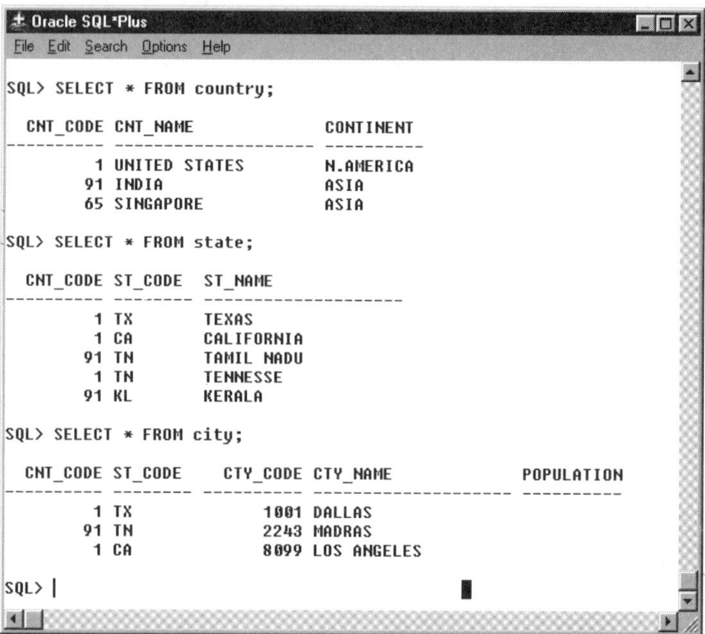


```
SQL> SELECT * FROM country;

  CNT_CODE CNT_NAME             CONTINENT
---------- -------------------- ----------
         1 UNITED STATES        N.AMERICA
        91 INDIA                ASIA
        65 SINGAPORE            ASIA

SQL> SELECT * FROM state;

  CNT_CODE ST_CODE  ST_NAME
---------- -------- --------------------
         1 TX       TEXAS
         1 CA       CALIFORNIA
        91 TN       TAMIL NADU
         1 TN       TENNESSE
        91 KL       KERALA

SQL> SELECT * FROM city;

  CNT_CODE ST_CODE    CTY_CODE CTY_NAME             POPULATION
---------- -------- ---------- -------------------- ----------
         1 TX             1001 DALLAS
        91 TN             2243 MADRAS
         1 CA             8099 LOS ANGELES

SQL> |
```

The CNT_CODE column relates the COUNTRY table and STATE table. The ST_CODE and CNT_CODE columns relate the STATE table and CITY table. The following examples show how to join the STATE and CITY tables to get information on the country code, state name, and city name.

Traditional Oracle Join

```
SQL> SELECT s.cnt_code, st_name, cty_name
  2  FROM   state s, city c
  3  WHERE  s.cnt_code  = c.cnt_code
```

```
  4  AND    s.st_code   = c.st_code
  5  AND    s.cnt_code  = 1;

  CNT_CODE ST_NAME              CTY_NAME
---------- -------------------- -------------
         1 CALIFORNIA           LOS ANGELES
         1 TEXAS                DALLAS

SQL>
```

ANSI Natural Join

```
SQL> SELECT cnt_code, st_name, cty_name
  2  FROM   state NATURAL JOIN city
  3  WHERE  cnt_code  = 1;

  CNT_CODE ST_NAME              CTY_NAME
---------- -------------------- --------------
         1 TEXAS                DALLAS
         1 CALIFORNIA           LOS ANGELES

SQL>
```

ANSI Using JOIN … USING

```
SQL> SELECT cnt_code, st_name, cty_name
  2  FROM   state JOIN city USING (cnt_code, st_code)
  3  WHERE  cnt_code  = 1;

  CNT_CODE ST_NAME              CTY_NAME
---------- -------------------- ----------------
         1 TEXAS                DALLAS
         1 CALIFORNIA           LOS ANGELES

SQL>
```

ANSI Using JOIN ... ON

```
SQL> SELECT s.cnt_code, s.st_name, c.cty_name
  2  FROM   state s
  3  JOIN   city c ON s.cnt_code = c.cnt_code
  4  AND    s.st_code  = c.st_code
  5* WHERE  s.cnt_code  = 1;

  CNT_CODE ST_NAME              CTY_NAME
---------- -------------------- -----------------
         1 CALIFORNIA           LOS ANGELES
         1 TEXAS                DALLAS

SQL>
```

Cartesian Joins

A *Cartesian join* occurs when data is selected from two or more tables and there is no common relation specified in the WHERE clause. If you do not specify a join condition for the tables listed in the FROM clause, Oracle joins each row from the first table to every row in the second table. If the first table has 3 rows and the second table has 4 rows, the result will have 12 rows. If you add another table with 2 rows without specifying a join condition, the result will have 24 rows.

You should avoid Cartesian joins. For the most part, they happen when there are many tables in the FROM clause and developers forget to include the join condition. To avoid a Cartesian join, there should be at least *n*-1 join conditions when joining *n* tables.

Consider the following example:

```
SQL> SELECT region_name, country_name
  2  FROM   regions, countries
  3* WHERE  countries.country_id LIKE 'I%';
```

```
REGION_NAME               COUNTRY_NAME
------------------------- ------------
Europe                    Israel
Americas                  Israel
Asia                      Israel
Middle East and Africa    Israel
Europe                    India
Americas                  India
Asia                      India
Middle East and Africa    India
Europe                    Italy
Americas                  Italy
Asia                      Italy
Middle East and Africa    Italy

12 rows selected.
SQL>
```

Although there is a `WHERE` clause, we did not specify a join condition between the COUNTRIES and REGIONS table. The query returns all the matching rows from the COUNTRIES table based on the `WHERE` clause and retrieves one row from the REGIONS table for every row from the COUNTRIES table. There are four rows in the REGIONS table and three rows in the COUNTRIES table with a country name beginning with *I*.

If a Cartesian join is made between a table having *m* rows and another table having *n* rows, the resulting query will have $m \times n$ rows.

Using ANSI Syntax

A Cartesian join in ANSI syntax is known as a *cross join*. A cross join is represented in ANSI/ISO SQL1999 syntax using the `CROSS JOIN` keywords. The previous example can be coded using ANSI syntax as follows:

```
SQL> SELECT region_name, country_name
  2  FROM   countries
  3  CROSS JOIN regions
  4* WHERE  countries.country_id LIKE 'I%';
```

```
REGION_NAME                COUNTRY_NAME
-------------------------- ------------
Europe                     Israel
Americas                   Israel
Asia                       Israel
Middle East and Africa     Israel
Europe                     India
Americas                   India
Asia                       India
Middle East and Africa     India
Europe                     Italy
Americas                   Italy
Asia                       Italy
Middle East and Africa     Italy

12 rows selected.
SQL>
```

Outer Joins

So far, we have seen inner joins, which return just the matched rows from both tables, and cross joins, which return a combination of all rows from both tables. Sometimes, you might want to see the data from one table, even if there is no corresponding row in the joining table. Oracle provides the *outer join* mechanism for this. The outer join returns results based on the inner-join condition, as well as the unmatched rows from one or both of the tables.

In traditional Oracle syntax, the plus symbol surrounded by parentheses, (+), denotes an outer join in the query. Enter `(+)` beside the column name of the table where there may not be a corresponding row. For example, to write a query that performs an outer join of tables A and B and returns all rows from A, apply the outer-join operator `(+)` to all columns of B in the join condition. For all rows in A that have no matching rows in B, the query returns `NULL` values for the columns in B.

Consider an example using the COUNTRIES and LOCATIONS tables. We want to list the country name and location city, and we also want to see all the countries in the COUNTRIES table. To perform this outer join, we place an outer-join operator beside all columns referencing LOCATIONS in the `WHERE` clause.

```
SELECT c.country_name, l.city
FROM   countries c, locations l
WHERE  c.country_id = l.country_id (+);
```

The outer-join operator (+) can appear only in the WHERE clause. If there are multiple join conditions between the tables, the outer-join operator should be used against all of the conditions. Consider the following query:

```
SQL> SELECT c.country_name, l.city
  2  FROM   countries c, locations l
  3  WHERE  c.country_id = l.country_id (+)
  4* AND    l.city LIKE 'B%';

COUNTRY_NAME                             CITY
---------------------------------------- --------
China                                    Beijing
India                                    Bombay
Switzerland                              Bern
SQL>
```

Even though we included the outer-join operator, Oracle just ignored it. This is because we did not place the outer-join operator beside all the columns from LOCATIONS table. The following query will return the desired result.

```
SELECT c.country_name, l.city
FROM   countries c, locations l
WHERE  c.country_id = l.country_id (+)
AND    l.city (+) LIKE 'B%';
```

An outer join (containing the (+) operator) cannot be combined with another condition using the OR or IN logical operators. For example, the following query is not valid.

```
SQL> SELECT c.country_name, l.city
  2  FROM   countries c, locations l
  3  WHERE  c.country_id = l.country_id (+)
  4* OR    l.city (+) LIKE 'B%';

OR    l.city (+) LIKE 'B%'
                 *
```

```
ERROR at line 4:
ORA-01719: outer join operator (+) not allowed in
operand of OR or IN
SQL>
```

The following query works, because the outer-join operator is used on the LOCATIONS table and the IN condition is on the column from COUNTRIES table.

```
SQL> SELECT c.country_name, l.city
  2  FROM   countries c, locations l
  3  WHERE  c.country_id = l.country_id (+)
  4* AND    c.country_name IN ('India','Israel');

COUNTRY_NAME                          CITY
------------------------------------- --------
Israel
India                                 Bombay
SQL>
```

Using ANSI Syntax

The ANSI syntax allows you to specify three types of outer joins: left outer join, right outer join, and full outer join.

Left Outer Joins

A *left outer join* is a join between two tables that returns rows based on the matching condition, as well as unmatched rows from the table to the left of the JOIN clause. For example, the following query returns the country name and city name from the COUNTRIES and LOCATIONS tables, as well as the entire country names from the COUNTRIES table.

```
SELECT c.country_name, l.city
FROM   countries c LEFT OUTER JOIN locations l
ON  c.country_id = l.country_id;
```

The keyword OUTER between LEFT and JOIN is optional. LEFT JOIN will return the same result, as in the following example:

```
SELECT country_name, city
FROM   countries LEFT JOIN locations
USING (country_id);
```

The same query can be written using NATURAL JOIN, since COUNTRY_ID is the only column common to both tables.

```
SELECT country_name, city
FROM   countries NATURAL LEFT JOIN locations;
```

In pre-9i or traditional Oracle left-outer-join syntax, the query is written as follows (note the order of tables in the FROM clause). If tables A and B are joined (FROM A, B), and you need all rows from A, the outer join operator is placed beside all columns of B. This is a left outer join.

```
SELECT c.country_name, l.city
FROM   countries c, locations l
WHERE  l.country_id (+) = c.country_id;
```

Right Outer Joins

A *right outer join* is a join between two tables that returns rows based on the matching condition, as well as unmatched rows from the table to the right of the JOIN clause. Let's rewrite the previous example using RIGHT OUTER JOIN.

```
SELECT country_name, city
FROM   locations NATURAL RIGHT OUTER JOIN countries;
```

or

```
SELECT c.country_name, l.city
FROM   locations l RIGHT JOIN countries c
ON  c.country_id = l.country_id;
```

In pre-9i or traditional Oracle right-outer-join syntax, you could write the query as follows (the order of tables in the FROM clause does matter, if you change the order, it becomes a left outer join):

```
SELECT c.country_name, l.city
FROM   locations l, countries c
WHERE  c.country_id  = l.country_id (+);
```

You cannot specify the traditional outer-join operator (+) in a query when the ANSI JOIN syntax is used.

Full Outer Joins

A *full outer join* is new to Oracle9i. This is a join between two tables that returns rows based on the matching condition, as well as unmatched rows from the table on the right and left of the JOIN clause. Suppose that you want to list all the employee last names with their department names. You want to include all the employees, even if they have not been assigned a department.

You also want to include all the departments, even if there are no employees working for that department. Here's the query:

```
SELECT e.employee_id, e.last_name,
       d.department_id, d.department_name
FROM   employees e FULL OUTER JOIN departments d
ON     e.department_id = d.department_id;
```

Trying to perform a similar query with the outer-join operator will produce an error:

```
SQL> SELECT e.employee_id, e.last_name, d.department_name
  2  FROM   employees e, departments d
  3* WHERE  e.department_id (+) = d.department_id (+)
SQL> /
WHERE  e.department_id (+) = d.department_id (+)
                             *
ERROR at line 3:
ORA-01468: a predicate may reference only one outer-joined
table
SQL>
```

The full outer join can be achieved using the UNION operator and the outer-join operator, as in the following query:

```
SELECT e.employee_id, e.last_name, d.department_name
FROM   employees e, departments d
WHERE  e.department_id (+) = d.department_id
UNION
SELECT e.employee_id, e.last_name, d.department_name
FROM   employees e, departments d
WHERE  e.department_id = d.department_id (+);
```

If you do not specify a join type before the JOIN keyword, Oracle assumes the default value of INNER. To specify an outer join, you must use the LEFT, RIGHT, or FULL keyword.

Other Multiple-Table Queries

In this section, we will consider other methods used to retrieve data from more than one table. These methods include self-joins, nonequality joins, and using the set operators.

Self-joins

A *self-join* joins a table to itself. The table name appears in the FROM clause twice, with different alias names. The two aliases are treated as two different tables, and they are joined as you would join any other tables, using one or more related columns. The following example lists the employees' names and their manager names from the EMPLOYEES table.

```
SELECT e.last_name Employee, m.last_name Manager
FROM   employees e, employees m
WHERE  m.employee_id = e.manager_id;
```

When performing self-joins in ANSI syntax, you must always use the JOIN … ON syntax. NATURAL join and JOIN … USING cannot be used. In the following example, the keyword INNER is optional.

```
SELECT e.last_name Employee, m.last_name Manager
FROM   employees e INNER JOIN employees m
ON     m.employee_id = e.manager_id;
```

Nonequality Joins

If the query is relating two tables using an equality operator (=), it is an equality join, also known as an inner join or an equijoin, as discussed earlier in this chapter. If any other operator is used to join the tables in the query, it is a *nonequality join*. Let's consider an example of a nonequality join. The EMPLOYEES table has a column named SALARY; the GRADES table has the range of salary values that correspond to each grade.

```
SQL> SELECT * FROM grades;

GRADE  LOW_SALARY HIGH_SALARY
------ ---------- -----------
P5              0        3000
P4           3001        5000
P3           5001        7000
P2           7001       10000
P1          10001
SQL>
```

To find out which grade each employee belongs to, use the following query. We limit the rows returned by using last_name LIKE 'R%'.

```
SQL> SELECT last_name, salary, grade
  2  FROM   employees, grades
  3  WHERE  last_name LIKE 'R%'
```

```
AND    salary >= low_salary
AND    salary <= NVL(high_salary, salary);

LAST_NAME                     SALARY GRADE
------------------------- ---------- ------
Raphaely                       11000 P1
Rogers                          2900 P5
Rajs                            3500 P4
Russell                        14000 P1
SQL>
```

The same query may be written using the ANSI syntax as follows:

```
SELECT last_name, salary, grade
FROM   employees JOIN grades
ON     salary >= low_salary
AND    salary <= NVL(high_salary, salary)
WHERE  last_name LIKE 'R%';
```

Using Set Operators

Set operators can be used to select data from multiple tables. Set operators basically combine the result of two queries into one. These queries are known as *compound queries*. All set operators have equal precedence. When multiple set operators are present in the same query, they are evaluated from left to right, unless another order is specified by using parentheses. The datatypes of the resulting columns, as well as the number of columns, should match in both queries. The column names of the first SELECT statement are used for the result set. Oracle has four set operators, which are listed in Table 5.1.

TABLE 5.1 Oracle Set Operators

Operator	Description
UNION	Returns all unique rows selected by either query.
UNION ALL	Returns all rows including duplicates selected by either query.
INTERSECT	Returns rows selected from both queries.
MINUS	Returns unique rows selected by the first query, but not the rows selected from second query.

Let's consider the EMPLOYEE table and the following two queries to illustrate the use of set operators.

```
SQL> SELECT last_name, hire_date
  2  FROM   employees
  3  WHERE  department_id = 90;

LAST_NAME                 HIRE DATE
------------------------- ---------
King                      17-JUN-87
Kochhar                   21-SEP-89
De Haan                   13-JAN-93
SQL>
SQL> SELECT last_name, hire_date
  2  FROM   employees
  3  WHERE  last_name LIKE 'K%';

LAST_NAME                 HIRE_DATE
------------------------- ---------
King                      17-JUN-87
Kochhar                   21-SEP-89
Khoo                      18-MAY-95
Kaufling                  01-MAY-95
King                      30-JAN-96
Kumar                     21-APR-00

6 rows selected.
SQL>
```

The UNION operator is used to return rows from either query, without any duplicate rows.

```
SQL> SELECT last_name, hire_date
  2  FROM   employees
  3  WHERE  department_id = 90
  4  UNION
  5  SELECT last_name, hire_date
  6  FROM   employees
  7  WHERE  last_name LIKE 'K%';
```

```
LAST_NAME                 HIRE_DATE
------------------------- ---------
De Haan                   13-JAN-93
Kaufling                  01-MAY-95
Khoo                      18-MAY-95
King                      17-JUN-87
King                      30-JAN-96
Kochhar                   21-SEP-89
Kumar                     21-APR-00

7 rows selected.
SQL>
```

Notice that even though there are total of nine rows in both queries, the UNION query returned only unique values. The employees with the last name King appear twice, but their hire dates are different.

The UNION ALL operator does not sort or filter the result set; it returns all rows from both queries. Let's consider this SQL:

```
SQL> SELECT last_name, hire_date
  2  FROM   employees
  3  WHERE  department_id = 90
  4  UNION ALL
  5  SELECT last_name, hire_date
  6  FROM   employees
  7* WHERE  last_name LIKE 'K%';

LAST_NAME                 HIRE_DATE
------------------------- ---------
King                      17-JUN-87
Kochhar                   21-SEP-89
De Haan                   13-JAN-93
King                      17-JUN-87
Kochhar                   21-SEP-89
Khoo                      18-MAY-95
Kaufling                  01-MAY-95
King                      30-JAN-96
Kumar                     21-APR-00
```

```
9 rows selected.
SQL>
```

The INTERSECT operator is used to return the rows returned by both queries. Let's find the employees common to both queries.

```
SQL> SELECT last_name, hire_date
  2  FROM   employees
  3  WHERE  department_id = 90
  4  INTERSECT
  5  SELECT last_name, hire_date
  6  FROM   employees
  7* WHERE  last_name LIKE 'K%';

LAST_NAME                 HIRE_DATE
------------------------- ---------
King                      17-JUN-87
Kochhar                   21-SEP-89
SQL>
```

Now, let's find the employees from the first query, but not in the second query. The MINUS operator can be used here.

```
SQL> SELECT last_name, hire_date
  2  FROM   employees
  3  WHERE  department_id = 90
  4  MINUS
  5  SELECT last_name, hire_date
  6  FROM   employees
  7* WHERE  last_name LIKE 'K%';

LAST_NAME                 HIRE_DATE
------------------------- ---------
De Haan                   13-JAN-93
SQL>
```

There can be only one ORDER BY clause in the query; you cannot specify an ORDER BY clause for each query appearing with the set operators. For example, the following query will produce an error.

```
SELECT last_name, hire_date
FROM   employees
```

```
WHERE  department_id = 90
ORDER BY last_name
UNION
SELECT first_name, hire_date
FROM   employees
WHERE  first_name LIKE 'K%'
ORDER BY first_name;
```

You can use the column name or alias name used in the first query or positional notation in the ORDER BY clause. Here are two examples:

```
SELECT last_name, hire_date "Join Date"
FROM   employees
WHERE  department_id = 90
UNION ALL
SELECT first_name, hire_date
FROM   employees
WHERE  first_name LIKE 'K%'
ORDER BY last_name, "Join Date";

SELECT last_name, hire_date "Join Date"
FROM   employees
WHERE  department_id = 90
UNION ALL
SELECT first_name, hire_date
FROM   employees
WHERE  first_name LIKE 'K%'
ORDER BY 1, 2;
```

Subqueries

A *subquery* is a query within a query. A subquery answers the queries that have multiple parts; the subquery answers one part of the question, and the parent query answers the other part. When you nest many subqueries, the innermost query is evaluated first. Subqueries can be used with all DML statements.

If you need to nest more than six subqueries, the query performance will be better if you write a PL/SQL program involving cursors. *Oracle PL/SQL Programming*, by Steven Feuerstein, *et al.* (O'Reilly & Associates) is a good book on PL/SQL.

Using subqueries in the FROM clause of a top-level query is known as an inline view. Inline views are discussed in Chapter 8, "Managing Views." You can nest any number of such queries; Oracle does not have a limit. Using the inline view, you can write queries to find top-*n* values. This is possible because Oracle allows an ORDER BY clause in the inline view. See Chapter 8 for details.

Using subqueries in the WHERE clause of a query is called *nested subquery*. You can have 255 levels of nested subqueries.

When a column from the table used in the parent query is referenced in the subquery, it is known as a *correlated subquery*. For each row processed in the parent query, the correlated subquery is evaluated once.

A *scalar subquery* returns a single row and a single column value. Scalar subqueries can be used anywhere a column name or expression can be used.

Single-Row Subqueries

Single-row subqueries return only one row of results. A single-row subquery uses a single-row operator; the common operator is the equality operator (=). Consider an example using our tables from the HR schema. To find the name of the employee with the highest salary, you first need to find the highest salary using a subquery. Then you can execute the parent query with the result from the subquery.

```
SQL> SELECT last_name, first_name, salary
  2  FROM   employees
  3  WHERE  salary = (SELECT MAX(salary) FROM employees);

LAST_NAME                 FIRST_NAME               SALARY
------------------------- -------------------- ----------
King                      Steven                    24000
SQL>
```

The parent query of a single-row subquery can return more than one row. For example, to find the names and salary of employees who work in the Accounting department, you need to find the department number for Accounting in a subquery, and then execute the parent query.

```
SQL> SELECT last_name, first_name, salary
  2  FROM   employees
  3  WHERE  department_id = (SELECT department_id
  4         FROM   departments
  5*        WHERE  department_name = 'Accounting');

LAST_NAME                 FIRST_NAME               SALARY
------------------------- -------------------- ----------
Higgins                   Shelley                   12000
Gietz                     William                    8300
SQL>
```

Multiple-Row Subqueries

Multiple-row subqueries return more than one row of results from the subquery. It is safer to provide the multiple-row operators in the subqueries if you are not sure of the results. In the previous query, if there is more than one department ID with the name Accounting, the query will fail. The following query returns three rows from the subquery. It lists all of the employees who work for the same department as John does.

```
SELECT last_name, first_name, department_id
FROM   employees
WHERE  department_id IN (SELECT department_id
       FROM   employees
       WHERE  first_name = 'John');
```

IN is the most commonly used multiple-row subquery operator. Other operators are EXISTS, ANY, and ALL. You may use NOT with the IN and EXISTS operators.

Correlated Subqueries

Oracle performs a correlated subquery when the subquery references a column from a table referred to in the parent statement. A correlated subquery is evaluated once for each row processed by the parent statement. The parent statement can be a SELECT, UPDATE, or DELETE statement. In the following example, the highest-paid employee of each department is selected. The subquery is executed for each row returned in the parent query. Notice that the parent table column is used inside the subquery.

```
SQL> SELECT department_id, last_name, salary
     FROM   employees e1
     WHERE  salary = (SELECT MAX(salary)
            FROM employees e2
            WHERE e1.department_id = e2.department_id)
     ORDER BY 1, 2, 3;

DEPARTMENT_ID LAST_NAME                     SALARY
------------- ------------------------- ----------
           10 Whalen                          4400
           20 Hartstein                      13000
           30 Raphaely                       11000
           40 Mavris                          6500
           50 Fripp                           8200
           60 Hunold                          9000
           70 Baer                           10000
           80 Russell                        14000
           90 King                           24000
          100 Greenberg                      12000
          110 Higgins                        12000

11 rows selected.
SQL>
```

The following example shows a correlated subquery using the EXISTS operator. The EXISTS operator checks for the existence of rows in the subquery based on the condition. The column results of the SELECT clause in the subquery are ignored when using the EXISTS operator. The query lists the names of employees who work with John (same department). The subquery selects a dummy value of 'x', which is ignored.

```
SELECT last_name, first_name, department_id
FROM   employees e1
```

```
WHERE  EXISTS (SELECT 'x'
               FROM   employees e2
               WHERE  first_name = 'John'
               AND    e1.department_id = e2.department_id);
```

The column names in the parent queries are available for reference in subqueries. The column names from the tables in the subquery cannot be used in the parent queries. The scope is only the current query level and its subqueries.

Scalar Subqueries

A scalar subquery returns exactly one column value from one row. Scalar subqueries can be used in most places where you would use a column name or expression, such as inside a single-row function as an argument, in the VALUES clause of an INSERT statement, in an ORDER BY clause, in a WHERE clause, and in a SELECT clause. Scalar subqueries can also be used in CASE expressions. Scalar subqueries cannot be used in GROUP BY or HAVING clauses. Let's review a few examples of using scalar subqueries.

A Scalar Subquery in a *CASE* Expression

To list the city name, country code, and if the city is in India, we use a CASE expression with a subquery to return the country code for India from the COUNTRIES table. To limit the rows, let's select only the cities that begin with *B*.

```
SQL> SELECT city, country_id, (CASE
            WHEN country_id IN (SELECT country_id
                                FROM   countries
                                WHERE  country_name = 'India')
            THEN 'Indian'
            ELSE 'Non-Indian'
            END) "INDIA?"
     FROM   locations
     WHERE  city LIKE 'B%';
```

```
CITY                           CO INDIA?
------------------------------ -- ----------
Beijing                        CN Non-Indian
Bombay                         IN Indian
Bern                           CH Non-Indian
SQL>
```

A Scalar Subquery in a *SELECT* Clause

To report the employee name, department, and the highest salary in that department, we use a subquery in the SELECT clause. This is also a correlated subquery.

```
SQL> SELECT last_name, department_id,
          (SELECT MAX(salary)
           FROM   employees sq
           WHERE  sq.department_id = e.department_id) HSAL
     FROM   employees e
     WHERE  last_name like 'R%';

LAST_NAME                 DEPARTMENT_ID       HSAL
------------------------- ------------- ----------
Raphaely                             30      11000
Rogers                               50       8200
Rajs                                 50       8200
Russell                              80      14000
SQL>
```

A Scalar Subquery in *SELECT* and *WHERE* Clauses

The following query may be confusing, but pay close attention to the flexibility of using subqueries to solve your queries. A scalar subquery is used in the SELECT clause. as well as in the WHERE clause. A multiple-row subquery is also used in the WHERE clause, after the IN operator. The purpose of the query is to find the department names and their manager names for all departments that are in United States or Canada. Since the country information is not available in the DEPARTMENTS table, we need to get this information from the LOCATIONS table. Also, we did not know the country IDs of United States and Canada, so we use a subquery to get them. The query also limits the number of rows retrieved by checking if a manager is assigned to the department (d.manager_id IS NOT NULL).

```
SQL> SELECT department_name, manager_id, (SELECT last_name
         FROM employees e
         WHERE e.employee_id = d.manager_id) MGR_NAME
   FROM  departments d
   WHERE ((SELECT country_id FROM locations l
        WHERE  d.location_id = l.location_id)
      IN (SELECT country_id FROM countries c
        WHERE  c.country_name = 'United States of America'
        OR     c.country_name = 'Canada'))
   AND   d.manager_id IS NOT NULL;

DEPARTMENT_NAME      MANAGER_ID MGR_NAME
-------------------- ---------- -------------
Administration              200 Whalen
Marketing                   201 Hartstein
Purchasing                  114 Raphaely
Shipping                    121 Fripp
IT                          103 Hunold
Executive                   100 King
Finance                     108 Greenberg
Accounting                  205 Higgins

8 rows selected.
SQL>
```

A Scalar Subquery in an *ORDER BY* Clause

Scalar subqueries also can be used in the ORDER BY clause. The following example sorts the city names by their country name order. Notice that country name is not included in the SELECT clause.

```
SELECT country_id, city, state_province
FROM   locations l
ORDER BY (SELECT country_name
          FROM   countries c
          WHERE  l.country_id = c.country_id);
```

If the scalar subquery returns more than one row, the query will fail. If the scalar subquery returns no rows, the value is NULL.

Multiple-Column Subqueries

A subquery is multiple-column when you have more than one column in the SELECT clause of the subquery. *Multiple-column subqueries* are generally used to compare column conditions or in an UPDATE statement. Let's consider a simple example using the STATE and CITY tables shown below. We'll list all the cities in Texas using a subquery on the STATE table.

```
SQL> SELECT * FROM state;

  CNT_CODE  ST_CODE    ST_NAME
----------  -------    ------------
         1  TX         TEXAS
         1  CA         CALIFORNIA
        91  TN         TAMIL NADU
         1  TN         TENNESSE
        91  KL         KERALA
SQL> SELECT * FROM city;

  CNT_CODE ST_CODE   CTY_CODE  CTY_NAME       POPULATION
---------- -------   --------  -------------- ----------
         1 TX            1001  DALLAS
        91 TN            2243  MADRAS
         1 CA            8099  LOS ANGELES

SQL> SELECT cty_name
  2  FROM   city
  3  WHERE  (cnt_code, st_code) IN
  4         (SELECT cnt_code, st_code
  5          FROM   state
  6          WHERE  st_name = 'TEXAS');

CTY_NAME
----------
DALLAS
SQL>
```

Subqueries in Other DML Statements

Subqueries can be used in DML statements such as INSERT, UPDATE, DELETE, and MERGE. DML statements and their syntax are discussed in Chapter 6, "Manipulating Data." Following are some examples of subqueries in DML statements.

- To update the salary of all employees to the maximum salary in the corresponding department (correlated subquery):

```
UPDATE employees e1
SET   salary = (SELECT MAX(salary)
      FROM   employees e2
      WHERE e1.department_id = e2.department_id);
```

- To delete the records of employees whose salary is below the average salary in the department (using a correlated subquery):

```
DELETE FROM employees e
WHERE salary < (SELECT AVG(salary) FROM employees
       WHERE  department_id = e.department_id);
```

- To insert records to a table using a subquery:

```
INSERT INTO employee_archive
SELECT * FROM employees;
```

- To specify a subquery in the VALUES clause of the INSERT statement:

```
INSERT INTO departments
       (department_id, department_name)
VALUES ((SELECT MAX(department_id)
         +10 FROM departments), 'EDP');
```

You can also have a subquery in the INSERT, UPDATE, and DELETE statements in place of the table name. Here is an example:

```
DELETE FROM
(SELECT * FROM departments
 WHERE department_id < 20)
WHERE department_id = 10;
```

The subquery can have an optional WITH clause. WITH READ ONLY specifies that the subquery cannot be updated. WITH CHECK OPTION specifies that, if the subquery is used in place of a table in an INSERT, UPDATE, or DELETE statement, Oracle will not allow any changes to the table that would produce rows that are not included in the subquery. Let's look at an example:

```
SQL> INSERT INTO (SELECT department_id, department_name
  2         FROM departments
  3          WHERE department_id < 20)
  4  VALUES (35, 'MARKETING');

1 row created.

SQL> INSERT INTO (SELECT department_id, department_name
  2         FROM departments
  3         WHERE department_id < 20 WITH CHECK OPTION)
  4* VALUES (45, 'EDP')
SQL> /
       FROM departments
            *
ERROR at line 2:
ORA-01402: view WITH CHECK OPTION where-clause violation
SQL>
```

Summary

Joins are used to relate two or more tables (or views). In a relational database, it is common to have a requirement to join data. The tables are joined by using a common column in the tables in the WHERE clause of the query. Oracle now supports ISO/ANSI SQL1999 syntax for joins. In this syntax, the tables are joined using the JOIN keyword and a condition can be specified using the ON clause.

If the join condition uses the equality operator (= or IN), it is known as an equality join. If any other operator is used to join the tables, it is a non-equality join. If you do not specify any join condition between the tables, the result will be a Cartesian product: each row from the first table joined to every row in the second table. To avoid Cartesian joins, there should be at least *n*–1 join conditions in the WHERE clause when there are *n* tables in the FROM clause. A table can be joined to itself. If you wish to select the results from a table, even if there are no corresponding rows in the joined table, you can use the outer-join operator: (+). In the ANSI syntax, you can use the NATURAL JOIN, CROSS JOIN, LEFT JOIN, RIGHT JOIN, and FULL JOIN keywords to specify the type of join.

A subquery is a query within a query. Writing subqueries is a powerful way to manipulate data. You can write single-row and multiple-row subqueries. Single-row subqueries must return zero or one row; multiple-row subqueries return zero or more rows. IN and EXISTS are the most commonly used subquery operators. Subqueries can appear in the WHERE clause or in the FROM clause. They can also replace table names in DELETE, INSERT, and UPDATE statements. Subqueries that return one row and one column result are known as scalar subqueries. Scalar subqueries can be used in most places where you would use an expression.

Exam Essentials

Understand joins. Make sure you know the different types of joins. Understand the difference between natural, cross, simple, complex, and outer joins.

Know the different outer join clauses. Outer joins can be specified using LEFT, RIGHT, or FULL. Know the syntax of each type of join.

Be sure of the join syntax. Since ANSI syntax is new to Oracle9i, spend time practicing using each type of join. Understand the restrictions of using each ANSI keyword in the JOIN and their implied column-naming conventions.

Know how to write subqueries. Understand the use and flexibility of subqueries. Practice using scalar subqueries and correlated queries.

Understand the use of the ORDER BY clause in the subqueries. The ORDER BY clause can be used in all subqueries, except the subqueries appearing the WHERE clause of the query.

Know the set operators. Understand the set operators that can be used in compound queries. Know the difference between the UNION and UNION ALL operators.

Key Terms

Before you take the exam, make sure you're familiar with the following terms:

- Cartesian join
- complex join
- compound query
- correlated subquery
- cross join
- equality join (equijoin)
- full outer join
- inner join
- join
- left outer join
- multiple-column subqueries
- multiple-row subqueries
- multi-table join
- natural join
- nested subquery
- nonequality join
- outer join
- right outer join
- scalar subquery
- self-join
- set operators
- single-row subqueries
- subquery
- table alias name

Review Questions

1. Which line of code has an error?

   A. `SELECT dname, ename`

   B. `FROM   emp e, dept d`

   C. `WHERE  emp.deptno = dept.deptno`

   D. `ORDER BY 1, 2;`

2. What will be the result of the following query?

```
SELECT c.cust_id, c.cust_name, o.ord_date, o.prod_id
FROM   customers c, orders o
WHERE  c.cust_id = o.cust_id (+);
```

   A. List all the customer names in the CUSTOMERS table and the orders they made from the ORDERS table, even if the customer has not placed an order

   B. List only the names of customer from the CUSTOMERS table who have placed an order in the ORDERS table

   C. List all orders from the ORDERS table, even if there is no valid customer record in the CUSTOMERS table

   D. For each record in the CUSTOMERS table, list the information from the ORDERS table

3. The CUSTOMERS and ORDERS tables have the following data:

```
SQL> SELECT * FROM customers;

CUST_ CUST_NAME            PHONE           CITY
----- -------------------- --------------- -----------
A0101 Abraham Taylor Jr.                   Fort Worth
B0134 Betty Baylor         972-555-5555    Dallas
B0135 Brian King                           Chicago
```

```
SQL> SELECT * FROM orders;

ORD_DATE     PROD_ID CUST_ID   QUANTITY      PRICE
--------- ---------- ------- ---------- ----------
20-FEB-00       1741 B0134            5       65.5
02-FEB-00       1001 B0134           25    2065.85
02-FEB-00       1001 B0135            3      247.9
```

When the following query is executed, what will be the value of *PROD_ID* and *ORD_DATE* for the customer Abraham Taylor Jr.?

```
SELECT c.cust_id, c.cust_name, o.ord_date, o.prod_id
FROM   customers c, orders o
WHERE  c.cust_id = o.cust_id (+);
```

A. NULL, 01-JAN-01

B. NULL, NULL

C. 1001, 02-FEB-00

D. The query will not return customer Abraham Taylor Jr.

4. When using ANSI join syntax, which clause is used to specify a join condition?

A. JOIN

B. USING

C. ON

D. WHERE

5. The EMPLOYEES table has EMPLOYEE_ID, DEPARTMENT_ID, and FULL_NAME columns. The DEPARTMENTS table has DEPARTMENT_ID and DEPARTMENT_NAME columns. Which two of the following queries return the department ID, name, and employee name, listing department names even if there is no employee assigned to that department?

   A.
   ```
   SELECT d.department_id, d.department_name, e.full_name
   FROM   departments d
   NATURAL LEFT OUTER JOIN employees e;
   ```

   B.
   ```
   SELECT department_id, department_name, full_name
   FROM   departments
   NATURAL LEFT JOIN employees;
   ```

   C.
   ```
   SELECT d.department_id, d.department_name, e.full_name
   FROM   departments d
   LEFT OUTER JOIN employees e
   USING (d.department_id);
   ```

   D.
   ```
   SELECT d.department_id, d.department_name, e.full_name
   FROM   departments d
   LEFT OUTER JOIN employees e
   ON  (d.department_id = e.department_id);
   ```

6. Which two operators are not allowed when using an outer-join operator in the query?

   A. OR

   B. AND

   C. IN

   D. =

7. Which two operators are used to add more joining conditions in a multiple-table query?

   A. NOT

   B. OR

   C. AND

   D. Comma (,)

8. The columns of the EMPLOYEES, DEPARTMENTS, and JOBS tables are shown below.

Table	Column Names	Datatype
EMPLOYEES	EMPLOYEE_ID	NUMBER (6)
	FIRST_NAME	VARCHAR2 (25)
	LAST_NAME	VARCHAR2 (25)
	SALARY	NUMBER (8,2)
	JOB_ID	VARCHAR2 (10)
	MANAGER_ID	NUMBER (6)
	DEPARTMENT_ID	NUMBER (2)
DEPARTMENTS	DEPARTMENT_ID	NUMBER (2)
	DEPARTMENT_NAME	VARCHAR2 (30)
	MANAGER_ID	NUMBER (6)
	LOCATION_ID	NUMBER (4)
JOBS	JOB_ID	VARCHAR2 (10)
	JOB_TITLE	VARCHAR2 (30)

Which assertion about the following query is correct?

```
SELECT e.last_name, d.department_name, j.job_title
FROM   jobs j
INNER JOIN employees e
ON (e.department_id = d.department_id)
JOIN departments d
ON (j.job_id = e.job_id);
```

A. The query returns all the rows from EMPLOYEE table, where there is a corresponding record in the JOBS table and DEPARTMENTS table.

B. The query fails with an invalid column name error.

C. The query fails because line 3 specifies `INNER JOIN`, which is not a valid syntax.

D. The query fails because line 5 does not specify the keyword `INNER`.

E. The query fails because the column names are qualified with the table alias.

9. The columns of the EMPLOYEES and DEPARTMENTS tables are shown in question 8. Consider the following three queries using those tables.

```
1. SELECT last_name, department_name
FROM   employees e, departments d
WHERE  e.department_id = d.department_id;
2. SELECT last_name, department_name
FROM   employees NATURAL JOIN departments;
3. SELECT last_name, department_name
FROM   employees JOIN departments
USING (department_id);
```

Which of the following assertions best describes the results?

A. Queries 1, 2, and 3 produce the same results.

B. Queries 2 and 3 produce the same result; query 1 produces a different result.

C. Queries 1, 2, and 3 produce different results.

D. Queries 1 and 3 produce the same result; query 2 produces a different result.

10. The data in the STATE table is as shown:

```
SQL> SELECT * FROM state;

  CNT_CODE ST_CODE ST_NAME
---------- ------- ------------
         1 TX      TEXAS
         1 CA      CALIFORNIA
        91 TN      TAMIL NADU
         1 TN      TENNESSE
        91 KL      KERALA
```

Consider the following query:

```
SELECT cnt_code
FROM   state
WHERE  st_name = (SELECT st_name FROM state
                  WHERE  st_code = 'TN');
```

Which of the following assertions best describes the results?

A. The query will return the CNT_CODE for the ST_CODE value `'TN'`.

B. The query will fail and will not return any rows.

C. The query will display 1 and 91 as CNT_CODE values.

D. The query will fail because an alias name is not used.

11. The data in the STATE table is shown in question 10. The data in the CITY table is as shown below.

```
SQL> SELECT * FROM city;

  CNT_CODE ST_CODE   CTY_CODE CTY_NAME
---------- ------- ---------- -------------
         1 TX            1001 DALLAS
        91 TN            2243 MADRAS
         1 CA            8099 LOS ANGELES
```

What is the result of the following query?

```
SELECT st_name "State Name"
FROM   state
WHERE  (cnt_code, st_code) =
       (SELECT cnt_code, st_code
        FROM   city
        WHERE  cty_name = 'DALLAS');
```

A. TEXAS

B. The query will fail because CNT_CODE and ST_CODE are not in the `WHERE` clause of the subquery.

C. The query will fail because more than one column appears in the `WHERE` clause.

D. TX

12. Which line of the code below has an error?

```
1  SELECT department_id, count(*)
2  FROM   employees
3  GROUP BY department_id
4  HAVING COUNT(department_id) =
5  (SELECT max(count(department_id))
6   FROM employees
7   GROUP BY department_id);
```

A. Line 3

B. Line 4

C. Line 5

D. Line 7

E. No error

13. Which query is a correlated subquery?

A.
```
select cty_name from city
where  st_code in (select st_code from state
where st_name = 'TENNESSE'
and  city.cnt_code = state.cnt_code);
```

B.
```
select cty_name
from   city
where  st_code in (select st_code from state
where st_name = 'TENNESSE');
```

C.
```
select cty_name
from city, state
where  city.st_code = state.st_code
and    city.cnt_code = state.cnt_code
and    st_name = 'TENNESSE';
```

D.
```
select cty_name
from city, state
where  city.st_code = state.st_code (+)
and    city.cnt_code = state.cnt_code (+)
and    st_name = 'TENNESSE';
```

14. The COUNTRY table has the following data:

```
SQL> SELECT * FROM country;

  CNT_CODE CNT_NAME          CONTINENT
---------- ----------------- ----------
         1 UNITED STATES     N.AMERICA
        91 INDIA             ASIA
        65 SINGAPORE         ASIA
```

What value is returned from the subquery when you execute the following?

```
SELECT CNT_NAME
FROM   country
WHERE  CNT_CODE =
(SELECT MAX(cnt_code) FROM country);
```

A. INDIA

B. 65

C. 91

D. SINGAPORE

15. Which line in the following query contains an error?

```
1 SELECT deptno, ename, sal
2 FROM   emp e1
3 WHERE  sal = (SELECT MAX(sal) FROM emp
4                WHERE  deptno = e1.deptno
5                ORDER BY deptno);
```

A. Line 2

B. Line 3

C. Line 4

D. Line 5

16. Consider the following query:

```
SELECT deptno, ename, salary salary, average,
       salary-average difference
FROM   emp,
(SELECT deptno dno, AVG(salary) average FROM emp
 GROUP BY deptno)
WHERE  deptno = dno
ORDER BY 1, 2;
```

Which of the following statements is correct?

A. The query will fail because no alias name is provided for the subquery.

B. The query will fail because a column selected inside the subquery is referenced outside the scope of the subquery.

C. The query will work without errors.

D. `GROUP BY` cannot be used inside a subquery.

17. The COUNTRY table has the following data:

```
SQL> SELECT * FROM country;

  CNT_CODE CNT_NAME             CONTINENT
---------- -------------------- ----------
         1 UNITED STATES        N.AMERICA
        91 INDIA                ASIA
        65 SINGAPORE            ASIA
```

What will be the result of the following query?

```
INSERT INTO (SELECT cnt_code FROM country
             WHERE continent = 'ASIA')
VALUES (971, 'SAUDI ARABIA', 'ASIA');
```

A. One row will be inserted into COUNTRY table.

B. `WITH CHECK OPTION` is missing in the subquery.

C. The query will fail because the `VALUES` clause is invalid.

D. The `WHERE` clause cannot appear in the subqueries used in `INSERT` statements.

18. In ANSI SQL, a self-join can be represented by using which of the following? (Choose the best answer.)

A. `NATURAL JOIN` clause

B. `CROSS JOIN` clause

C. `JOIN .. USING` clause

D. `JOIN ... ON` clause

E. All of the above

19. Consider the following queries:

```
1. SELECT last_name, salary,
          (SELECT (MAX(sq.salary) - e.salary)
           FROM   employees sq
           WHERE  sq.department_id = e.department_id) DSAL
FROM   employees e
WHERE  department_id = 20;
2. SELECT last_name, salary, msalary - salary dsal
FROM   employees e,
       (SELECT department_id, MAX(salary) msalary
        FROM   employees
        GROUP BY department_id) sq
WHERE e.department_id = sq.department_id
AND   e.department_id = 20;
3. SELECT last_name, salary, msalary - salary dsal
FROM   employees e INNER JOIN
       (SELECT department_id, MAX(salary) msalary
        FROM   employees
        GROUP BY department_id) sq
ON      e.department_id = sq.department_id
WHERE   e.department_id = 20;
4. SELECT last_name, salary, msalary - salary dsal
FROM   employees INNER JOIN
       (SELECT department_id, MAX(salary) msalary
        FROM   employees
        GROUP BY department_id) sq
USING   (department_id)
WHERE   department_id = 20;
```

Which of the following assertions best describes the results?

A. Queries 1 and 2 produce identical results, and queries 3 and 4 produce identical results, but queries 1 and 3 produce different results.

B. Queries 1, 2, 3, and 4 produce identical results.

C. Queries 1, 2, and 3 produce identical results; query 4 will produce errors.

D. Queries 1 and 3 produce identical results; queries 2 and 4 will produce errors.

E. Queries 1, 2, 3, and 4 produce different results.

F. Queries 1 and 2 are valid SQL; queries 3 and 4 are not valid.

20. The columns of the EMPLOYEES and DEPARTMENTS tables are shown in question 8. Which query will show us the top-five highly paid employees in the company?

A.
```
SELECT last_name, salary
FROM   employees
WHERE ROWNUM <= 5
ORDER BY salary DESC;
```

B.
```
SELECT last_name, salary
FROM (SELECT *
FROM   employees
WHERE ROWNUM <= 5
ORDER BY salary DESC )
WHERE ROWNUM <= 5;
```

C.
```
SELECT * FROM
(SELECT last_name, salary
FROM   employees
ORDER BY salary)
WHERE ROWNUM <= 5;
```

D.
```
SELECT * FROM
(SELECT last_name, salary
FROM   employees
ORDER BY salary DESC)
WHERE ROWNUM <= 5;
```

Answers to Review Questions

1. C. When table aliases are defined, you should qualify the column names with the table alias only. In this case, the table name cannot be used to qualify column names. The line in option C should read `WHERE e.deptno = d.deptno`.

2. A. An outer-join operator (+) indicates an outer join and is used to display the records, even if there are no corresponding records in the table mentioned on the other side of the operator. Here, the outer-join operator is next to the ORDERS table, so even if there are no corresponding orders from a customer, the result set will have the customer ID and name.

3. B. When an outer join returns values from a table that does not have corresponding records, a `NULL` is returned.

4. C. The join condition is specified in the `ON` clause. The `JOIN` clause specifies the table to be joined. The `USING` clause specifies the column names that should be used in the join. The `WHERE` clause is used to specify additional search criteria to restrict the rows returned.

5. B, D. Option A does not work because you cannot qualify column names when using a natural join. Option B works, because the only common column between these two tables is DEPARTMENT_ID. The keyword `OUTER` is optional. Option C does not work, again because you cannot qualify column names when specifying the `USING` clause. Option D specifies the join condition explicitly in the `ON` clause.

6. A, C. `OR` and `IN` are not allowed in the `WHERE` clause on the columns where an outer-join operator is specified. You can use `AND` and = in the outer join.

7. B, C. The operators `OR` and `AND` are used to add more joining conditions to the query. `NOT` is a negation operator, and a comma is used to separate column names and table names.

8. B. The query fails because the `d.department_id` column is referenced before the DEPARTMENTS table is specified in the `JOIN` clause. A column can be referenced only after its table is specified.

9. D. Since DEPARTMENT_ID and MANAGER_ID are common columns in the EMPLOYEES and DEPARTMENTS tables, a natural join will relate these two tables using the two common columns.

10. B. There are two records in the STATE table with the ST_CODE value as `'TN'`. Since we are using a single-row operator for the subquery, it will fail. Option C would be correct if it used the `IN` operator instead of = for the subquery.

11. A. The query will succeed, because there is only one row in the city table with the CTY_NAME value `'DALLAS'`.

12. E. There is no error in the statement. The query will return the department number where the most employees are working.

13. A. A subquery is correlated when a reference is made to a column from a table in the parent statement.

14. C. The subquery returns 91 to the main query.

15. D. You cannot have an `ORDER BY` clause in the subquery used in a `WHERE` clause.

16. C. The query will work fine, producing the difference between employee's salary and average salary in the department. You do not need to use the alias names because the column names returned from the subquery are different from the column names returned by the parent query.

17. C. Because only one column is selected in the subquery to which we are doing the insert, only one column value should be supplied in the `VALUES` clause. The `VALUES` clause can have only `CNT_CODE value (971)`.

18. D. `NATURAL JOIN` and `JOIN .. USING` clauses will not allow alias names to be used. Since a self-join is getting data from the same table, you must include alias names and qualify column names.

19. B. All four queries produce the same result. The first query uses a scalar subquery in the `SELECT` clause. The rest of queries use an inline view. All of the queries display the last name, salary, and difference of salary from the highest salary in the department for all employees in department 20.

20. D. To find the top-*n* rows, you can select the necessary columns in an inline view with an `ORDER BY DESC` clause. An outer query limiting the rows to *n* will give the result.

Modifying Data

INTRODUCTION TO ORACLE9i: SQL EXAM OBJECTIVES COVERED IN THIS CHAPTER:

✓ **Manipulating Data**

- Describe each DML statement
- Insert rows into a table
- Update rows in a table
- Delete rows from a table
- Merge rows in a table
- Control transactions

Exam objectives are subject to change at any time without prior notice and at Oracle's sole discretion. Please visit Oracle's Certification website (`http://www.oracle.com/education/certification/`) for the most current exam objectives listing.

In this chapter, we will cover how to modify data. In an Oracle database, you change data using SQL *Data Manipulation Language* (*DML*) statements. You will learn how to coordinate multiple changes using transactions. Oracle is a multiuser database, and more than one user or session can change data at the same time. You will read about locks and how they are used to control this concurrency. Another effect of a multiuser database is that data can change during the execution of *statements*. You can exercise some control over the consistency or visibility of these changes within a transaction.

The exam will assess your knowledge of how to change data and control these changes. This chapter will solidify your understanding of these concepts in preparation for the exam.

Using DML Statements

DML is the subset of SQL that is employed to change data. Table 6.1 summarizes the DML statements that Oracle supports.

TABLE 6.1 DML Statements Supported by Oracle

Statement	Purpose
INSERT	Adds rows to a table
UPDATE	Changes the value stored in a table
MERGE	Updates or inserts rows from one table into another
DELETE	Removes rows from a table

TABLE 6.1 DML Statements Supported by Oracle *(continued)*

Statement	Purpose
SELECT FOR UPDATE	Prevents other sessions from performing DML on selected rows
LOCK TABLE	Prevents other sessions from performing DML on a table

Inserting Rows into a Table

The INSERT statement is used to add rows to one or more tables. Rows can be added with specific data values, or the rows can be created from existing data using a subquery.

Inserting into a Single Table

Figure 6.1 shows the syntax for the single-table INSERT statement.

FIGURE 6.1 The syntax of the single-table INSERT statement

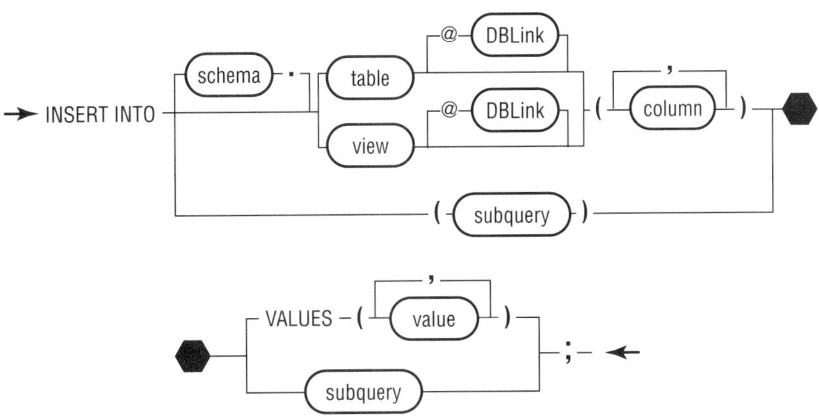

The column list is optional. The default list is all columns, in order of their column ID. You can see the column ID in the data dictionary views ALL_TAB_COLUMNS, USER_TAB_COLUMNS, and DBA_TAB_COLUMNS.

You cannot insert into a view that contains any of the following:

- An aggregate function
- A distinct operator

- A set operator (UNION, INTERSECT, MINUS, and UNION ALL)
- A GROUP BY, ORDER BY, or CONNECT BY clause
- A subquery in the SELECT list

Here are some examples of single-table INSERT statements:

```
INSERT INTO checking (account_id, create_date, balance)
  VALUES ('Kiesha' , SYSDATE, 5000);

INSERT INTO brokerage (account_id, create_date, balance)
  SELECT account_id, SYSDATE, 0
  FROM checking
  WHERE account_type = 'C';

INSERT INTO e_checking
  SELECT * from checking
  WHERE account_type = 'C';
```

The number and datatypes of values inserted must match the number and datatypes in the column list. Implicit data conversion will be performed if possible to achieve the correct datatypes for the values. A NULL string will implicitly insert a NULL into the appropriate column. The keyword NULL can be used to explicitly assign NULL to a column. The following statements are equivalent:

```
INSERT INTO customers (cust_id, state, postal_code)
  VALUES ('Ariel', NULL, '94501');
```

or

```
INSERT INTO customers (cust_id, state, postal_code)
  VALUES ('Ariel','', '94501');
```

Inserting into Multiple Tables

Beginning with Oracle9i, the INSERT statement can be used to add rows to more than one table at a time. In prior releases, this functionality required multiple statements or multiple passes through the source table. This multiple-table insert is very useful for efficiently loading data, because you can add the data to multiple target tables via a single pass through the source table, with a minimum of database calls. Figure 6.2 shows the syntax of the multiple-table INSERT statement.

FIGURE 6.2 The syntax of the multiple-table INSERT statement

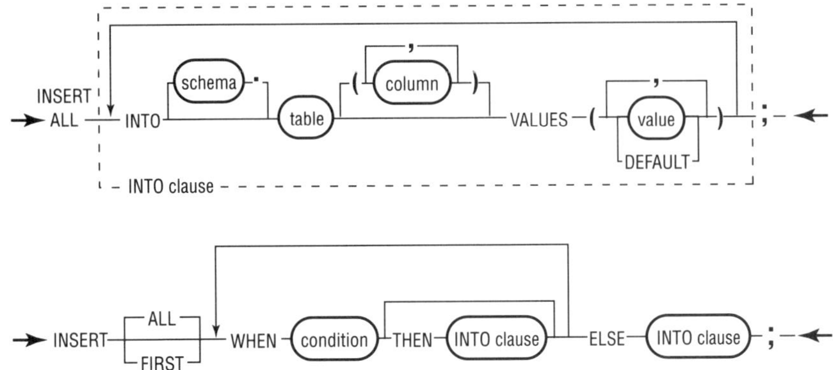

The keyword ALL tells Oracle to evaluate each and every WHEN clause, whether or not any evaluate to TRUE. In contrast, the FIRST keyword tells Oracle to stop evaluating WHEN clauses after encountering the first one that evaluates to TRUE. The INTO clause and the WHEN clause can be repeated.

Suppose that our company, Sales Inc., sells books, videos, and audio CDs. We have a SALES_DETAIL table that contains information about all of the sales and is used by the selling system. We need to load this information into three other tables that focus specifically on the three product categories: Book, Audio, and Video. These category-specific tables are used by the analysis systems. Here are the structure and contents of the source SALES_DETAIL table:

```
Name                          Null?    Type
----------------------------- -------- ------------
TXN_ID                        NOT NULL NUMBER
PRODUCT_ID                             NUMBER
PROD_CATEGORY                          VARCHAR2(2)
CUSTOMER_ID                            VARCHAR2(10)
SALE_DATE                              DATE
SALE_QTY                               NUMBER
SALE_PRICE                             NUMBER
```

```
SELECT * FROM sales_detail;

TXN_ID PRODUCT_ID PR CUST SALE_DATE  SALE_QTY SALE_PRICE
------ ---------- -- ---- ---------- -------- ----------
     1  304329743 B  43   17-JUN-02         2       19.1
     2  304943209 B  22   17-JUN-02         1       8.95
     3  211524098 A  16   17-JUN-02         1       11.4
     4  413354981 V  41   17-JUN-02         1      12.95
     5  304957315 B  48   17-JUN-02         1       38.5
     6  304183648 B  32   17-JUN-02         2       17.9
     7  211681559 A  32   18-JUN-02         1       11.4
     8  211944553 A  21   18-JUN-02         1       11.4
     9  304155687 B  26   18-JUN-02         1       8.95
    10  304776352 B  18   18-JUN-02         3      48.45
    11  413753861 V  30   18-JUN-02         1      12.95
    12  413159654 V  29   18-JUN-02         1      19.99
    13  304357689 B  11   18-JUN-02         2       72.3
    14  211153246 A  14   18-JUN-02         2       26.4
    15  304852369 B  44   18-JUN-02         1      15.95
```

The target table structures are described in the following output.

```
DESC book_sales

Name                          Null?    Type
----------------------------- -------- ------------
PROD_ID                       NOT NULL NUMBER
CUST_ID                       NOT NULL VARCHAR2(10)
QTY_SOLD                      NOT NULL NUMBER
AMT_SOLD                      NOT NULL NUMBER
ISBN                                   VARCHAR2(24)

DESC video_sales
Name                          Null?    Type
----------------------------- -------- ------------
PROD_ID                       NOT NULL NUMBER
CUST_ID                       NOT NULL VARCHAR2(10)
```

```
QTY_SOLD                      NOT NULL NUMBER
AMT_SOLD                      NOT NULL NUMBER
RATING                                 VARCHAR2(5)
YEAR_RELEASED                          NUMBER

DESC audio_sales
Name                          Null?    Type
----------------------------- -------- ------------
PROD_ID                       NOT NULL NUMBER
CUST_ID                       NOT NULL VARCHAR2(10)
QTY_SOLD                      NOT NULL NUMBER
AMT_SOLD                      NOT NULL NUMBER
ARTIST                                 VARCHAR2(64)
```

The multiple-table insert that follows selects from the SALES_DETAIL table and, based on the value of PROD_CATEGORY, inserts a row into the BOOK_SALES, VIDEO_SALES, or AUDIO_SALES table.

```
INSERT ALL
WHEN prod_category='B' THEN
  INTO book_sales(prod_id,cust_id,qty_sold,amt_sold)
      VALUES(product_id,customer_id,sale_qty,sale_price)
WHEN prod_category='V' THEN
  INTO video_sales(prod_id,cust_id,qty_sold,amt_sold)
      VALUES(product_id,customer_id,sale_qty,sale_price)
WHEN prod_category='A' THEN
  INTO audio_sales(prod_id,cust_id,qty_sold,amt_sold)
      VALUES(product_id,customer_id,sale_qty,sale_price)
SELECT prod_category ,product_id ,customer_id ,sale_qty
      ,sale_price
FROM sales_detail;
```

This multiple-table insert will create eight rows in the BOOK_SALES table, four rows in the AUDIO_SALES table, and three rows in the VIDEO_SALES table.

In most SQL statements, you can prefix column names with a table alias. In fact, this aids readability even if it's not strictly required for parsing. If you try to use an alias for the table name and then prefix the column names with either this alias or the schema-qualified table name in a multiple-table insert, you may raise an exception.

Updating Rows in a Table

The UPDATE statement is used to modify existing rows in a table. Figure 6.3 shows the syntax of the UPDATE statement.

FIGURE 6.3 The syntax of the UPDATE statement

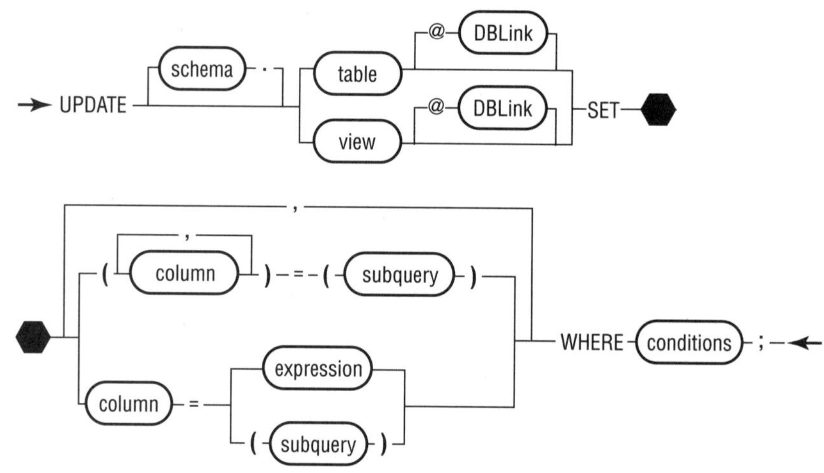

The column list can be either a single column or a number of columns delimited by commas:

```
UPDATE order_rollup
SET (qty, price) = (SELECT SUM(qty), SUM(price)
                    FROM order_lines
                    WHERE customer_id = 'KOHL')
WHERE customer_id = 'KOHL'
 AND  order_period = TO_DATE('01-Oct-2001');
```

or

```
UPDATE order_rollup
SET phone = '3125551212'
   ,fax   = '7735551212'
WHERE customer_id = 'KOHL';
```

Merging Rows into a Table

The MERGE statement is used to both update and insert rows in a table. The MERGE statement has a join specification that describes how to determine if an update or insert should be executed. Figure 6.4 shows the syntax of the MERGE statement.

FIGURE 6.4 The syntax of the MERGE statement

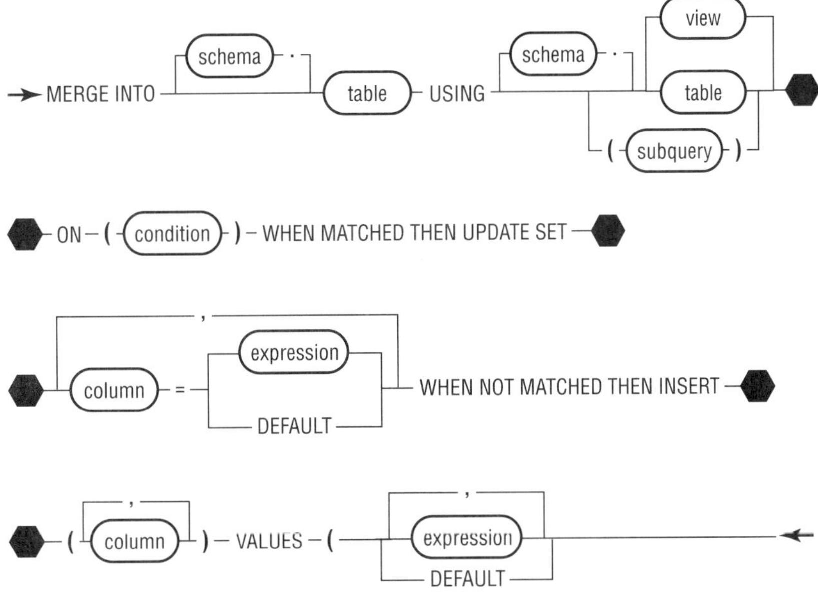

The WHEN MATCHED predicate specifies how to update the existing rows. The WHEN NOT MATCHED predicate specifies how to create rows that do not exist.

In the following example, we have a new pricing sheet for products in category 33. This new pricing data has been loaded into the NEW_PRICES table. We need to update the PRODUCT_INFORMATION table with these new prices. The NEW_PRICES table contains updates to existing rows in the PRODUCT_INFORMATION table as well as new products. The new products need to be inserted and the existing products need to be updated.

```
SELECT product_id,category_id,list_price,min_price
FROM oe.product_information
WHERE category_id=33;

PRODUCT_ID CATEGORY_ID LIST_PRICE  MIN_PRICE
---------- ----------- ---------- ----------
      2986          33        125        111
      3163          33         35         29
      3165          33         40         34
      3167          33         55         47
      3216          33         30         26
      3220          33         45         36

SELECT *
FROM new_prices;

PRODUCT_ID LIST_PRICE  MIN_PRICE
---------- ---------- ----------
      2986        135        121
      3163         40         32
      3164         40         35
      3165         40         37
      3166         50         45
      3167         55         50
      3216         30         26
      3220         45         36
```

We use the MERGE statement to perform an update/insert of the new pricing data into the PRODUCT_INFORMATION table, as follows:

```
MERGE INTO oe.product_information pi
USING (SELECT product_id, list_price, min_price
    FROM new_prices) NP
```

```
ON (pi.product_id = np.product_id)
WHEN MATCHED THEN UPDATE SET pi.list_price =np.list_price
                            ,pi.min_price = np.min_price
WHEN NOT MATCHED THEN INSERT (pi.product_id,pi.category_id
                            ,pi.list_price,pi.min_price)
  VALUES (np.product_id, 33,np.list_price, np.min_price);

PRODUCT_ID CATEGORY_ID LIST_PRICE  MIN_PRICE
---------- ----------- ---------- ----------
      2986          33        135        121 (updated)
      3163          33         40         32 (updated)
      3164          33         40         35 (inserted)
      3165          33         40         37 (updated)
      3166          33         50         45 (inserted)
      3167          33         55         50 (updated)
      3216          33         30         26 (updated)
      3220          33         45         36 (updated)
```

Deleting Rows from a Table

The DELETE statement is used to remove rows from a table. You can see the DELETE statement's syntax in Figure 6.5.

After executing DML, you must execute a commit to make the changes permanent or execute a rollback to undo the changes.

FIGURE 6.5 The syntax of the DELETE statement

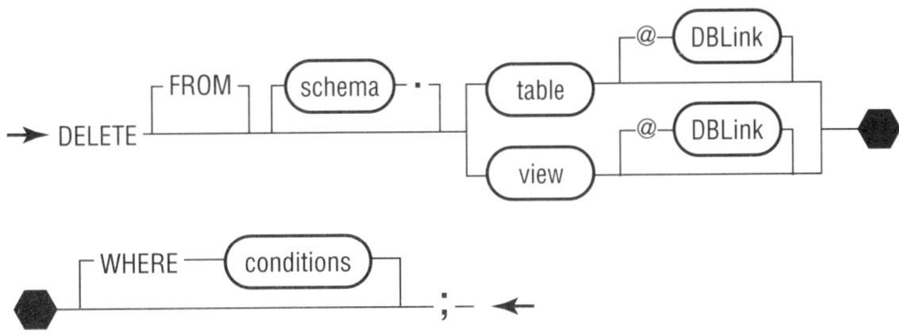

Here are some examples of the DELETE statement:

```
--Remove old orders shipped to some states
DELETE FROM po_lines
WHERE ship_to_state IN ('TX','NY','IL')
 AND  order_date < TRUNC(SYSDATE) - 90

--Remove customer Gomez
DELETE FROM customers
WHERE customer_id = 'GOMEZ';

--Remove duplicate line_detail_ids
--Note keyword FROM is not needed
DELETE line_details
WHERE rowid NOT IN (SELECT MAX(rowid)
                    FROM line_detail
                    GROUP BY line_detail_id)

--Remove all rows from the table order_staging
DELETE FROM order_staging;
```

The WHERE clause is optional; when it is missing, all rows are removed from the table. Removing all rows from a large table can take a long time and require significant rollback segment space. If you are truncating a table, consider using the TRUNCATE statement, as described in the next section.

Truncating a Table

If you want to empty a table of all rows, consider using the *Data Definition Language (DDL)* statement TRUNCATE. Like a DELETE statement without a WHERE clause, TRUNCATE will remove all rows from a table. However, TRUNCATE is not DML—it is DDL, and therefore, it has different characteristics from the DELETE statement. DDL is the subset of SQL that is employed to define database objects. One of the key differences between DML and DDL is that DDL statements will implicitly perform a commit, affecting not only the change in object definition, but also committing any pending DML. A DDL statement cannot be rolled back; only DML statements can be rolled back. DDL statements include CREATE, ALTER, and DROP statements, together with the TRUNCATE statement covered here. (For more information about DDL, see Chapter 7, "Managing Tables and Constraints.")

Figure 6.6 shows the syntax for TRUNCATE. The STORAGE clause is optional, and the default is to DROP STORAGE, which shrinks the table and its indexes down to the MINEXTENT number of extents and resets the NEXT parameter to the last deallocated extent. In most cases, this space deallocation resets the segments back to their original size and original NEXT parameter. REUSE STORAGE will not shrink the table or adjust the NEXT parameter.

FIGURE 6.6 The syntax for the TRUNCATE statement

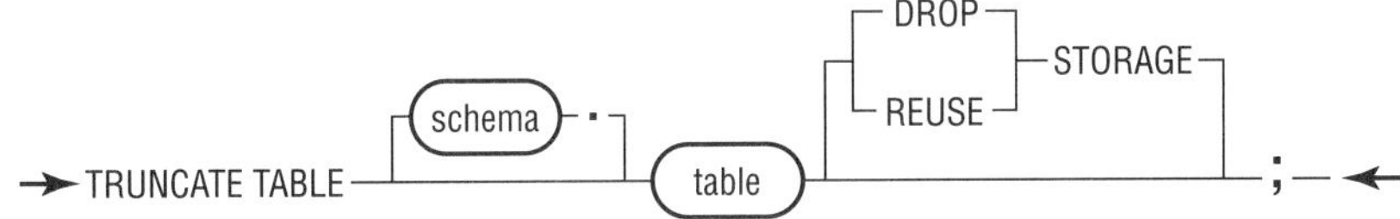

For example, to remove all rows from the ORDER_STAGING table, shrink the table and indexes to the original size, reset the high-water mark, and commit the change, truncate the table as follows:

```
TRUNCATE TABLE order_staging;
```

Alternatively, if you want to keep the storage (so that Oracle doesn't need to reallocate it when you reload the table), remove all rows, reset the high-water mark, and commit the change, truncate the table as follows:

```
TRUNCATE TABLE order_staging REUSE STORAGE;
```

TRUNCATE versus *DELETE*

The TRUNCATE statement is similar to a DELETE statement without a WHERE clause, except for the following:

- TRUNCATE is very fast on both large and small tables. DELETE will generate undo information, in case a rollback is issued, but TRUNCATE will not generate undo.
- TRUNCATE is DDL and, like all DDL, performs an implicit commit—you cannot roll back a TRUNCATE. Any uncommitted DML changes will also be committed with the TRUNCATE.

- TRUNCATE resets the high-water mark in the table and all indexes. Since full-table scans and index fast full scans read all data blocks up to the high-water mark, full-scan performance after a DELETE will not improve; after a TRUNCATE, it will be very fast.
- TRUNCATE does not fire any DELETE triggers.
- There is no object privilege that can be granted to allow a user to truncate another user's table. The DROP ANY TABLE system privilege is required to truncate a table in another schema. See Chapter 10, "User Access and Security," for more information about getting around this limitation.
- When a table is truncated, the storage for the table and all indexes can be reset back to the initial size. A DELETE will never shrink the size of a table or its indexes.
- You cannot truncate the parent table from an enabled referential integrity constraint. You must first disable the foreign key constraints that reference the parent table, and then you can truncate the parent table. The following example demonstrates this:

```
ALTER TABLE employees
  DISABLE CONSTRAINT emp_dept_fk;
ALTER TABLE job_history
  DISABLE CONSTRAINT jhist_dept_fk;
TRUNCATE TABLE departments;
```

Understanding the TRUNCATE statement—how it differs from the DELETE statement and especially the fact that it will perform a commit—is important and may appear as an exam question.

TRUNCATE versus *DROP TABLE*

Using TRUNCATE is also different from dropping and re-creating a table. Compared to dropping and recreating a table, TRUNCATE does *not* do the following:

- Invalidate dependent objects
- Drop indexes, triggers, or referential integrity constraints
- Require privileges to be regranted

Selecting Rows *FOR UPDATE*

The SELECT FOR UPDATE statement is used to lock specific rows, preventing other sessions from changing or deleting those locked rows. When the rows are locked, other sessions can select these rows, but they cannot change or lock these rows. The syntax for this statement is identical to a SELECT statement, except you append the keywords FOR UPDATE to the statement. The locks acquired for a SELECT FOR UPDATE will not be released until the transaction ends with a COMMIT or ROLLBACK, even if no data changes.

```
SELECT product_id, warehouse_id, quantity_on_hand
FROM   oe.inventories
WHERE  quantity_on_hand < 5
FOR UPDATE;
```

Locking a Table

The LOCK statement is used to lock an entire table, preventing other sessions from performing most or all DML on it. Figure 6.7 shows the LOCK statement's syntax.

FIGURE 6.7 The syntax for the LOCK statement

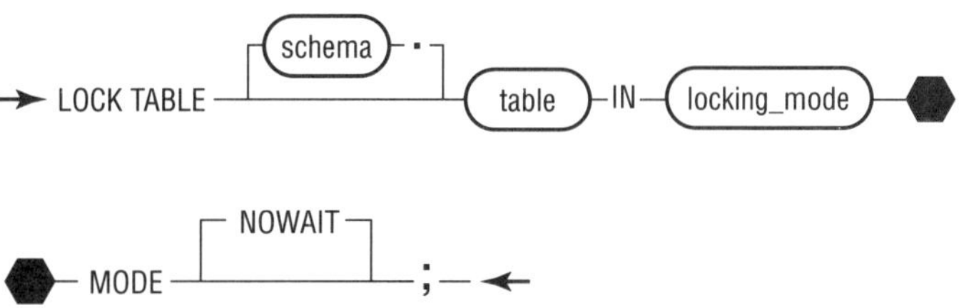

Locking can be in either shared or exclusive mode. Shared mode prevents other sessions from acquiring an exclusive lock but allows other sessions to acquire a shared lock. Exclusive mode prevents other sessions from acquiring either a shared or an exclusive lock.

```
LOCK TABLE inventories IN EXCLUSIVE MODE;
```

Changes to data require an exclusive lock on the rows changed. When table locks are explicitly used, the chances for deadlocks increase. Therefore, use table locks cautiously and sparingly.

Deadlocks

A *deadlock* occurs when two transactions hold locks and each is waiting for a lock held by the other session. In the sample sessions below, two users hold clashing locks. Oracle detects this deadlock condition (usually within a couple of seconds) and raises an exception in one of the sessions. Table 6.2 shows how this works.

TABLE 6.2 Deadlock Detection

Jerie's Session	Time Point	Aly's Session
`UPDATE oe.customers SET credit_limit=1200 WHERE customer_id=754;` *RX locks acquired for updated rows*	101	
	102	`UPDATE oe.customers SET account_mgr_id=149 WHERE customer_id=843;` *RX locks acquired for updated rows*
`UPDATE oe.customers SET credit_limit=1200 WHERE customer_id=843;` *Waiting for Aly's session to complete*	103	
	104	`UPDATE oe.customers SET account_mgr_id=149 WHERE customer_id=754;` *Waiting for Jerie's session to complete*

TABLE 6.2 Deadlock Detection *(continued)*

Jerie's Session	Time Point	Aly's Session
ERROR at line 1: *ORA-00060: deadlock detected while waiting for resource*		

DML Locks in Oracle

Oracle uses DML locks to manage *concurrency*: multiple sessions modifying the same data at the same time. Oracle employs both table and row locks. Row locks are always exclusive, and table locks can be either share or exclusive. *Share locks* prevent other exclusive locks but allow other share locks. *Exclusive locks* prevent both other share locks and other exclusive locks. However, no DML locks prevent read access. To change data, Oracle must acquire an exclusive row-level lock on the rows that are changed. `INSERT`, `UPDATE`, `DELETE`, and `SELECT FOR UPDATE` statements implicitly acquire the necessary row locks. The five types of table locks that Oracle uses are described in the paragraphs that follow and are listed in Table 6.3.

Row Share (SS) A *row share (SS)* lock is acquired implicitly via a `SELECT FOR UPDATE` statement or explicitly with a `LOCK TABLE IN ROW SHARE MODE` statement. An SS lock does not prevent changes to data rows but does prevent another session from getting an exclusive table lock. An SS lock allows multiple, concurrent row share and row exclusive locks, as well as a table share or a share row exclusive lock.

Row Exclusive (RX) A *row exclusive (RX)* lock is acquired implicitly via an `INSERT`, `UPDATE`, or `DELETE` statement or explicitly with a `LOCK TABLE IN ROW EXCLUSIVE MODE` statement. This lock prevents other sessions from acquiring a share, share row exclusive, or exclusive lock.

Share (S) A *share (S)* lock is explicitly acquired with a `LOCK TABLE IN SHARE MODE` statement. This lock prevents other sessions from acquiring RX locks (`INSERT`, `UPDATE`, or `DELETE`) or other table locks (share row exclusive or exclusive). It allows multiple, concurrent SS and S locks on the table. Locking a table in share mode can give your session a transaction-level consistency for the locked table, because no other sessions can make changes to the locked table until you commit or roll back the transaction, releasing the table lock.

Share Row Exclusive (SRX) A *share row exclusive (SRX)* lock is explicitly acquired with a `LOCK TABLE IN SHARE ROW EXCLUSIVE MODE` statement. This lock prevents other sessions from acquiring a share, row exclusive, or exclusive lock. It allows other RS locks. It is similar to the share lock, except that only one SRX lock can be placed on a table at a time. If session Y has an SRX lock on a table, session Z can perform a `SELECT FOR UPDATE` (SS lock), but will wait if it tries to then update (RX) the rows selected.

Exclusive (X) An *exclusive (X)* lock is explicitly acquired on a table with a `LOCK TABLE IN EXCLUSIVE MODE` statement. This lock prevents other sessions from acquiring any other share or exclusive locks on the table. Other sessions are limited to selecting from the exclusively locked table.

TABLE 6.3 Lock Modes

Lock	Prevents	Allows	Acquiring Statements
SS (Row Share)	X	SS, RX, S, SRX	`SELECT FOR UPDATE` `LOCK TABLE`

RX (Row Exclusive)	X, SRX, S	SS	`INSERT`
			`MERGE`
			`UPDATE`
			`DELETE`
			`LOCK TABLE`

S (Share)	X, SRX, RX	SS, S	`LOCK TABLE`
SRX (Share Row Exclusive)	X, SRX, S, RX	SS	`LOCK TABLE`
X (Exclusive)	X, SRX, S, RX, SS		`LOCK TABLE`

Table 6.4 shows two hypothetical sessions: user Alan and user Molly executing DDL and DML on the same table.

TABLE 6.4 Examples of Locking Sessions

Molly's Session	Time Point	Alan's Session
`UPDATE oe.customers SET credit_limit=1200 WHERE customer_id=754;` *RX locks acquired for updated rows*	201	
	202	`TRUNCATE TABLE customers;` *ERROR at line 1:* *ORA-00054: resource busy and acquire with NOWAIT specified* ***DDL is blocked by the RX lock***
	203	`LOCK TABLE oe.customers IN EXCLUSIVE MODE NOWAIT;` *...ORA-00054: resource busy...*
	204	`LOCK TABLE oe.customers IN EXCLUSIVE MODE;` *Waiting for Molly's session*
`COMMIT;`	205	*Table locked*
`UPDATE oe.customers SET credit_limit=1200 WHERE customer_id=843;` *Waiting for Alan's session*	206	
Update complete	207	`ROLLBACK;`
`LOCK TABLE oe.customers IN ROW EXCLUSIVE MODE;`	208	
	209	`LOCK TABLE oe.customers IN SHARE ROW EXCLUSIVE MODE NOWAIT;` *...ORA-00054: resource busy...*
	210	`LOCK TABLE oe.customers IN ROW EXCLUSIVE MODE;`

TABLE 6.4 Examples of Locking Sessions *(continued)*

Molly's Session	Time Point	Alan's Session
	211	`UPDATE oe.customers SET account_mgr_id=149 WHERE customer_id=754;`
	212	`COMMIT;`
`UPDATE oe.customers SET credit_limit=1200 WHERE customer_id=930;`	213	
`COMMIT;`	214	
`LOCK TABLE customers IN SHARE ROW EXCLUSIVE MODE;`	215	
	216	`LOCK TABLE oe.customers IN SHARE MODE NOWAIT;` *...ORA-00054: resource busy...*
	217	`UPDATE oe.customers SET account_mgr_id=149 WHERE customer_id=931;` *Waiting on Molly's session*
`COMMIT;`	218	*Customers updated*
`SELECT credit_limit FROM oe.customers WHERE customer_id=931 FOR UPDATE NOWAIT;` *...ORA-00054: resource busy...*	219	
	220	`COMMIT;`
`LOCK TABLE oe.customer IN ROW SHARE MODE;`	221	

TABLE 6.4 Examples of Locking Sessions *(continued)*

Molly's Session	Time Point	Alan's Session
	222	`INSERT INTO oe.customer...`
	223	`COMMIT;`
`LOCK TABLE oe.customer IN SHARE MODE;`	224	
	225	`INSERT INTO oe.customer...` *Waiting for Molly's session*
`COMMIT;`	226	
	227	`COMMIT;`

Understanding Transaction Control

Transaction control involves coordinating multiple concurrent access to the same data. When one session is changing data that another session is accessing, Oracle uses *transactions* to control who has visibility to what changing data, and when they can see that data. Transactions represent an atomic unit of work. All changes to data in a transaction are applied together or rolled back (undone) together.

There are a number of statements in SQL that let the programmer control transactions. Using transaction-control statements, the programmer can do the following:

- Explicitly begin a transaction, choosing statement-level consistency or transaction-level consistency
- Set undo savepoints and undo changes back to a savepoint
- End a transaction by making the changes permanent or undoing the changes
- Explicitly begin a transaction, allocating a specific rollback segment for use in the transaction

Table 6.5 summarizes the transaction-control statements.

TABLE 6.5 Transaction Control Statements

Statement	Purpose
COMMIT	Ends the current transaction, making data changes permanent and visible to other sessions
ROLLBACK	Undoes all data changes in the current transaction
ROLLBACK TO SAVEPOINT	Undoes all data changes in the current transactions going chronologically backwards to the optionally named savepoint
SET TRANSACTION	Enables transaction or statement consistency; specifies named rollback segment for transaction use

Throughout this section, we will use a banking example to clarify transactional concepts and the control statements used to ensure data is changed as designed. In our example, we have a banking customer named Kiesha, who has a checking account and a brokerage account with her bank.

When Kiesha transfers $5,000 from her checking account to her brokerage account, the balance in her checking account is reduced by $5,000, and the cash balance in her brokerage account is increased by $5,000. We cannot allow only one account to change—they must both change or neither must change. To couple these changes, we issued the two UPDATE statements and the two log statements in a single transaction. If there is any failure in one of these four statements (say, perhaps, an index on the CHECKING_LOG table hits MAXEXTENTS), then none of the changes will go through. The changes will only be committed and made permanent if all four statements succeed. See Figure 6.8 for an example of a transaction.

A transaction will implicitly begin with an INSERT, UPDATE, DELETE, or SELECT FOR UPDATE statement. The transaction will always end with either an implicit or explicit COMMIT or ROLLBACK statement. A ROLLBACK TO SAVEPOINT statement will not end a transaction.

FIGURE 6.8 An example of a banking transaction

Implicitly begin the transaction → UPDATE checking

Keep the changes and the transaction → COMMIT;

Undo the changes and end the transaction → ROLLBACK;

```
BEGIN
  -- Change the checking account
  UPDATE checking
    SET balance = balance - 5000
    WHERE account = 'Kiesha';

  -- Record the transaction in the checking log table
  INSERT INTO checking_log (action_date, action, amount)
    VALUES (SYSDATE, 'Transfer to brokerage', 5000);

  -- Change the brokerage account
  UPDATE brokerage
    SET cash_balance = cash_balance + 5000
    WHERE account = 'Kiesha'

  -- Record the transaction in the brokerage log table
  INSERT INTO brokerage_log (action_date, action, amount)
    VALUES (SYSDATE, 'Transfer from checking',5000);

  -- Make the changes permanent
  -- and visible to other sessions
  COMMIT;

  EXCEPTION
    WHEN OTHERS THEN
      ROLLBACK;
END;
```

Savepoints and Partial Rollbacks

Savepoints are intermediate fallback positions in SQL code. The ROLLBACK TO SAVEPOINT statement is used to undo changes chronologically back to the last savepoint or to the named savepoint. Savepoints are not used extensively in industry. However, you must understand them, because there will likely be a question related to savepoints on the exam. Savepoints are not labels for goto statements, and ROLLBACK TO SAVEPOINT is not a goto. The code after a savepoint does not get re-executed after a ROLLBACK TO SAVEPOINT—only the data changes made since that savepoint are undone.

Again, an example will help clarify. Kiesha tries to withdraw $100 from her checking account. We want to log her request in the ATM activity log, but if she has insufficient funds, we don't want to change her balance and will deny her request.

```
INSERT INTO ATM_LOG(who, when, what, where)
  VALUES('Kiesha', SYSDATE, 'Withdrawal of $100','ATM54');
SAVEPOINT ATM_logged;
```

```
UPDATE checking
  SET balance = balance - 100
  RETURNING balance INTO new_balance;

IF new_balance < 0
THEN
  ROLLBACK TO ATM_logged; -- undo update
  COMMIT; -- keep changes prior to savepoint (insert)
  RAISE insufficient_funds; -- Raise error/deny request
END IF;
COMMIT; -- keep insert and update
```

The keyword SAVEPOINT is optional, so the following two statements are equivalent:

```
ROLLBACK TO ATM_logged;
ROLLBACK TO SAVEPOINT ATM_logged;
```

Because savepoints are not frequently used, always include the keyword SAVEPOINT in any ROLLBACK TO SAVEPOINT statement. That way, anyone reading the code will be reminded of the keyword SAVEPOINT, making it easier to recognize that a partial rollback has occurred.

Consistency and Transactions

Consistency is one of the key concepts underlying the use of transaction-control statements. Understanding Oracle's consistency model will enable you to employ transaction control appropriately and answer exam questions on transaction control correctly. Oracle implements consistency to guarantee that the data seen by a statement or transaction does not change until that statement or transaction completes. This support is only germane to multiuser databases, where one database session can change (and commit) data that is being read by another session.

Oracle always uses statement-level consistency, which ensures that the data visible to a statement does not change during the life of that statement. Transactions can consist of one or more statements. When used, transaction-level consistency will ensure that the data visible to all statements in a transaction does not change for the life of the transaction.

Our banking example will help clarify: Matt starts running a total-balance report against the checking account table at 10:00 a.m.; this report takes five minutes. During those five minutes, the data that he is reporting on changes when Kiesha transfers $5,000 from her checking account to her brokerage account. When Matt's session gets to Kiesha's checking account record, it will need to reconstruct what the record looked like at 10:00 a.m. Matt's session will examine the rollback segment that Kiesha used during her account-transfer transaction and re-create the image of what the checking account table looked like at 10:00 a.m.

Next, at 10:05 a.m., Matt runs a total balance report on the cash in the brokerage account table. If he is using transaction-level consistency, his session will re-create what the brokerage account table looked like at 10:00 a.m. (and exclude Kiesha's transfer). If Matt's session is using the default statement-level consistency, his session will report on what the brokerage account table looked like at 10:05 a.m. (and include Kiesha's transfer).

Oracle never uses locks for reading operations, since reading operations will never block writing operations. Instead, the rollback segments are used to re-create the image needed. Rollback segments are released for reuse when the transaction writing to them commits or if `undo_management` is set to `auto` and the `undo_retention` period is exceeded, so sometimes a consistent image cannot be re-created. When this happens, Oracle raises either a "snapshot too old" exception or a "can't serialize access for this transaction" exception. Using our example, if Matt's transaction can't locate Kiesha's transaction in the rollback segments because it was overwritten, Matt's transaction will not be able to re-create the 10:00 a.m. image of the table and will fail.

Oracle implements consistency internally through the use of System Change Numbers (SCNs). An SCN is a time-oriented, database internal key. The SCN only increases, never decreases, and represents a point in time for comparison purposes. So, in our previous example, Oracle internally assigns Matt's first statement the current SCN when it starts reading the checking account table. This starting SCN is compared to each data block's SCN. If the data block SCN is higher (newer), then the rollback segments are examined to find the older version of the data.

Enabling Transaction-Level or Statement-Level Consistency

One of the uses of the `SET TRANSACTION` statement is to enable either transaction-level or statement-level consistency. The keywords `ISOLATION LEVEL READ COMMITTED` indicate statement-level consistency (this is the default). The keywords ISOLATION LEVEL SERIALIZABLE indicate transaction-level consistency. Here are some examples:

```
SET TRANSACTION ISOLATION LEVEL SERIALIZABLE;

SET TRANSACTION ISOLATION LEVEL READ COMMITTED;
```

Transaction-level consistency can also be enabled for transactions that only read (do not modify) data, with this statement:

```
SET TRANSACTION READ ONLY;
```

Any attempts to change data in a read-only transaction will raise an exception. Therefore, read-only transactions can use only the following statements:

- SELECT (without a FOR UPDATE clause)
- LOCK TABLE
- SET ROLE
- ALTER SYSTEM
- ALTER SESSION

To end the read-only transaction, you must execute a COMMIT or ROLLBACK statement. The COMMIT or ROLLBACK is necessary to end the transaction, even though no data has changed.

Specifying a Rollback Segment for a Transaction

The other use of the SET TRANSACTION statement is to direct Oracle to use a specifically named rollback segment for the transaction. This usage is most common in environments that have mostly small transactions, with a few large transactions that require significant rollback segment space for undo. This use is not applicable to system-managed undo.

By default, Oracle allocates rollback segments to transactions using a round-robin algorithm. A particularly large transaction can therefore be assigned to any rollback segment and cause that rollback segment to grow significantly in size. This dynamic space management can have negative performance and disk-space implications. To avoid the random assignment of the large transaction to any rollback segment, begin the large transaction with a SET TRANSACTION statement such as this one:

```
SET TRANSACTION USE ROLLBACK SEGMENT rb_large;
```

where *rb_large* is the name of the large rollback segment. By specifically assigning the large transaction to a large rollback segment, the other (small) rollback segments will not undergo dynamic space management.

When Would You Assign a Transaction to a Rollback Segment?

Suppose that we have a rollback segment tablespace that is 2GB in size, and we need ten rollback segments to accommodate our peak online users. These peak online users have only small transactions. Once a week, we have four large transactions run one after another. These large transactions, which delete and load data, require 1GB of undo each. Our rollback segments are sized as follows:

```
rb_large (INITIAL 100M NEXT 100M MINEXTENTS 2)

rb1 (INITIAL 1M NEXT 1M MINEXTENTS 5)

rb2 (INITIAL 1M NEXT 1M MINEXTENTS 5)

rb3 (INITIAL 1M NEXT 1M MINEXTENTS 5)

rb4 (INITIAL 1M NEXT 1M MINEXTENTS 5)

rb5 (INITIAL 1M NEXT 1M MINEXTENTS 5)

rb6 (INITIAL 1M NEXT 1M MINEXTENTS 5)

rb7 (INITIAL 1M NEXT 1M MINEXTENTS 5)

rb8 (INITIAL 1M NEXT 1M MINEXTENTS 5)

rb9 (INITIAL 1M NEXT 1M MINEXTENTS 5)
```

These ten rollback segments all fit nicely in the 2GB tablespace. If we used the default round-robin allocation, our four large transactions would use four separate rollback segments, and they would try to expand each of these four to 1GB. Four 1GB segments won't fit in our 2GB tablespace, and the DBA would get paged at 2 A.M., when the job fails. To avoid this, we begin each of our four large transactions with the following statements:

```
SET TRANSACTION USE ROLLBACK SEGMENT rb_large;
```

Now, our four large transactions, which run serially, reuse the same large rollback segment. We can keep our rollback segment tablespace at 2GB (and the DBA can sleep all night).

Summary

In this chapter, you saw how to modify data. This includes the DML statements `INSERT`, `UPDATE`, `MERGE`, and `DELETE`, along with `SELECT FOR UPDATE` and `LOCK TABLE`. The DDL statement `TRUNCATE` has similarities to `DELETE`, but the two statements also have important differences.

We discussed concurrency and how to use locks to manage concurrent changes, as well as what causes deadlocks. We also discussed consistency and how to use transactions to manage consistency. The `SET TRANSACTION` statement is usually used to set statement-level or transaction-level consistency, but it can also be used to explicitly assign a transaction to a specific rollback segment.

Exam Essentials

Know the syntax for a multiple-table insert. The multiple-table `INSERT` statement is new in Oracle9i and slightly different from the traditional single-table `INSERT` statement. The multiple-table `INSERT` statement can specify `ALL` or `FIRST` and uses a `WHEN` *`condition`* `THEN` clause.

Know what a deadlock is and how Oracle resolves one. A deadlock occurs when two sessions are blocked, waiting on locks held by the other session. Oracle recognizes a deadlock condition and terminates one of the sessions. No DBA involvement is required.

Know how a TRUNCATE statement differs from a DELETE statement. The `TRUNCATE` statement will immediately commit the data changes (no `ROLLBACK` is allowed), will not fire the `after delete` triggers (if any exist), and will reset the high-water mark on the table. The `DELETE` statement requires a `COMMIT` or `ROLLBACK` to confirm the data changes, fires all appropriate triggers, and does not affect the table's high-water mark.

Understand what will begin and end a transaction. A transaction will begin with an `INSERT`, `UPDATE`, `DELETE`, `MERGE`, `SELECT FOR UPDATE`, or `SET TRANSACTION` statement. A `COMMIT` or `ROLLBACK` will end a transaction.

Know how to set and roll back to savepoints. Savepoints are set with the `SAVEPOINT` statement. Data changes made after a savepoint are undone when a `ROLLBACK TO SAVEPOINT` statement is executed. A `ROLLBACK TO SAVEPOINT` is a *partial* undo operation.

Understand the scope of data changes and consistency. Statement-level consistency is automatic and will ensure that each `SELECT` will see an image of the database consistent with the beginning of the statement's execution. Transaction-level consistency will ensure that all `SELECT` statements within a transaction will see an image of the database consistent with the beginning of the transaction.

Key Terms

Before you take the exam, make sure you're familiar with the following terms:

concurrency	consistency
Data Definition Language (DDL)	Data Manipulation Language (DML)
deadlock	exclusive lock
row exclusive lock	row share lock
savepoint	share lock
share row exclusive lock	statement
transaction	

Review Questions

1. Which of the following statements will succeed?

```
1. merge into product_descriptions p
   using (select product_id, language_id
                ,translated_name
   from products_for_2003) p2003
   where (p.product_id = p2003.product_id)
   when matched then update
   set p.language=p2003.language_id
      ,p.translated_name = p2003.translated_name
   when not matched then insert
      (p.product_id, p.language_id
       ,p.translated_name)
      values (p2003.product_id,p2003.language_id
             ,p2003.translated_name);

2. merge into product_descriptions p
   using (select product_id, language_id
                ,translated_name
   from products_for_2003) p2003
   on (p.product_id = p2003.product_id)
   when matched then update
   set p.language=p2003.language_id
      ,p.translated_name = p2003.translated_name
   when not matched then insert
      (p.product_id, p.language_id
       ,p.translated_name)
      values (p2003.product_id,p2003.language_id
             ,p2003.translated_name);

3. merge into product_descriptions p
   using (select product_id, language_id
                ,translated_name
   from products_for_2003) p2003
   join on (p.product_id = p2003.product_id)
```

```
when matched then update
set p.language=p2003.language_id
   ,p.translated_name = p2003.translated_name
when not matched then insert
   (p.product_id, p.language_id
    ,p.translated_name)
   values (p2003.product_id,p2003.language_id
          ,p2003.translated_name);
```

A. Statement 1

B. Statement 2

C. Statement 3

D. They all fail.

2. Which of the following statements will not implicitly begin a transaction?

   A. `INSERT`

   B. `UPDATE`

   C. `DELETE`

   D. `SELECT FOR UPDATE`

   E. None of the above; they all implicitly begin a transaction.

3. If Julio executes a `LOCK TABLE IN SHARE ROW EXCLUSIVE MODE` statement, with which of the following statements will Marisa *not* wait for Julio's commit or rollback?

   A. `INSERT`

   B. `SELECT FOR UPDATE`

   C. `LOCK TABLE IN SHARE MODE`

   D. `LOCK TABLE IN EXCLUSIVE MODE`

   E. None of the above; all will wait.

4. Which of the following statements does not end a transaction?

   A. `LOCK TABLE IN EXCLUSIVE MODE`

   B. `COMMIT`

   C. `ALTER USER`

   D. `CREATE INDEX`

5. Choose the maximum number of tables into which rows can be inserted via a single `INSERT` statement.

   A. 1

   B. 2

   C. No more than 16

   D. Unlimited

6. Can you execute an `ALTER INDEX REBUILD` while there are uncommitted updates on a table?

   A. No, it will always fail with a resource busy error.

   B. Yes, but you must specify the keyword `WAIT` to wait for the commit or rollback.

   C. Yes, the row exclusive locks from the `UPDATE` statements only block other changes to the same rows.

   D. Yes, but only if the updates do not change the indexed columns.

7. Which of the following statements will begin a transaction using transaction-level read consistency?

   A. `ALTER SESSION USE TRANSACTION CONSISTENCY;`

   B. `BEGIN TRANSACTION USING TRANSACTION CONSISTENCY;`

   C. `BEGIN SERIALIZABLE TRANSACTION;`

   D. `SET TRANSACTION ISOLATION LEVEL SERIALIZABLE;`

8. Which of the following statements will improve the performance of a full-table scan on the PROCESS_ORDER_STAGE table?

   A. `DELETE FROM process_order_stages;`

   B. `TRUNCATE TABLE process_order_stage;`

   C.
   ```
   CREATE INDEX ord_idx2 ON
   process_order_stage (customer_id);
   ```

   D.
   ```
   ALTER SESSION
   SET hash_area_size 16613376;
   ```

9. The following table shows two concurrent transactions. What happens at time point 9?

Session A	Time	Session B
`UPDATE customers SET region='H' WHERE state='43' and county='046';`	6	
	7	`UPDATE customers SET mgr=4567 WHERE state='47' and county='072';`
`UPDATE customers SET region='H' WHERE state='47' and county='072';`	8	
	9	`UPDATE customers SET mgr=4567 WHERE state='43' and county='046';`

A. Session B will wait for session A to commit or roll back.

B. Session A will wait for session B to commit or roll back.

C. A deadlock will occur, and both sessions will hang until the DBA kills one or until one of the users cancels their statement.

D. A deadlock will occur, and Oracle will cancel one of the statements.

E. Both sessions are not updating the same column, so no waiting or deadlocks will occur.

10. The following table shows two concurrent transactions. Which statement about the result returned in session A at time point 16 is most true?

Session A	Time	Session B
`SELECT SUM(deposit_amt) FROM transaction_log WHERE deposit_date > TRUNC(SYSDATE);`	12	
	13	`INSERT INTO transaction_log (deposit_date, deposit_amt) VALUES (SYSDATE, 6247.00);`
	14	`COMMIT;`
Table scan for the active SELECT reaches the data block where session B's row was inserted.	15	
Table scan complete results returned.	16	

A. The results would include the changes committed by transaction B at time point 14.

B. The results would not include the changes committed by transaction B at time point 14.

C. The results would include the changes committed by transaction B at time point 14 if the two sessions were connected to the database as the same user.

D. Session A would raise a "snapshot too old" exception.

11. The following table shows two concurrent transactions. Which statement about the results returned in session A at time points 16 and 18 is most true?

Session A	Time	Session B
`SET TRANSACTION ISOLATION LEVEL READ COMMITTED;`	11	
`SELECT SUM(deposit_amt) FROM transaction_log WHERE deposit_date > TRUNC(SYSDATE);`	12	
	13	`INSERT INTO transaction_log (deposit_date, deposit_amt) VALUES (SYSDATE, 6247.00);`
	14	`COMMIT;`
Table scan for the active SELECT reaches the data block where session B's row was inserted.	15	
Table scan complete, results returned.	16	
`SELECT SUM(deposit_amt) FROM transaction_log WHERE deposit_date > TRUNC(SYSDATE);`	17	
Table scan complete, results returned.	18	

A. The results would be identical.

B. The results would be different.

C. The results would be identical only if the two sessions were connected to the database as the same user.

D. Both statements would include the data committed by transaction B at time point 14.

12. The following table shows two concurrent transactions. Which statement about the results returned in session A at time point 16 and 18 is most true?

Session A	Time	Session B
`SET TRANSACTION ISOLATION LEVEL SERIALIZABLE;`	11	
`SELECT SUM(deposit_amt) FROM transaction_log WHERE deposit_date > TRUNC(SYSDATE);`	12	
	13	`INSERT INTO transaction_log (deposit_date, deposit_amt) VALUES (SYSDATE, 6247.00);`
	14	`COMMIT;`
Table scan for the active SELECT reaches the data block where session B's row was inserted.	15	
Table scan complete results returned.	16	
`SELECT SUM(deposit_amt) FROM transaction_log WHERE deposit_date > TRUNC(SYSDATE);`	17	
Table scan complete results returned.	18	

A. The results would be identical.

B. The results would be different.

C. The results would be identical only if the two sessions were connected to the database as the same user.

D. Both statements would include the data committed by transaction B at time point 14.

13. You have a DELETE statement that will generate a large amount of undo. One rollback segment, named RB_LARGE, is larger than the others. How would you force the use of this rollback segment for the DELETE operation?

    A. `ALTER SESSION USE ROLLBACK SEGMENT rb_large;`

    B. `SET TRANSACTION USE ROLLBACK SEGMENT rb_large;`

    C. `BEGIN WORK USING ROLLBACK SEGMENT rb_large`

    D. You cannot force the use of a specific rollback segment.

14. The following table describes the DEPARTMENTS table.

Column Name	dept_id	dept_name	mgr_id	location_id
Key Type	pk			
NULLs/Unique	NN			
FK Table				
Datatype	NUMBER	VARCHAR2	NUMBER	NUMBER
Length	4	30	6	4
Default Value	None	None	None	None

Which of the following INSERT statements will raise an exception?

A.
```
INSERT INTO departments (dept_id, dept_name, location_
id)
VALUES(280,'Security',1700);
```

B.
```
INSERT INTO departments
VALUES(280,'Security',1700);
```

C.
```
INSERT INTO departments
VALUES(280,'Corporate Giving',266,1700);
```

D. None of these statements will raise an exception.

15. The SALES table contains the following data:

```
SELECT channel_id, COUNT(*)
FROM sales
WHERE channel_id IN ('T','I')
GROUP BY channel_id;

C   COUNT(*)
- ----------
T      12000
I      24000
```

How many rows will be inserted into the NEW_CHANNEL_SALES table with the following SQL statement?

```
INSERT FIRST
 WHEN channel_id ='C' THEN
   INTO catalog_sales (prod_id,time_id,promo_id
                      ,amount_sold)
        VALUES (prod_id,time_id,promo_id,amount_sold)
 WHEN channel_id ='I' THEN
   INTO internet_sales (prod_id,time_id,promo_id
                       ,amount_sold)
        VALUES (prod_id,time_id,promo_id,amount_sold)
 WHEN  channel_id IN ('I','T') THEN
   INTO new_channel_sales (prod_id,time_id,promo_id
                          ,amount_sold)
        VALUES (prod_id,time_id,promo_id,amount_sold)
SELECT channel_id,prod_id,time_id,promo_id,amount_sold
FROM sales;
```

A. 0

B. 12,000

C. 24,000

D. 36,000

16. How many rows will be counted in the last SQL statement that follows?

```
SELECT COUNT(*) FROM emp;
  120 returned

INSERT INTO emp (emp_id)
   VALUES (140);
SAVEPOINT emp140;

INSERT INTO emp (emp_id)
   VALUES (141);
INSERT INTO emp (emp_id)
   VALUES (142);
INSERT INTO emp (emp_id)
   VALUES (143);
TRUNCATE TABLE emp;
INSERT INTO emp (emp_id)
   VALUES (144);

ROLLBACK;

SELECT COUNT(*) FROM emp;
```

A. 121

B. 1

C. 0

D. 143

17. Which of the following statements will raise an exception in a transaction that starts with `SET TRANSACTION READ ONLY`?

A. `ALTER SYSTEM`

B. `SELECT`

C. `ALTER USER`

D. `SET ROLE`

18. Which of the following statements will raise an exception?

A. `LOCK TABLE SALES IN EXCLUSIVE MODE;`

B. `LOCK TABLE SALES IN ROW SHARE EXCLUSIVE MODE;`

C. `LOCK TABLE SALES IN SHARE ROW EXCLUSIVE MODE;`

D. `LOCK TABLE SALES IN ROW EXCLUSIVE MODE;`

19. Which of the following INSERT statements will raise an exception?

A. `INSERT INTO EMP SELECT * FROM NEW_EMP;`

B. `INSERT FIRST WHEN DEPT_NO IN (12,14) THEN INSERT INTO EMP SELECT * FROM NEW_EMP;`

C. `INSERT FIRST WHEN DEPT_NO IN (12,14) THEN INTO EMP SELECT * FROM NEW_EMP;`

D. `INSERT ALL WHEN DEPT_NO IN (12,14) THEN INTO EMP SELECT * FROM NEW_EMP;`

20. What will the salary of employee Arsinoe be at the completion of the following SQL statements?

```
UPDATE emp
  SET salary = 1000
  WHERE name = 'Arsinoe';
SAVEPOINT Point_A

UPDATE emp
  SET  salary = salary * 1.1
  WHERE name = 'Arsinoe';
SAVEPOINT Point_B;

UPDATE emp
  SET  salary = salary * 1.1
  WHERE name = 'Berenike';
SAVEPOINT point_C;

ROLLBACK TO SAVEPOINT point_b;
COMMIT;
```

```
UPDATE emp
  SET salary = 1500
  WHERE name = 'Arsinoe';
SAVEPOINT point_d;

ROLLBACK TO point_d;

COMMIT;
```

A. 1000

B. 1100

C. 1111

D. 1500

Answers to Review Questions

1. B. The correct syntax uses an ON clause as in option B. The WHERE in option A and the JOIN ON clause in option C are not valid.

2. E. If a transaction is not currently open, any INSERT, UPDATE, MERGE, DELETE, SELECT FOR UPDATE, or LOCK statement will implicitly begin a transaction.

3. B. The row share exclusive mode will block other share, exclusive, and row exclusive locks, but not row share locks.

4. A. COMMIT, ROLLBACK, and any DDL statement ends a transaction —DDL is automatically committed. LOCK TABLE is DML, like INSERT, UPDATE, DELETE, or MERGE, and requires a commit or rollback.

5. D. A single INSERT statement can insert data into an unlimited number of tables. This multiple-table insert capability is new in Oracle9i.

6. A. The row exclusive locks from the update will block all DDL, including DDL on the indexes—it does not matter which columns the index is on. You cannot specify WAIT on DDL.

7. D. Transaction-level consistency is obtained with a serializable isolation level. An isolation level of read committed identifies statement-level read consistency.

8. B. A TRUNCATE operation will reset the high-water mark on a table, so when a full-table scan (that scans to the high-water mark) is executed against the table, it will run very fast. Delete operations do not affect the high-water mark or full-scan performance. Indexes and hash_area_size do not affect full-scan performance.

9. D. At time point 8, session A will wait for session B. At time point 9, a deadlock will occur; Oracle will recognize it and cancel one of the statements. Oracle locks to the granularity of a row, so even though the columns are different, the locks will still block each other.

10. B. Statement-level read consistency would ensure that the data visible to each statement does not change while the statement is executing. The "snapshot too old" exception might be raised if there were a lot of other transactions committing to the database between time points 12 and 16, but if this exception were raised, the table scan would neither complete nor return results.

11. B. The read-consistent isolation level is statement-level read consistency, so each statement sees the committed data that existed at the beginning of the statement. The committed data at time point 17 includes session B's commit at time point 14.

12. A. The serializable isolation level is transaction-level read-consistency, so both of session A's `SELECT` statements see the same data image. Neither would include the changes committed at time point 14.

13. B. The `SET TRANSACTION` statement can be used to force the use of a specific rollback segment, provided that the `SET TRANSACTION` statement begins the transaction.

14. B. Option B will raise an exception because there are not enough column values for the implicit column list (all columns).

15. B. The `FIRST` clause tells Oracle to execute only the first `WHEN` clause that evaluates to `TRUE`. This statement will insert 12,000 rows into the INTERNET_SALES table and 0 rows into the NEW_CHANNEL_SALES table. If the `ALL` clause were used, 36,000 rows would be inserted into the NEW_CHANNEL_SALES table.

16. C. The `TRUNCATE` statement is DDL and performs an implicit commit. After the `TRUNCATE` statement, there are 0 rows in the table. The one row that was inserted was removed when the `ROLLBACK` statement was executed.

17. C. A read-only transaction will raise an exception if data is changed. Altering a user will change data.

18. B. There are five types of table locks: row share, row exclusive, share, share row exclusive, and exclusive. Row share exclusive mode does not exist.

19. B. The keywords `INSERT INTO` are required in single-table `INSERT` statements, but are not valid in multiple-table `INSERT` statements.

20. D. The final rollback (to point_d) will roll the changes back to just after setting the salary to 1500.

Managing Tables and Constraints

INTRODUCTION TO ORACLE9i: SQL EXAM OBJECTIVES COVERED IN THIS CHAPTER:

✓ **Creating and Managing Tables**

- Describe the main database objects
- Create tables
- Describe the datatypes that can be used when specifying column definition
- Alter table definitions
- Drop, rename and truncate tables

✓ **Including Constraints**

- Describe constraints
- Create and maintain constraints

Exam objectives are subject to change at any time without prior notice and at Oracle's sole discretion. Please visit Oracle's Certification website (`http://www.oracle.com/education/certification/`) for the most current exam objectives listing.

The table is the basic structure of data storage in Oracle. A table has columns as part of the definition and stores rows of data. In a relational database, the data in various tables may be related. A constraint can be considered as a rule or policy defined in the database to enforce data integrity and business rules. In this chapter, we will discuss creating tables and using constraints.

Database Objects Review

Data in the Oracle database is stored in tables. A *table* is the main database object. Many other database objects, whether or not they store data, are based on the tables. Let's review the main database objects in Oracle that are relevant for this test.

Table Defined with columns and stores rows of data. A table should have at least one column. In Oracle, a table normally refers to a relational table. You can also create object tables and temporary tables. Temporary tables are used to hold temporary data specific to a transaction or session. Object tables are created with user-defined datatypes. A table can store a wide variety of data. Apart from storing text and numeric information, you can store date, timestamp, binary, or raw data (such as images, documents, and information about external files).

View A customized representation of data from one or more tables and/or views. Views are used as a window to show information from tables in a certain way or to restrict the information. Views are queries stored in the database that select data from one or more tables. They also provide a way to restrict data from certain users, thus providing an additional level of security. (Views are discussed in detail in Chapter 8, "Managing Views.")

Sequence A way to generate continuous numbers. Sequences are useful for generating unique serial numbers or key values. The sequence definition is stored in the data dictionary. Sequence numbers are generated independently of other database objects. Sequences are discussed in Chapter 9, "Other Database Objects."

Synonym An alias for any table, view, sequence, or other accessible database object. Because a synonym is simply an alias, it requires no storage other than its definition in the data dictionary. Synonyms are useful because they hide the identity of the underlying object. The object can even be part of another database. A public synonym is accessible to all users of the database; and a private synonym is accessible only to its owner. Synonyms are discussed in Chapter 9.

Index A structure associated with tables used to speed up the queries. An index is an access path to reach the desired row faster. Oracle has B-tree and bitmap indexes. Creating and dropping indexes does not affect the storage of data in the underlying tables. You can create unique or nonunique indexes. In most cases unique indexes are created automatically by Oracle when you create a primary key or a unique key constraint in a table. A composite index has more than one column in the index. Indexes are discussed in Chapter 9.

Oracle9i has a wide array of database objects to suit various application requirements. These objects are not discussed in this book because they are not part of this test at this time. Some of the other database objects that may be used in application development are cluster, dimension, directory, function, Java source/class, library, materialized view, and type.

Built-in Datatypes

When creating tables, you must specify a *datatype* for each column you define. Oracle9i is rich with various datatypes to store different kinds of information. By choosing the appropriate datatype, you will be able to store and retrieve data without compromising its integrity. A datatype associates a predefined set of properties with the column.

The datatypes in Oracle9i can be classified into five major categories. Figure 7.1 shows the categories and the datatype names.

FIGURE 7.1 Oracle built-in datatypes

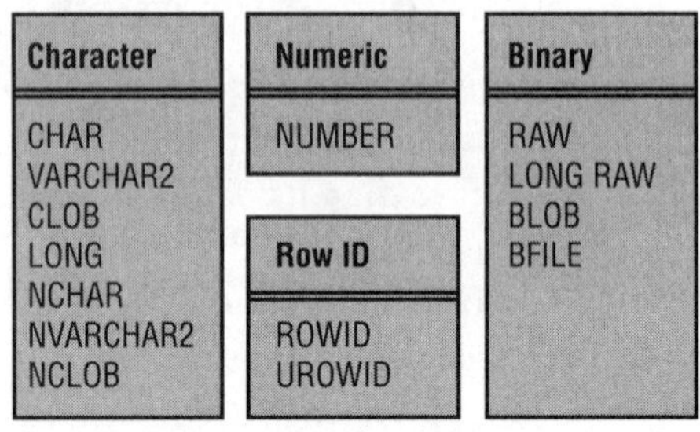

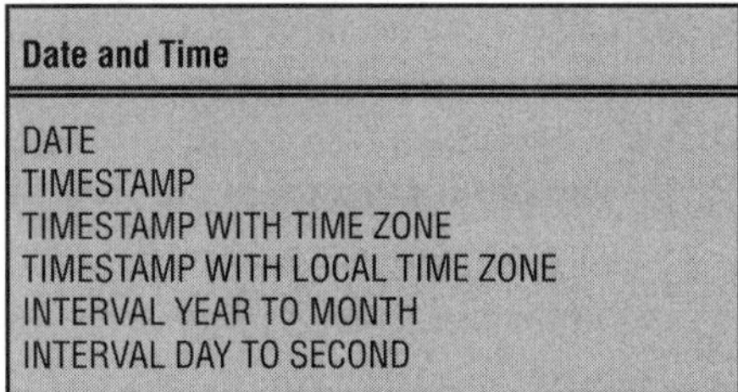

In Chapter 1, "Basic SQL SELECT Statements," we introduced four basic datatypes: CHAR, VARCHAR2, NUMBER, and DATE. Here, we will review those and describe the other datatypes that can be specified while creating a table.

Character Datatypes

There are seven character datatypes that can be used for defining columns in a table:

- CHAR
- VARCHAR2
- CLOB
- LONG
- NCHAR
- NVARCHAR2
- NCLOB

Character datatypes store alphanumeric data, in the database character set or in the Unicode character set. The database character set is specified when you create the database.

The character set determines which languages can be represented in the database. For example, US7ASCII is a 7-bit ASCII character set that can represent the English language and any other language that uses the English alphabet set. WE8ISO8859P1 is an 8-bit character set that can support multiple European languages such as English, German, French, Albanian, Spanish, Portuguese, Irish, and so on, because they all use a similar writing script. Unicode, the Universal Encoded character set, allows you to store any language character using a single character set. Unicode uses either 16-bit encoding (UTF-16) or 8-bit encoding (UTF-8). You can choose the Unicode datatypes to be used in the database while creating the database. The default is the AL16UTF16 character set, which is UTF-16 encoding.

If you try to insert a value into a character datatype column that is larger than its maximum specified size, Oracle will return an error. Oracle will not chop or truncate the inserted value to store it in the database column.

CHAR

Specification `CHAR [(<size> [BYTE | CHAR ] ) ]`

The CHAR datatype is fixed length, with the maximum size of the column specified in parentheses. You may also include the optional keywords BYTE or CHAR inside parentheses along with the size to indicate if the size is in bytes or in characters. BYTE is the default.

For single-byte database character sets (such as US7ASCII), the size specified in bytes and the size specified in characters are the same. If the column value is shorter than the size defined, trailing spaces are added to the column value. Specifying the size is optional, and the default size is 1 byte. The maximum allowed size in a CHAR datatype column is 2000 bytes. Here are a few examples of specifying a CHAR datatype column:

```
employee_id  CHAR (5)
employee_name CHAR (100 CHAR)
employee_sex CHAR
```

NCHAR

Specification `NCHAR [ ( <size> ) ]`

The NCHAR datatype is similar to CHAR, but it is used to store Unicode character set data. The NCHAR datatype is fixed length, with a maximum size of 2000 bytes and a default size of 1 character.

The size in the NCHAR datatype definition is always specified in characters. Trailing spaces are added if the value inserted into the column is shorter than the column's maximum length. Here is an example of specifying an NCHAR datatype column:

```
emp_name NCHAR (100)
```

Several built-in Oracle9i functions have options to represent NCHAR data. An NCHAR string may be represented by prefixing the string with `N`, as in this example:

```
SELECT  emp_name FROM employee_records
WHERE emp_name = N'John Smith';
```

VARCHAR2 or VARCHAR

Specification `VARCHAR2 (<size> [BYTE | CHAR] )`

VARCHAR2 and VARCHAR are synonymous datatypes. VARCHAR2 specifies variable-length character data. A maximum size for the column should be defined; Oracle9i will not assume any default value. Unlike CHAR columns, VARCHAR2 columns are not blank-padded with trailing spaces if the column value is shorter than its maximum specified length. You can specify the size in bytes or characters; by default, the size is in bytes. The range of values allowed for size is from 1 to 4000 bytes. For storing variable-length data, Oracle recommends using VARCHAR2 rather than VARCHAR, because the behavior of the VARCHAR datatype may change in a future release.

NVARCHAR2

Specification `NVARCHAR2 (<size>)`

The NVARCHAR2 datatype is used to store Unicode variable-length data. The size is specified in characters, and the maximum size allowed is 4000 bytes.

CLOB

Specification `CLOB`

CLOB is one of the Large Object datatypes provided to store variable-length character data. The maximum amount of data you can store in a CLOB column is 4GB. You do not specify the size with this datatype definition.

NCLOB

Specification `NCLOB`

NCLOB is one of the Large Object datatypes and stores variable-length Unicode character data. The maximum amount of data you can store in a NCLOB column is 4GB. You do not specify the size with this datatype definition.

LONG

Specification `LONG`

Using the LONG datatype is discouraged by Oracle. It is provided only for backward compatibility. You should use the CLOB datatype instead of LONG. LONG columns can store up to 2GB of data. There can be only one LONG column in the table definition. LONG datatypes cannot appear in `WHERE`, `GROUP BY`, or `ORDER BY` clauses.

Numeric Datatype

There is one built-in numeric datatype that can be used for defining columns in a table: NUMBER.

NUMBER

Specification `NUMBER [ (<precision> [, <scale>] )]`

You can represent all non-Oracle numeric datatypes such as float, integer, decimal, double, and so on, using the NUMBER datatype. The NUMBER datatype can store both fixed-point and floating-point numbers. Oracle also supports the ANSI datatype FLOAT.

Date and Time Datatypes

In pre-Oracle9i databases, the only date/time datatype available is DATE, which stores the date and time. In Oracle9i, the TIMESTAMP and INTERVAL datatypes have been added to enhance the storage and manipulation of date and time data. There are six date/time datatypes that can be used for defining columns in a table:

- DATE
- TIMESTAMP
- TIMESTAMP WITH TIME ZONE
- TIMESTAMP WITH LOCAL TIME ZONE
- INTERVAL YEAR TO MONTH
- INTERVAL DAY TO SECOND

DATE

Specification `DATE`

The DATE datatype stores date and time information. You can store the dates from January 1, 4712 BC to December 31, 9999 AD. If you specify a date value without the time component, the default time is 12 A.M. (midnight, 00:00:00 hours). If you specify a date value without the date component, the default value is the first day of the current month. The DATE datatype stores century, year, month, date, hour, minute, and seconds internally. You can display the dates in various formats using the `NLS_DATE_FORMAT` parameter or by specifying a format mask with the `TO_CHAR` function. The various date format masks are discussed in Chapter 3, "Single-Row Functions."

TIMESTAMP

Specification `TIMESTAMP [(<precision>)]`

The TIMESTAMP datatype stores date and time information with fractional seconds precision. The only difference between the DATE and TIMESTAMP datatypes is the ability to store fractional seconds up to a precision of nine digits. The default precision is 6 and can range from 0 to 9. The TIMESTAMP datatype is new to Oracle9i.

TIMESTAMP WITH TIME ZONE

Specification `TIMESTAMP [(<precision>)] WITH TIME ZONE`

The TIMESTAMP WITH TIME ZONE datatype is similar to the TIMESTAMP datatype, but it stores the *time zone displacement*. Displacement is the difference between the local time and the Coordinated Universal Time (UTC, also known as Greenwich Mean Time). The displacement is represented in hours and minutes. Two TIMESTAMP WITH TIME ZONE values are considered identical if they represent the same time in UTC. For example, 5 P.M. CST is equal to 6 P.M. EST or 3 P.M. PST.

TIMESTAMP WITH LOCAL TIME ZONE

Specification `TIMESTAMP [(<precision>)] WITH LOCAL TIME ZONE`

The TIMESTAMP WITH LOCAL TIME ZONE datatype is similar to the TIMESTAMP datatype, but like the TIMESTAMP WITH TIME ZONE datatype, it also includes the time zone displacement. TIMESTAMP WITH LOCAL TIME ZONE does not store the displacement information in the database, but stores the time as a normalized form of the database time zone. The data is always stored in the database time zone, but when the user retrieves data, it is shown in the user's local session time zone.

The following example demonstrates how the DATE, TIMESTAMP, TIMESTAMP WITH TIME ZONE, and TIMESTAMP WITH LOCAL TIME ZONE datatypes store data. The `NLS_xx _FORMAT` parameter is explicitly set to display the values in the nondefault format. The data is inserted at CDT (Central Daylight Time), which is seven hours behind the UTC. (The output shown for the example was reformatted for better readability.)

```
SQL> CREATE TABLE date_time_demo (
  2   r_no         NUMBER (2),
  3   c_date       DATE DEFAULT SYSDATE,
  4   c_timezone   TIMESTAMP DEFAULT SYSTIMESTAMP,
  5   c_timezone2  TIMESTAMP (2) DEFAULT SYSTIMESTAMP,
  6   c_ts_wtz     TIMESTAMP (0) WITH TIME ZONE
                              DEFAULT SYSTIMESTAMP,
  7   c_ts_wltz    TIMESTAMP (9) WITH LOCAL TIME ZONE
                              DEFAULT SYSTIMESTAMP)
```

```
SQL> /
Table created.

SQL> INSERT INTO date_time_demo (r_no) VALUES (1);
1 row created.

SQL> ALTER SESSION SET NLS_DATE_FORMAT =
                              'YYYY-MM-DD HH24:MI:SS';
Session altered.
SQL> ALTER SESSION SET NLS_TIMESTAMP_FORMAT
                          = 'YYYY-MM-DD HH24:MI:SS.FF';
Session altered.
SQL> ALTER SESSION SET NLS_TIMESTAMP_TZ_FORMAT
                         = 'YYYY-MM-DD HH24:MI:SS.FFTZH:TZM';
Session altered.
SQL> SELECT * FROM date_time_demo;

R_NO C_DATE              C_TIMEZONE
---------------------    ---------------------------
1 2001-10-24 13:09:14    2001-10-24 13:09:14. 000001

C_TIMEZONE2               C_TS_WTZ
----------------------    --------------------------
2001-10-24 13:09:14.00    2001-10-24 13:09:14.-07:00

C_TS_WLTZ
-----------------------------
2001-10-24 13:09:14.000001000
```

INTERVAL YEAR TO MONTH

Specification `INTERVAL YEAR [(precision)] TO MONTH`

The INTERVAL YEAR TO MONTH datatype is used to represent a period of time as years and months. The *precision* specifies the precision needed for the year field, and its default is 2. Valid precision values are from 0 to 9. This datatype can be used to store the difference between two date/time values, where the only significant portions are the year and month.

INTERVAL DAY TO SECOND

Specification `INTERVAL DAY [(precision)] TO SECOND`

The INTERVAL DAY TO SECOND datatype is used to represent a period of time as days, hours, minutes, and seconds. The *precision* specifies the precision needed for the day field, and its default is 6. Valid precision values are from 0 to 9. Larger precision values allow a greater difference between the dates; for example, a precision of 2 allows values from 0 through 99, and a precision of 4 allows values from 0 through 9999. This datatype can use used to store the difference between two date/time values, including seconds.

The following example demonstrates the INTERVAL datatypes. We create a table with the INTERVAL datatypes, insert data to it, and select data from the table.

```
SQL> CREATE TABLE interval_demo (
  2  ts1     TIMESTAMP (2),
  3  iy2m    INTERVAL YEAR (3) TO MONTH,
  4  id2s    INTERVAL DAY (4) TO SECOND);
Table created.

SQL> INSERT INTO interval_demo VALUES (
  2  TO_TIMESTAMP('010101-102030.45',
  3  'YYMMDD-HH24MISS.FF'),
  4  TO_YMINTERVAL('3-7'),
  5* TO_DSINTERVAL('4 02:20:30.30'));
1 row created.

SQL> SELECT * FROM interval_demo;
TS1                         IY2M     ID2S
-------------------------- -------- ---------------------
2001-01-01 10:20:30.45      +003-07  +0004 02:20:30.300000
SQL>
```

Date Arithmetic

Date/time datatypes can be used in expressions with the + or - operator. You can use the +, -, *, and / operators with the INTERVAL datatypes. Dates are stored in the database as Julian numbers with a fraction component for the time. A *Julian date* refers to the number of days since January 1, 4712 BC.

Due to the time component of the date, comparing dates can result in fractional differences, even though the date is the same. Oracle provides a number of functions, such as TRUNC, that help you to remove the time component when you want to compare only the date portions.

Adding 1 to the date simply moves the date ahead one day. You can add time to the date by adding a fraction of a day. One day equals 24 hours, or 24 × 60 minutes, or 24 × 60 × 60 seconds. Table 7.1 shows the numbers used to add or subtract time for a date/time datatype.

TABLE 7.1 Date Arithmetic

Time to Add or Subtract	Fraction	Date Difference
1 day	1	1
1 hour	1/24	1/24
1 minute	1/(24 × 60)	1/1440
1 second	1/(24 × 60 × 60)	1/86400

Subtracting two dates gives you the difference between the dates in days. This usually results in a fractional component that represents the time difference. If the time components are the same, there will be no fractional results.

A date/time value operation using a numeric value results in a date/time value. The following example adds 2 days and 12 hours to a date value.

```
SQL> SELECT TO_DATE('2001-10-24 13:09:14') + 2.5
  2  FROM dual;
2001-10-27 01:09:14
```

This example subtracts 6 hours from a timestamp value:

```
SQL> SELECT TO_TIMESTAMP('2001-10-24 13:09:14.05')
  2  - 0.25 FROM dual;
2001-10-24 07:09:14
SQL>
```

A date/time value subtracted from another date/time value results in a numeric value (the difference in days). You cannot add two date/time values. Here is an example that results in the difference between dates as a fraction of a day:

```
SQL> SELECT SYSDATE,
  2  SYSDATE - TO_DATE('2001-10-24 13:09:14')
  3  FROM dual;
SYSDATE             SYSDATE-TO_DATE('2001-10-2413:09:14')
------------------- -------------------------------------
2001-10-24 15:32:21                             .099386574
```

This example converts the fraction of days to hours, minutes, and seconds using the NUMTODSINTERVAL function:

```
SQL> SELECT SYSDATE,
  2  NUMTODSINTERVAL(SYSDATE
  3  - TO_DATE('2001-10-24 13:09:14'), 'DAY')
  4  FROM DUAL;
SYSDATE              NUMTODSINTERVAL(SYSDATE
-------------------- -----------------------------
2001-10-24 15:53:04  +000000000 02:43:49.999999999
SQL>
```

A date/time value operation using an interval value results in a date/time value. The following example adds 1 year and 3 months to today's date.

```
SQL> SELECT TRUNC(SYSDATE),
  2  TRUNC(SYSDATE)+TO_YMINTERVAL('1-3')
  3  FROM dual;
TRUNC(SYSDATE)      TRUNC(SYSDATE)+TO_Y
------------------- -------------------
2001-10-24 00:00:00 2003-01-24 00:00:00
```

An interval datatype operation on another interval or numeric value results in an interval value. You can use + and – between two interval datatypes, and * and / between interval and numeric values. The following example converts a string (which represents 1 day, 3 hours, and 30 minutes) to an INTERVAL DAY TO SECOND datatype and multiplies that value by 2, which results in 2 days and 7 hours.

```
SQL> SELECT TO_DSINTERVAL('1 03:30:00.0') * 2 FROM dual;

TO_DSINTERVAL('103:30:00.0')*2
-------------------------------
+000000002 07:00:00.000000000
SQL>
```

The following example shows arithmetic between two INTERVAL DAY TO SECOND datatype values. The interval value of 3 hours and 30 minutes is subtracted from 1 day, 3 hours, and 30 minutes, resulting in 1 day.

```
SQL> SELECT TO_DSINTERVAL('1 03:30:00.0')
          - TO_DSINTERVAL('0 03:30:00.0') FROM dual;

TO_DSINTERVAL('103:30:00.0')-TO_DSINTERVAL('003:30:00.0')
---------------------------------------------------------
+000000001 00:00:00.000000000
SQL>
```

Binary Datatypes

Binary datatypes store information without converting them to the database's character set. This type of storage is required to store images, audio/video, executable files, and similar data. There are four datatypes available to store binary data:

- RAW
- LONG RAW
- BLOB
- BFILE

RAW

Specification RAW (<*size*>)

RAW is used to store binary information up to 2000 bytes. You must specify the maximum size of the column in bytes. RAW is a variable-length datatype.

BLOB

Specification BLOB

BLOB can store binary data up to 4GB. There is no size specification for this datatype.

BFILE

Specification `BFILE`

BFILE is used to store information on external files. The external file size can be up to 4GB. Oracle stores only the file pointer in the database. The actual file is stored on the operating system. Of the four Large Object datatypes (CLOB, BLOB, NCLOB, and BFILE), only BFILE stores actual data outside the Oracle database.

LONG RAW

Specification `LONG RAW`

LONG RAW is supported in Oracle9i for backward compatibility. Use BLOB instead. You can have only one LONG RAW column in a table.

Row ID Datatypes

Physical storage of each row in a table can be represented using a unique value called the ROWID. Every table has a pseudo-column called the ROWID. To store such values, Oracle provides two datatypes: ROWID and UROWID.

ROWID

Specification `ROWID`

ROWID can store the physical address of a row. Physical ROWIDs store the addresses of rows in ordinary tables (excluding index-organized tables), clustered tables, table partitions and subpartitions, indexes, and index partitions and subpartitions. Logical ROWIDs store the addresses of rows in index-organized tables. Physical ROWIDs provide the fastest possible access to a row of a given table.

UROWID

Specification `UROWID`

UROWID can store the logical ROWIDs of index-organized tables or non-Oracle database tables. Oracle creates logical ROWIDs based on an index-organized table's primary key. The logical ROWIDs do not change as long as the primary key does not change.

Creating Tables

You can think of a table as a spreadsheet with columns and rows. It is a structure that holds data in a relational database. The table is created with a name to identify it and columns defined with valid column names and column attributes, such as the datatype and size. CREATE TABLE is a comprehensive statement with many options. Here is the simplest format to use to create a table:

```
SQL> CREATE TABLE products
  2  ( prod_id    NUMBER (4),
  3    prod_name  VARCHAR2 (20),
  4    stock_qty  NUMBER (15,3)
  5  );

Table created.
SQL>
```

You specify the table name following the keywords CREATE TABLE. This example creates a table named PRODUCTS under the user (schema) connected to the database. The table name can be qualified with the username; you must qualify the table when creating a table in another user's schema. Table and column names are discussed in more detail in the next section.

The column definitions are enclosed in parentheses. The table we created has three columns, each identified by a name and datatype. Commas separate the column definitions. This table has two columns with the NUMBER datatype and one column with VARCHAR2 datatype. A datatype must be specified for each column.

When creating tables, you can specify the following:

- Default values for columns
- Constraints for the columns and/or table (discussed later in this chapter, in the "Managing Constraints" section)
- The type of table: relational (heap), temporary, index-organized, external, or object (index-organized and object tables are not covered in the exam)
- Table storage, including any index storage and storage specification for the Large Object columns (LOBs) in the table
- The tablespace where the table/index should be stored
- Any partitioning and subpartitioning information

Naming Tables and Columns

Table names are used to identify each table. You should make table names as descriptive as possible. Table and column names are *identifiers* and can be up to 30 characters long. An identifier name should begin with a letter and may contain numeric digits. The only special characters allowed in an identifier name are the dollar sign ($), the underscore (_), and the pound sign (#). The underscore can be used for meaningful separation of the words in an identifier name. These names are case insensitive. Oracle converts the names to uppercase and stores them in the data dictionary. If, however, you enclose the identifier name in double quotation marks ("), it will be case sensitive in the Oracle dictionary.

Creating table names enclosed in quotation marks with mixed case can cause serious problems when you do a query if you do not know the exact case of the table name.

You can use the DESCRIBE or DESC (SQL*Plus) command to list all of the columns in the table, along with their datatype, size, nullity, and order. The syntax is DESCRIBE <*table name*>. The case sensitivity of names and describing tables are illustrated in the following examples:

```
SQL> CREATE TABLE MyTable (
  2   Column_1  NUMBER,
  3   Column_2  CHAR);
Table created.

SQL> DESC mytable
 Name                    Null?    Type
 ------------------- -------- --------
 COLUMN_1                         NUMBER
 COLUMN_2                         CHAR(1)

SQL> SELECT table_name FROM user_tables
  2  WHERE  table_name = 'MyTable';
no rows selected

SQL> CREATE TABLE "MyTable" (
  2   "Column1" number,
```

```
  3   "Column2" char);
Table created.

SQL> DESC "MyTable"
 Name                    Null?    Type
 ----------------------- -------- --------
 Column1                          NUMBER
 Column2                          CHAR(1)

SQL> SELECT table_name FROM user_tables
  2   WHERE  upper(table_name) = 'MYTABLE';

TABLE_NAME
------------------------------
MYTABLE
MyTable
SQL>
```

It is a good practice to give the other objects directly related to a table a name that reflects the table name. For example, consider the EMPLOYEE table. The primary key of the table may be named PK_EMPLOYEE, indexes might be named EMPLOYEE_NDX1 and EMPLOYEE_NDX2, a check constraint could be named CK_EMPLOYEE_STATUS, a trigger could be named TRG_EMPLOYEE_HIRE, and so on.

Creating a Temporary Table

When you create a table without any specific keywords to indicate the type of the table, the table created is a relational table that is permanent. If you include the keywords GLOBAL TEMPORARY, Oracle9i creates a temporary relational table whose definition is available to all sessions in the database, but the data is available only to the session that inserted to it. The ON COMMIT clause can be included to specify if the data in the temporary table is session-specific (ON COMMIT PRESERVE ROWS) or transaction-specific (ON COMMIT DELETE ROWS). ON COMMIT DELETE ROWS is the default. Here is an example of creating a temporary table whose inserted data will be available throughout the session:

```
SQL> CREATE GLOBAL TEMPORARY TABLE emp_bonus_temp  (
  2  emp_id  NUMBER (10),
  3  bonus   NUMBER (15,2))
  4  ON COMMIT PRESERVE ROWS;

Table created.
SQL>
```

Specifying Default Values for Columns

When creating or altering a table, you can specify *default values* for columns. The default value specified will be used when you do not specify any value for the column while inserting data. The default value specified in the definition should satisfy the datatype and length of the column. If a default value is not explicitly set, the default for the column is implicitly set to NULL. Default values cannot refer to another column, and they cannot have the pseudo-columns LEVEL, NEXTVAL, CURRVAL, ROWNUM, or PRIOR. The default values can include SYSDATE, USER, USERENV, and UID.

In the following example, the table ORDERS is created with a column STATUS that has a default value of PENDING.

```
SQL> CREATE TABLE orders (
  2  order_number NUMBER (8),
  3  status       VARCHAR2 (10) DEFAULT 'PENDING');

Table created.

SQL> INSERT INTO orders (order_number) VALUES (4004);

1 row created.

SQL> SELECT * FROM orders;

ORDER_NUMBER STATUS
------------ ----------
        4004 PENDING
SQL>
```

Here is an example of creating a table that includes default values for two columns:

```
SQL> CREATE TABLE emp_punch (
emp_id      NUMBER (6) NOT NULL,
time_in     DATE,
time_out    DATE,
updated_by  VARCHAR2 (30) DEFAULT USER,
update_time TIMESTAMP WITH LOCAL TIME ZONE
                              DEFAULT SYSTIMESTAMP
);

Table created.
SQL> DESCRIBE emp_punch
 Name                          Null?    Type
 ----------------------------- -------- ------------------
 EMP_ID                        NOT NULL NUMBER(6)
 TIME_IN                                DATE
 TIME_OUT                               DATE
 UPDATED_BY                             VARCHAR2(30)
 UPDATE_TIME                            TIMESTAMP(6) WITH
                                        LOCAL TIME ZONE

SQL> INSERT INTO emp_punch (emp_id, time_in)
VALUES (1090, TO_DATE('062801-2121','MMDDYY-HH24MI'));

1 row created.

SQL> SELECT * FROM emp_punch;

EMP_ID TIME_IN   TIME_OUT  UPDATED_BY UPDATE_TIME
------ --------- --------- ---------- ------------------
1090   28-JUN-01           JOHN       02.55.58.000000 PM
SQL>
```

This example uses a NOT NULL constraint in the table definition. A NOT NULL constraint prevents NULL values from being entered into the column. Constraints are discussed in details in the "Managing Constraints" section later in this chapter.

If you explicitly insert a NULL value for a column with DEFAULT defined, the value in the DEFAULT clause will not be used. You can explicitly specify DEFAULT in the INSERT statement to use the DEFAULT value, as in the following example:

```
SQL> INSERT INTO emp_punch
  2  VALUES (104, TO_DATE('062801-2121','MMDDYY-HH24MI'),
  3          DEFAULT, DEFAULT, NULL);

1 row created.

SQL> SELECT * FROM emp_punch;

EMP_ID TIME_IN   TIME UPDATED UPDATE_TIME
                 _OUT   _BY
------ --------- ---- ------- ---------------------------
1090   28-JUN-01        JOHN  29-JUN-01 02.55.58.000000 PM
 104   28-JUN-01        JOHN
SQL>
```

Adding Comments

The purpose of the table and the column can be documented in the database using the COMMENT statement. Let's provide comments for our sample table:

```
SQL> COMMENT ON TABLE mytable IS
 2   'Oracle9i Study Guide Example Table';
Comment created.

SQL> COMMENT ON COLUMN mytable.column_1 is
 2   'First column in MYTABLE';
Comment created.
SQL>
```

You can query the table and column information from the Oracle dictionary using the following views: USER_TABLES, ALL_TABLES, USER_TAB_COLUMNS, and ALL_TAB_COLUMNS.

Creating a Table from Another Table

You can create a table using a query based on one or more existing tables or views. The column datatype and width will be determined by the query result. A table created in this fashion can select all the columns from another table (you may use *), or a subset of columns or expressions and functions applied on columns (these are called derived columns). The syntax used for creating a table using an existing table is as follows:

```
CREATE TABLE <table characteristics> AS SELECT <query>
```

This syntax is generally known as CTAS. The table characteristics include the new table name and its storage properties.

For example, suppose that you need to duplicate the structure and data of the EMP table in the EMPLOYEES table. You can use CTAS, like this:

```
SQL> CREATE TABLE employees
  2  AS SELECT * FROM emp;

Table created.
SQL>
```

You can have complex query statements in the CREATE TABLE statement. The table is created with no rows if the query returned no rows. If you just want to copy the structure of the table, make sure that the query returns no rows:

```
CREATE TABLE Y AS SELECT * FROM X WHERE 1 = 2;
```

You can provide column alias names to have different column names in the newly created table. The following example shows a table structure, displays the data, then creates a new table with the data and displays it.

```
SQL> DESCRIBE city
```

```
 Name                          Null?    Type
 ------------------- -------- -------------
 CNT_CODE                      NOT NULL NUMBER(4)
 ST_CODE                       NOT NULL VARCHAR2(2)
 CTY_CODE                      NOT NULL NUMBER(4)
 CTY_NAME                               VARCHAR2(20)
 POPULATION                             NUMBER

SQL> SELECT COUNT(*) FROM city;

  COUNT(*)
----------
         3
SQL> CREATE TABLE new_city AS
  2  SELECT cty_code CITY_CODE, cty_name CITY_NAME
  3  FROM city;

Table created.
SQL> SELECT COUNT(*) FROM new_city;

  COUNT(*)
----------
         3
SQL> DESC new_city
 Name                          Null?    Type
 ------------------- -------- -------------
 CITY_CODE                     NOT NULL NUMBER(4)
 CITY_NAME                              VARCHAR2(20)
SQL>
```

The CREATE TABLE…AS SELECT… statement will not work if the query refers to columns of the LONG datatype.

When you create a table using the subquery, only the NOT NULL constraints associated with the columns are copied to the new table. Other constraints and column default definitions are not copied.

Modifying Tables

After you've created a table, there are several reasons why you might want to modify it. You can modify a table to change its column definition or default values, add a new column, or drop an existing column. You cannot rename columns. You might also modify a table if you need to change or add constraint definitions. The ALTER TABLE statement is used to change table definitions. You can also drop and rename tables.

The TRUNCATE command allows you to empty a table of all rows, leaving the table structure. See Chapter 6, "Modifying Data," for details on using TRUNCATE.

Adding Columns

Here is the syntax to add a new column to an existing table:

```
ALTER TABLE [<schema>.]<table_name> ADD <column_definitions>;
```

When a new column is added, it is always at the bottom of the table. For the existing rows, the new column value will be NULL.

Let's add a new column, ORDER_DATE, to the ORDERS table.

```
SQL> DESCRIBE orders
 Name                          Null?    Type
 ----------------------------- -------- -------------
 ORDER_NUMBER                  NOT NULL NUMBER(8)
 STATUS                                 VARCHAR2(10)

SQL> SELECT * FROM orders;

ORDER_NUMBER STATUS
------------ ----------
        4004 PENDING
        5005 COMPLETED

SQL> ALTER TABLE orders ADD order_date DATE;
```

```
Table altered.

SQL> DESC orders
 Name                      Null?    Type
 ------------------------- -------- ---------------
 ORDER_NUMBER              NOT NULL NUMBER(8)
 STATUS                             VARCHAR2(10)
 ORDER_DATE                         DATE

SQL> SELECT * FROM orders;

ORDER_NUMBER STATUS     ORDER_DAT
------------ ---------- ---------
        4004 PENDING
        5005 COMPLETED
SQL>
```

If you are adding more than one column, the column definitions should be enclosed in parentheses and separated by commas. If you specify a DEFAULT value for a newly added column, all the rows in the table will have the default value automatically assigned. The following example adds two more columns to ORDERS table.

```
SQL> ALTER TABLE orders ADD
  2  (quantity NUMBER (13,3),
  3  update_dt DATE DEFAULT SYSDATE);

Table altered.
SQL> SELECT * FROM orders;

ORDER_NUMBER STATUS     ORDER_DAT   QUANTITY UPDATE_DT
------------ ---------- --------- ---------- ---------
        4004 PENDING                         23-MAR-02
        5005 COMPLETED                       23-MAR-02
SQL>
```

When adding a new column, you cannot specify the NOT NULL constraint if the table already has rows. To add a NOT NULL column, you need to follow three steps:

1. Modify the table to add the column.
2. Update the column with values for all the existing rows.
3. Add a NOT NULL constraint.

You may add a NOT NULL constraint with a DEFAULT clause, even if the table has rows. Here is an example:

```
SQL> ALTER TABLE orders
       ADD updated_by VARCHAR2 (30) NOT NULL;
ALTER TABLE orders
       ADD updated_by VARCHAR2 (30) NOT NULL
           *
ERROR at line 1:
ORA-01758: table must be empty to add mandatory
(NOT NULL) column

SQL> ALTER TABLE orders ADD updated_by VARCHAR2 (30)
  2  DEFAULT 'JOHN' NOT NULL;

Table altered.
SQL>
```

Modifying Columns

The syntax to modify an existing column in a table is as follows:

```
ALTER TABLE [<schema>.]<table_name>
MODIFY <column_name> <new_attributes>;
```

If you omit any of the parts of the column definition (datatype, default value, or column constraint), the omitted parts remain unchanged. If you are modifying more than one column at a time, enclose the column definitions in parentheses. For example, to modify the ORDERS table, increasing the STATUS column to 15 and reducing the QUANTITY column to 10,3, do this:

```
ALTER TABLE orders MODIFY (quantity NUMBER (10,3),
                           status VARCHAR2 (15));
```

You can add or drop constraints in the column and modify the DEFAULT values for the column. The DEFAULT value included using the MODIFY clause affects only the new rows inserted to the table; the existing rows with NULL column values are not affected. To remove the DEFAULT value for a column, redefine the DEFAULT clause with a NULL value. For example, the following statement removes the default SYSDATE value from the UPDATE_DT column of the ORDERS table.

```
ALTER TABLE orders
MODIFY update_dt DEFAULT NULL;
```

These are the rules for modifying column definitions:

- You can increase the length of the character column and precision of the numeric column. If your table has many rows, increasing the length of a CHAR column will require a lot of resources, because the column data for all the rows needs to blank-padded with the additional length.
- You may decrease the length of a VARCHAR2 column and reduce the precision or increase the scale of a numeric column, if all of the data in the column fits the new length.
- You may decrease the length of a nonempty CHAR column, if the parameter BLANK_TRIMMING is set to TRUE.
- The column values must be NULL to change its datatype. If you do not reduce the length, you can change the datatype from CHAR to VARCHAR2 or vice versa, even if the column is not empty.

Dropping Columns

You can drop a column that is not used, or you can mark the column as not used and drop it later. Here is the syntax for dropping a column:

```
ALTER TABLE [<schema>.]<table_name>
DROP {COLUMN <column_name> | (<column_names>)}
[CASCADE CONSTRAINTS]
```

DROP COLUMN drops the column name specified from the table. You can provide more than one column name separated by commas inside parentheses. The indexes and constraints on the column are also dropped. You must specify CASCADE CONSTRAINTS if the dropped column is part of a multicolumn constraint; the constraint will be dropped.

The syntax for marking a column as unused is as follows:

```
ALTER TABLE [<schema>.]<table_name>
SET UNUSED {COLUMN <column_name> | (<column_names>)}
[CASCADE CONSTRAINTS]
```

You usually mark a column as unused instead of dropping it immediately, especially at peak hours, if the table is a very large, because Oracle rebuilds the entire table— it takes a lot of resources to rebuild a large table. In such cases, you would mark the column as unused and drop it later. Once the column is marked as unused, you will not see it as part of the table definition. Let's mark the UPDATE_DT column in the ORDERS table as unused:

```
SQL> ALTER TABLE orders SET UNUSED COLUMN update_dt;

Table altered.

SQL> DESCRIBE orders
 Name                       Null?    Type
 -------------------------- -------- -------------
 ORDER_NUMBER               NOT NULL NUMBER(8)
 STATUS                              VARCHAR2(15)
 ORDER_DATE                          DATE
 QUANTITY                            NUMBER(10,3)
SQL>
```

Here is the syntax for dropping a column already marked as unused:

```
ALTER TABLE [<schema>.]<table_name>
DROP {UNUSED COLUMNS | COLUMNS CONTINUE}
```

Use the `COLUMNS CONTINUE` clause to continue a `DROP` operation that was previously interrupted. The `DROP UNUSED COLUMNS` clause will drop all the columns that are marked as unused. You cannot selectively drop column names after marking them as unused. The following example clears data from the UPDATE_DT column in the ORDERS table:

```
ALTER TABLE orders DROP UNUSED COLUMNS;
```

The data dictionary views DBA_UNUSED_COL_TABS, ALL_UNUSED_COL_TABS, and USER_UNUSED_COL_TABS provide the names of tables in which you have columns marked as unused.

Dropping Tables

Dropping a table is simple. The syntax is as follows:

```
DROP TABLE [schema.]table_name [CASCADE CONSTRAINTS]
```

When you drop a table, the data and definition of the table are removed. The indexes, constraints, triggers, and privileges on the table are also dropped. Once you drop a table, the action cannot be undone.

Oracle does not drop the views, materialized views, or other stored programs that reference the table, but it marks them as invalid. You must specify the CASCADE CONSTRAINTS clause if there are referential integrity constraints referring to the primary key or unique key of this table. Here's how to drop the table TEST owned by user SCOTT:

```
DROP TABLE scott.test;
```

A method for emptying a table of all rows is to use the TRUNCATE statement. This is different from dropping and re-creating a table, because TRUNCATE does not invalidate dependent objects or drop indexes, triggers, or referential integrity constraints. See Chapter 6 for more information about using TRUNCATE.

Renaming Tables

The RENAME statement is used to rename a table and other database objects, such as views, private synonyms, or sequences. The syntax for the RENAME statement is as follows:

```
RENAME old_name TO new_name;
```

Here, *old_name* and *new_name* are names of table, view, private synonym, or sequence.

When you rename a table, Oracle automatically transfers integrity constraints, indexes, and grants on the old table to the new table. Oracle invalidates all objects that depend on the renamed table, such as views, synonyms, stored procedures, and functions.

The following example renames the ORDERS table to PURCHASE_ORDERS:

```
SQL> RENAME orders TO purchase_orders;

Table renamed.

SQL> DESCRIBE purchase_orders
```

```
 Name               Null?    Type
 ------------------ -------- ---------------
 ORDER_NUMBER       NOT NULL NUMBER(8)
 STATUS                      VARCHAR2(15)
 ORDER_DATE                  DATE
 QUANTITY                    NUMBER(10,3)

SQL>
```

You can use the RENAME statement to rename only the objects you own. You cannot rename an object owned by another user.

You can also use the RENAME TO clause of the ALTER TABLE statement to rename a table. Using this technique, you can qualify the table name with the schema. You must use the ALTER TABLE statement to rename a table owned by another user (and you need the ALTER privilege on the table or the ALTER ANY TABLE system privilege). Here is an example:

```
SQL> ALTER TABLE scott.purchase_orders
  2  RENAME TO orders;

Table altered.
SQL>
```

Managing Constraints

Constraints are created in the database to enforce a business rule in the database and to specify relationships between various tables. Business rules can also be enforced using database triggers and application code. *Integrity constraints* prevent bad data from being entered into the database. Oracle supports five types of integrity constraints:

NOT NULL Prevents NULL values from being entered into the column. These types of constraints are defined on a single column. By default, Oracle allows NULL values in any column.

CHECK Checks whether the condition specified in the constraint is satisfied.

UNIQUE Ensures that there are no duplicate values for the column(s) specified. Every value or set of values is unique within the table.

PRIMARY KEY Uniquely identifies each row of the table and prevents NULL values. A table can have only one *primary key* constraint.

FOREIGN KEY Establishes a parent-child relationship between tables by using common columns. The *foreign key* defined on a table refers to the primary key or unique key of another table.

Creating Constraints

Constraints are created using the CREATE TABLE or ALTER TABLE statements. You can specify the constraint definition at the column level if the constraint is defined on a single column. Multiple-column constraints must be defined at the table level; the columns should be specified in parentheses and separated by commas.

If you do not provide a name for the constraints, Oracle assigns a system-generated unique name that begins with SYS_. A name is provided for the constraint by specifying the keyword CONSTRAINT followed by the constraint name.

You should not rely on system-generated names for constraints. If you want to compare table characteristics, such as between production and test databases, the inconsistent system-generated names will make this comparison difficult.

In this section, we will discuss the rules for each constraint type and provide examples of creating constraints.

NOT NULL Constraint

A NOT NULL constraint is defined at the column level; it cannot be defined at the table level. The syntax for a NOT NULL constraint is as follows:

```
[CONSTRAINT <constraint name>] [NOT] NULL
```

The following example creates a table with two columns that have NOT NULL constraints.

```
CREATE TABLE orders (
 order_num   NUMBER (4) CONSTRAINT nn_order_num NOT NULL,
```

```
  order_date  DATE NOT NULL,
  product_id)
```

The example provides a name for the constraint on the ORDER_NUM column. Since no name is specified for the constraint on the ORDER_DATE column, it will get a system-generated name.

Use ALTER TABLE MODIFY to add or remove a NOT NULL constraint on the columns of an existing table. The following examples remove a constraint and add a constraint to an existing table.

```
ALTER TABLE orders MODIFY order_date NULL;
ALTER TABLE orders MODIFY product_id NOT NULL;
```

Check Constraints

A check constraint can be defined at the column level or table level. For both the column and table level, the syntax is as follows:

```
[CONSTRAINT <constraint name>] CHECK ( <condition> )
```

The condition specified in the CHECK clause should evaluate to a Boolean result and can refer to values in other columns of the same row; the condition cannot use queries. Environment functions (such as SYSDATE, USER, USERENV, and UID) and pseudo-columns (such as ROWNUM, CURRVAL, NEXTVAL, and LEVEL) cannot be used to evaluate the check condition. One column can have more than one check constraint defined.

The following are examples of check constraints defined at the table level:

```
CREATE TABLE bonus (
 emp_id    VARCHAR2 (40) NOT NULL,
 salary    NUMBER (9,2),
 bonus     NUMBER (9,2),
CONSTRAINT ck_bonus check (bonus > 0));

ALTER TABLE bonus
ADD CONSTRAINT ck_bonus2 CHECK (bonus < salary);
```

The check constraint can be defined at the column level if the constraint refers to only that column.

You cannot use the ALTER TABLE MODIFY clause to add or modify check constraints (only NOT NULL constraints can be modified this way). Column-level constraints can be defined when using the CREATE TABLE statement or when using the ALTER TABLE statement with ADD clause. Here is an example:

```
ALTER TABLE orders ADD cust_id number (5)
CONSTRAINT ck_cust_id CHECK (cust_id > 0);
```

You can use the check constraint to implement a NOT NULL constraint also. This is especially useful if you need to disallow NULL values in multiple columns together. For example, the following constraint definition for the BONUS table allows a NULL value for the BONUS and SALARY columns if both column values are NULL, or else both columns should have valid non-NULL value.

```
ALTER TABLE bonus ADD CONSTRAINT ck_sal_bonus
CHECK ((bonus IS NULL AND salary IS NULL) OR
      (bonus IS NOT NULL AND salary IS NOT NULL));
```

Unique Constraints

A unique constraint protects one or more columns in a table, ensuring that no two rows contain duplicate data in the protected columns. Unique constraints can be defined at the column level for single-column unique keys. Here is the column-level syntax:

```
[CONSTRAINT <constraint name>] UNIQUE
```

For a multiple-column unique key (composite key—the maximum number of columns specified can be 32), the constraint should be defined at the table level. Here is the table-level syntax:

```
[CONSTRAINT <constraint name>]
UNIQUE (<column>, <column>, …)
```

Oracle creates a unique index on the unique key columns to enforce uniqueness. If a unique index or nonunique index already exists on the table with the same column order prefix, Oracle uses the existing index. To use the existing nonunique index for enforcing uniqueness, there must not be any duplicate values in the unique key columns.

Unique constraints allow NULL values in the constraint columns. The following example defines a unique constraint with two columns.

```
ALTER TABLE employee
ADD CONSTRAINT uq_emp_id UNIQUE (dept, emp_id);
```

The next example adds a new column to the EMP table and creates a unique key at the column level.

```
ALTER TABLE employee ADD
ssn VARCHAR2 (11) CONSTRAINT uq_ssn unique;
```

Primary Key Constraints

All characteristics of the unique key are applicable to the primary key constraint, except that NULL values are not allowed in the primary key columns. A table can have only one primary key. The column-level syntax is as follows:

```
[CONSTRAINT <constraint name>] PRIMARY KEY
```

Here is the table-level syntax:

```
[CONSTRAINT <constraint name>]
PRIMARY KEY (<column>, <column>, …)
```

Oracle creates a unique index and NOT NULL constraints for each column in the key. The following example defines a primary key when creating the table.

```
CREATE TABLE employee (
 dept_no VARCHAR2 (2),
 emp_id  NUMBER (4),
 name    VARCHAR2 (20) NOT NULL,
 ssn     VARCHAR2 (11),
 salary  NUMBER (9,2) CHECK (salary > 0),
CONSTRAINT pk_employee primary key (dept_no, emp_id),
CONSTRAINT uq_ssn unique (ssn))
```

To add a primary key to an existing table, use the ALTER TABLE statement. Here is an example:

```
ALTER TABLE employee
ADD CONSTRAINT pk_employee PRIMARY KEY (dept_no, emp_id);
```

Indexes created to enforce unique keys and primary keys can be managed in the same way as any other index. However, these indexes cannot be dropped explicitly using the DROP INDEX statement.

Foreign Key Constraints

A foreign key constraint protects one or more columns in a table by ensuring that for each non-NULL value there is data available elsewhere in the database with a primary or unique key. The foreign key is the column or columns in the table (child table) where the constraint is created. The referenced key is the primary key or unique key column or columns in the table (parent table) that is referenced by the constraint. The column data types in parent table and child table should match.

A foreign key constraint can be defined at the column level or table level. Here is the syntax for the column-level constraint:

```
[CONSTRAINT <constraint name>]
REFERENCES [<schema>.]<table> [(<column>, <column>, …]
[ON DELETE {CASCADE | SET NULL}]
```

Multiple-column foreign keys should be defined at the table level. Here is the table-level syntax:

```
[CONSTRAINT <constraint name>]
FOREIGN KEY (<column>, <column>, …)
REFERENCES [<schema>.]<table> [(<column>, <column>, …]
[ON DELETE {CASCADE | SET NULL}]
```

The foreign key column(s) and referenced key column(s) can be in the same table (self-referential integrity constraint). NULL values are allowed in the foreign key columns.

The following is an example of creating a foreign key constraint on the COUNTRY_CODE and STATE_CODE columns of the CITY table, which refers to the COUNTRY_CODE and STATE_CODE columns of the STATE table (the composite primary key of the STATE table).

```
ALTER TABLE city ADD CONSTRAINT fk_state
FOREIGN KEY (country_code, state_code)
REFERENCES state (country_code, state_code);
```

You can omit the column listing of the referenced table, if referring to the primary key of the table. For example, if the COUNTRY_CODE and STATE_CODE columns are the primary key of STATE table, the above statement could be written like this:

```
ALTER TABLE city ADD CONSTRAINT fk_state
FOREIGN KEY (country_code, state_code)
REFERENCES state;
```

The ON DELETE clause specifies the action to be taken when a row in the parent table is deleted and child rows exist for the deleted parent primary key. You can delete the child rows (CASCADE) or set the foreign key column values to NULL (SET NULL). If you omit this clause, Oracle will not allow you to delete from the parent table if child records exist. You must delete the child rows first, and then delete the parent row. Following are two examples of specifying the delete action in a foreign key.

```
ALTER TABLE city ADD CONSTRAINT fk_state
 FOREIGN KEY (country_code, state_code)
 REFERENCES state (country_code, state_code)
 ON DELETE CASCADE;

ALTER TABLE city ADD CONSTRAINT fk_state
 FOREIGN KEY (country_code, state_code)
 REFERENCES state (country_code, state_code)
 ON DELETE SET NULL;
```

You can query the constraint information from the Oracle dictionary using the following views: USER_CONSTRAINTS, ALL_CONSTRAINTS, USER_CONS_COLUMNS, and ALL_CONS_COLUMNS.

Disabled Constraints

When a constraint is created, it is enabled automatically. You can create a *disabled* constraint by specifying the DISABLE keyword after the constraint definition. Here is an example:

```
ALTER TABLE city ADD CONSTRAINT fk_state
 FOREIGN KEY (country_code, state_code)
 REFERENCES state (country_code, state_code) DISABLE;

ALTER TABLE bonus
ADD CONSTRAINT ck_bonus CHECK (bonus > 0) DISABLE;
```

Dropping Constraints

Constraints are dropped using the ALTER TABLE statement. Any constraint can be dropped by specifying the constraint name, as in this example:

```
ALTER TABLE bonus DROP CONSTRAINT ck_bonus2;
```

To drop the NOT NULL constraint, use the ALTER TABLE MODIFY statement, like this:

```
ALTER TABLE employee MODIFY employee_name NULL;
```

To drop unique key constraints with referenced foreign keys, specify the CASCADE clause to drop the foreign key constraints and the unique constraint. Specify the unique key columns(s). Here is an example:

```
ALTER TABLE employee DROP UNIQUE (emp_id) CASCADE;
```

To drop primary key constraints with referenced foreign key constraints, use the CASCADE clause to drop all foreign key constraints and then the primary key. Here is an example:

```
ALTER TABLE bonus DROP PRIMARY KEY CASCADE;
```

Enabling and Disabling Constraints

When you create a constraint, the constraint is automatically enabled (unless you specify the DISABLE clause). You can disable a constraint by using the DISABLE clause of the ALTER TABLE statement. When you disable unique or primary key constraints, Oracle drops the associated unique index. When you reenable these constraints, Oracle builds the index.

You can disable any constraint by specifying the clause DISABLE CONSTRAINT followed by the constraint name. Specifying UNIQUE and the column name(s) can disable unique keys, and specifying PRIMARY KEY can disable the table's primary key. You cannot disable a primary key or unique key if foreign keys that are enabled reference it. To disable all the referenced foreign keys and the primary or unique key, specify CASCADE. The following three examples demonstrate disabling constraints.

```
ALTER TABLE bonus DISABLE CONSTRAINT ck_bonus;

ALTER TABLE employee DISABLE CONSTRAINT uq_employee;

ALTER TABLE state DISABLE PRIMARY KEY CASCADE;
```

Using the ENABLE clause of the ALTER TABLE statement enables a constraint. When you enable a disabled unique or primary key, Oracle creates an index if an index with the unique or primary key columns does not already exist. You can specify storage for the unique or primary key while enabling these constraints, as in this example:

```
ALTER TABLE state ENABLE PRIMARY KEY USING INDEX
TABLESPACE user_INDEX STORAGE (INITIAL 2M NEXT 2M);
```

Validated Constraints

You have seen how to enable and disable a constraint. ENABLE and DISABLE affect only future data that will be added or modified in the table. In contrast, the VALIDATE and NOVALIDATE keywords in the ALTER TABLE statement act on the existing data. Therefore, a constraint can have four states:

ENABLE VALIDATE This is the default for the ENABLE clause. The existing data in the table is validated to verify that it conforms to the constraint.

ENABLE NOVALIDATE This does not validate the existing data, but enables the constraint for future constraint checking.

DISABLE VALIDATE The constraint is disabled (any index used to enforce the constraint is also dropped), but the constraint is kept valid. No DML operation is allowed on the table because future changes cannot be verified.

DISABLE NOVALIDATE This is the default for the DISABLE clause. The constraint is disabled, and no checks are done on future or existing data.

Suppose that you have a large data warehouse table, where bulk data loads are performed every night. The primary key of this table is enforced using a nonunique index because Oracle does not drop the nonunique index when disabling the constraint. When you do batch loads, you can disable the primary key constraint as follows:

```
ALTER TABLE wh01 MODIFY CONSTRAINT pk_wh01
DISABLE NOVALIDATE;
```

After the batch load completes, you can enable the primary key like this:

```
ALTER TABLE wh01 MODIFY CONSTRAINT pk_wh01
ENABLE NOVALIDATE;
```

Oracle does not allow any INSERT, UPDATE, or DELETE operations on a table with a DISABLE VALIDATE constraint. This is a quick way to make a table read-only.

Deferring Constraint Checks

By default, Oracle checks whether the data conforms to the constraint when the statement is executed. Oracle allows you to change this behavior if the constraint is created using the DEFERRABLE clause (NOT DEFERRABLE is the default). It specifies that the transaction can set the constraint-checking behavior.

INITIALLY IMMEDIATE specifies that the constraint should be checked for conformance at the end of each SQL statement (this is the default). INITIALLY DEFERRED specifies that the constraint should be checked for conformance at the end of the transaction.

The DEFERRABLE status of a constraint cannot be changed using ALTER TABLE MODIFY CONSTRAINT; you must drop and re-create the constraint. The INITIALLY {DEFERRED|IMMEDIATE} clause can be changed using ALTER TABLE.

If the constraint is DEFERRABLE, you can set the behavior by using the SET CONSTRAINTS command or by using the ALTER SESSION SET CONSTRAINT command. You can enable or disable *deferred constraint checking* by listing all the constraints or by specifying the ALL keyword. The SET CONSTRAINTS command is used to set the constraint-checking behavior for the current transaction, and the ALTER SESSION command is used to set the constraint-checking behavior for the current session.

As an example, let's create a primary key constraint on the CUSTOMER table and a foreign key constraint on the ORDERS table as DEFERRABLE. Although the constraints are created as DEFERRABLE, they are not deferred because of the INITIALLY IMMEDIATE clause.

```
ALTER TABLE customer ADD CONSTRAINT pk_cust_id
PRIMARY KEY (cust_id) DEFERRABLE
INITIALLY IMMEDIATE;

ALTER TABLE orders ADD CONSTRAINT fk_cust_id
FOREIGN KEY (cust_id)
```

```
REFERENCES customer (cust_id)
ON DELETE CASCADE DEFERRABLE;
```

Primary key and unique constraints defined as DEFERRABLE will create/use nonunique indexes to enforce the constraint.

If you try to add a row to the ORDERS table with a CUST_ID value that is not available in the CUSTOMER table, Oracle returns an error immediately, even though you plan to add the CUSTOMER row soon. Since the constraints are verified for conformance as each SQL statement is executed, you must insert the row in the CUSTOMER table first and then add to the ORDERS table. Since the constraints are defined as DEFERRABLE, you can change this behavior by using this command:

```
SET CONSTRAINTS ALL DEFERRED;
```

Now, you can insert rows to these tables in any order. Oracle checks the constraint conformance only at commit time.

If you want deferred constraint checking as the default, create or modify the constraint by using INITIALLY DEFERRED, as in this example:

```
ALTER TABLE customer MODIFY CONSTRAINT pk_cust_id
INITIALLY DEFERRED;
```

Real World Scenario

Creating Tables and Constraints for an Application

You have been provided the following information to create tables and constraints for an application developed in your company to maintain geographic information:

- The COUNTRY table stores the country name and country code. The country code uniquely identifies each country. The country name must be present.
- The STATE table stores the state code, name, and its capital. The country code in this table refers to a valid entry in the COUNTRY table. The state name must be present. The state code and country code together uniquely identify each state.

- The CITY table stores the city code, name, and population. The city code uniquely identifies each city. The state and country where the city belongs are also stored in the table, which refers to the STATE table. The city name must be present.
- Each table should have a column identifying the created-on timestamp, with the system date as the default.
- The user should not be able to delete from the COUNTRY table if there are records in the STATE table for that country.
- The records in the CITY table should be automatically removed when their corresponding state is removed from the STATE table.
- All foreign key and primary key constraints should be provided with meaningful names.

Let's start by creating the COUNTRY table.

```
SQL> CREATE TABLE country (
  2  code    NUMBER (4) PRIMARY KEY,
  3  name    VARCHAR2 (40));
Table created.
SQL>
```

Oops, CODE and NAME are not very descriptive column names, and we also have other columns in tables to store codes and names. Let's name the columns COUNTRY_CODE and COUNTRY_NAME. To rename a column, we need to re-create the table. While we're re-creating it, we'll also provide a name for the primary key constraint.

```
SQL> DROP TABLE country;
Table dropped.
SQL> CREATE TABLE country (
  2  country_code  NUMBER (4) CONSTRAINT pk_country
  3                           PRIMARY KEY,
  4  country_name  VARCHAR2 (40));
```

```
Table created.

SQL>
```

Oops again, the table should include a column to store the created-on date, and the country name cannot be NULL.

Before we continue, realize that if you have a good logical and physical design before you start creating tables, you will not have any of these problems. This is not the typical or recommended approach to creating tables for the application. The objective here is to demonstrate the various options available.

```
SQL> ALTER TABLE country MODIFY country_name NOT NULL
  2 ADD created  DATE DEFAULT SYSDATE;

Table altered.

SQL>
```

Review the table created.

```
SQL> DESCRIBE country
 Name                   Null?    Type
 ------------------ -------- ------------
 COUNTRY_CODE           NOT NULL NUMBER(4)
 COUNTRY_NAME           NOT NULL VARCHAR2(40)
 CREATED                         DATE

SQL>
```

Let's create the STATE table. Notice that multiple column constraints can be defined only at the table level.

```
SQL> CREATE TABLE state (
  2 state_code    VARCHAR2 (3),
  3 state_name    VARCHAR2 (40) NOT NULL,
  4 country_code  NUMBER (4) REFERENCES country,
```

```
  5  capital_city  VARCHAR2 (40),
  6  created       DATE DEFAULT SYSDATE,
  7  CONSTRAINT pk_state PRIMARY KEY
  8    (country_code, state_code));
Table created.
SQL>
```

Since we did not provide a name for the COUNTRY_CODE foreign key, Oracle assigns a name. To rename this constraint to provide a meaningful name, we must drop the constraint and re-create it. Let's find the constraint name from the USER_CONSTRAINTS view, drop it, and re-create it.

```
SQL> SELECT constraint_name, constraint_type
  2  FROM   user_constraints
  3  WHERE  table_name = 'STATE';
CONSTRAINT_NAME                C
------------------------------ -
SYS_C002811                    C
PK_STATE                       P
SYS_C002813                    R
SQL> ALTER TABLE state DROP CONSTRAINT SYS_C002813;
Table altered.
SQL> ALTER TABLE state ADD CONSTRAINT fk_state
  2  FOREIGN KEY (country_code) REFERENCES country;
Table altered.
SQL>
```

Now, we'll create the CITY table. Notice the foreign key constraint is created with the `ON DELETE CASCADE` clause.

```
SQL> CREATE TABLE city (
city_code    VARCHAR2 (6),
city_name    VARCHAR2 (40) NOT NULL,
country_code NUMBER (4) NOT NULL,
state_code   VARCHAR2 (3) NOT NULL,
population   NUMBER (15),
created      DATE DEFAULT SYSDATE,
constraint   pk_city PRIMARY KEY (city_code),
constraint   fk_cigy FOREIGN KEY
             (country_code, state_code)
             REFERENCES state ON DELETE CASCADE);
Table created.
SQL>
```

Summary

Tables are the basic structure of data storage. A table comprises columns and rows, as in a spreadsheet. Each column has a characteristic that restricts and verifies the data that it stores. There are several datatypes that can be used to define columns. CHAR, NCHAR, VARCHAR2, CLOB, and NCLOB are the character datatypes. BLOB, BFILE, and RAW are the binary datatypes. DATE, TIMESTAMP, and INTERVAL are the date datatypes. TIMESTAMP datatypes can store the time zone information also.

The `CREATE TABLE` statement is used to create a new table. A table should have at least one column, and a datatype should be assigned to the column. The table name and column name should begin with a letter and may contain letters, numbers, or special characters. You can create a new table from an existing table using the `CREATE TABLE…AS SELECT…` (CTAS) statement. You can add, modify, or drop columns from an existing table using the ALTER TABLE statement. Before changing the datatype of a column, the column should be empty.

Constraints are created in the database to enforce a business rule and to specify relationships between various tables. NOT NULL constraints can be defined only with a column definition and are used to prevent NULL values (absence of data). Check constraints are used to verify if the data conforms to certain conditions. Primary key constraints uniquely identify a row in the table. There can be only one primary key for a table, and the columns in the primary key cannot have NULL values. A unique key is similar to a primary key, but you can have more than one unique key in a table, as well as NULL values in the unique key columns.

Constraints can be enabled and disabled using the ALTER TABLE statement. The constraint can be in four different states. ENABLE VALIDATE is the default state.

Exam Essentials

Understand datatypes. Know each datatype's limitations and accepted values. Concentrate on the new TIMESTAMP and INTERVAL datatypes.

Know how date arithmetic works. Know the resulting datatype of date arithmetic, especially between INTERVAL and DATE datatypes.

Know how to modify column characteristics. Understand how to change datatypes, add and modify constraints, and make other modifications.

Understand the rules associated with changing datatype definitions of columns with rows in table. When the table is not empty, you can only change a datatype from CHAR to VARCHAR2 or vice versa. Reducing the length is allowed only if the existing data fits in the new length specified.

Understand the DEFAULT clause on the column definition. The DEFAULT clause provides a value for the column if the INSERT statement omits a value for the column. When modifying a column to have default values, the existing rows with NULL values in the table are not updated with the default value. When adding a new column with DEFAULT value, all the rows in the table will have the default value for the newly added column.

Understand constraints. Know the difference between a primary key and a unique key constraints, and how to use a nonunique index for primary/unique keys.

Know how a constraint can be defined. You can use the `CREATE TABLE` or `ALTER TABLE` statement to define a constraint on the table.

Key Terms

Before you take the exam, be certain you are familiar with the following terms:

datatype	default value
deferred constraint checking	foreign key
identifier	integrity constraint
Julian date	primary key
table	time zone displacement

Review Questions

1. The STATE table has the following constraints (the constraint status is shown in parentheses):

Primary key	pk_state (enabled)
Foreign key	COUNTRY table–fk_statc (cnabled)
Check constraint	ck_cnt_code (disabled)
Check constraint	ck_st_code (enabled)
Not null constraint	nn_st_name (enabled)

You execute the following SQL:

```
CREATE TABLE STATE_NEW AS SELECT * FROM STATE;
```

How many constraints will there be in the new table?

A. 0

B. 1

C. 3

D. 5

E. 2

2. Which line of code has an error?

```
1  CREATE TABLE FRUITS_VEGETABLES
2  (FRUIT_TYPE VARCHAR2,
3   FRUIT_NAME CHAR (20),
4   QUANTITY   NUMBER);
```

A. 1

B. 2

C. 3

D. 4

3. Which statement successfully adds a new column ORDER_DATE to the table ORDERS?

   A. `ALTER TABLE ORDERS ADD COLUMN ORDER_DATE DATE;`

   B. `ALTER TABLE ORDERS ADD ORDER_DATE (DATE);`

   C. `ALTER TABLE ORDERS ADD ORDER_DATE DATE;`

   D. `ALTER TABLE ORDERS NEW COLUMN ORDER_DATE TYPE DATE;`

4. What are the special characters allowed in a table name? (Choose two answers.)

   A. &

   B. #

   C. @

   D. $

5. Consider the following statement:

```
CREATE TABLE MY_TABLE (
1ST_COLUMN  NUMBER,
2ND_COLUMN  VARCHAR2 (20));
```

   Which of the following best describes this statement?

   A. Tables cannot be created without a defining a primary key. The table definition here is missing the primary key.

   B. The reserved word `COLUMN` cannot be part of the column name.

   C. The column names are invalid.

   D. There is no maximum length specified for the first column definition. You must always specify a length for character and numeric columns.

   E. There is no error in the statement.

6. Which dictionary view would you query to list only the tables you own?

   A. ALL_TABLES

   B. DBA_TABLES

   C. USER_TABLES

   D. USR_TABLES

7. The STATE table has six rows. You issue the following command:

```
ALTER TABLE STATE ADD UPDATE_DT DATE DEFAULT SYSDATE;
```

   Which of the following is correct?

   A. A new column, UPDATE_DT, is added to the STATE table, and its contents for the existing rows are NULL.

   B. Since the table is not empty, you cannot add a new column.

   C. The DEFAULT value cannot be provided if the table has rows.

   D. A new column, UPDATE_DT, is added to STATE and is populated with the current system date and time.

8. The HIRING table has the following data:

```
EMPNO      HIREDATE
---------  ----------
1021       12-DEC-00
3400       24-JAN-01
2398       30-JUN-01
```

   What will be result of the following query?

```
SELECT hiredate+1 FROM hiring WHERE empno = 3400;
```

   A. 4-FEB-01

   B. 25-JAN-01

   C. N-02

   D. None of the above

9. What is the default length of a CHAR datatype column, if no length is specified in the table definition?

   A. 256

   B. 1000

   C. 64

   D. 1

   E. You must always specify a length for CHAR columns.

10. Which statement will remove the column UPDATE_DT from table STATE?

    A. `ALTER TABLE STATE DROP COLUMN UPDATE_DT;`

    B. `ALTER TABLE STATE REMOVE COLUMN UPDATE_DT;`

    C. `DROP COLUMN UPDATE_DT FROM STATE;`

    D. `ALTER TABLE STATE SET UNUSED COLUMN UPDATE_DT;`

    E. You cannot drop a column from the table.

11. Which option is not available in Oracle when modifying tables?

    A. Add new columns

    B. Rename existing column

    C. Drop existing column

    D. All of the above

12. Which one of the following statements will create a primary key for the CITY table with columns STATE_CD and CITY_CD?

    A. `CREATE PRIMARY KEY ON CITY (STATE_CD, CITY_CD);`

    B. `CREATE CONSTRAINT PK_CITY PRIMARY KEY ON CITY (STATE_CD, CITY_CD);`

    C. `ALTER TABLE CITY ADD CONSTRAINT PK_CITY PRIMARY KEY (STATE_CD, CITY_CD);`

    D. `ALTER TABLE CITY ADD PRIMARY KEY (STATE_CD, CITY_CD);`

    E. `ALTER TABLE CITY ADD PRIMARY KEY CONSTRAINT PK_CITY ON (STATE_CD, CITY_CD);`

13. Which of the following check constraints will raise an error? (Choose all that apply.)

A. `CONSTRAINT ck_gender CHECK (gender IN ('M', 'F'))`

B. `CONSTRAINT ck_old_order CHECK (order_date > (SYSDATE - 30))`

C. `CONSTRAINT ck_vendor CHECK (vendor_id IN (SELECT vendor_id FROM vendors))`

D. `CONSTRAINT ck_profit CHECK (gross_amt > net_amt)`

14. Consider the datatypes DATE, TIMESTAMP (TS), TIMESTAMP WITH LOCAL TIME ZONE (TSLTZ), INTERVAL YEAR TO MONTH (IY2M), INTERVAL DAY TO SECOND (ID2S). Which operations are not allowed by the Oracle9i database? (Choose all that apply.)

A. DATE + DATE

B. TSLTZ - DATE

C. TSLTZ + IY2M

D. TS * 5

E. ID2S / 2

F. IY2M + IY2M

G. ID2S + IY2M

H. DATE – IY2M

15. A constraint is created with the `DEFERRABLE INITIALLY IMMEDIATE` clause. What does this mean?

A. Constraint checking is done only at commit time.

B. Constraint checking is done after each SQL statement is executed, but you can change this behavior by specifying `SET CONSTRAINTS ALL DEFERRED`.

C. Existing rows in the table are immediately checked for constraint violation.

D. The constraint is immediately checked in a DML operation, but subsequent constraint verification is done at commit time.

16. What is the default precision for fractional seconds in a TIMESTAMP datatype column?

    A. 0

    B. 2

    C. 6

    D. 9

17. Which datatype stores the time zone information along with the date value?

    A. TIMESTAMP

    B. TIMESTAMP WITH LOCAL TIME ZONE

    C. TIMESTAMP WITH TIME ZONE

    D. DATE

    E. Both options B and C

18. You have a large job that will load many thousands of rows into your ORDERS table. To speed up the loading process, you want to temporarily stop enforcing the foreign key constraint FK_ORDERS. Which of the following statements will satisfy your requirement?

    A. `ALTER CONSTRAINT FK_ORDERS DISABLE;`

    B. `ALTER TABLE ORDERS DISABLE FOREIGN KEY FK_ORDERS;`

    C. `ALTER TABLE ORDERS DISABLE CONSTRAINT FK_ORDERS;`

    D. `ALTER TABLE ORDERS DISABLE ALL CONSTRAINTS;`

19. You are connected to the database as user JOHN. You need to rename a table named NORDERS to NEW_ORDERS, owned by SMITH. Consider the following two statements:

```
1. RENAME SMITH.NORDERS TO NEW_ORDERS;
2. ALTER TABLE SMITH.NORDERS RENAME TO NEW_ORDERS;
```

Which of the following is correct?

A. Statement 1 will work; statement 2 will not.

B. Statements 1 and 2 will work.

C. Statement 1 will not work; statement 2 will work.

D. Statements 1 and 2 will not work

20. Which two declarations define the maximum length of a CHAR datatype column in bytes?

A. `CHAR (20)`

B. `CHAR (20) BYTE`

C. `CHAR (20 BYTE)`

D. `BYTE (20 CHAR)`

E. `CHAR BYTE (20)`

Answers to Review Questions

1. B. When you create a table using CTAS (`CREATE TABLE AS`), only the `NOT NULL` constraints are copied.

2. B. A VARCHAR2 datatype should always specify the maximum length of the column.

3. C. The correct statement is C. When adding only one column, the column definition need not be enclosed in parentheses.

4. B, D. Only three special characters ($, _, and #) are allowed in the table names along with letters and numbers.

5. C. All identifiers (column names, table names, and so on) must begin with an alphabetic character. An identifier can contain alphabetic characters, numbers, and the special characters $, #, and _.

6. C. The USER_TABLES view provides information on the tables owned by the user who has logged on that session. DBA_TABLES will have all the tables in the database, and ALL_TABLES will have the tables owned by you as well as the tables to which you have access. USR_TABLES is not a valid dictionary view.

7. D. When a default value is specified in the new column added, the column values for the existing rows are populated with the default value.

8. B. In date arithmetic, adding 1 is equivalent to adding 24 hours. To add 6 hours to a date value with time, add 0.25.

9. D. If you do not specify a length for a CHAR datatype column, the default length of 1 is assumed.

10. A. You can use the `DROP COLUMN` clause with the `ALTER TABLE` statement to drop a column. There is no separate `DROP COLUMN` statement or a `REMOVE` clause in the `ALTER TABLE` statement. The `SET UNUSED` clause is used to mark the column as unused. This column can be dropped later using the `DROP UNUSED COLUMNS` clause.

11. B. You cannot rename an existing column using the ALTER TABLE statement. To rename the column, you must re-create the table with the new name.

12. C. The ALTER TABLE statement is used to create and remove constraints. Option D would work if the keyword CONSTRAINT were included between ADD and PRIMARY.

13. B, C. Check constraints cannot reference the SYSDATE function or other tables.

14. A, D, G. You cannot add two DATE datatypes, but you can subtract to find the difference in days. Multiplication and division operators are permitted only on INTERVAL datatypes. When adding or subtracting INTERVAL datatypes, both INTERVAL datatypes should be of the same category.

15. B. DEFERRABLE specifies that the constraint can be deferred using the SET CONSTRAINTS command. INITIALLY IMMEDIATE specifies that the constraint's default behavior is to validate the constraint for each SQL statement executed.

16. C. The default precision is 6 digits. The precision can range from 0 to 9.

17. C. Only TIMESTAMP WITH TIME ZONE stores the time zone information as a displacement from UTC. TIMESTAMP WITH LOCAL TIME ZONE adjusts the time to database's time zone before storing it.

18. C. You can disable constraints by specifying its constraint name. You may enable the constraint after the load and avoid the constraint checking while enabling using the ALTER TABLE ORDERS MODIFY CONSTRAINT FK_ORDERS ENABLE NOVALIDATE; command.

19. C. RENAME can be used to rename objects owned the user. ALTER TABLE should be used to rename tables owned by another user. To do so, you must have the ALTER privilege on the table or the ALTER ANY TABLE privilege.

20. A, C. The maximum lengths of CHAR and VARCHAR2 columns can be defined in characters or bytes. BYTE is the default.

Managing Views

INTRODUCTION TO ORACLE9i: SQL EXAM OBJECTIVES COVERED IN THIS CHAPTER:

✓ **Creating Views**

- Describe a view
- Create, alter the definition, and drop a view
- Retrieve data through a view
- Insert, update and delete data through a view
- Create and use an inline view
- Perform Top 'N' Analysis

Exam objectives are subject to change at any time without prior notice and at Oracle's sole discretion. Please visit Oracle's Certification website (`http://www.oracle.com/education/certification/`) for the most current exam objectives listing.

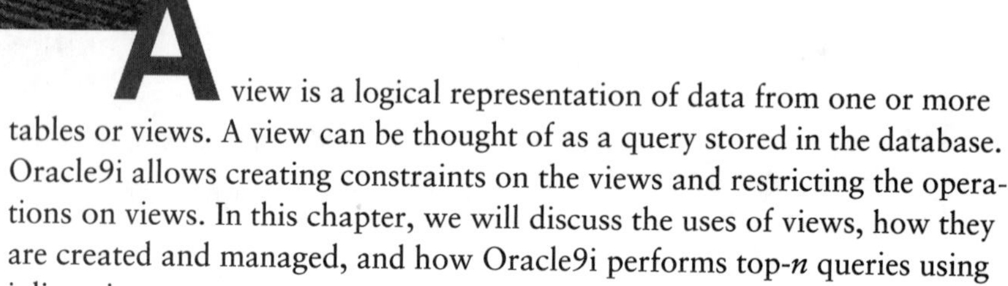

A view is a logical representation of data from one or more tables or views. A view can be thought of as a query stored in the database. Oracle9i allows creating constraints on the views and restricting the operations on views. In this chapter, we will discuss the uses of views, how they are created and managed, and how Oracle9i performs top-*n* queries using inline views.

Creating and Modifying Views

A *view* is a customized representation of data from one or more tables. The tables that the view is referencing are known as *base tables*. A view can be considered as a stored query or a virtual table. Only the query is stored in the Oracle data dictionary; the actual data is not copied anywhere. This means that creating views does not take any storage space, other than the space in dictionary.

The maximum number of columns that can be defined in a view is 1000, just as for a table.

Use the `CREATE VIEW` statement to create a view. The query that defines the view can refer to one or more tables, to materialized views, or to other views. Let's begin by creating a simple view. We'll use the EMPLOYEES table of the HR schema as the base table.

```
SQL> DESCRIBE employees
 Name                          Null?    Type
 ----------------------------- -------- -------------
 EMPLOYEE_ID                   NOT NULL NUMBER(6)
 FIRST_NAME                             VARCHAR2(20)
 LAST_NAME                     NOT NULL VARCHAR2(25)
 EMAIL                         NOT NULL VARCHAR2(25)
 PHONE_NUMBER                           VARCHAR2(20)
 HIRE_DATE                     NOT NULL DATE
 JOB_ID                        NOT NULL VARCHAR2(10)
 SALARY                                 NUMBER(8,2)
 COMMISSION_PCT                         NUMBER(2,2)
 MANAGER_ID                             NUMBER(6)
 DEPARTMENT_ID                          NUMBER(4)
```

The following code creates a view named ADMIN_EMPLOYEES, with the employee information for employees who belong to the Administration department (department 10). Notice that the LAST_NAME and FIRST_NAME columns are joined to display just a NAME column. You can rename columns by using alias names in the view definition. The datatype of the view's columns are derived by Oracle.

```
SQL> CREATE VIEW admin_employees AS
  2  SELECT first_name || last_name NAME,
  3         email, job_id POSITION
  4  FROM   employees
  5  WHERE  department_id = 10;

View created.
SQL> DESCRIBE admin_employees
 Name                          Null?    Type
 ----------------------------- -------- -------------
 NAME                                   VARCHAR2(45)
 EMAIL                         NOT NULL VARCHAR2(25)
 POSITION                      NOT NULL VARCHAR2(10)
SQL>
```

When numeric operations are performed using numeric datatypes in the view definition, the resulting column will be a floating datatype, which is NUMBER without any precision or scale. The following example uses SALARY (defined `NUMBER (8,2)`) and COMMISSION_PCT (defined `NUMBER (2,2)`) in an arithmetic operation. The resulting column value is the NUMBER datatype.

```
SQL> CREATE VIEW emp_sal_comm AS
  2  SELECT employee_id, salary,
  3         salary * NVL(commission_pct,0) commission
  4  FROM   employees;

View created.

SQL> DESCRIBE emp_sal_comm
 Name                        Null?    Type
 --------------------- -------- ----------
 EMPLOYEE_ID                 NOT NULL NUMBER(6)
 SALARY                               NUMBER(8,2)
 COMMISSION                           NUMBER
SQL>
```

Using Defined Column Names

You can also specify the column names immediately following the view name to have different column names in the view. Let's create another view using defined column names. This view joins the DEPARTMENTS table to the EMPLOYEES table, uses a function on the HIRE_DATE column, and also derives a new column named COMMISSION_AMT. Notice the `ORDER BY` clause in the view definition. The derived column COMMISSION_AMT is the NUMBER datatype, so there is no maximum length.

```
SQL> CREATE VIEW emp_hire
  2  (employee_id, employee_name, department_name,
  3   hire_date, commission_amt)
  4  AS SELECT employee_id, first_name || ' ' || last_name,
  5      department_name, TO_CHAR(hire_date,'DD-MM-YYYY'),
  6      salary * NVL(commission_pct, .5)
  7  FROM employees JOIN departments USING (department_id)
  8  ORDER BY first_name || ' ' || last_name;
```

```
View created.
SQL> DESC emp_hire
 Name                          Null?    Type
 ----------------------------- -------- ------------
 EMPLOYEE_ID                   NOT NULL NUMBER(6)
 EMPLOYEE_NAME                          VARCHAR2(46)
 DEPARTMENT_NAME               NOT NULL VARCHAR2(30)
 HIRE_DATE                              VARCHAR2(10)
 COMMISSION_AMT                         NUMBER
SQL>
```

If you use an asterisk (*) to select all columns from a table in the query to create a view, and you later modify the table to add columns, you should re-create the view to reflect the new columns. When * is used, Oracle expands it to the column list and stores the definition in the database.

Creating Views with Errors

You can create views with errors using the FORCE option (NO FORCE is the default). Normally, if the base tables do not exist, the view will not be created. If, however, you need to create the view with errors, you can do so. The view will be INVALID. Later, you can fix the error, such as creating the underlying table, and then the view can be recompiled. Oracle recompiles invalid views (all invalid stored objects, for that matter) when the view is accessed.

As an example, suppose that we try to create a new view named TEST_VIEW on a nonexisting base table named TEST_TABLE:

```
SQL> CREATE VIEW test_view AS
  2  SELECT c1, c2 FROM test_table;
SELECT c1, c2 FROM test_table
                   *
ERROR at line 2:
ORA-00942: table or view does not exist
```

Since we did not use the FORCE option, the view was not created. When we use the FORCE option, Oracle creates the view. However, trying to access the view gives an error, because the table TEST_TABLE does not exist yet.

```
SQL> CREATE FORCE VIEW test_view AS
  2  SELECT c1, c2 FROM test_table;
```

```
Warning: View created with compilation errors.

SQL> SELECT * FROM test_view;
SELECT * FROM test_view
              *
ERROR at line 1:
ORA-04063: view "HR.TEST_VIEW" has errors
```

Now, let's create the TEST_TABLE and access the view.

```
SQL> CREATE TABLE test_table (
  2  c1 NUMBER (10),
  3  c2 VARCHAR2 (20));

Table created.
SQL> SELECT * FROM test_view;

no rows selected
SQL>
```

This time, it works!

The subquery that defines the view cannot contain the FOR UPDATE clause, and the columns should not reference the CURRVAL or NEXTVAL pseudo-columns.

Creating Read-Only Views

You can create a view as read-only using the WITH READ ONLY option. Such views can be used only in queries; no DML operations can be performed on the view. Let's create a read-only view.

```
SQL> CREATE VIEW all_locations
  2  AS SELECT country_id, country_name, location_id, city
  3  FROM  locations NATURAL JOIN countries
  4  WITH READ ONLY;

View created.
SQL>
```

Creating Constraints on Views

Oracle9i allows creating constraints on views. Constraints on views are not enforced—they are *declarative constraints*. To enforce constraints, you must define them on the base tables. When creating constraints on views, you must always include the DISABLE NOVALIDATE clause. You can define primary key, unique key, and foreign key constraints on views. The syntax for creating constraints on views is the same as for creating constraints on a table (see Chapter 7, "Managing Tables and Constraints").

The following example creates a view with constraints. Line 2 defines a column-level foreign key constraint, line 5 defines a column-level unique constraint, and line 7 defines a view-level foreign key constraint.

```
SQL> CREATE VIEW emp_details
  2  (employee_no CONSTRAINT fk_employee_no
  3                 REFERENCES employees DISABLE NOVALIDATE,
  4   manager_no,
  5   phone_number CONSTRAINT uq_email unique
  6                  DISABLE NOVALIDATE,
  7   CONSTRAINT fk_manager_no FOREIGN KEY (manager_no)
  8                 REFERENCES employees DISABLE NOVALIDATE)
  9  AS SELECT employee_id, manager_id, phone_number
 10  FROM   employees
 11* WHERE  department_id = 40
SQL> /

View created.
SQL>
```

Modifying Views

To change the definition of the view, use the CREATE VIEW statement with the OR REPLACE option. The ALTER VIEW statement can be used to compile an invalid view or to add and drop constraints.

Changing a View's Definition

When using the OR REPLACE option, if the view exists, it will be replaced with the new definition; otherwise, a new view will be created. When you use the CREATE OR REPLACE option instead of dropping and re-creating the view, the privileges granted on the view are preserved. The dependent stored programs and views become invalid.

In the ADMIN_EMPLOYEES view defined earlier, we forgot to include a space between the first name and last name of the employee. Let's fix that now using the OR REPLACE option.

```
SQL> CREATE OR REPLACE VIEW admin_employees AS
  2  SELECT first_name ||' '|| last_name NAME,
  3         email, job_id
  4  FROM   employees
  5  WHERE  department_id = 10;

View created.
SQL>
```

Recompiling a View

Views become invalid when the base tables are altered. Oracle automatically recompiles the view when it is accessed, but you can explicitly recompile the view using the ALTER VIEW statement. When the view is recompiled, the objects dependent on the view become invalid.

Let's change the length of a column in the TEST_TABLE table we created earlier. The TEST_VIEW view is dependent on this table. The status of the database objects can be seen in the USER_OBJECTS view. The following example queries the status of the view, modifies the table, queries the status of the view, compiles the view, and again queries the status of the view.

```
SQL> SELECT last_ddl_time, status FROM user_objects
  2  WHERE  object_name = 'TEST_VIEW';

LAST_DDL_TIME           STATUS
----------------------- -------
25-OCT-2001 11:17:24 AM VALID

SQL> ALTER TABLE test_table MODIFY c2 VARCHAR2 (8);
Table altered.

SQL> SELECT last_ddl_time, status FROM user_objects
  2  WHERE  object_name = 'TEST_VIEW';
```

```
LAST_DDL_TIME           STATUS
----------------------- -------
25-OCT-2001 11:17:24 AM INVALID

SQL> ALTER VIEW test_view compile;
View altered.

SQL> SELECT last_ddl_time, status FROM user_objects
  2 WHERE  object_name = 'TEST_VIEW';

LAST_DDL_TIME           STATUS
----------------------- -------
25-OCT-2001 05:47:46 PM VALID
SQL>
```

The syntax for adding or dropping constraints on a view is similar to that for modifying the constraints on a table, but you use the `ALTER VIEW` statement instead of the `ALTER TABLE` statement. The following example adds a primary key constraint on the TEST_VIEW view.

```
SQL> ALTER VIEW hr.test_view
  2 ADD CONSTRAINT pk_test_view
  3 PRIMARY KEY (C1) DISABLE NOVALIDATE;

View altered.
SQL>
```

The next example drops the constraint we just added.

```
SQL> ALTER VIEW test_view DROP CONSTRAINT pk_test_view;

View altered.
SQL>
```

Dropping a View

To drop a view, use the `DROP VIEW` statement. The view definition is dropped from the dictionary, and the privileges and grants on the view are also dropped. Other views and stored programs that refer to the dropped view become invalid.

```
SQL> DROP VIEW test_view;

View dropped.
SQL>
```

Using Views

A view can be used in most places where a table is used, such as in queries and in DML operations. If certain conditions are met, most single-table views and many join views can be used to insert, update, and delete data from the base table. All operations on views affect the data in the base tables; therefore, they should satisfy any integrity constraints defined on the base tables.

The following are some common uses of views:

To represent a subset of data For security reasons, you many not want certain users to see all of the rows of your table. You may create a view on the columns that the users need to access with a WHERE clause to limit the rows, and then grant privileges on the view.

To represent a superset of data You can use views to represent information from multiple normalized tables in one unnormalized view.

To hide complex joins Since views are stored queries, you can have complex queries defined as views, where the end user need not worry about the relationship between tables or know SQL.

To provide more meaningful names for columns If your tables are defined with short and cryptic column names, you may create a view and provide more meaningful column names that the users will understand better.

To minimize application and data source changes You may develop an application referring to views, and if the data source changes or the data is derived in a different manner, only the view needs to be changed.

Using Views in Queries

You can use views in queries and subqueries. You can use all SQL functions and all the clauses of the SELECT statement when querying against a view, as you would when querying against a table.

When you issue a query against a view, most of the time, Oracle merges the query with the query that defines the view, then executes the resulting query as if the query were issued directly against the base tables. This helps to use the indexes, if there are any defined on the table.

Let's query the results of the EMPLOYEE_DETAILS view we created earlier.

```
SQL> SELECT * FROM emp_details;

EMPLOYEE_NO MANAGER_NO PHONE_NUMBER
----------- ---------- --------------
        203        101 515.123.7777
SQL>
```

Let's consider another example using a `WHERE` clause and a `GROUP BY` clause. This example finds the total commission paid for each department from the EMP_HIRE view for all commissions above $100.

```
SQL> SELECT department_name, SUM(commission_amt) comm_amt
  2  FROM   emp_hire
  3  WHERE  commission_amt > 100
  4  GROUP BY department_name;

DEPARTMENT_NAME                  COMM_AMT
------------------------------ ----------
Accounting                          10150
Administration                       2200
Executive                           29000
Finance                             25800
Human Resources                      3250
IT                                  14400
Marketing                            9500
Public Relations                     5000
Purchasing                          12450
Sales                               72640
Shipping                            78200

11 rows selected.
SQL>
```

Inserting, Updating, and Deleting Data through Views

You can update, insert, and delete rows through a view, but with some restrictions. You can perform DML statements on a view only if the view definition does not have the following:

- DISTINCT clause
- GROUP BY clause
- START WITH clause
- CONNECT BY clause
- ROWNUM clause
- Set operators (UNION, UNION ALL, INTERSECT, or MINUS)
- Subquery in the SELECT clause

All DML operations on the view are performed on the base tables.

Let's create a simple view based on the DEPARTMENTS table. The following view includes all of the columns that are part of any constraint in the DEPARTMENTS table, so we can insert a row through the view without violating any constraints.

```
SQL> CREATE OR REPLACE VIEW dept_above_250
  2  AS SELECT department_id DID, department_name
  3  FROM   departments
  4  WHERE  department_id > 250;

View created.
SQL> SELECT * FROM dept_above_250;

       DID DEPARTMENT_NAME
---------- -----------------
       260 Recruiting
       270 Payroll
SQL>
```

Let's insert a new department through the view and verify that the department is added to the DEPARTMENTS table. (The SET NULL * SQL*Plus command displays an asterisk whenever the column value is NULL.)

```
SQL> SET NULL *
SQL> INSERT INTO dept_above_250
  2  VALUES (199, 'Temporary Dept');
```

```
1 row created.
SQL> SELECT * FROM departments
  2  WHERE  department_id = 199;

DEPARTMENT_ID DEPARTMENT_NAME      MANAGER_ID LOCATION_ID
------------- -------------------- ---------- -----------
          199 Temporary Dept       *          *
SQL>
```

Although the view is defined with a WHERE clause to verify DEPARTMENT_ID > 250, Oracle did not enforce this condition when you inserted a new row. If you want the DML statements through the view to conform to the view definition, use the WITH CHECK OPTION clause. The WITH CHECK OPTION clause creates a check constraint on the view to enforce the condition (such constraints will have the constraint type "V", when you query the USER_CONSTRAINTS view).

Let's re-create the DEPT_ABOVE_250 view to include the WITH CHECK OPTION clause. The CONSTRAINT keyword can be followed by a constraint name. If you do not provide a constraint name, Oracle creates a constraint whose name begins with SYS_C, followed by a unique string.

```
SQL> CREATE OR REPLACE VIEW dept_above_250
  2  AS SELECT department_id DID, department_name
  3  FROM   departments
  4  WHERE  department_id > 250
  5  WITH CHECK OPTION;

View created.
SQL> INSERT INTO dept_above_250
  2  VALUES (199, 'Temporary Dept');
INSERT INTO dept_above_250
            *
ERROR at line 1:
ORA-01402: view WITH CHECK OPTION where-clause violation

SQL> SELECT constraint_name, table_name
  2  FROM   user_constraints
  3  WHERE  constraint_type = 'V';
```

```
CONSTRAINT_NAME                TABLE_NAME
------------------------------ ----------------
SYS_C002779                    DEPT_ABOVE_250
SQL>
```

Let's provide a name for the constraint and query the USER_CONSTRAINTS view again.

```
SQL> CREATE OR REPLACE VIEW dept_above_250
  2  AS SELECT department_id DID, department_name
  3  FROM   departments
  4  WHERE  department_id > 250
  5  WITH CHECK OPTION CONSTRAINT check_dept_250;

View created.
SQL> SELECT constraint_name, table_name
  2  FROM   user_constraints
  3  WHERE  constraint_type = 'V';

CONSTRAINT_NAME                TABLE_NAME
------------------------------ ---------------
CHECK_DEPT_250                 DEPT_ABOVE_250
SQL>
```

Real World Scenario

Controlling Access with a View

You may need to make sure that users cannot view or modify records that do not belong to them. You can use a view to control access in this way.

The EMPLOYEE_INFO table in the HR schema holds the personal information of employees. The business requirement is for the employees to be able to update their own address information. EMPLOYEE_ID is the primary key of this table.

The SQL variable `USER` gives the username used to connect to the database. We'll use this variable to restrict the rows available to the user. The EMPLOYEE_INFO table has a column named LOGIN_ID. The view can be defined as follows:

```
CREATE OR REPLACE VIEW employee_address AS
SELECT employee_id, street, city, zip, home_phone
FROM   employee_info
WHERE  login_id = USER
WITH CHECK OPTION;
```

For updating the address, the user needs to be given `UPDATE` privileges on the view, not on the base table. The `WITH CHECK OPTION` clause is optional if you do not give the user access to add records to the view.

Using Join Views

A join view is a view with more than one base table in the top-level `FROM` clause. An *updatable join view* (or modifiable join view) is a view that can be used to update the base tables through the view. Any `INSERT`, `UPDATE`, or `DELETE` operation on the join view can modify data from only one base table in any single SQL operation.

A table in the join view is *key-preserved*, if the primary and unique keys of the table are unique on the view's result set. For example, let's create a view using the base tables COUNTRIES and REGIONS.

```
SQL> CREATE OR REPLACE VIEW country_region AS
     SELECT a.country_id, a.country_name, a.region_id,
            b.region_name
     FROM   countries a, regions b
     WHERE  a.region_id = b.region_id;

View created.
```

```
SQL> DESC country_region
 Name                          Null?    Type
 ----------------------------- -------- ------------
 COUNTRY_ID                    NOT NULL CHAR(2)
 COUNTRY_NAME                           VARCHAR2(40)
 REGION_ID                              NUMBER
 REGION_NAME                            VARCHAR2(25)
SQL>
```

In the COUNTRY_REGION view, the COUNTRIES table is key-preserved because the primary key in the COUNTRIES table is also unique in the view. The REGIONS table is not key-preserved because its primary key REGION_ID is duplicated several times, for each country.

You can update only a key-preserved table through a view. If the view is defined with the `WITH CHECK OPTION` clause, you cannot update the columns that join the base tables. For example, if we define the COUNTRY_REGION view with the `WITH CHECK OPTION` clause, even though the COUNTRY table is key-preserved, we will not be able to update the REGION_ID column.

`INSERT` statements cannot refer to any columns of the non-key-preserved table. If the view is created with the `WITH CHECK OPTION` clause, no `INSERT` operation is permitted on the view.

Let's try a few examples. Updating the REGION_NAME column in the COUNTRY_REGION view produces an error.

```
SQL> UPDATE country_region
  2  SET    region_name = 'Testing Update'
  3  WHERE  region_id = 1;
SET    region_name = 'Testing Update'
       *
ERROR at line 2:
ORA-01779: cannot modify a column which maps to a
non key-preserved table
SQL>
```

Updating the REGION_ID column does not cause an error because the column belongs to a key-preserved table.

```
SQL> UPDATE country_region
  2  SET    region_id = 1
  3  WHERE  country_id = 'EG';
```

```
1 row updated.
SQL>
```

Let's redefine the COUNTRY_REGION view with the `WITH CHECK OPTION` clause and try the same `UPDATE` statement again.

```
SQL> CREATE OR REPLACE VIEW country_region AS
  2  SELECT a.country_id, a.country_name, a.region_id,
  3         b.region_name
  4  FROM   countries a, regions b
  5  WHERE  a.region_id = b.region_id
  6  WITH CHECK OPTION;

View created.
SQL> UPDATE country_region
  2  SET    region_id = 1
  3  WHERE  country_id = 'EG';
SET    region_id = 1
       *
ERROR at line 2:
ORA-01733: virtual column not allowed here
SQL>
```

Viewing Allowable DML Operations

Oracle provides data dictionary views with information on what DML operations are allowed on each column of the view: the USER_UPDATABLE_COLUMNS view has information on columns of the views owned by the user, the ALL_UPDATABLE_COLUMNS view has information on the columns of views to which the user has access, and the DBA_UPDATABLE_COLUMNS view has information on columns of all the views in the database.

Let's query the USER_UPDATABLE_COLUMNS view to see what information is available on the COUNTRY_REGION view.

```
SQL> SELECT column_name, updatable, insertable, deletable
  2  FROM   user_updatable_columns
  3  WHERE  owner = 'HR'
  4  AND    table_name = 'COUNTRY_REGION';
```

```
COLUMN_NAME                    UPD INS DEL
------------------------------ --- --- ---
COUNTRY_ID                     YES YES YES
COUNTRY_NAME                   YES YES YES
REGION_ID                      YES YES YES
REGION_NAME                    NO  NO  NO
SQL>
```

You can query information on the views from the data dictionary using USER_VIEWS (or DBA_VIEWS or ALL_VIEWS). This view contains the view definition SQL. The column names of the view can be queried from USER_TAB_COLUMNS.

Using Inline Views

A subquery can appear in the FROM clause of the SELECT statement. This is similar to defining and using a view, hence the name *inline view*. The subquery in the FROM clause is enclosed in parentheses and may be given an alias name. The columns selected in the subquery can be referenced in the parent query, just as you would select from any normal table or view.

Inline views can be considered as temporary views; you need not create these views to use them in queries. The columns of the inline view result set can be accessed in the same way that you access the columns of a view in DML statements.

Let's consider an example using the EMPLOYEES table of the sample HR schema. The following query can be used to report the employee names, their salary, and the average salary in their department. We'll limit the result set to the employees whose names begin with *B*.

```
SQL> SELECT first_name, salary, avg_salary
     FROM   employees, (SELECT department_id,
            AVG(salary) avg_salary FROM employees e2
            GROUP BY department_id) dept
     WHERE  employees.department_id = dept.department_id
     AND    first_name like 'B%';
```

```
FIRST_NAME                SALARY AVG_SALARY
-------------------- ---------- ----------
Britney                     3900 3475.55556
Bruce                       6000       5760
SQL>
```

The same query written using the ANSI syntax is as follows:

```
SQL> SELECT first_name, salary, avg_salary
     FROM   employees
     NATURAL JOIN (SELECT department_id,
            AVG(salary) avg_salary FROM employees e2
            GROUP BY department_id) dept
     WHERE  first_name like 'B%';

FIRST_NAME                SALARY AVG_SALARY
-------------------- ---------- ----------
Britney                     3900 3475.55556
Bruce                       6000       5760
SQL>
```

You cannot have an ORDER BY clause in the subquery appearing in a WHERE clause. A FROM clause subquery (inline view) can have an ORDER BY clause.

As another example, suppose that we want to find the newest employee in each department. We need to get the MAX(HIRE_DATE) for all employees in each department and get the name of employee, as follows:

```
SQL> SELECT department_name, first_name, last_name,
            hire_date
     FROM   employees JOIN departments
            USING (department_id)
     JOIN   (SELECT department_id, max(hire_date) hire_date
             FROM   employees
             GROUP BY department_id)
     USING  (department_id, hire_date);
```

```
DEPARTMENT_NAME    FIRST_NAME LAST_NAME  HIRE_DATE
------------------ ---------- ---------- ---------
Administration     Jennifer   Whalen     17-SEP-87
Marketing          Pat        Fay        17-AUG-97
Purchasing         Karen      Colmenares 10-AUG-99
Human Resources    Susan      Mavris     07-JUN-94
Shipping           Steven     Markle     08-MAR-00
IT                 Diana      Lorentz    07-FEB-99
Public Relations   Hermann    Baer       07-JUN-94
Sales              Sundita    Kumar      21-APR-00
Sales              Amit       Banda      21-APR-00
Executive          Lex        De Haan    13-JAN-93
Finance            Luis       Popp       07-DEC-99
Accounting         William    Gietz      07-JUN-94
Accounting         Shelley    Higgins    07-JUN-94

13 rows selected.
SQL>
```

The same query written using standard Oracle join syntax would be:

```
SQL> SELECT d.department_name, e.first_name, e.last_name,
            mhd.hire_date
     FROM   employees e, departments d,
            (SELECT department_id, max(hire_date) hire_date
             FROM   employees
             GROUP BY department_id) mhd
     WHERE e.department_id = d.department_id
     AND   e.department_id = mhd.department_id
     AND   e.hire_date     = mhd.hire_date;

DEPARTMENT_NAME    FIRST_NAME LAST_NAME  HIRE_DATE
------------------ ---------- ---------- ---------
Executive          Lex        De Haan    13-JAN-93
IT                 Diana      Lorentz    07-FEB-99
Finance            Luis       Popp       07-DEC-99
Purchasing         Karen      Colmenares 10-AUG-99
Shipping           Steven     Markle     08-MAR-00
```

```
Sales               Amit       Banda     21-APR-00
Sales               Sundita    Kumar     21-APR-00
Administration      Jennifer   Whalen    17-SEP-87
Marketing           Pat        Fay       17-AUG-97
Human Resources     Susan      Mavris    07-JUN-94
Public Relations    Hermann    Baer      07-JUN-94
Accounting          Shelley    Higgins   07-JUN-94
Accounting          William    Gietz     07-JUN-94

13 rows selected.
SQL>
```

Performing Top-'N' Analysis

Using an inline view, you can write queries to find *top-'n'* values. This is possible because Oracle allows an ORDER BY clause in the inline view. So, you sort the rows in the inline view and retrieve the top rows using the ROWNUM variable. The ROWNUM variable gives the row number; the row number is assigned only when the query is fetched. For example, here is a query intended to find the top five highest-paid employees:

```
SQL> SELECT last_name, salary
  2  FROM   employees
  3  WHERE  rownum <= 5
  4  ORDER BY salary DESC ;

LAST_NAME                     SALARY
------------------------- ----------
King                           24000
Kochhar                        17000
De Haan                        17000
Hunold                          9000
Ernst                           6000
SQL>
```

Since the ROWNUM is assigned only when each row is returned, the result set is not right. What we got is just five rows from the table sorted by salary. The following query will return the top five highest-paid employees.

```
SQL> SELECT * FROM
  2  (SELECT last_name, salary
  3  FROM   employees
  4  ORDER BY salary DESC)
  5  WHERE ROWNUM <= 5;

LAST_NAME                      SALARY
------------------------- ----------
King                           24000
Kochhar                        17000
De Haan                        17000
Russell                        14000
Partners                       13500
SQL>
```

The Oracle9i optimizer recognizes the top-*n* analysis queries, and hence does not sort all the rows in the subquery.

Summary

A view is a tailored representation of data from one or more tables or views. The view is a stored query. Views can be used to present a different perspective of data, to limit the data access, or to hide a complex query.

Views can be used as you would use table in queries. You can update, delete, and insert into the base tables through the view (with restrictions), but the operation can affect only one table at a time if there is more than one table in the view definition.

To change the definition of the view, you must re-create the view using `CREATE OR REPLACE` statement. To recompile a view or add or drop constraints, use the `ALTER VIEW` statement.

Declarative constraints can be created on views; the constraints are not enforced. Primary key, unique key, and foreign key are the valid constraint types.

An inline view is a query that can be used instead of a table or view in the `FROM` clause of a query. By using the `ORDER BY` clause in views (and inline views), you can perform top-*n* analyses.

Exam Essentials

Understand how join views work. Know the restrictions on the columns that can be updated in a join view.

Learn how to do a top-'*n*' analysis. Know how to write a query to get the top few rows of a table.

Understand how constraints are used with views. Understand the type of constraints that can be defined on table and a constraint's only valid state.

Understand how inline views are used. Inline views are subqueries used in the `FROM` clause. These subqueries can have an `ORDER BY` clause.

Know how to change the definition of a view. The `CREATE OR REPLACE VIEW` statement is used to change the definition of the view. The `ALTER VIEW` statement is used to recompile a view or to manage constraints on a view.

Key Terms

Before you take the exam, make sure you're familiar with the following terms:

base tables

inline view

top-'*n*'

view

declarative constraints

key-preserved

updatable join view

Review Questions

1. A view created with which option makes sure that rows added to the base table through the view are accessible to the view?

   A. WHERE

   B. WITH READ ONLY

   C. WITH CHECK OPTION

   D. CREATE OR REPLACE VIEW

2. A view is created using the following code. What operations are permitted on the view?

```
CREATE VIEW USA_STATES
AS SELECT * FROM STATE
WHERE  CNT_CODE = 1
WITH READ ONLY;
```

   A. SELECT

   B. SELECT, UPDATE

   C. SELECT, DELETE

   D. SELECT, INSERT

3. How do you remove the view USA_STATES from the schema?

   A. ALTER VIEW USA_STATES REMOVE;

   B. DROP VIEW USA_STATES;

   C. DROP VIEW USA_STATES CASCADE;

   D. DROP USA_STATES;

4. Which data dictionary view has information on the columns in a view that are updatable?

   A. USER_VIEWS

   B. USER_UPDATABLE_COLUMNS

   C. USER_COLUMNS

   D. USER_COLUMNS_UPDATABLE

5. Which option in view creation creates a view even if there are syntax errors?

   A. CREATE FORCE VIEW…

   B. CREATE OR REPLACE VIEW…

   C. CREATE OR REPLACE VIEW FORCE…

   D. CREATE VIEW … IGNORE ERRORS

6. In a join view, on how many base tables can you perform a DML operation (UPDATE/INSERT/DELETE) in a single step?

   A. One

   B. The number of base tables in the view definition

   C. The number of base tables minus one

   D. None

7. The following code is used to define a view. The EMP table does not have a primary key or any other constraints.

   ```
   CREATE VIEW MYVIEW AS
   SELECT DISTINCT ENAME, SALARY
   FROM   EMP
   WHERE  DEPT_ID = 10;
   ```

   Which operations are allowed on the view?

   A. SELECT, INSERT, UPDATE, DELETE

   B. SELECT, UPDATE

   C. SELECT, INSERT, DELETE

   D. SELECT

   E. SELECT, UPDATE, DELETE

8. Which two statements are used to modify a view definition?

A. `ALTER VIEW`

B. `CREATE OR REPLACE VIEW`

C. `REPLACE VIEW`

D. `CREATE FORCE VIEW`

E. `CREATE OR REPLACE FORCE VIEW`

9. You create a view based on the EMPLOYEES table using the following SQL.

```
CREATE VIEW MYVIEW AS SELECT * FROM EMPLOYEES;
```

You modify the table to add a column named EMP_SSN. What do you need to do to have this new column appear in the view?

A. Nothing, since the view definition is selecting all columns, the new column will appear in the view automatically.

B. Recompile the view using `ALTER VIEW MYVIEW RECOMPILE`.

C. Re-create the view using `CREATE OR REPLACE VIEW`.

D. Add the column to the view using `ALTER VIEW MYVIEW ADD EMP_SSN`.

10. You can view the constraints on the objects in your schema in the USER_CONSTRAINTS dictionary view. The CONSTRAINT_TYPE column shows the type of constraint. What is the type of constraint created when you create a view with the `WITH CHECK OPTION` clause?

A. R

B. C

C. V

D. F

11. Which types of constraints can be created on a view?

    A. Check, NOT NULL

    B. Primary key, foreign key, unique key

    C. Check, NOT NULL, primary key, foreign key, unique key

    D. No constraints can be created on a view.

12. Which is a valid status of a constraint created on a view?

    A. DISABLE VALIDATE

    B. DISABLE NOVALIDATE

    C. ENABLE NOVALIDATE

    D. All of the above

13. The SALARY column of the EMPLOYEE table is defined as NUMBER (8,2), and the COMMISSION_PCT column is defined as NUMBER(2,2). A view is created with the following code.

```
CREATE VIEW EMP_COMM AS
SELECT LAST_NAME,
SALARY * NVL(COMMISSION_PCT,0) Commission
FROM   EMPLOYEES;
```

    What is the datatype of the COMMISSION column in the view?

    A. NUMBER (8,2)

    B. NUMBER (10,2)

    C. NUMBER

    D. FLOAT

14. Which clause in the SELECT statement is not supported in a view definition subquery?

    A. GROUP BY

    B. HAVING

    C. CUBE

    D. FOR UPDATE OF

    E. ORDER BY

15. The EMPLOYEE table has the following columns:

```
EMP_ID        NUMBER (4)
EMP_NAME      VARCHAR2 (30)
SALARY        NUMBER (5,2)
DEPT_ID       VARCHAR2 (2)
```

Which query will show the top-five highest paid employees?

A.
```
SELECT * FROM
(SELECT EMP_NAME, SALARY
 FROM    EMPLOYEES
 ORDER BY SALARY ASC)
WHERE ROWNUM <= 5;
```

B.
```
SELECT EMP_NAME, SALARY FROM
(SELECT *
 FROM    EMPLOYEES
 ORDER BY SALARY DESC)
WHERE ROWNUM < 5;
```

C.
```
SELECT * FROM
(SELECT EMP_NAME, SALARY
 FROM    EMPLOYEES
 ORDER BY SALARY DESC)
WHERE ROWNUM <= 5;
```

D.
```
SELECT EMP_NAME, SALARY
(SELECT *
 FROM    EMPLOYEES
 ORDER BY SALARY DESC)
WHERE ROWNUM = 5;
```

16. The EMPLOYEE table has the following columns:

```
EMP_ID        NUMBER (4) PRIMARY KEY
EMP_NAME      VARCHAR2 (30)
SALARY        NUMBER (6,2)
DEPT_ID       VARCHAR2 (2)
```

A view is defined using the following SQL.

```
CREATE VIEW EMP_IN_DEPT10 AS
SELECT * FROM EMPLOYEE
WHERE  DEPT_ID = 'HR';
```

Which INSERT statement will succeed through the view?

A. `INSERT INTO EMP_IN_DEPT10 VALUES (1000, 'JOHN',1500,'HR');`

B. `INSERT INTO EMP_IN_DEPT10 VALUES (1001, NULL,1700,'AM');`

C. `INSERT INTO EMP_IN_DEPT10 VALUES (1002, 'BILL',2500,'AC');`

D. All of the above

17. To be able to modify a join view, the view definition should not contain which of the following in the top-level query? (Choose all that apply.)

A. `DISTINCT` operator

B. `ORDER BY` clause

C. Aggregate functions such as `SUM`, `AVG`, and `COUNT`

D. `WHERE` clause

E. `GROUP BY` clause

F. `ROWNUM` pseudo-column

18. What is an inline view?

A. A subquery appearing in the `WHERE` clause

B. A subquery appearing in the `FROM` clause

C. A view created using the same column names of the base table

D. A view created with an `ORDER BY` clause

19. Which of the following two statements are true?

A. A view can be created before creating the base table.

B. A view cannot be created before creating the base table.

C. A view will become invalid if the base table's column referred to in the view is altered.

D. A view will become invalid if any column in the base table is altered.

20. Which pseudo-column (with an inline view) can be used to get the top-*n* rows from a table?

A. `ROWID`

B. `ROW_ID`

C. `ROWNUM`

D. `ROW_NUM`

Answers to Review Questions

1. C. `WITH CHECK OPTION` makes sure that the new rows added or the rows updated are accessible to the view. The `WHERE` clause in the view definition limits the rows selected in the view from the base table.

2. A. When the view is created with the `READ ONLY` option, only reads are allowed from the view.

3. B. A view is dropped using the `DROP VIEW` *`view_name`*`;` command.

4. B. The USER_UPDATABLE_COLUMNS view shows the columns that can be updated.

5. A. The `CREATE FORCE VIEW` statement creates an invalid view, even if there are syntax errors. Normally, a view will not be created if there are compilation errors.

6. A. You can perform an `INSERT`, `UPDATE`, or `DELETE` operation on the columns involving only one base table at a time. There are also some restrictions on the DML operations you perform on a join view.

7. D. Since the view definition includes a `DISTINCT` clause, only queries are allowed on the view.

8. B, E. The `OR REPLACE` option in the `CREATE VIEW` statement is used to modify the definition of the view. The `FORCE` option can be used to create the view with errors. The `ALTER VIEW` statement is used to compile a view or to add or modify constraints on the view.

9. C. When you modify the base table, the view becomes invalid. Recompiling the view will make it valid, but the new column will not be available in the view. This is because when you create the view using *, Oracle expands the column names and stores the column names in the dictionary.

10. C. The constraint type will be V for the constraints created on views with the `WITH CHECK OPTION` clause.

11. B. You can create primary key, foreign key, and unique key constraints on a view. The constraints on views are not enforced by Oracle. To enforce a constraint it must be defined on a table.

12. B. Since the constraints on the view are not enforced by Oracle, the only valid status of a constraint can be `DISABLE NOVALIDATE`. You must specify this status when creating constraints on a view.

13. C. When numeric operations are performed using numeric datatypes in the view definition, the resulting column will be a floating datatype, which is NUMBER without any precision or scale.

14. D. The `FOR UPDATE OF` clause is not supported in the view definition. The `FOR UPDATE` clause locks the rows, so it is not allowed.

15. C. The top five salaries can be found using an inline view with the `ORDER BY` clause. Oracle9i optimizer understands the top-'*n*' rows query.

16. D. The view is based on a single table and the only constraint on the table is the primary key. Although the view defined with a `WHERE` clause, we have not enforced that check while using DML statements through the `WITH CHECK OPTION` clause.

17. A, C, E, F. To be able to update a base table using the view, the view definition should not have a `DISTINCT` clause, `GROUP BY` clause, `START WITH` clause, `CONNECT BY` clause, `ROWNUM`, set operators (`UNION`, `UNION ALL`, `INTERSECT`, or `MINUS`), or subquery in the `SELECT` clause.

18. B. A subquery appearing in the `FROM` clause of the `SELECT` statement is similar to defining and using a view, hence the name inline view. The subquery in the `FROM` clause is enclosed in parentheses and may be given an alias name. The columns selected in the subquery can be referenced in the parent query, just as you would select from any normal table or view.

19. A, D. The `CREATE FORCE VIEW` statement can be used to create a view before its base table is created. Any modification to the table will invalidate the view. Use the `ALTER VIEW <view name> COMPILE` statement to recompile the view.

20. C. The `ROWNUM` pseudo-column gives a record number for each row returned. The row number is assigned as the record is fetched; the number is not stored in the database.

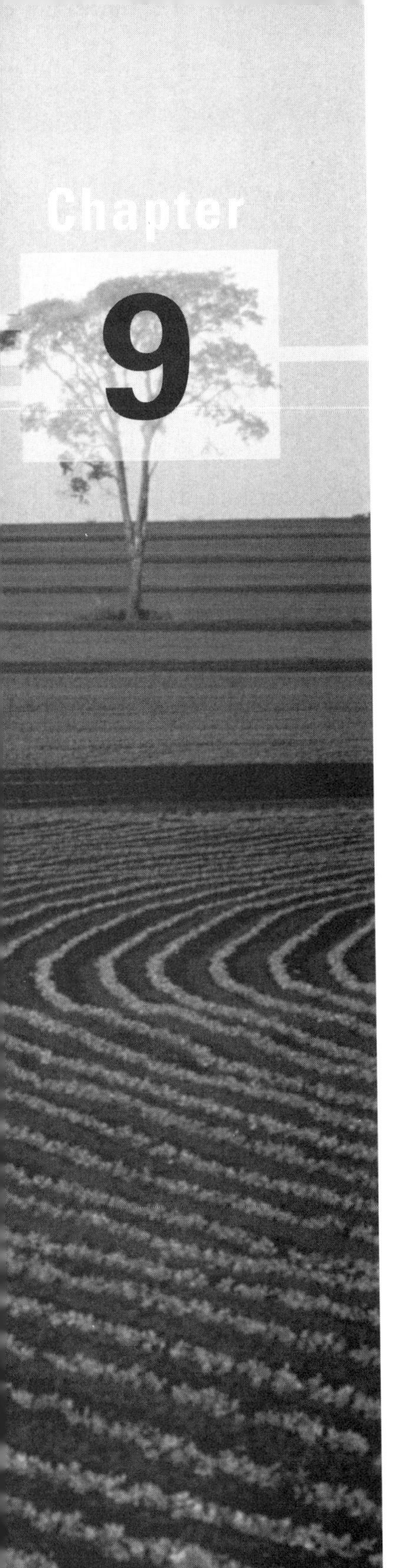

Other Database Objects

INTRODUCTION TO ORACLE9i: SQL EXAM OBJECTIVES COVERED IN THIS CHAPTER:

✓ **Creating Other Database Objects**

- Create, maintain and use sequences
- Create and maintain indexes
- Create private and public synonyms

Exam objectives are subject to change at any time without prior notice and at Oracle's sole discretion. Please visit Oracle's Certification website (`http://www.oracle.com/education/certification/`) for the most current exam objectives listing.

An Oracle database can contain far more than simply tables and views. Sequences can be used to generate artificial keys. Synonyms provide aliases for objects. Several types of indexes can be deployed to enhance the performance of queries. To perform database administrative tasks, you must know how to use packages, procedures, and functions.

Sequences, synonyms, and indexes are basic database tools that you'll need to understand for the exam, as well as for your database administration work. Additionally, with each new release of the database, Oracle delivers more and more functionality to database administrators in the form of built-in or supplied packages. For example, to collect optimizer statistics, you need to call a built-in package. To tune or troubleshoot a database, you need to call packages. Since there is so much functionality that requires database administrators to call stored programs (such as functions and procedures), you should also grasp these fundamental concepts, both for the exam and for your work.

Creating and Managing Sequences

An Oracle *sequence* is a named sequential number generator. Sequences are often used for artificial keys or to order rows that otherwise have no order. Like constraints (discussed in Chapter 7, "Managing Tables and Constraints"), sequences exist only in the data dictionary. Sequences can be configured to increase or decrease without bounds or to repeat (cycle) upon reaching a boundary value.

Creating and Dropping Sequences

Sequences are created with the CREATE SEQUENCE statement. Figure 9.1 shows the syntax of the CREATE SEQUENCE statement.

FIGURE 9.1 CREATE SEQUENCE syntax

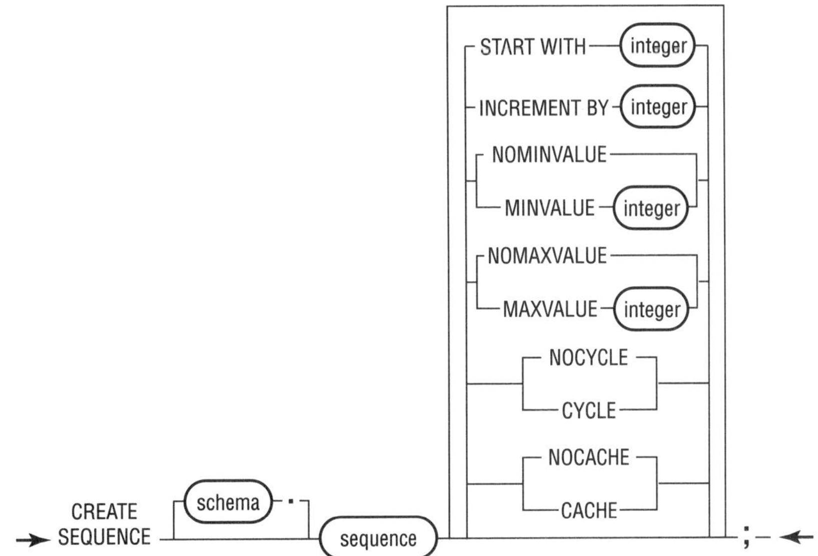

The following keywords may be used to create a sequence:

START WITH Defines the first number that the sequence will generate. The default is 1.

INCREMENT BY Defines the increase or decrease amount for subsequently generated numbers. To specify a decreasing sequence, use a negative INCREMENT BY value. The default is 1.

MINVALUE Defines the lowest number the sequence will generate. This is the bounding value in a decreasing sequence. The default MINVALUE is NOMINVALUE, which evaluates to 1 for an increasing sequence and to -10^{26} for a decreasing sequence.

MAXVALUE Defines the largest number that the sequence will generate. This is the bounding value in the default, increasing sequence. The default

MAXVALUE is the NOMAXVALUE, which evaluates to 10^{27} for an increasing sequence and to –1 for a decreasing sequence.

CYCLE Configures the sequence to repeat numbers after reaching the bounding value.

NOCYCLE Configures the sequence to not repeat numbers after reaching the bounding value. This is the default. When you try to generate MAXVALUE+1, an exception will be raised.

CACHE Defines the size of the block of sequence numbers held in memory. The default is 20.

NOCACHE Forces the data dictionary to be updated for each sequence number generated, guaranteeing no gaps in the generated numbers, but decreasing performance of the sequence.

When you create the sequence, the START WITH value must be equal to or greater than MINVALUE. Sequence numbers can be configured so that a set of numbers is fetched from the data dictionary and cached or held in memory for use. Caching the sequence improves its performance because the data dictionary table does not need to be updated for each generated number, only for each set of numbers.

Sequences are removed with the DROP SEQUENCE statement:

```
DROP SEQUENCE sequence_name
```

Using Sequences

To access the next number in the sequence, you simply select from it, using the pseudo-column *NEXTVAL*. To get the last sequence number that your session has generated, you select from it using the pseudo-column *CURRVAL*. If your session has not yet generated a new sequence number, CURRVAL will be undefined.

The syntax for accessing the next sequence number is as follows:

```
sequence_name.nextval
```

Here is the syntax for accessing the last-used sequence number:

```
sequence_name.currval
```

Sequence Initialization

One problem that you may encounter using sequences involves selecting CURRVAL from the sequence before initializing it within your session by selecting NEXTVAL from it. Here is an example:

```
CREATE SEQUENCE emp_seq NOMAXVALUE NOCYCLE;

Sequence created.

SELECT emp_seq.currval FROM dual;

ERROR at line 1:
ORA-08002: sequence POLICY_SEQ.CURRVAL is not yet defined
in this session
```

Make sure that your code initializes a sequence within your session by selecting its NEXTVAL before you try to reference CURRVAL:

```
SELECT emp_seq.nextval FROM dual;

   NEXTVAL
----------
         1

SELECT policy_seq.currval FROM dual;

   CURRVAL
----------
         1
```

Missing Sequence Values

Another potential problem in the use of sequences involves "losing" sequence values when a rollback occurs. A sequence's NEXTVAL increments outside any user transactions, so a rollback will not put the selected sequence values back into the sequence. These rolled back values simply disappear and may create a gap in the use of the sequence numbers. This is not a bad thing—you don't want one session's use of a sequence to block others until it commits. However, you do need to understand how gaps happen. To demonstrate this, suppose that we have a table with the old Acme employee identifiers and we need to assign new employee IDs to them using our new EMP_SEQ sequence:

```
SELECT * FROM old_acme_employees;

 EMP_ID ACME_ID          HOLDER_NAME
------- ---------------- -----------
        C23              Joshua
        C24              Elizabeth
        D31              David
        D34              Sara
        A872             Jamie
        A891             Jeff
        A884             Jennie

UPDATE old_acme_employees SET emp_id = emp_seq.nextval;

7 rows updated.

SELECT * FROM old_acme_employees;

    EMP_ID ACME_ID          HOLDER_NAME
---------- ---------------- -----------
         5 C23              Joshua
         6 C24              Elizabeth
         7 D31              David
         8 D34              Sara
         9 A872             Jamie
        10 A891             Jeff
        11 A884             Jennie
```

Now suppose that we encounter an error, such as a rollback segment unable to extend, before we commit these changes, and this error causes the process to roll back. We can simulate the error and rollback by simply executing a rollback before the update is committed:

```
ROLLBACK;
```

After we fix the problem and run the update again, we find that there are "missing" sequence values (values 5, 6, 7, and so on).

```
UPDATE old_acme_employees SET emp_id = emp_seq.nextval;

7 rows updated.

SELECT * FROM old_acme_employees;

    EMP_ID ACME_ID          HOLDER_NAME
---------- ---------------- ------------
        12 C23              Joshua
        13 C24              Elizabeth
        14 D31              David
        15 D34              Sara
        16 A872             Jamie
        17 A891             Jeff
        18 A884             Jennie

COMMIT;
```

Maximum and Minimum Values

Another potential pitfall occurs when you reach MAXVALUE on an ascending sequence (or MINVALUE on a descending sequence). If the sequence is set to NOCYCLE, Oracle will raise an exception if you try to select NEXTVAL after the sequence reaches MAXVALUE:

```
CREATE SEQUENCE emp_seq MAXVALUE 10 NOCYCLE;

Sequence created.

SELECT  emp_seq.nextval
FROM hr.employees;

ERROR:
ORA-08004: sequence EMP_SEQ.NEXTVAL exceeds MAXVALUE
and cannot be instantiated
```

Altering Sequences

A common problem with sequences is how to go about altering them to change the NEXTVAL. You cannot simply alter the sequence and set the NEXTVAL. If you use a sequence to generate keys in your table, and reload the development table from production, your sequence may be out of sync with the table. You may get primary key violations when you run the application in development and it tries to insert key values that already exist.

You cannot directly alter the sequence and change its NEXTVAL. Instead, you can take one of the following approaches:

- Drop and re-create it (invalidating all dependent objects and losing the grants).
- Select NEXTVAL from it enough times to bring the sequence up to a desired value.
- Alter the sequence by changing the INCREMENT BY value to a large number, select NEXTVAL from the sequence to make it increment by the large number, then alter the INCREMENT BY value back down to the original small value.

The following session log shows an example of the third technique. We start with the sequence SALE_SEQ that has a LAST_NUMBER value of 441:

```
SELECT sequence_name, cache_size, last_number
FROM user_sequences;

SEQUENCE_NAME  CACHE_SIZE LAST_NUMBER
-------------- ---------- -----------
SALE_SEQ               20         441
```

Our SALES table needs this sequence to be larger than 111555888. So, we alter the sequence's INCREMENT BY value, increment it with a SELECT of its NEXTVAL, and then alter the INCREMENT BY value back to 1. Now our program won't try to generate duplicate keys and will work fine in development.

```
SELECT sequence_name, cache_size, last_number
FROM user_sequences;

SEQUENCE_NAME  CACHE_SIZE LAST_NUMBER
-------------- ---------- -----------
SALE_SEQ               20         441
```

```
ALTER SEQUENCE sale_seq INCREMENT BY 111555888;

Sequence altered.

SELECT sale_seq.nextval FROM dual;

   NEXTVAL
----------
 111556309

ALTER SEQUENCE sale_seq INCREMENT BY 1;

Sequence altered.

SELECT sequence_name, cache_size, last_number
FROM user_sequences;

SEQUENCE_NAME  CACHE_SIZE LAST_NUMBER
-------------- ---------- -----------
SALE_SEQ               20   111556310
```

Creating and Managing Synonyms

A *synonym* is an alias for another database object. A *public synonym* is available to all users, while a *private synonym* is available only to the owner or to the accounts to whom that owner grants privileges. A synonym can point to a table, view, sequence, procedure, function, or package in the local database or, via a database link, to an object in another database. Synonyms are frequently used to simplify SQL by giving a universal name to a local or remote object. Synonyms also can be used to give different or multiple names to individual objects. Unlike views or stored SQL, synonyms don't become invalid if the objects they point to are dropped. Likewise, you can create a synonym that points to an object that does not exist or for which the owner does not have privileges.

For example, user SCOTT owns a table EMP. All users log in to the database under their own username, and so must reference the table with the owner as SCOTT.EMP. But when we create a public synonym EMP for SCOTT.EMP, then anyone who has privileges on the table can simply reference it in their SQL (or PL/SQL) as EMP, without needing to specify the owner. When the statement is parsed, Oracle will resolve the name EMP via the synonym to SCOTT.EMP.

Creating and Dropping Synonyms

The syntax for creating a synonym is as follows:

```
CREATE [PUBLIC] SYNONYM synonym_name
FOR [schema.]object[@db_link];
```

To create a public synonym called EMPLOYEES for the table HR.EMPLOYEES, execute the following statement:

```
CREATE PUBLIC SYNONYM employees FOR hr.employees;
```

Alternatively, to create a private synonym called EMPLOYEES for the table HR.EMPLOYEES, you simply remove the keyword `PUBLIC`, as in the following statement:

```
CREATE SYNONYM employees FOR hr.employees;
```

To remove a synonym, use the `DROP SYNONYM` statement. For a public synonym, you need to make sure that you include the keyword `PUBLIC`, as in this example:

```
DROP PUBLIC SYNONYM employees;
```

To drop a private synonym, issue the `DROP SYNONYM` statement without the `PUBLIC` keyword:

```
DROP SYNONYM employees;
```

Public Synonyms

Public synonyms are used to identify "well-known" objects (tables, views, sequences, procedures, functions, and packages). These well-known objects do not require an owner name prepended to them. In fact, if you try to prepend the owner PUBLIC to a public synonym, it will raise an exception.

The data dictionary views are good examples of public synonyms. These synonyms are created when you run `catalog.sql` at database creation time. When you write SQL code that references the dictionary view ALL_TABLES, you do not need to select from SYS.ALL_TABLES, you can simply select from ALL_TABLES. Your code can use the fully qualified SYS.ALL_TABLES or the unqualified ALL_TABLES and resolve to the same view, owned by user SYS. When you reference SYS.ALL_TABLES, you explicitly denote the object owned by user SYS. When you reference ALL_TABLES, you actually denote the public synonym ALL_TABLES, which then resolves to SYS.ALL_TABLES. Sound confusing? Let's look at some examples to help clarify this concept.

Suppose that the DBA creates a public synonym EMPLOYEES for the HR table EMPLOYEES:

```
CREATE PUBLIC SYNONYM employees FOR hr.employees;
```

Now, user SCOTT, who does not own an EMPLOYEES table but has SELECT privileges on the HR.EMPLOYEES table, can reference that table without including the schema owner (HR.):

```
SELECT COUNT(*) FROM employees;

  COUNT(*)
----------
       107
```

As another example, suppose that you want to create a public synonym NJ_EMPLOYEES for the HR.EMPLOYEES table in the New_Jersey database (using the database link New_Jersey). To create this synonym, execute the following statement:

```
CREATE PUBLIC SYNONYM nj_employees for hr.employees@new_jersey;
```

Private Synonyms

Private synonyms can be created for objects that you own or objects that are owned by other users. You can even create a private synonym for an object in another database by incorporating a database link.

Private synonyms can be useful when a table is renamed and both the old and new names are needed. The synonym can be either the old or new name, with both the old and new names referencing the same object.

Private synonyms are also useful in a development environment. A developer can own a modified local copy of a table, create a private synonym that points to this local table, and test code and table changes without affecting everyone else. For example, developer Derek runs the following statements to set up a private version of the HR.EMPLOYEES table so he can test some new functionality, without affecting anyone else using the HR.EMPLOYEES table.

```
CREATE TABLE my_employees AS SELECT * FROM hr.employees;
ALTER TABLE my_employees ADD pager_nbr VARCHAR2(10);
CREATE SYNONYM employees FOR my_employees;
```

Now Derek can test changes to his program that will use the new PAGER_NBR column. The code in the program will reference the table as EMPLOYEES, but Derek's private synonym will redirect Derek's access to the MY_EMPLOYEES table. When the code is tested and then promoted, the code won't need to change, but the reference to employees will resolve via the public synonym to the HR.EMPLOYEES table.

Use of a private synonym is not restricted to the owner of that synonym. If another user has privileges on the underlying object, she can reference the private synonym as if it were an object itself. For example, user HR grants SELECT privileges on the EMPLOYEES table to both ALICE and CHIPD:

```
GRANT SELECT ON employees TO alice, chipd;
```

Then user CHIPD creates a private synonym to alias this HR-owned object:

```
CREATE SYNONYM emp_tbl FOR hr.employees;
```

User ALICE can now reference CHIPD's private synonym:

```
SELECT COUNT(*) FROM chipd.empl_tbl;

  COUNT(*)
----------
       107
```

This redirection can be a useful technique to change the objects that SQL code references, without changing the code itself. At the same time, this kind of indirection can add layers of obfuscation to code. Exercise care in the use of private synonyms.

Resolving Object References

The key to avoiding confusion (and to passing the exam questions on synonyms) is to know the order that Oracle follows in trying to resolve object references. When your code references an unqualified table, view, procedure, function, or package, there are three places that Oracle will look for the referenced object, in this order:

1. An object owned by the current user
2. A private synonym owned by the current user
3. A public synonym

Real World Scenario

Creating Database Links

An Oracle database link is an object that gives you visibility into another database. Unlike other objects, a database link cannot be used by itself. Instead it acts as a modifier for table or view reference in a remote database. The syntax for creating a database link is as follows:

```
CREATE [SHARED] [PUBLIC] DATABASE LINK link_name

[CONNECT TO username IDENTIFIED BY password] USING 'tns_name';
```

Like a synonym, the keyword PUBLIC makes the database link available to all users in the database. When the CONNECT TO clause is used, it specifies the username and password that will be used to establish a session in the remote database. This password is stored in the data dictionary in an unencrypted form, which is only visible in the data dictionary view USER_DB_LINKS or directly in the SYS.LINK$ table. By default, only user SYS has SELECT privileges on SYS.LINK$. The *tns_name* parameter specifies the service name for the remote database. The keyword SHARED tells Oracle that all users of a public database link should share a single network connection to the remote database.

To create a public database link called NEW_JERSEY that connects as the HOME_OFFICE user with the password SECRET in the NJ database, execute the following:

```
CREATE PUBLIC DATABASE LINK new_jersey

 CONNECT TO home_office IDENTIFIED BY secret USING 'NJ';
```

If you don't want everyone to share the same username in the remote database, create the database link without the CONNECT TO clause, like this:

```
CREATE PUBLIC DATABASE LINK new_jersey USING 'NJ';
```

This will tell Oracle that each user should connect to the NJ database via their own username and password. Each user that references the database link must then have an account in both the local and remote databases.

Unlike a private synonym, a private database link really is private and is not available to other users. So, if user SYSTEM created a private database link to the NJ database that specifically connected to user SYSTEM in the NJ database, the DBA would not need to worry about non-DBA user BERNICE accessing the NJ database with DBA privileges. She could not use SYSTEM's private database link.

To use this new database link you concatenate the @ symbol and the link name to the table reference, like this:

```
SELECT * FROM hr.employees@new_jersey;
```

Creating and Managing Indexes

Indexes are data structures that can offer improved performance in obtaining specific rows over the default full-table scan. Indexes do not always improve performance, however. In this section we will review the indexing technologies covered on the exam: B-tree and bitmap. We will also look at when and how indexes can improve performance.

How Indexes Work

Oracle usually retrieves rows from a table in only one of two ways:

- By ROWID
- By full-table scan

Both B-tree and bitmap indexes map column data to ROWIDs for the columns of interest, but they do so in different ways. When one or more indexes are accessed, Oracle will use the known column values to find the corresponding ROWIDs. The rows are then retrieved by ROWID.

Indexes may improve the performance of `SELECT`, `UPDATE`, and `DELETE` operations. An index can be used if a leading subset of the indexed columns appear in the `SELECT` or `WHERE` clause. Additionally, if all of the columns needed to satisfy a query appear in an index, Oracle may access only the index and not the table. As an example, consider our HR.EMPLOYEES table, which has an index on the columns (LAST_NAME and FIRST_NAME). If we run the following query to get a count of the employees named Taylor, Oracle only needs to access the index, not the table, because all of the necessary columns are in the index:

```
SELECT COUNT(*)
```

```
FROM hr.employees
WHERE last_name = 'Taylor';
```

Although indexes can improve the performance of data retrieval, they degrade performance for data changes (DML). This is because the indexes must be modified in addition to the table.

Using B-Tree Indexes

B-tree indexes are the most common index type, as well as the default. They can be either unique or nonunique and either simple (one column) or concatenated (multiple columns).

B-tree indexes provide the best performance on high-*cardinality* columns, which are columns that have many distinct values. For example, in the HR.EMPLOYEES table, the columns LAST_NAME and PHONE_NUMBER are high-cardinality columns.

B-tree indexes offer an efficient method to retrieve a small number of interesting rows. However, if more than about 10 percent of the table must be examined, a full-table scan is the preferred method.

As the name implies, a B-tree index is based on a binary tree, constructed with branch blocks and leaf blocks. Branch blocks contain the index columns (the *key*) and an address to another index block. Leaf blocks contain the key and the ROWID for each matching row in the table. Additionally, the leaf blocks are a doubly linked list, so they can be range-scanned in either direction. Figure 9.2 shows how the B-tree index key values are constructed into a binary tree.

FIGURE 9.2 The structure of a B-tree index on names

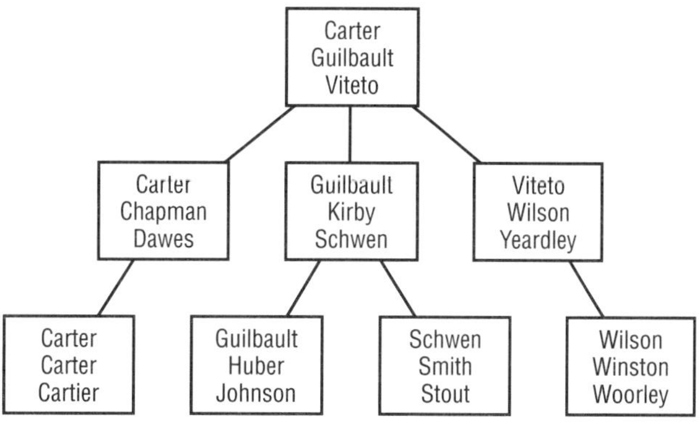

B-tree indexes may be used if any combinations of the leading columns of the index are used in the SQL statement. For example, The OE.INVENTORIES table has the index INVENTORY_PK on the PRODUCT_ID and WAREHOUSE_ID columns. We can use this INVENTORY_PK index with the following query, which returns the number of product ID 3191 items that we have on hand in warehouse ID 3:

```
SELECT SUM(quantity_on_hand)
FROM oe.inventories
WHERE product_id = 3191
 AND  warehouse_id=3;

SUM(QUANTITY_ON_HAND)
---------------------
                  181
```

We could also use the INVENTORY_PK index to find the total number of product ID 3191 that we have on hand in all warehouses, since PRODUCT_ID is a leading subset of columns in the index:

```
SELECT SUM(quantity_on_hand)
FROM oe.inventories
WHERE product_id = 3191;

SUM(QUANTITY_ON_HAND)
---------------------
                  846
```

We would not be able to use the INVENTORY_PK index if we ran the following query to see how many items are in warehouse ID 3, because WAREHOUSE_ID is *not* a leading subset of columns in the index:

```
SELECT SUM(quantity_on_hand)
FROM oe.inventories
WHERE warehouse_id = 3;
```

Using Bitmap Indexes

Bitmap indexes are primarily used for decision-support systems or static data, because they do not support row-level locking. Bitmap indexes can be simple (one column) or concatenated (multiple columns), but in practice, bitmap indexes are almost always simple.

Bitmap indexes are best used for low- to medium-cardinality columns where multiple bitmap indexes can be combined with AND and OR conditions. Each key value has a bitmap, which contains a TRUE, FALSE, or NULL value for every row in the table. The bitmap index is constructed by storing the bitmaps in the leaf nodes of a B-tree structure. The B-tree structure makes it easy to find the bitmaps of interest quickly. Additionally, the bitmaps are stored in a compressed format, so they take up significantly less disk space than regular B-tree indexes.

Figure 9.3 shows how a bitmap index on the PROD_PACK_SIZE column of the SH.PRODUCTS table would be structured. The bitmaps are in the leaf blocks of a B-tree structure. Each row (ROWID) in the table has an entry in each bitmap. These entries are TRUE or FALSE (1, 0).

FIGURE 9.3 The structure of a bitmap index on the PROD_PACK_SIZE column

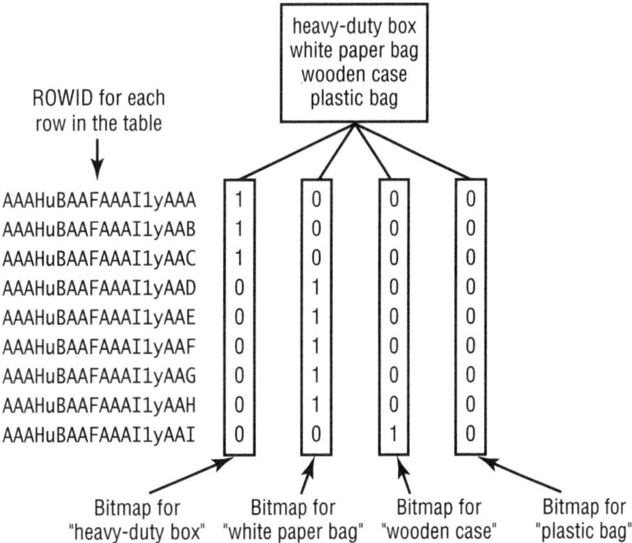

When a query references a number of bitmap-indexed columns, the bitmaps can be combined with AND and OR operations to find the interesting data. For example, the SH.PRODUCTS table contains a number of low-cardinality columns that are descriptive attributes of the product, including PROD_PACK_SIZE, PROD_WEIGHT_CLASS, and PROD_CATEGORY. The Marketing department wants to do some analysis on various combinations of these attributes. For this example, you must find the products that match these criteria:

- In either category 'Women' or 'Girls'
- Have a PROD_PACK_SIZE of 'wooden case', 'plastic bag', or 'card box'
- Have a PROD_WEIGHT_CLASS of 8 or 9

The following SQL will retrieve the required products.

```
SELECT prod_id
FROM sh.products
WHERE prod_category in ('Women','Girls')
 AND  prod_pack_size in ('wooden case', 'plastic bag'
                         ,'card box')
 AND  prod_weight_class BETWEEN 8 AND 9;
```

To combine the bitmaps, Oracle will perform a bitwise OR for the two PROD_CATEGORY bitmaps of interest, a bitwise OR for the three PROD_PACK_SIZE bitmaps of interest, and a bitwise OR for the two PROD_WEIGHT_CLASS bitmaps of interest, as shown in Figure 9.4.

FIGURE 9.4 Bitmap merge collapsing each predicate

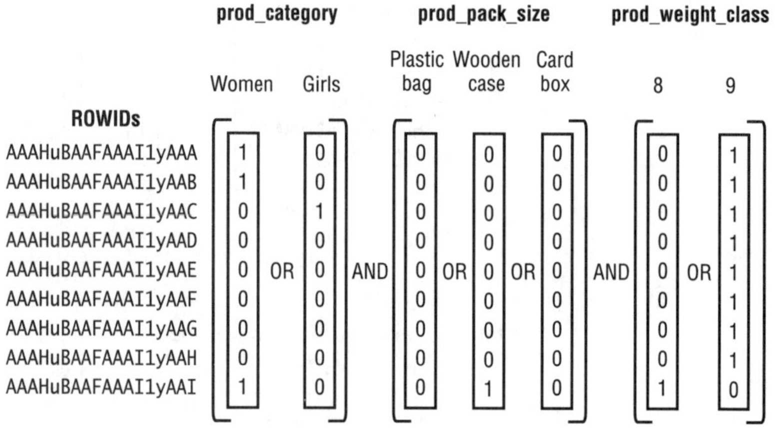

	prod_category			prod_pack_size			prod_weight_class	
ROWIDs	Women	Girls		Plastic bag	Wooden case	Card box	8	9
AAAHuBAAFAAAI1yAAA	1	0		0	0	0	0	1
AAAHuBAAFAAAI1yAAB	1	0		0	0	0	0	1
AAAHuBAAFAAAI1yAAC	0	1		0	0	0	0	1
AAAHuBAAFAAAI1yAAD	0	0		0	0	0	0	1
AAAHuBAAFAAAI1yAAE	0	OR 0	AND	0	OR 0	OR 0	AND 0	OR 1
AAAHuBAAFAAAI1yAAF	0	0		0	0	0	0	1
AAAHuBAAFAAAI1yAAG	0	0		0	0	0	0	1
AAAHuBAAFAAAI1yAAH	0	0		0	0	0	0	1
AAAHuBAAFAAAI1yAAI	1	0		0	1	0	1	0

Next, Oracle will perform a bitwise AND of the three derived bitmaps to locate the single ROWID of interest (AAAHuBAAFAAAI1yAAI). This operation is illustrated in Figure 9.5.

FIGURE 9.5 Bitmap merge combining the predicates

ROWIDs	prod_category		prod_pack_size		prod_weight_class		
AAAHuBAAFAAAI1yAAA	1		0		1		0
AAAHuBAAFAAAI1yAAB	1		0		1		0
AAAHuBAAFAAAI1yAAC	1		0		1		0
AAAHuBAAFAAAI1yAAD	0		0		1		0
AAAHuBAAFAAAI1yAAE	0	AND	0	AND	1	=	0
AAAHuBAAFAAAI1yAAF	0		0		1		0
AAAHuBAAFAAAI1yAAG	0		0		1		0
AAAHuBAAFAAAI1yAAH	0		0		1		0
AAAHuBAAFAAAI1yAAI	1		1		1		1

As you learned in the previous section, B-tree indexes work well as a single index and not as well in combinations. Bitmap indexes work best where various combinations of multiple indexed columns are specified.

Since bitmap indexes are usually on low-cardinality columns, a single bitmap index may not afford improved performance over a full-table scan. In the products example described here, a single three-column concatenated B-tree index should perform slightly better than the combination of three bitmap indexes. However, if the queries did not always use all three of these columns or used other combinations of columns, the number of B-tree indexes required would grow to be quite large, especially if you have many of these attribute columns. With bitmap indexes, you create a bunch of single-column indexes, and then use them in various combinations to support the nonuniform queries typical of a decision-support system.

Calling Stored Programs

Stored programs can be written in the PL/SQL or Java language and take the form of procedures, functions, packages, and triggers. These objects incorporate procedural code with loops, cursors, and conditional branching. It is not within the scope of this text to cover all these constructs, but knowing how to call stored programs is important and may appear on the Oracle9i exam.

Oracle ships a number of built-in programs that a database administrator will use. Some of these built-in programs include DBMS_STATS and the Oracle XML SQL utility.

Using Procedures and Functions

Procedures and *functions* are named programs that are stored in the database. Functions take zero or more parameters and return a value. Procedures take zero or more parameters and return no values. PL/SQL functions and procedures can receive or return zero or more values through their parameter list. Void Java methods are called as procedures, and Java methods that return a value are called as functions.

Procedures are called from SQL*Plus with an EXEC statement, as in:

```
exec dbms_stats.gather_table_stats(ownname=>'HR' ,
tabname=>'EMPLOYEES' ,cascade=>TRUE ,degree=>4);
```

Functions are called anywhere an expression is valid:

- In an assignment:

  ```
  order_volume := open_orders(SYSDATE, 30);
  ```

- In a Boolean expression:

  ```
  IF (open_orders(SYSDATE, 30) < 500 )
  THEN ...
  ```

- In a default value assignment:

  ```
  DECLARE
     order_volume NUMBER
         DEFAULT open_orders(SYSDATE, 30);
  BEGIN ...
  ```

- In a SQL statement:

  ```
  SELECT vendor_name
  FROM vendors
  WHERE open_orders(SYSDATE, 30, vendor_id) = 0;
  ```

- In the parameter list of another program:

  ```
  process_vendor(vendor_id,open_orders(
        vendor=>vendor_id));
  ```

Parameter Passing

When calling procedures and functions, there are two techniques that you can use to pass parameters to the programs:

- Positional notation
- Named notation

As the name implies, positional notation passes parameters based on their position in the parameter list, regardless of name. With named notation, the programmer specifically assigns a value to a named parameter, and the order in which the parameters appear does not matter. The names of the parameters are available from the package specification. As you can see in the example below, named notation is more verbose, but it is also more self-documenting. For our example, we want to use the packaged procedure `DBMS_UTILITY.ANALYZE_SCHEMA` to analyze user Scott's schema estimating the statistics, by sampling 10 percent of each table:

```
--positional notation
dbms_utility.analyze_schema('SCOTT'
   ,'ESTIMATE',NULL,10);

--named notation
dbms_utility.analyze_scheam(
schema=>'SCOTT'
,method=>'ESTIMATE'
,estimate_percent=>10);

--named notation with parms in different order
dbms_utility.analyze_scheam(
schema=>'SCOTT'
,estimate_percent=>10
,method=>'ESTIMATE');
```

Using Packages

Packages are containers that bundle together procedures, functions, and data structures. Oracle provides a number of built-in or "supplied" PL/SQL packages that are used for a variety of database administrative tasks. See the Oracle "Supplied PL/SQL Packages and Types Reference" for complete specifications.

Packages consist of an externally visible package specification, which contains the function headers, procedure headers, and externally visible data structures. The package also consists of a package body, which contains the declaration, executable, and exception sections of all the bundled procedures and functions.

There are a number of differences between packaged and nonpackaged programs. Package data is persistent for the duration of the user's session. Package data thus persists across commits in the session. When you grant the EXECUTE privilege on a package, it is for all programs and data structures in the package specification. You cannot grant privileges on only one procedure or function within a package.

PL/SQL packages can overload procedures and functions, declaring multiple programs with the same name. The correct program to be called is decided at runtime, based on the number or datatypes of the parameters. An example of an overloaded function is the TRUNC function declared in the package STANDARD. There is one TRUNC function for a DATE datatype and another for numeric data. The PL/SQL engine decides which to call at runtime based on which datatype is passed to TRUNC.

For more information on writing PL/SQL see *Oracle PL/SQL Programming* by Steven Feuerstein (O'Reilly & Associates), or *Oracle9i PL/SQL Programming* by Scott Urman (Osborne McGraw Hill).

Summary

In this chapter, we reviewed sequences, synonyms, indexes, and stored programs. Sequences are number generators, and you can use them with the NEXTVAL and CURRVAL keywords.

Oracle synonyms are a mechanism to alias other objects, either locally or in another database accessed through database links. Synonyms can be globally available (public) or restricted to limited users (private).

The two main types of Oracle indexes are B-tree and bitmap indexes. You learned how each type works, when indexes may speed up access to data, and also that they slow down INSERT, UPDATE, and DELETE operations.

Finally, we reviewed stored programs, including procedures, functions, and packages. You learned how to call them with either named notation or positional notation.

Exam Essentials

Know the precise syntax for obtaining sequence values. You should understand how to use *sequence_name*.NEXTVAL and *sequence_name*.CURRVAL to obtain the next and most recently generated number from a sequence.

Understand when indexes degrade performance. Know that indexes degrade the performance of DML operations (INSERT, UPDATE, and DELETE).

Recognize when indexes improve performance. Indexes can improve the performance of SELECT, UPDATE, DELETE, and MERGE statements if the statement's criteria reference indexed columns. A B-tree index can be used if a leading subset of columns from that index is referenced.

Know when a bitmap index is more appropriate than a B-tree index. Bitmap indexes work best on low- to medium-cardinality columns where row-level locking is not needed. In contrast, B-tree indexes work best on high- to medium-cardinality columns and do support row-level locking.

Know that a table does not need to be accessed if an index contains all of the needed information. When an index contains all of the columns needed to satisfy a query, Oracle may not examine the base table.

Know how Oracle will resolve table references. Oracle will first search for a table or view that matches the referenced name. If no table or view is found, private synonyms are then examined. Finally, public synonyms are examined. If no matching name is found, Oracle will raise an exception.

Key Terms

Before you take the exam, make sure you're familiar with the following terms:

- B-tree index
- bitmap index
- cardinality
- `CURRVAL`
- function
- key
- `NEXTVAL`
- package
- procedure
- private synonym
- public synonym
- sequence

Review Questions

1. Which statement will create a sequence that starts with 0 and gets smaller one whole number at a time?

   A. `create sequence desc_seq start with 0 increment by -1 maxvalue 1;`

   B. `create sequence desc_seq increment by -1;`

   C. `create sequence desc_seq start with 0 increment by -1;`

   D. Sequences can only increase.

2. Which statement is most correct in describing what happens to a synonym when the underlying object is dropped?

   A. The synonym's status is changed to `INVALID`.

   B. You can't drop the underlying object if a synonym exists unless the `CASCADE` clause is used in the `DROP` statement.

   C. The synonym is automatically dropped with the underlying object.

   D. Nothing happens to the synonym.

3. The built-in packaged procedure `DBMS_APPLICATION_INFO.SET_MODULE` has, in the package specification, the following declaration:

```
PROCEDURE DBMS_APPLICATION_INFO.SET_MODULE
(module_name IN VARCHAR2
,action_name IN VARCHAR2);
```

Which of the following statements will successfully call this procedure passing 'Monthly Load' and 'Rebuild Indexes' for the MODULE_NAME and ACTION_NAME, respectively? (Choose all that apply.)

A.
```
dbms_application_info.set_module('Monthly Load'
'Rebuild Indexes');
```

B.
```
dbms_application_info.set_module(
 module_name=>'Monthly Load'
,action_name=>'Rebuild Indexes');
```

C.
```
dbms_application_info.set_module('Rebuild Indexes'
,'Monthly Load');
```

D.
```
dbms_application_info.set_module(
 module_name->'Monthly Load'
,action_name->'Rebuild Indexes');
```

4. With which of the following statements could you expect improved performance over a full-table scan, when a B-tree index is created on the two columns HIRE_DATE and SALARY in the HR.EMPLOYEES table?

A.
```
select max(salary)
from hr.employees
where hire_date < sysdate -90;
```

B.
```
select last_name, first_name
from hr.employees
where salary > 90000;
```

C.
```
update hr.employees
set salary = salary * 1.05
where department_id = 102;
```

D. None of these statements would benefit from the index.

5. Which of the following statements will raise an exception?

A. `alter sequence emp_seq nextval 23050;`

B. `alter sequence emp_seq nocycle;`

C. `alter sequence emp_seq increment by -5;`

D. `alter sequence emp_seq maxvalue 10000;`

6. Rajiv has created a private synonym NEW_PRODUCTS for the MEG.PRODUCTS table. Who can select from RAJIV.NEW_PRODUCTS?

   A. The users that Rajiv has granted SELECT on NEW_PRODUCTS to and Meg has granted SELECT on PRODUCTS to.

   B. The users that Rajiv has granted SELECT on NEW_PRODUCTS to.

   C. The users that Meg has granted SELECT on PRODUCTS to, even if Rajiv does not grant privileges to his synonym.

   D. The users that Rajiv has granted SELECT on NEW_PRODUCTS to, if Meg has granted him SELECT WITH ADMIN OPTION.

7. Which type of stored program must return a value?

   A. PL/SQL procedure

   B. PL/SQL function

   C. Java trigger

   D. Java procedure

8. What does the following SQL statement enable all users in the database to do?

```
create public synonym plan_table
for system.plan_table;
```

   A. Use the EXPLAIN PLAN feature of the database

   B. Save execution plans in the system repository

   C. Reference a table as PLAN_TABLE instead of SYSTEM.PLAN_TABLE

   D. Turn on SQL tracing

9. There is a public synonym named PLAN_TABLE for SYSTEM .PLAN_TABLE. Which of the following statements will remove this public synonym from the database?

   A. `drop table system.plan_table;`

   B. `drop synonym plan_table;`

   C. `drop table system.plan_table cascade;`

   D. `drop public synonym plan_table;`

10. A developer reports that she is receiving the following error:

```
SELECT key_seq.currval FROM dual;

ERROR at line 1:
ORA-08002: sequence KEY_SEQ.CURRVAL is not yet defined
```

   Which of the following statements does the developer need to run to fix this condition?

   A. `create sequence key_seq;`

   B. `create synonym key_seq;`

   C. `select key_seq.nextval from dual;`

   D. `grant create sequence to public;`

11. A power user is running some reports and has asked you to put two new B-tree indexes on a large table so that her reports will run faster. You acknowledge that the indexes would speed up her reports. Can thc proposed indexes slow other processes? (Choose the best answer.)

   A. No, indexes only speed up queries.

   B. Yes, the indexes will make the optimizer take longer to decide the best execution plan.

   C. Yes, DML will run more slowly.

   D. Yes, table reorganization operations will be slower.

12. Bitmapped indexes are best suited for which type of environment?

    A. High-cardinality columns

    B. Online transaction processing (OLTP) applications

    C. Full-table scan access

    D. Low- to medium-cardinality columns

13. The INSURED_AUTOS table has one index on the columns YEAR, MAKE, and MODEL, and one index on VIN. Which of the following SQL statements could not benefit from using these indexes?

    A. `select vin from insured_autos`
       `where make='Ford' and model = 'Taurus';`

    B. `select count(*) from insured_autos`
       `where make='Ford' and year = 1998;`

    C. `select vin from insured_autos`
       `where year = 1998 and owner = 'Dahlman';`

    D. `select min(year) from insured_autos`
       `where make='Ford' and model = 'Taurus';`

14. Which clauses in a SELECT statement can an index be used for? (Choose all that apply.)

    A. SELECT

    B. FROM

    C. WHERE

    D. HAVING

15. You need to generate artificial keys for each row inserted into the PRODUCTS table. You want the first row to use a sequence value of 1000, and you want to make sure that no sequence value is skipped. Which of the following statements will meet these requirements?

    A.
    ```
    CREATE SEQUENCE product_key2
    START WITH 1000
    INCREMENT BY 1
    NOCACHE;
    ```

    B.
    ```
    CREATE SEQUENCE product_key2
    START WITH 1000
    NOCACHE;
    ```

    C.
    ```
    CREATE SEQUENCE product_key2
    START WITH 1000
    NEXTVAL 1
    NOCACHE;
    ```

    D. Options A and B meet the requirements.

    E. None of the above statements meet all of the requirements.

16. Which statement will display the last number generated from the EMP_SEQ sequence?

    A. `select emp_seq.curr_val from dual;`

    B. `select emp_seq.currval from dual;`

    C. `select emp_seq.lastval from dual;`

    D. `select last_number from all_sequences where sequence_name ='EMP_SEQ';`

    E. You cannot get the last sequence number generated.

17. Which statement will create a sequence that will rotate through 100 values in a round-robin manner?

    A. `create sequence roundrobin cycle maxvalue 100;`

    B. `create sequence roundrobin cycle to 100;`

    C. `create sequence max_value 100 roundrobin cycle;`

    D. `create rotating sequence roundrobin min 1 max 100;`

18. The following statements are executed:

```
create sequence my_seq;
select my_seq.nextval from dual;
select my_seq.nextval from dual;
rollback;
select my_seq.nextval from dual;
```

What will be selected when the last statement is executed?

A. 0

B. 1

C. 2

D. 3

19. Which of the following can you not do with a package?

A. Overload procedures and functions

B. Hide data

C. Retain data across commits

D. Grant EXECUTE privileges on one procedure in a package

20. Which of the following calls to the stored function my_sine() will raise an exception?

A. `Theta := my_sine(45);`

B. `IF (my_sine(45) > .3 ) THEN`

C.
```
DECLARE
   Theta   NUMBER DEFAULT my_sine(45);
BEGIN …
```

D. `my_sine(45);`

Answers to Review Questions

1. A. For a descending sequence, the default START WITH value is –1, and the default MAXVALUE value is -1. To start the sequence with 0, you must explicitly override both of these defaults.

2. D. Synonyms do not have a status. The CASCADE CONSTRAINTS option does not drop synonyms. Synonyms can point to nonexisting objects.

3. B. Option A almost uses the correct positional notation, except the delimiting comma is missing. Option B uses the correct named notational style. Option C transposes the module and action name using positional notation. Option D uses the wrong assignment syntax.

4. A. The index could be used if a leading subset of columns in the index is referenced. Options B and C do not reference the leading subset of columns in their WHERE clauses.

5. A. You cannot explicitly change the next value of a sequence. You can set the MAXVALUE or INCREMENT BY value to a negative number, and NOCYCLE tells Oracle to not reuse a sequence number.

6. C. Private synonyms can be referenced by anyone who has privileges on the underlying objects. You cannot grant privileges on synonyms, only on the underlying object. Option D is close, but the WITH ADMIN OPTION is only for roles and system privileges, not for table privileges.

7. B. Functions must include a RETURN statement and must return a value.

8. C. This statement creates a public synonym or global alias, which allows users to reference the underlying table without needing to explicitly specify the owner. A table named PLAN_TABLE is needed to use the EXPLAIN PLAN feature, but the statement above creates a public synonym. Also, the existence of a public synonym does not grant to public any privileges on the underlying object. An ALTER SESSION statement is used to enable and disable SQL tracing.

9. D. To remove a public synonym, use the `DROP PUBLIC SYNONYM` statement. The `DROP TABLE` statement will remove a table from the database, but will not affect any synonyms on the table.

10. C. A sequence is not yet defined if `NEXTVAL` has not yet been selected from it within the current session. It has nothing to do with creating a sequence, creating a synonym, or granting privileges.

11. C. This one's a little tricky. B, C, and D are all true, but C is the best answer. Two additional indexes should not appreciably slow the optimizer, and table reorganization in Oracle (unlike in other databases) is usually not needed. DML (`INSERT`, `UPDATE`, and `DELETE`) operations will definitely be slowed, as the new indexes will need to be maintained.

12. D. Bitmapped indexes are not suited for high-cardinality columns (those with highly selective data). OLTP applications tend to need row-level locking, which is not available with bitmap indexes. Full-table scans do not use indexes. Bitmap indexes are best suited for multiple combinations of low- to medium-cardinality columns.

13. A. Option A does not use a leading subset of columns in an index, nor do all of the columns come from the index. A full-table scan on the table will be needed. Options B and C use a leading subset of the three-column index, so that index could be used. Option D uses data that is found completely in the three-column index, and a full scan of this index would likely be faster than a full scan of the larger table.

14. A, C. The obvious answer is C, but an index also can be used for the `SELECT` clause. If an index contains all of the columns needed to satisfy the query, the table does not need to be accessed.

15. D. Both options A and B produce identical results, because the `INCREMENT BY 1` clause is the default if it is not specified. Option C is invalid because `NEXTVAL` is not a valid keyword within a `CREATE SEQUENCE` statement.

16. B. Option D is close, but it shows the greatest number in the cache, not the latest generated. The correct answer is from the sequence itself, using the pseudo-column `CURRVAL`.

17. A. The keyword CYCLE will cause the sequence to wrap and reuse numbers. The keyword MAXVALUE will set the largest value the sequence will cycle to. The name roundrobin is there to confuse to you.

18. D. The CREATE SEQUENCE statement will create an increasing sequence that will start with 1, increment by 1, and be unaffected by the rollback. A rollback will never stuff vales back into a sequence.

19. D. You can only grant EXECUTE privileges on the entire package, not on individual packaged programs.

20. D. Functions cannot be called as stand-alone statements; only procedures can be called this way.

User Access and Security

INTRODUCTION TO ORACLE9i: SQL EXAM OBJECTIVES COVERED IN THIS CHAPTER:

✓ **Controlling User Access**

- Create users
- Create Roles to ease setup and maintenance of the security model
- Use the GRANT and REVOKE statements to grant and revoke object privileges

Exam objectives are subject to change at any time without prior notice and at Oracle's sole discretion. Please visit Oracle's Certification website (`http://www.oracle.com/education/certification/`) for the most current exam objectives listing.

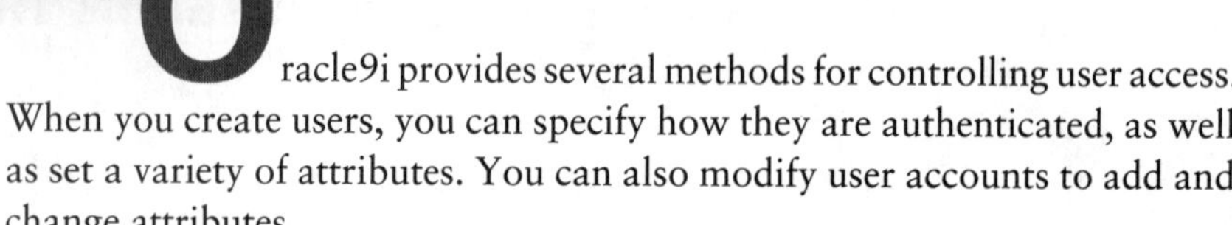

Oracle9i provides several methods for controlling user access. When you create users, you can specify how they are authenticated, as well as set a variety of attributes. You can also modify user accounts to add and change attributes.

A primary way to control user access is through privileges. Oracle9i includes object privileges, system privileges, and role privileges. By granting and revoking privileges, you can specify what users can do with various database objects. Another method for controlling how users use system resources and passwords is through profiles.

In this chapter, we will cover how to create and modify user accounts and use account licensing controls. Then we will discuss how to allow or prevent changes using privileges and how to manage privilege assignments using roles. Finally, we'll describe how to assign profiles.

Creating and Modifying User Accounts

The `CREATE USER` statement is employed to create a user (sometimes called an account or schema) and optionally to assign additional attributes to that user. The `ALTER USER` statement is used to assign any combination of account attributes to the user account, but the account must already exist.

Configuring Account Authentication

When a user connects to an Oracle database, he must be authenticated. Oracle can be configured for one of three types of authentication:

- The default is database authentication. With database authentication, Oracle checks that the user is a legitimate user for that database and has supplied the correct password.

- With external authentication, Oracle only checks that the user is a legitimate user for that database; the password is validated by the operating system or network.
- With global authentication, Oracle only checks that the user is a legitimate user for that database. The password is validated by the Oracle Security Service, a separately licensed and configured service.

Database-Authenticated User Accounts

Database-authenticated accounts are the default type of account, and probably the most common. To create a database-authenticated account for username `piyush` with a password of `welcome`, you would execute the following:

```
CREATE USER piyush IDENTIFIED BY welcome;
```

The keywords `IDENTIFIED BY` *<password>* tell Oracle that the account is a database-authenticated account.

Externally Authenticated User Accounts

User accounts can be configured not to check a password in the database, but instead to rely on password checking from the client's operating system. These externally identified accounts are sometimes called OPS$ accounts, because when they were initially introduced in Oracle6, the Oracle account needed to be prefixed with the key string `OPS$`. This is also why the default for the `init.ora` parameter `os_authent_prefix` is `OPS$`.

The `os_authent_prefix` defines the string that must be prepended to the operating system account name for Oracle externally identified accounts. If this parameter is left as the default of `OPS$`, the operating system user `appl` would be created in Oracle as follows:

```
CREATE USER ops$appl IDENTIFIED EXTERNALLY;
```

Frequently, the `os_authent_prefix` parameter will be set to a blank string (`os_authent_prefix=""`), so no prefix is required. The same `appl` account would then be created like this:

```
CREATE USER appl IDENTIFIED EXTERNALLY;
```

The keywords `IDENTIFIED EXTERNALLY` tell Oracle that the account is an externally authenticated account. Externally identified accounts are used extensively in cron jobs, batch jobs, or other noninteractive programs, where incorporating a password would violate security protocols or result in broken processes when passwords are changed.

Globally Authenticated User Accounts

User accounts can be configured not to check a password in the database, but instead to rely on password checking from an X.509 enterprise directory service. These types of accounts will be most common in large organizations where a single sign-on system is used. Here's an example:

```
CREATE USER scott IDENTIFIED GLOBALLY AS 'CN=scott,
OU=division1, O=sybex, C=US';
```

The keywords `IDENTIFIED GLOBALLY AS` *<directory_name>* tell Oracle that the account uses global authentication.

Assigning Attributes to Accounts

Account characteristics are assigned with the `CREATE` or `ALTER USER` statements. The `CREATE USER` statement must minimally include the username and the password clause. Users can change their own password with the `ALTER USER` statement, as in:

```
ALTER USER piyush IDENTIFIED BY saraswati;
```

You can create or alter user accounts to assign default and temporary tablespaces, tablespace quotas, profiles, roles, and password restrictions. (For more information on temporary tables, see Chapter 7, "Managing Tables and Constraints.")

Assigning a Default Tablespace

The default tablespace is where the user's objects (tables, indexes, and clusters) will be placed if an explicit `TABLESPACE` clause is not included in that object's `CREATE` statement. The default is the SYSTEM tablespace, which is generally not a good place to put non-data dictionary objects.

```
CREATE USER piyush IDENTIFIED BY saraswati
DEFAULT TABLESPACE user_data;

CREATE USER manoj IDENTIFIED EXTERNALLY;

ALTER USER manoj DEFAULT TABLESPACE devl_data;
```

Assigning a Temporary Tablespace

The temporary tablespace is where temporary tables and temporary segments from large sorting operations are placed. As with the default tablespace, the default for the temporary tablespace is SYSTEM, which should be changed.

```
CREATE USER piyush IDENTIFIED BY saraswati
TEMPORARY TABLESPACE temp;

ALTER USER manoj TEMPORARY TABLESPACE temp;
```

To avoid changing the temporary tablespace for each user that you create, change the database default with an `ALTER DATABASE` statement, such as `ALTER DATABASE DEFAULT TEMPORARY TABLESPACE temp`.

Assigning Tablespace Quotas

Tablespace quotas limit the amount of disk space that a user can consume within a tablespace. These quotas can be specified in bytes, kilobytes, megabytes, or the special quota `UNLIMITED`, which allows the user to consume any amount of disk space in the specified tablespace. The quota amount is interpreted as bytes if no suffix is included (`32768`), as kilobytes if the suffix `K` is included (`512K`), and as megabytes if the suffix `M` is included (`8M`).

```
CREATE USER piyush IDENTIFIED BY saraswati
DEFAULT TABLESPACE user_data
QUOTA UNLIMITED ON user_data
QUOTA 20M ON tools;

ALTER USER manoj QUOTA 2500K ON tools;
```

Using Profiles

Profiles can be used to limit the resources that a user's session can consume. Some of these limiting resources include connect time, idle time, logical reads per session, failed login attempts, and the password verification function. The default profile allows unlimited resource usage. Before using profiles to limit resource consumption, the init.ora parameter resource_limit must be set to TRUE.

```
CREATE USER piyush IDENTIFIED BY saraswati
PROFILE instructor;

ALTER USER manoj PROFILE engineer;
```

Profiles are discussed in the "Managing User Groups with Profiles" section later in this chapter.

Enabling or Disabling Roles

A role is an instrument for administering privileges. The role attribute can be set only with the ALTER USER statement. Attempts to set this attribute with a CREATE USER statement will raise an exception.

```
ALTER USER manoj DEFAULT ROLE ALL EXCEPT salary_adm;
```

Roles are discussed in the "Creating and Using Roles" section later in this chapter.

Setting Password Expiration

When a user's password expires, the user will be forced to change passwords on the next connection to the database. Oracle will first prompt the user for the old password, then for the new password, and finally for the new password a second time in order to confirm it. This functionality is frequently used for new accounts when default passwords are assigned and the new users must change their passwords immediately. Another common use is when users forget their passwords. The DBA changes and expires it, then lets the user know the temporary password. With expired passwords, users must change their password on the next login.

```
ALTER USER manoj IDENTIFIED BY welcome;
ALTER USER manoj PASSWORD EXPIRE;
```

Account Locking

Account locking is frequently used for application schema accounts where no one actually logs in to the database as that user, but that user owns tables used by an application.

```
ALTER USER gl ACCOUNT LOCK;
```

Account Unlocking

When an account is locked because of failed password attempts (which you can set using the profile parameter FAILED_LOGON_ATTEMPTS, as discussed in the "Managing User Groups with Profiles" section later in this chapter), the UNLOCK attribute unlocks the account. You may also need to unlock an application schema account for upgrades, and then lock it again after the maintenance operation.

```
ALTER USER scott ACCOUNT UNLOCK;
ALTER USER general_ledger ACCOUNT UNLOCK;
```

Using Account Licensing Controls

Oracle offers either concurrent user or named user licensing and includes some database controls to assist you in complying with your license. You can limit the number of sessions allowed to connect to your database, as well as the number of user accounts that can be created in your database. There are three `init.ora` parameters that you can set to help enforce your licensing restrictions: `license_max_users`, `license_sessions_warning`, and `license_max_sessions`.

You should keep in mind that these parameters can assist you in enforcing your licensing, but the licensing rules do not completely follow the rules that these parameters use. As an informed and intelligent DBA, you should exercise good judgment in their use.

Even without setting any of these controls, Oracle will write to the alert log the high number of concurrent sessions that were connected to the database since the last startup. This maximum number of concurrent sessions can be useful in auditing your licensing compliance.

Limiting the Number of User Accounts

The `license_max_users` parameter limits the number of user accounts that can be created in your database and is useful if you have a named user license. Oracle counts the number of users in your database with the following query:

```
SELECT COUNT(*) FROM dba_users
```

In setting this parameter, you need to keep in mind that some user accounts (such as SYS and SYSTEM) exist in every database and will be counted toward the `license_max_users` limit, even though they do not count toward a named user licensing limit. Setting the `license_max_users=2` to enforce a two–named user license will, in fact, prohibit you from creating any accounts. You need to adjust this parameter based on your system and application account usage.

When you try to create an account above the `license_max_users` limit, Oracle will raise the following exception:

```
CREATE USER lucy IDENTIFIED BY ricky
                  ..                *
ERROR at line 1:
ORA-01985: cannot create user as LICENSE_MAX_USERS
parameter exceeded
```

If you set the `license_max_users` parameter to a value lower than the number of current users in your database, the next time you start up your database, the following error message will be written to the alert log:

```
Number of users (30) more than maximum
allowed (20) at database open time
```

If the number of users is over the `license_max_users` limit, you will not be able to create any new accounts.

Managing Concurrent User Licenses

The `license_sessions_warning` parameter is designed to help manage concurrent user licenses. When this parameter is set, Oracle will log a warning into the alert log file whenever the number of concurrent session exceeds this threshold value. The warning will look like this:

```
License warning limit (20) exceeded
```

The `alert.log` file is found in the directory specified by the `init.ora` parameter `background_dump_dest`. The default location for this file is in `$ORACLE_HOME/rdbms/log`.

Enforcing Concurrent User Licenses

The `license_max_sessions` parameter is designed to help you enforce your concurrent user licenses. Concurrent user licenses count each user, not the number of sessions that each user has open. For example, if you are running DBA Studio, Top Sessions, and SQL*Plus, your concurrent user licensing count would be one, but the `license_max_sessions` count would be three.

When the number of database sessions exceeds this threshold value, Oracle will record a message in the alert log for DBA accounts, such as the following:

```
License maximum (3) exceeded, DBA logon allowed
```

For non-DBA accounts, the logon fails with this message:

```
CONNECT scott/tiger
ERROR:
ORA-00019: maximum number of session licenses exceeded
```

Also, for non-DBA accounts, a message is written to the alert log, like this:

```
Non-DBA logon denied; current logons equal maximum (3)
```

Creating and Using Roles

A *role* is an instrument for administering privileges. Privileges (discussed in the next section) can be granted to a role, and then that role can be granted to another role or to a user. Users can thus inherit privileges via roles. Roles serve no other purpose than to administer privileges.

To take advantage of the administrative relief that a role may provide, you must first create the role with the `CREATE ROLE` statement. Figure 10.1 shows the `CREATE ROLE` statement's syntax.

FIGURE 10.1 The syntax for the CREATE ROLE statement

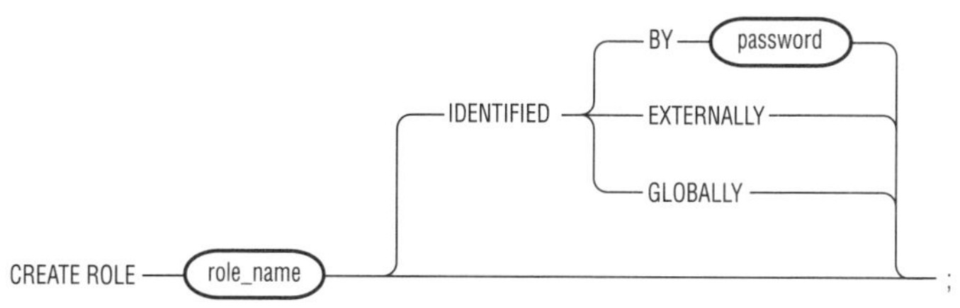

By default, a role will be created without a password or other authentication. If a role is created with the IDENTIFIED BY clause, that role is disabled by default. To enable the role, use the SET ROLE statement:

```
SET ROLE role_name IDENTIFIED BY password;
```

The SET ROLE statement can be used to enable or disable any combination of roles that have been granted to a user.

Externally and globally identified roles are authenticated by the operating system and by Oracle Security Service, respectively. Often, users will need privileges to modify data in application tables, but only when running the application, not when using ad hoc tools. This context-sensitive security can be achieved by a role that has a password. When a user connects to the database inside the application, the application code, without the user's knowledge, will execute a SET ROLE statement, passing the secret password to the database. The user does not need to know the role's password, and therefore may not be able to manually execute the SET ROLE with a password while using an ad hoc tool, such as SQL*Plus or TOAD.

Granting and Revoking Privileges

Privileges allow a user account to access objects or execute programs that are owned by another user or to perform system-level operations, such as creating or dropping objects. Privileges can be granted (assigned) to a user, to the special user PUBLIC, or to a role. Once granted, privileges can be revoked (canceled).

Oracle has three types of privileges:

- *Object privileges* are permissions on schema objects, such as tables, views, programmer-defined functions, and libraries.
- *System privileges* give the grantee the ability to perform system-level activities, such as connecting to the database, altering the user session, creating tables, or creating users.
- *Role privileges* are those privileges that a user owns by way of a role.

You can see a complete list of system privileges in the data dictionary view SYSTEM_PRIVILEGE_MAP.

Object Privileges

There are nine different types of object privileges that can be granted to a user or role, as shown in Table 10.1. There is also the special ALL privilege, for objects that can have more than one privilege.

TABLE 10.1 Object Privileges

	Privilege								
Object	**Alter**	**Delete**	**Execute**	**Index**	**Insert**	**Read**	**Reference**	**Select**	**Update**
Directory	No	No	No	No	No	Yes	No	No	No
Function	No	No	Yes	No	No	No	No	No	No
Procedure	No	No	Yes	No	No	No	No	No	No
Package	No	No	Yes	No	No	No	No	No	No
DB Object	No	No	Yes	No	No	No	No	No	No
Library	No	No	Yes	No	No	No	No	No	No
Operator	No	No	Yes	No	No	No	No	No	No
Sequence	Yes	No	No	No	No	No	No	Yes	No
Table	Yes	Yes	No	Yes	Yes	No	Yes	Yes	Yes
Type	No	No	Yes	No	No	No	No	No	No
View	No	Yes	No	No	Yes	No	No	Yes	Yes

The *ALTER* Privilege

The ALTER privilege allows the grantee to execute the ALTER TABLE or LOCK TABLE statement on the table. An ALTER TABLE statement can rename the table, add columns, drop columns, change the datatype and size of columns, and convert the table into a partitioned table. The ALTER privilege on a sequence allows the grantee to execute the ALTER SEQUENCE statement on the sequence, which lets the grantee do such things as reset the minimum value, increment, and cache size.

The *DELETE* Privilege

The DELETE privilege allows the grantee to execute a DELETE statement to remove rows from the table or view. The SELECT privilege must be granted together with the DELETE privilege, or the grantee will be unable to select the rows, and therefore, unable to delete them. DELETE also allows the grantee to lock the table.

The *EXECUTE* Privilege

The EXECUTE privilege gives the grantee the permission to execute the specified program. The EXECUTE privilege on a package allows the grantee to execute or use any program or program object (such as a record type or cursor) declared in the package specification. The EXECUTE privilege on an operator or type will allow the grantee to use that operator in SQL or PL/SQL. On a database object, EXECUTE will allow the grantee to use that database object and invoke its methods.

The *INDEX* Privilege

The INDEX privilege allows the grantee to create indexes on or to lock that table. Confusion can arise when one schema owns a table but another schema owns the indexes. Use care when granting this privilege.

The *INSERT* Privilege

The INSERT privilege gives the grantee the ability to create rows in that table or view. If the INSERT privilege is on specific columns of the table or view, the grantee will only be able to populate the columns on which that user has been granted INSERT privileges. INSERT also implicitly gives the grantee the ability to lock the table.

The *READ* Privilege

The READ privilege can be granted only on a directory and lets the grantee read BFILEs in the specified directory. This privilege should not be confused with SELECT, which allows a user to read a table or view.

The *REFERENCE* Privilege

The REFERENCE privilege can be granted only on a table to a user (not a role). It allows the grantee to create integrity constraints that reference that table.

The grantee can also lock the table. SELECT does not need to be granted with REFERENCE for the database to enforce referential integrity constraints. However, this can give rise to situations in which the parent schema cannot read the child records and the child schema cannot read the parent records, but the database will enforce the parent-child relationship. Use care when granting this privilege.

The *SELECT* Privilege

The SELECT privilege gives the grantee permission to execute SELECT statements on the table or view, allowing the grantee to read the table or view's contents. The SELECT privilege on a sequence allows the grantee to obtain the current value (CURRVAL) or to increment the value by selecting NEXTVAL.

The *UPDATE* Privilege

The UPDATE privilege allows the grantee to change data values in the table or view. The SELECT privilege must be granted together with the UPDATE privilege, which implicitly gives the grantee the ability to lock the table.

The *ALL* Privilege

For objects that can have more than one privilege, the special privilege ALL can be granted or revoked. For tables, ALL includes SELECT, INSERT, UPDATE, and DELETE, as well as INDEX, ALTER, and REFERENCE. Take care before granting ALL on a table, because you might not wish to grant the INDEX, ALTER, and REFERENCE privileges.

Privileges on Table or View Columns

At a finer granularity, you can grant the privileges INSERT, UPDATE, and REFERENCE on specific columns of tables. On views, you can grant INSERT and UPDATE on specific columns. Revoking column privileges, however, must be done on a table-wide basis.

For example, suppose that Norman grants UPDATE on the SURNAME, ADDRESS, and CITY columns, and then later needs to revoke UPDATE on the ADDRESS and CITY columns, leaving UPDATE on the SURNAME column. Norman must first revoke UPDATE on the whole table, and then regrant the UPDATE privilege on the SURNAME column.

System Privileges

System privileges allow the grantee to create, alter, drop, and manage database objects or features. There are many system privileges—the 9.0.1 release for Linux used with this book includes 140 in the data dictionary view SYSTEM_PRIVILEGE_MAP. The exam does not require you to know all of these privileges, as many are for features that are outside the scope of the exam. The following sections summarize the system privileges that may appear on exam.

Cluster Privileges

The following system privileges allow the grantee to manage clusters:

- `CREATE CLUSTER` allows the grantee to create, alter, and drop clusters in the grantee's own schema.
- `CREATE ANY CLUSTER` allows the grantee to create new clusters in any schema.
- `ALTER ANY CLUSTER` allows the grantee to alter clusters in any schema.
- `DROP ANY CLUSTER` allows the grantee to drop any cluster in any schema.

Database Privileges

The following system privileges allow the grantee to manage databases:

- `ALTER DATABASE` allows the grantee to execute the `ALTER DATABASE` statement.
- `ALTER SYSTEM` allows the grantee to execute the `ALTER SYSTEM` statement.
- `AUDIT SYSTEM` allows the grantee to execute the `AUDIT` and `NOAUDIT` statements.

Index Privileges

The following system privileges allow the grantee to manage indexes:

- `CREATE ANY INDEX` allows the grantee to create indexes in any schema.
- `ALTER ANY INDEX` allows the grantee to alter indexes in any schema.
- `DROP ANY INDEX` allows the grantee to drop indexes in any schema.

Procedure Privileges

The following system privileges allow the grantee to manage procedures:

- CREATE PROCEDURE allows the grantee to create, alter, or drop procedures, functions, and packages in the grantee's own schema.
- CREATE ANY PROCEDURE allows the grantee to create new procedures, functions, and packages in any schema.
- ALTER ANY PROCEDURE allows the grantee to alter existing procedures, functions, and packages in any schema.
- DROP ANY PROCEDURE allows the grantee to drop any procedure, function, or package in any schema.
- EXECUTE ANY PROCEDURE allows the grantee to execute or reference procedures in any schema.

Profile Privileges

The following system privileges allow the grantee to manage profiles:

- CREATE PROFILE allows the grantee to create new profiles.
- ALTER PROFILE allows the grantee to alter existing profiles.
- DROP PROFILE allows the grantee to drop profiles from the database.

Role Privileges

The following system privileges allow the grantee to manage roles:

- CREATE ROLE allows the grantee to create new roles.
- ALTER ANY ROLE allows the grantee to alter existing roles.
- DROP ANY ROLE allows the grantee to drop roles.
- GRANT ANY ROLE allows the grantee to grant any role in the database to any other role or to a user. (Note that there is no corresponding REVOKE ANY ROLE privilege.)

Rollback Segment Privileges

The following system privileges allow the grantee to manage rollback segments:

- CREATE ROLLBACK SEGMENT allows the grantee to create new rollback segments.
- ALTER ROLLBACK SEGMENT allows the grantee to alter any existing rollback segment.
- DROP ROLLBACK SEGMENT allows the grantee to drop rollback segments from the database.

Sequence Privileges

The following system privileges allow the grantee to manage sequences:

- CREATE SEQUENCE allows the grantee to create, alter, drop, and select sequences in the grantee's own schema.
- CREATE ANY SEQUENCE allows the grantee to create new sequences in any schema.
- ALTER ANY SEQUENCE allows the grantee to alter existing sequences in any schema.
- DROP ANY SEQUENCE allows the grantee to drop sequences in any schema.
- SELECT ANY SEQUENCE allows the grantee to select from any sequence in any schema.

Session Privileges

The following system privileges allow the grantee to manage sessions:

- CREATE SESSION allows the grantee to log on (connect) to the database.
- ALTER SESSION allows the grantee to execute the ALTER SESSION statement.
- ALTER RESOURCE COST allows the grantee to change the way that Oracle calculates resource costs for resource restrictions in a profile.
- RESTRICTED SESSION allows the grantee to connect to the database when the database is in restricted session mode.

Synonym Privileges

The following system privileges allow the grantee to manage synonyms:

- `CREATE SYNONYM` allows the grantee to create and drop private synonyms in the grantee's own schema.
- `CREATE ANY SYNONYM` allows the grantee to create private synonyms in any schema.
- `CREATE PUBLIC SYNONYM` allows the grantee to create public synonyms.
- `DROP ANY SYNONYM` allows the grantee to drop private synonyms in any schema.
- `DROP PUBLIC SYNONYM` allows the grantee to drop public synonyms.

Table Privileges

The following system privileges allow the grantee to manage tables:

- `CREATE TABLE` allows the grantee to create, alter, and drop tables in the grantee's own schema.
- `CREATE ANY TABLE` allows the grantee to create tables in any schema.
- `ALTER ANY TABLE` allows the grantee to alter existing tables in any schema.
- `DROP ANY TABLE` allows the grantee to drop tables from any schema.
- `SELECT ANY TABLE` allows the grantee to select from or lock any table in any schema.
- `INSERT ANY TABLE` allows the grantee to insert rows into any table in any schema.
- `UPDATE ANY TABLE` allows the grantee to update rows from any table in any schema.
- `DELETE ANY TABLE` allows the grantee to truncate or delete rows from any table in any schema.
- `LOCK ANY TABLE` allows the grantee to lock tables in any schema.

Tablespace Privileges

The following system privileges allow the grantee to manage tablespaces:

- `CREATE TABLESPACE` allows the grantee to create new tablespaces.

- ALTER TABLESPACE allows the grantee to alter any existing tablespace.
- DROP TABLESPACE allows the grantee to drop any tablespace, optionally including the tables, indexes, and clusters in the tablespace.
- MANAGE TABLESPACE allows the grantee to take tablespaces online or offline, as well as to begin and end backup mode for V7-compatible hot backups.
- UNLIMITED TABLESPACE allows the grantee to override any tablespace quotas and use as much disk space in any tablespace as the grantee requests.

The UNLIMITED TABLESPACE privilege can be granted only to accounts. Like the object privilege REFERENCE, UNLIMITED TABLESPACE cannot be inherited from a role.

User Privileges

The following system privileges allow the grantee to manage users:

- CREATE USER allows the grantee to create new users.
- ALTER USER allows the grantee to change user account attributes.
- BECOME USER allows the grantee to become another user, such as during a full database import operation.
- DROP USER allows the grantee to drop users from the database.

View Privileges

The following system privileges allow the grantee to manage views:

- CREATE VIEW allows the grantee to create, alter, and drop views in the grantee's own schema.
- CREATE ANY VIEW allows the grantee to create views in any schema.
- DROP ANY VIEW allows the grantee to drop views from any schema.

Special Privileges

SYSDBA is one of two special privileges that are not limited to a single database. This privilege allows the grantee to do the following:

- Create a new database.
- Start up and shut down a database.
- Alter a database with the OPEN, MOUNT, BACKUP, CHANGE CHARACTER SET, ARCHIVELOG, and RECOVER options.
- Create an SP file.

SYSOPER is the other special privilege that is not limited to a single database. This privilege allows the grantee to do the following:

- Start up and shut down a database.
- Alter a database with the OPEN, MOUNT, BACKUP, ARCHIVELOG, and RECOVER options.
- Create an SP file.

Other Privileges

The following are some other important system privileges:

- ANALYZE ANY allows the grantee to execute the ANALYZE statement against any table, cluster, or index.
- AUDIT ANY allows the grantee to audit any database object if auditing is enabled.
- COMMENT ANY allows the grantee to add comments to any table, view, or column in any schema.
- GRANT ANY PRIVILEGE allows the grantee to grant any system privilege. (There is no corresponding GRANT ANY OBJECT privilege.)
- GRANT ANY ROLE allows the grantee to grant any role.

Assigning Privileges

When you want to assign one or more privileges to a user or a role, use the GRANT statement. You can see the GRANT statement's syntax in Figure 10.2.

FIGURE 10.2 The syntax for the GRANT statement

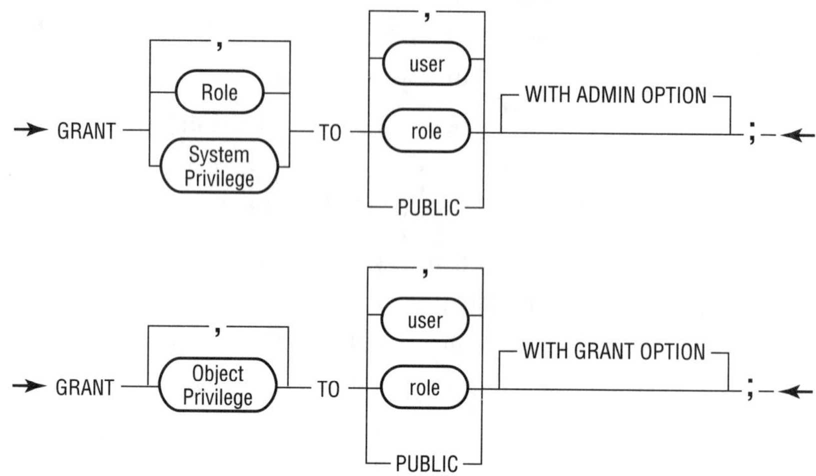

Granting a privilege to the special user `PUBLIC` implicitly grants that privilege to any user who connects to the database. Granting a privilege to `PUBLIC` is analogous to granting that privilege to everyone. When privileges are granted, they take effect immediately; there is no need for the user to log off and log back on to begin using those privileges.

Granting Object Privileges

Object privileges can be granted `WITH GRANT OPTION`, which gives the grantee permission to grant those privileges to any other user or role, or to `PUBLIC`. For example, suppose that Oliver grants SELECT on SALES to Bill using the `WITH GRANT OPTION`. Bill can then grant SELECT on SALES to Bonnie. If user Bill is dropped, however, the chain is broken, and Bonnie loses her SELECT privilege. Figure 10.3 illustrates this example.

Because both the grantor and grantee for object privileges are kept in the data dictionary, a user or role can be granted the same privilege from multiple grantees. When this happens, all grantors must revoke the privilege before the grantee actually loses the ability to exercise the privilege.

Let's take our previous example of Oliver, Bill, and Bonnie, and add another user, Dennis. Oliver has granted to Bill, who has granted to Bonnie. Oliver has also granted to Dennis, and Dennis has granted to Bonnie, as well. You can see this in Figure 10.4.

FIGURE 10.3 Object privileges are lost when the chain is broken.

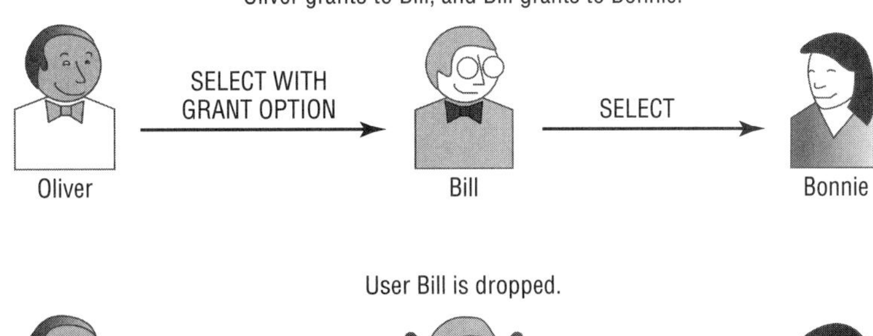

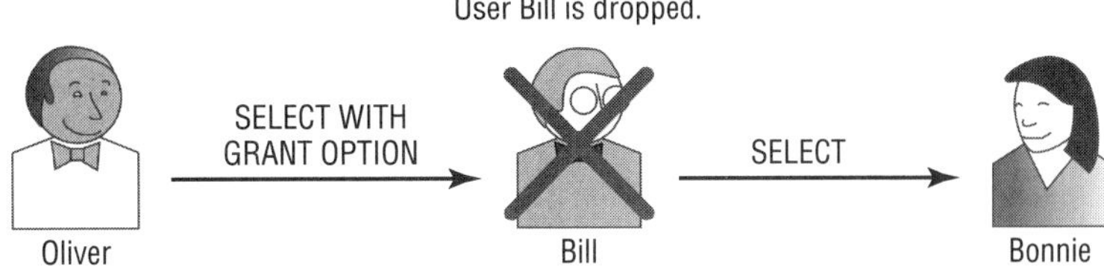

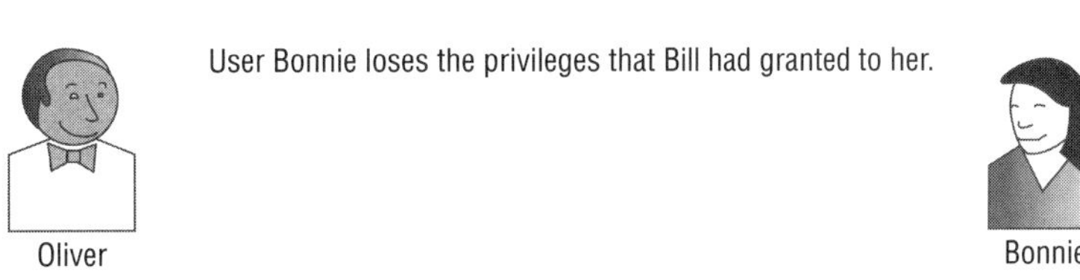

FIGURE 10.4 Receiving a privilege from multiple grantors

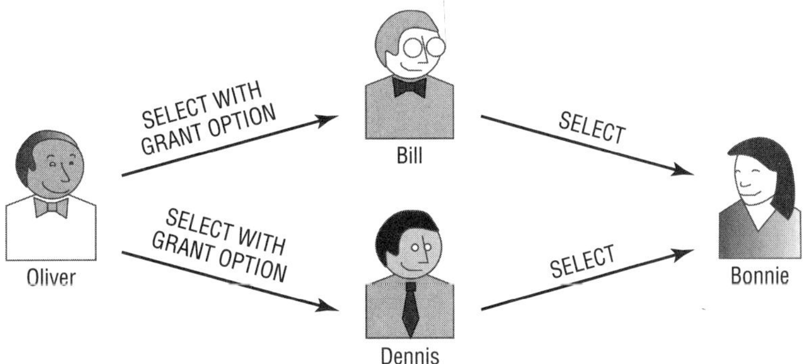

Now, when user Bill is dropped, Bonnie only loses one of her two privileges. She can still execute SELECT statements on the SALES table, as shown in Figure 10.5.

FIGURE 10.5 Bonnie retains her privilege if any granted path remains.

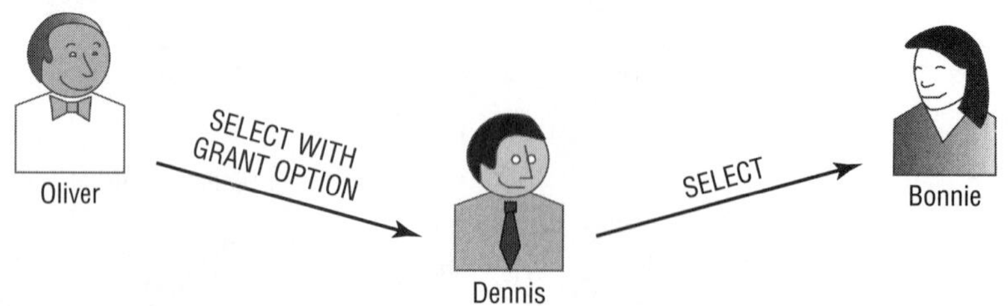
Oliver
SELECT WITH GRANT OPTION
Dennis
SELECT
Bonnie
Bill is dropped, but Bonnie still has the privilege from Dennis.

Granting System Privileges

Like object privileges, system privileges are assigned with the GRANT statement. A notable syntactical difference between system and object privileges is how you pass along the ability for the recipient to grant that privilege. With object privileges, you use the WITH GRANT OPTION clause, but with system privileges you use the WITH ADMIN OPTION clause. The functionality is identical, but the syntax is different. This syntax difference is trivial in practice, because if you try to grant system privileges using WITH GRANT OPTION, the error message says:

```
Only the ADMIN OPTION can be specified.
```

On the exam, however, you must know the syntax and not rely on an error message.

A notable difference between object privileges and system or role privileges is that the grantor of the system or role privilege is not kept. Thus, if Oliver grants DBA to Bill using WITH ADMIN OPTION, then Bill grants DBA to Bonnie, the database does not record that Bill granted to Bonnie—only that Bonnie has the role privilege. If Bill is dropped, Bonnie still retains the system and role privileges that Bill granted to her. See Figure 10.6 for an illustration of how this works.

FIGURE 10.6 System and role privileges remain when the grantor is dropped.

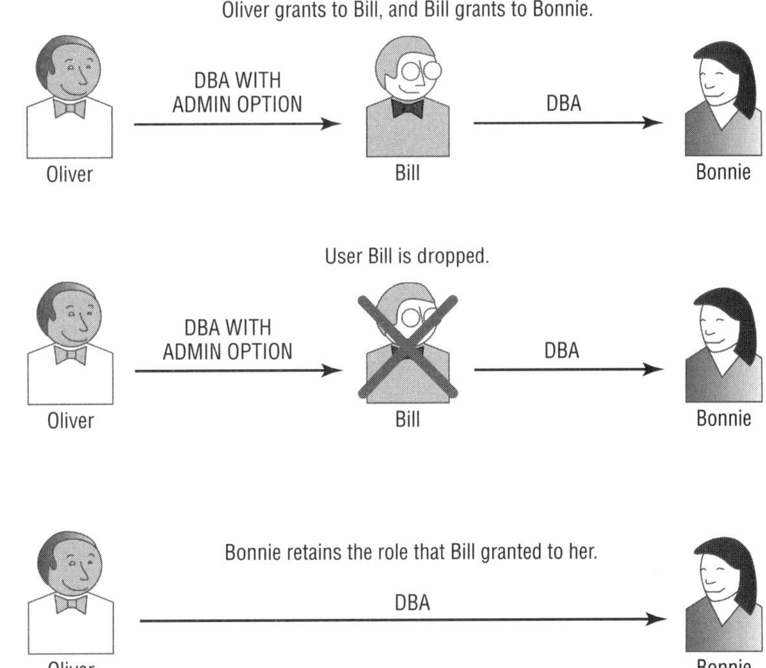

Granting Role Privileges

Any combination of system privileges, object privileges, and role privileges may be granted to a role. As with system privileges, passing along the ability for the recipient to grant the privilege in turn requires the `WITH ADMIN OPTION` clause. Role privileges can be enabled and disabled during a session with the `SET ROLE` statement.

Role privileges cannot be relied upon for privileges on stored SQL. If a function, procedure, package, trigger, or method uses an object owned by another schema, privileges on that object must be granted directly to the owner of the stored SQL. Since granted privileges cannot vary from session to session, they will always be in effect.

Real World Scenario

Using a Role to Facilitate Granting Developer Privileges

One of the more common uses for a role is to bundle a collection of system privileges into one role, so that you need to grant only that single role to a new developer.

In your shop, the developers must be able to create and alter a session, as well as tables, clusters, views, sequences, and synonyms. The developers also need the SELECT privilege on the data dictionary views SYS.V_$SESSION and SYS.V_$SESSION_LONGOPS. You could grant all the privileges to each individual developer when he or she starts to work on a new database, but this is tedious and prone to error. Instead, you can create a role called DEVELOPER that will be granted to each of your developers. This role will incorporate all the system privileges and will be granted to the developers Chuck, Dave, and Erik, as follows:

```
CREATE ROLE developer;

GRANT CREATE SESSION, ALTER SESSION TO developer;

GRANT CREATE CLUSTER, CREATE TABLE, CREATE VIEW,

     ,CREATE SEQUENCE, CREATE SYNONYM TO developer;

GRANT SELECT ON v_$session TO developer;

GRANT SELECT ON v_$session_longops TO developer;


GRANT developer TO chuck, dave, erik;
```

After the role is created and the privileges are granted, the development manager discovers the need to use stored SQL (procedures, functions, packages, and triggers). You need to grant the necessary privileges to the developers so they can create and use these objects. You could grant the CREATE PROCEDURE and CREATE TRIGGER privileges to each developer, but since you have the DEVELOPER role, the better solution is to simply grant the privileges to the role, and then the users will inherit this new privilege.

```
GRANT CREATE PROCEDURE, CREATE TRIGGER TO developer;
```

A couple of months later, the development manager wants her team to create and use materialized views for the new data mart, so the developers now need the CREATE SNAPSHOT, CREATE DIMENSION, QUERY_REWRITE, and GLOBAL QUERY REWRITE privileges. Also, there are two new developers, Karen and Annie, who need all the privileges granted to Chuck, Dave, and Erik. Again, with your DEVELOPER role, you don't need to grant these privileges to each individual developer. Instead, you just grant these privileges to the role, and the developers inherit these privileges.

```
GRANT CREATE SNAPSHOT, CREATE DIMENSION, QUERY REWRITE
   ,GLOBAL QUERY REWRITE TO developer;
GRANT developer TO karen, annie;
```

As you can see, the use of roles has a greater benefit over time than the direct granting of privileges. Maintenance and the introduction of new features or systems are less tedious and error prone.

Revoking Privileges

To rescind privileges, use the REVOKE statement, whose syntax is shown in Figure 10.7. Object privileges can only be revoked by the grantor. But systems and role privileges can be revoked by anyone with the appropriate privileges.

FIGURE 10.7 The syntax for the REVOKE statement

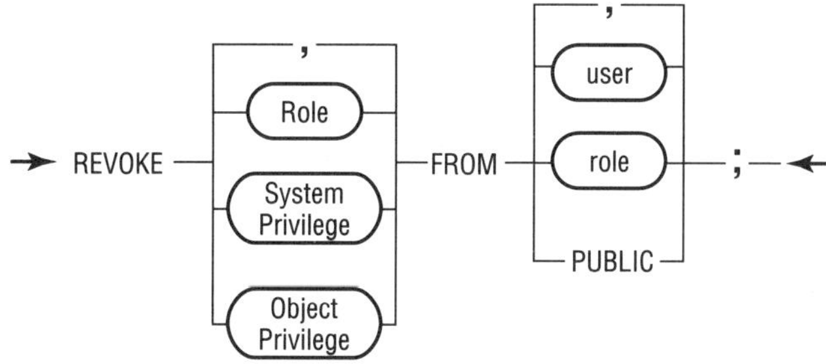

The WITH GRANT OPTION and the WITH ADMIN OPTION of the GRANT statement confer upon the recipient the ability to grant the privileges to other users or roles. To rescind only the WITH GRANT OPTION or WITH ADMIN OPTION, the entire privilege must be dropped and regranted. However, this can have unintended consequences. For example, if Joshua has used his grant option and granted David object privileges, then when Joshua's privilege is revoked, David's privilege is revoked along with Joshua's.

Viewing Privileges in the Data Dictionary

You can examine the data dictionary to see what privileges have been granted. DBA_TAB_PRIVS contains the object privileges that have been granted from any user to any user and shows whether they were granted using `WITH GRANT OPTION`. Don't let the name confuse you—DBA_TAB_PRIVS is not for just tables; it also includes privileges granted on functions, packages, sequences, libraries, and so on.

Table 10.2 lists the data dictionary views related to privileges and their contents. Rote memorization is not much fun, but knowing the contents of these dictionary views is very important, because you are likely to encounter one or more questions about them on the exam. In a professional setting, you can simply look up the view definitions in a reference or describe them in a tool like SQL*Plus. On the exam, however, you must rely on your memory of this material.

You can help yourself to memorize these views by closing this book, pulling out a sheet of paper, and seeing how many of the privilege views in Table 10.2 you can write down. The very act of writing them down will stimulate your memory and help you to recall them later.

TABLE 10.2 Data Dictionary Views on Privileges

Dictionary View	Contents
ALL_COL_PRIVS	The column privileges that have been granted to the user or to `PUBLIC`, or for which the user is the owner
ALL_COL_PRIVS_MADE	The column privileges that have been granted on tables and views where the user is either the owner or the grantor

TABLE 10.2 Data Dictionary Views on Privileges *(continued)*

ALL_COL_PRIVS_RECD	The column privileges that have been granted to the user or to PUBLIC
ALL_TAB_PRIVS	The object privileges that have been granted to the user or to PUBLIC or for which the user is the owner
ALL_TAB_PRIVS_MADE	The object privileges in which the user is either the owner of the object or the grantor of the privilege
ALL_TAB_PRIVS_RECD	The object privileges that have been granted to the user or to PUBLIC
DBA_COL_PRIVS	All column privileges that have been granted
DBA_ROLE_PRIVS	All roles that have been granted to users or to other roles
DBA_SYS_PRIVS	All system privileges that have been granted to users or to roles
DBA_TAB_PRIVS	All object privileges that have been granted
ROLE_ROLE_PRIVS	Roles that have been granted to the user both directly and indirectly
ROLE_SYS_PRIVS	System privileges that have been granted to the user via roles directly and indirectly
ROLE_TAB_PRIVS	Object privileges that have been granted to the user via roles directly and indirectly
SESSION_PRIVS	All system privileges that are available to the user in the current session
USER_COL_PRIVS	The column privileges that have been granted for which the user is owner, grantor, or grantee

TABLE 10.2 Data Dictionary Views on Privileges *(continued)*

USER_COL_PRIVS_MADE	The column privileges that have been granted for which the user is owner or grantor
USER_COL_PRIVS_RECD	The column privileges that have been granted for which the user is owner or grantee
USER_ROLE_PRIVS	The roles that have been granted directly to the user
USER_SYS_PRIVS	The system privileges that have been granted directly to the user
USER_TAB_PRIVS	The object privileges that have been granted directly to the user
USER_TAB_PRIVS_MADE	The object privileges that have been granted to others
USER_TAB_PRIVS_RECD	The object privileges that have been granted to the user

Managing User Groups with Profiles

Profiles allow you to manage groups of users by limiting resource consumption or setting password policies. All user accounts have a profile. The default profile is used if one is not explicitly assigned to an account.

Enabling Resource Settings

Profile settings fall into one of two categories:

- Password resource settings are always in effect and include settings like `failed_logon_attempts` or `password_life_time`.
- Kernel resources are enforced only if they are enabled and include settings like `idle_time` and `logical_reads_per_session`.

To enable kernel resource limits, set the `init.ora` parameter `resource_limit=TRUE`. You can also enable resource limits dynamically with the following statement:

```
ALTER SYSTEM SET resource_limit=TRUE;
```

Creating and Altering Profiles

Each database starts out with one profile, named default, that has all parameters set to unlimited values. To create a new profile, use the `CREATE PROFILE` statement. The syntax for this statement is shown in Figure 10.8.

FIGURE 10.8 The syntax for the CREATE PROFILE statement

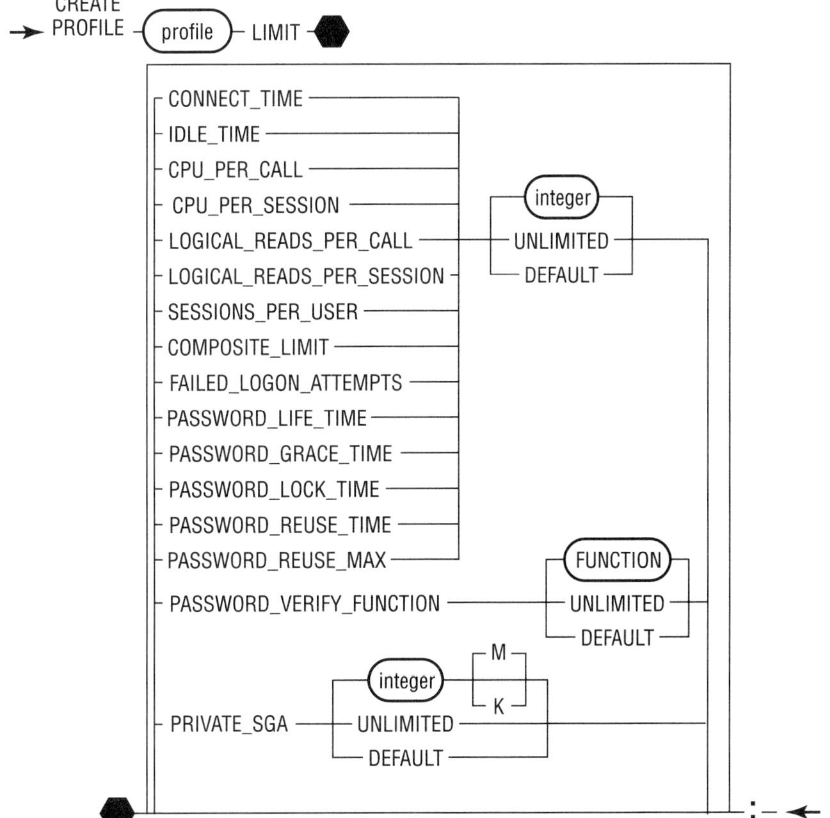

To alter an existing profile, use the ALTER PROFILE statement. The syntax for ALTER PROFILE is shown in Figure 10.9.

FIGURE 10.9 The syntax for the ALTER PROFILE statement

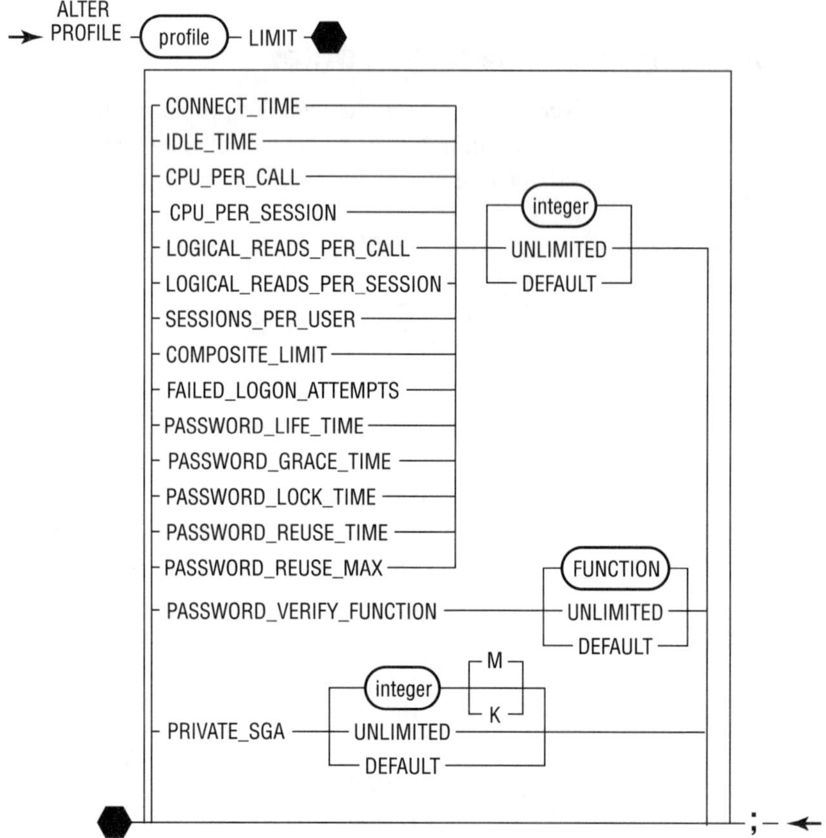

When you create a new profile, you must limit one or more parameters. Those parameters that you don't explicitly limit are inherited from the default profile. You can alter the default profile with the ALTER PROFILE statement.

When creating a new profile, the keyword DEFAULT indicates that the value should be inherited from the default profile. Any parameter not explicitly limited in the CREATE statement is set to inherit its value from the default profile. When altering a profile, the keyword DEFAULT indicates that the parameter should inherit the value in the default profile. If the default profile is changed, all other profiles that inherit the changed parameter will implicitly be changed as well.

```
CREATE PROFILE dba_users LIMIT PASSWORD_LIFE_TIME default;
ALTER PROFILE default LIMIT IDLE_TIME 5;
```

The keyword UNLIMITED specifies that no limit should be enforced for that resource.

```
CREATE PROFILE power_users LIMIT IDLE_TIME UNLIMITED;
ALTER PROFILE dba_users LIMIT CPU_PER_SESSION UNLIMITED;
```

Kernel Resource Settings

The parameters for setting kernel resource limits are described in the following sections. Remember that these limits must first be enabled by setting the init.ora parameter resource_limit to TRUE (or by using the ALTER SYSTEM SET command).

CONNECT_TIME

The kernel parameter CONNECT_TIME limits a session to the specified number of minutes. CONNECT_TIME is sometimes referred to as "wall clock time" to differentiate it from CPU time. When the CONNECT_TIME value is exceeded, Oracle rolls back the current transaction and ends the session. The next call to the database will return an error.

```
CREATE PROFILE power_users LIMIT CONNECT_TIME UNLIMITED;
ALTER PROFILE agents LIMIT CONNECT_TIME 240;
```

IDLE_TIME

The kernel parameter IDLE_TIME sets the maximum number of minutes that Oracle will wait between calls. When the IDLE_TIME value is exceeded, Oracle rolls back the current transaction and ends the session. The next call to the database will return an error. Long-running statements are not affected by this setting. It limits only the time that Oracle waits on a "SQL*Net message from client" event, as reported in the V$SESSION_WAIT view.

```
CREATE PROFILE dba_users LIMIT IDLE_TIME 15;
ALTER PROFILE gate_agent LIMIT IDLE_TIME 5;
```

CPU_PER_CALL

The kernel parameter CPU_PER_CALL limits the amount of CPU time each database call can consume, in hundredths of a second. A database call is a parse, execute, or fetch. These separate calls are usually made from PL/SQL or OCI programs. If you execute a SQL statement in SQL*Plus, all three are performed together and are transparent to the user. If a database call exceeds this setting, the statement fails and rolls back, an error is returned, and the user can then commit or roll back the transaction.

```
CREATE PROFILE power_users LIMIT CPU_PER_CALL UNLIMITED;
ALTER PROFILE students LIMIT CPU_PER_CALL 18000;
```

CPU_PER_SESSION

The kernel parameter CPU_PER_SESSION limits the total amount of CPU time each session can consume, in hundredths of a second. If a session exceeds this setting, the statement fails and rolls back, an error is returned, and the user must either commit or roll back the transaction and end the session.

```
CREATE PROFILE power_users
  LIMIT CPU_PER_SESSION UNLIMITED;
ALTER PROFILE students LIMIT CPU_PER_SESSION 120000;
```

LOGICAL_READS_PER_CALL

The kernel parameter LOGICAL_READS_PER_CALL limits the number of logical reads that each database call can perform. A database call is a parse, execute, or fetch. These separate calls are usually made from PL/SQL or OCI programs. If you execute a SQL statement in SQL*Plus, all three are performed together and are transparent to the user. If a database call exceeds this setting, the statement fails and rolls back, an error is returned, and the user can then commit or roll back the transaction. Logical reads are computed as the sum of consistent gets and current mode gets.

```
CREATE PROFILE power_users
  LIMIT LOGICAL_READS_PER_CALL UNLIMITED;
ALTER PROFILE students
  LIMIT LOGICAL_READS_PER_CALL 1000000;
```

The logical reads values, both per call and per session, are reasonable measures of the amount of work the database must perform. Logical reads are computed as the sum of consistent gets and current mode gets. Limiting logical reads is an accurate way to limit work. Unlike time-based measures, such as elapsed time or CPU time, logical reads values do not vary with system load.

LOGICAL_READS_PER_SESSION

The kernel parameter LOGICAL_READS_PER_SESSION limits the number of logical reads that a session can perform. If a session exceeds this setting, the statement fails and rolls back, an error is returned, and the user must either commit or roll back the transaction and end the session.

```
CREATE PROFILE dba_users
  LIMIT LOGICAL_READS_PER_SESSION UNLIMITED;
ALTER PROFILE sales_staff
  LIMIT LOGICAL_READS_PER_SESSION 1000000;
```

SESSIONS_PER_USER

The kernel parameter SESSIONS_PER_USER limits the number of database sessions that a user may have open concurrently. This setting can be useful to discourage users from all connecting to a shared administrative account to do their work when corporate policy indicates that they should be connecting to their individual accounts.

```
CREATE PROFILE admin_account LIMIT SESSIONS_PER_USER 2;
ALTER PROFILE problem_children LIMIT SESSIONS_PER_USER 3;
```

COMPOSITE_LIMIT

The kernel parameter COMPOSITE_LIMIT puts a ceiling on the number of service units that can be consumed during a user session. Service units are calculated as the weighted sum of CPU_PER_SESSION, LOGICAL_READS_PER_SESSION, CONNECT_TIME, and PRIVATE_SGA values. The weightings are established with the ALTER RESOURCE COST statement and are viewable from the RESOURCE_COST data dictionary view. This COMPOSITE_LIMIT allows you to cap the resource consumption of user groups in more complex ways than a single resource limit.

```
CREATE PROFILE power_users
  LIMIT COMPOSITE_LIMIT UNLIMITED;
ALTER PROFILE ticket_agents LIMIT COMPOSITE_LIMIT 100000;
```

PRIVATE_SGA

The kernel parameter PRIVATE_SGA limits the amount of SGA memory that a session connecting through a shared server (via multithreaded server, or MTS) can allocate to the UGA (User Global Area). The UGA contains private SQL areas, sort areas, and bitmap merge areas. This parameter is useful if you typically grant ALTER SESSION privilege to users so they can enable SQL_TRACE, but you want to limit the SORT_AREA_SIZE that they can allocate.

With the ALTER SESSION privilege, users can enable SQL_TRACE to assist in tuning SQL, but can also change settings that the DBA may not want them to change, such as increasing SORT_AREA_SIZE. A profile with a limit to the PRIVATE_SGA value can allow the DBA to manage the SGA more effectively. The units are bytes, kilobytes if a K is used, or megabytes if an M is used.

```
CREATE PROFILE mts_users LIMIT PRIVATE_SGA 512K;
ALTER PROFILE dba_users LIMIT PRIVATE_SGA UNLIMITED;
```

Password Resource Settings

The parameters for setting password resource limits can be useful for enhancing password security. These parameters are described in the following sections.

FAILED_LOGON_ATTEMPTS

The password parameter FAILED_LOGIN_ATTEMPTS limits the number of times a user account can be accessed unsuccessfully. After this limit is reached, the account becomes locked.

```
CREATE PROFILE power_users LIMIT FAILED_LOGIN_ATTEMPTS
UNLIMITED;
ALTER PROFILE problem_children
  LIMIT FAILED_LOGIN_ATTEMPTS 5;
```

PASSWORD_LIFE_TIME

The password parameter PASSWORD_LIFE_TIME limits the number of days that a password will remain valid. After this limit is reached, the password will expire and need to be changed. If you set PASSWORD_LIFE_TIME, you must also set PASSWORD_GRACE_TIME to a value other than UNLIMITED to actually prevent a user from logging on after the password expiration.

```
CREATE PROFILE regular_users
  LIMIT PASSWORD_LIFE_TIME UNLIMITED;
ALTER PROFILE dba_users LIMIT PASSWORD_LIFE_TIME 30;
```

PASSWORD_GRACE_TIME

The password parameter PASSWORD_GRACE_TIME sets the number of days after the PASSWORD_LIFE_TIME expiration date that a user will receive a warning about the password expiring. When the grace time is up, the password expires. The DBA can see which accounts have expired passwords by examining the data dictionary view DBA_USERS looking for accounts with a status of EXPIRED(GRACE). Both PASSWORD_GRACE_TIME and PASSWORD_LIFE_TIME must be set to effectively limit a lifetime for passwords.

```
CREATE PROFILE power_users LIMIT PASSWORD_GRACE_TIME 7;
ALTER PROFILE problem_children
  LIMIT PASSWORD_GRACE_TIME 14;
```

PASSWORD_LOCK_TIME

The password parameter PASSWORD_LOCK_TIME sets the number of days after which a locked password will automatically unlock. This parameter is useful only if you have FAILED_LOGON_ATTEMPTS set as well. A value of UNLIMITED indicates that the account will never automatically unlock.

```
CREATE PROFILE regular_users LIMIT PASSWORD_LOCK_TIME 1;
ALTER PROFILE dba_users
  LIMIT PASSWORD_LOCK_TIME UNLIMITED;
```

PASSWORD_REUSE_TIME

The password parameter PASSWORD_REUSE_TIME sets the minimum number of days before which a password can be reused. If PASSWORD_REUSE_TIME is set to a value other than UNLIMITED, then PASSWORD_REUSE_MAX must be set to UNLIMITED.

```
CREATE PROFILE regular_users LIMIT PASSWORD_REUSE_TIME 30;
ALTER PROFILE dba_users
  LIMIT PASSWORD_REUSE_TIME UNLIMITED;
```

PASSWORD_REUSE_MAX

The password parameter PASSWORD_REUSE_MAX sets the minimum number of password changes before which a password can be reused. If PASSWORD_REUSE_MAX is set to a value other than UNLIMITED, then PASSWORD_REUSE_TIME must be set to UNLIMITED.

```
CREATE PROFILE regular_users
  LIMIT PASSWORD_REUSE_MAX UNLIMITED;
ALTER PROFILE dba_users LIMIT PASSWORD_REUSE_MAX 3;
```

PASSWORD_VERIFY_FUNCTION

The password parameter PASSWORD_VERIFY_FUNCTION sets the PL/SQL password certification function. This function certifies that the password meets the minimum complexity or other verification rules. Setting PASSWORD_VERIFY_FUNCTION to NULL disables password verification.

```
CREATE PROFILE regular_users
  LIMIT PASSWORD_VERIFY_FUNCTION password_checker;
ALTER PROFILE dba_users
  LIMIT PASSWORD_VERIFY_FUNCTION NULL;
```

Summary

In this chapter, you learned how to create and manage user accounts, including setting the various attributes of those accounts. Next, you learned about object and system privileges as well as how to manage these privileges through the use of roles. You learned how to assign and rescind privileges using the GRANT and REVOKE statements. We also reviewed many of the data dictionary views that provide information about privileges.

Finally, we covered how to managing user groups with profiles. Profiles allow you to use kernel resource settings to limit resource consumption for groups of users, as well as password resource settings to manage password usage rules.

Exam Essentials

Understand the three types of authentication and how they work. With database authentication, the database requires and verifies a password. With external authentication, the database only checks to see that the user exists, relying on the server's operating system to authenticate the user. Global authentication uses an X.509 single sign-on service to authenticate the user; the database only validates that the user exists.

Know what you can do with an ALTER USER statement. There are a number of attributes that can be changed with an ALTER USER statement, including enabling/disabling roles by default and changing a user's password.

Know which object privileges apply to which objects. There are only nine object privileges. The READ privilege does not bestow upon the grantee any ability to read a table. READ is for a directory; SELECT is for a table. Likewise, EXECUTE does not allow the grantee to use a sequence number generator; the SELECT privilege is required.

Know which privileges go along with the WITH ADMIN OPTION option and which privileges go with the WITH GRANT OPTION. Both the admin and grant options confer upon the grantee the ability to grant the privilege to other users or roles. Object privileges can be granted using WITH GRANT OPTION. System and role privileges can be granted using WITH ADMIN OPTION.

Know how revoking object privileges and system/role privileges differ. When object privileges are revoked, the revocation cascades down the chain of granted privileges, but with system and role privileges, there is no cascading revocation. Object privileges can be granted from multiple grantors, so removing object privileges requires all grantors to revoke the privilege. A system or role privilege requires only a single revoke to remove it, regardless of how many grantors granted the privilege to the grantee.

Remember which data dictionary views provide information about privileges. Even the esoteric views like USER_COL_PRIVS_MADE or USER_COL_PRIVS_RECD might make their way onto the exam. You'll need to memorize these views for the exam.

Key Terms

Before you take the exam, make sure you're familiar with the following terms:

object privilege

profile

role

role privilege

system privilege

Review Questions

1. Which of the following assertions most correctly describes the privileges in force after the SQL below is executed?

```
connect athos/musketeer
grant select,insert,update,delete on
   athos.services to porthos
   with grant option;
grant all on athos.services to aramis;
connect porthos/musketeer
grant select,delete,insert,update on
   athos.services to aramis
   with grant option;
connect athos/musketeer
revoke all on athos.services from aramis;
```

   A. Aramis can create an index on athos.services.

   B. Aramis has no privileges on athos.services.

   C. Aramis can select from athos.services.

   D. Aramis can select, insert, update, and delete rows from athos.services.

2. Which of the following assertions most correctly describes the privileges in force after the SQL below is executed?

```
connect system/manager
grant select any table to jon with admin option;
grant select any table to jason;
connect jon/seekrit
grant select any table to jason;
revoke select any table from jason;
```

   A. Jason can select from any table regardless of any individual table privileges.

   B. Jason can only select from tables that he has been granted `SELECT` privileges on or has acquired via a role.

   C. Jason can only select from his own tables.

   D. Jason continues to enjoy the `SELECT ANY TABLE` privilege.

3. You need to create a database-authenticated account named selena. This account should have the password welcome, and Selena should be required to change this password as soon as she connects. Which of the following SQL statements most completely meets these requirements?

    A. `create user selena password welcome expired;`

    B. `create user selena identified by welcome expire;`

    C. `create user selena identified by welcome expire password;`

    D. `create user selena identified by welcome password expire;`

4. You have an account called sales that owns the tables for an application. You have created the tables and need to ensure that no one will be able to connect as this account. Which of the following SQL statements most completely meets these requirements?

    A. `alter user sales account lock;`

    B. `alter user sales disable account;`

    C. `alter user sales lock account;`

    D. `alter account sales lock;`

5. Which of the following queries will include the privileges on another user's procedure that you have granted to a third party?

    A. `SELECT owner, proc_name, grantor, grantee FROM all_sql_privs;`

    B. `SELECT owner, sql_name, grantor, grantee FROM all_sql_privs;`

    C. `SELECT owner, table_name, grantor, grantee, privilege FROM all_tab_privs_made;`

    D. `SELECT owner, sql_name, grantor, grantee FROM user_table_privs;`

6. You have a few developers who insist on connecting to the database as the well-known table-owning account HR, which is reserved for system testing. These developers need to periodically connect to the HR account to promote changes, but the corporate guidelines say that development should be done in each of the developer's personal accounts so they don't conflict with each other. The development manager has asked you to enable any database settings that might help discourage these developers from all connecting to the HR account at the same time. Which of the following options will best assist the development manager?

   A. Give the development manager SELECT privileges on the V$SESSION table, so she can monitor her team's connection activity.

   B. Lock the HR account and make the developers come to a DBA when they need to promote changes to system test.

   C. Use a profile to limit the number of concurrent sessions for user HR to one.

   D. Create an `after logon` trigger that causes the logon to fail if someone else is logged into the HR account.

7. Which of the following actions cannot be done with an `ALTER USER` statement?

   A. Expire a password.

   B. Enable DBA privileges.

   C. Set the default tablespace for tables.

   D. Set different default tablespaces for indexes and tables.

8. Which `init.ora` parameter will limit the number of concurrent session from non-DBA accounts to 16?

   A. `sessions=16`

   B. `license_max_sessions =16`

   C. `processes=16`

   D. `max_concurrent_logons=16`

9. What cannot be done with a profile?

   A. Limit the number of physical reads per session to 100,000.

   B. Limit the number of logical reads per session to 1,000,000.

   C. Limit passwords to expire after 90 days.

   D. Limit the duration of each session to 9 hours.

10. Which of the following assertions most correctly describes the privileges in force after the SQL below is executed?

```
connect system/manager
grant dba to arsal with admin option;
grant dba to gretchen;
connect arsal/troodon
grant dba to gretchen;
revoke dba from gretchen;
```

   A. Gretchen can exercise DBA privileges.

   B. Gretchen can grant DBA privileges to other accounts.

   C. Arsal loses DBA privileges.

   D. Gretchen loses DBA privileges.

11. Which statement will configure the principle_user profile to lock any account after three failed logon attempts?

   A. `alter profile principle_user set failed_logon_attempts=3;`

   B. `alter profile principle_user limit failed_logon_attempts 3;`

   C. `alter principle_user profile set failed_logon_attempts=3;`

   D. `alter profile principle_user lock account when failed_logon_attempts=3;`

   E. You can't limit failed logon attempts.

12. Which of the following SQL statements will give user Nikki the privileges to assign SELECT authority on HR.EMPLOYEES to other user accounts?

    A. `grant select on hr.employees to nikki;`

    B. `grant select on hr.employees to nikki with grant option;`

    C. `grant select on hr.employees to nikki with admin option;`

    D. `grant select on hr.employees to nikki cascade;`

13. Which statement will set a five-minute limit to the maximum time that a user with the default profile can remain idle?

    A. `alter user default set profile max_idle_time=300;`

    B. `alter profile default limit max_idle_time 300;`

    C. `alter profile default limit idle_time 5;`

    D. `alter profile default limit idle_time 300;`

14. Which `init.ora` parameter will assist you in enforcing named user licensing, by limiting the number of user accounts that can be created in your database?

    A. `max_users`

    B. `license_max_users`

    C. `max_named_users`

    D. `named_users_max`

15. Which of the following statements will give user Zachary the privilege to modify only the COMMENTS column in the CUSTOMER table?

    A. `grant update on customer(comments) to zachary;`

    B. `grant update (comments) on customer to zachary;`

    C. `grant update on customer.comments to zachary;`

    D. `grant update on customer columns(comments) to zachary;`

16. Mary has granted INSERT WITH GRANT OPTION, UPDATE WITH GRANT OPTION, and DELETE WITH GRANT OPTION privileges on the CHART_OF_ACCOUNTS table to Charlie. Charlie is changing jobs and should not have the grant option. How can Mary leave the INSERT, UPDATE, and DELETE privileges, but remove the WITH GRANT OPTION? Mary also wants to ensure that whomever Charlie granted the privileges to will retain the privileges.

    A. Grant the privileges on CHART_OF_ACCOUNTS without the grant option, and then revoke the privileges WITH GRANT OPTION.

    B. Simply revoke the grant option.

    C. Revoke the privileges, so that the grant option goes away, and then grant the privileges without the grant option.

    D. Extract all the grants that Charlie made from the data dictionary, revoke the privileges on CHART_OF_ACCOUNTS, grant the privileges on CHART_OF_ACCOUNTS without the grant option, and regrant all the extracted privileges.

17. You need to report on all of the column privileges that you have made on your BONUS table. You must include the name of the account receiving the privilege, which column, and which privilege. Which of the following statements will accomplish this task?

    A.
    ```
    select grantor, table_name, column_name, privilege
    from user_col_privs_recd
    where table_name ='BONUS';
    ```

    B.
    ```
    select * from all_col_privs_made
    where table_name='BONUS';
    ```

    C.
    ```
    select table_name, column_name, privilege, grantee
    from user_col_privs_made
    where table_name ='BONUS';
    ```

    D.
    ```
    select grantee, table_name, column_name, privilege
    from all_tab_col_privs
    where owner=user and table_name='BONUS';
    ```

18. EMP is a table. Mary is a user. Sales_mgr is a role. Which one of the following statements will fail?

    A. `grant sales_mgr to mary with admin option;`

    B. `grant read on emp to mary;`

    C. `grant insert,update,delete on emp to mary with grant option;`

    D. `grant reference on emp to mary;`

19. Which of the following table privileges cannot be granted to a role (can only be granted to a user)?

    A. `INDEX`

    B. `ALTER`

    C. `REFERENCE`

    D. `TRUNCATE`

20. If Judy grants `ALL` on her table FORMAT_CODES to `PUBLIC`, which operation will user Jerry not be able to perform without being granted other privileges?

    A. `create index on judy.format_codes`

    B. `alter table judy.format_codes`

    C. `delete table judy.format_codes`

    D. `truncate table judy.format_codes`

Answers to Review Questions

1. D. Object privileges can be obtained from more than one grantor. To completely remove object privileges from an account, all grantors must revoke these privileges. Aramis was granted the four privileges SELECT, INSERT, UPDATE, and DELETE on athos.services from Porthos, as well as ALL (SELECT, INSERT, UPDATE, DELETE, ALTER, INDEX, and REFERENCE) from Athos. After Athos revokes the privileges that he granted, Aramis still retains the privileges that were granted from Porthos.

2. B. Oracle does not retain the grantor on system privileges, so if anyone revokes a system privilege, that privilege is gone, even if the grantee obtained it from more than one grantor. This behavior is the same as role privileges, but different from object privileges, such as SELECT, INSERT, or EXECUTE.

3. D. You create a database-authenticated account with the CREATE USER statement. You assign the password with the IDENTIFIED BY clause and expire the password with the PASSWORD EXPIRE clause. When the password expires, the user will be required to change it on the next connection to the database.

4. A. To lock an account, disabling logons for that account, you alter the account with the ACCOUNT LOCK option.

5. C. All of the other data dictionary tables are fictitious.

6. C. This one is really tricky. All of the options would work technically. However, the development manager probably has better things to do than monitor who on her team is connecting as which user. Unless the corporate standards say a DBA must promote changes to system test, the DBA probably has better things to do than slow down the development efforts by getting involved in promotions to system test. The `after logon` trigger is a clever bit of engineering, but it actually does the same thing as the profile with added complexity, overhead, and maintenance.

7. D. It would be nice, but Oracle does not (yet) let you set a default tablespace for indexes. DBA privileges can be enabled by default with an `ALTER USER` statement if the role was granted to the user previously and set to disabled.

8. B. Option A is a hard limit that includes restricted session logons. The `processes` setting includes such non-logon processes as pmon, lgwr, and parallel I/O slaves. The `max_concurrent_logons` parameter is fictitious. When the number of logon sessions reaches `license_max_sessions`, only restricted session (DBA) logons are allowed.

9. A. You can limit a number of resources with a profile, but the number of physical reads can be dependent on how warm the cache is and cannot be limited via a profile.

10. D. Oracle does not retain the grantor on role privileges, so if anyone revokes a role privilege, that privilege is gone, even if the grantee obtained it from more than one grantor. This behavior is the same as system privileges, but different from object privileges, such as `SELECT`, `INSERT`, or `EXECUTE`.

11. B. Know the syntax for changing resource limits in a profile.

12. B. The `WITH GRANT OPTION` clause is used to give the grantee the ability to grant the privilege to other accounts. The `WITH ADMIN OPTION` does the same thing with system and role privileges.

13. C. The `ALTER PROFILE` statement is used to change a profile, and the `idle_time` parameter is set in minutes, not seconds.

14. B. `license_max_users` can be used to limit the number of user accounts created. The other options are fictitious.

15. B. Any additional columns would appear as a comma-delimited list within the parentheses.

16. D. There is no simple and easy way to remove the `WITH GRANT OPTION` while retaining the privilege. Revoking a privilege from someone will cascade through and revoke it from all grantees, so it would be crucial to first extract these privileges before revoking them.

17. C. The grantee is the recipient of the privilege. Every one of the ALL_DATA dictionary views contains not only the user's own objects, but also those that the user has access to, so ALL_COL_PRIVS_MADE may contain privileges on other schemas' tables. ALL_TAB_COL_PRIVS is not a valid data dictionary view.

18. B. The `READ` privilege is valid only on directories.

19. C. `TRUNCATE` is not a table privilege. `INDEX` and `ALTER` can be granted to either a user or a role, but `REFERENCE` can be granted only to a user.

20. D. `TRUNCATE` is not a table privilege.

Glossary

A

aggregate functions Functions that operate on groups of rows, also known as group functions. The exact number of inputs for aggregate functions is not determined until the query is executed and all rows are fetched. This differs from *single-row functions*, in which the number of inputs is known at parse time, before the query is executed.

arithmetic operators Operators used to manipulate information in the arithmetic expressions. Addition (+), subtraction (–), multiplication (*), and division (/) are the arithmetic operators.

B

base tables The tables used to define a view.

binary operators Operators that take two operands. All operators are binary, except the + or – used to represent the sign of a numeric value.

bitmap index An index database object that organizes table data in a series of bitmaps. A bitmap index is analogous to a two-dimensional matrix, where index keys and table rows are the axes.

B-tree index An index database object that organizes table data in a binary tree format.

C

cardinality The number of distinct values. If a table has a cardinality of 1,000, it has 1,000 rows. If a column has a cardinality of 30, it has 30 distinct values (there may be 1,000 rows, but only 30 distinct values).

Cartesian join A join that joins two tables with no common condition, also known as a *cross join*. Each row from the first table is joined against every row in the second table.

CASE An expression that can be used to derive IF...THEN...ELSE logic in SQL.

column alias Another name for the column to display with the query results. Alias names can provide meaningful names for the result set.

comparison operators Operators that compare two values or expressions and give a Boolean result of `TRUE`, `FALSE`, or `NULL`.

complex join A join that includes additional filter criteria along with the join conditions in the `WHERE` clause.

compound query A query that includes a set operator to join two or more queries.

concurrency The condition where many users/sessions can access and modify data at the same time.

consistency A state maintained by the database. A statement/transaction sees a time-consistent image of the data plus any uncommitted data from the statement/transaction.

correlated subquery A subquery that references the column names of the parent query.

cross join A join that joins two tables with no common condition, also known as a *Cartesian join*. Each row from the first table is joined against every row in the second table.

CURRVAL The sequence pseudo-column that will return the last number generated from the sequence number generator.

D

Data Definition Language (DDL) The subset of SQL that is used to change database object structures.

Data Manipulation Language (DML) The subset of SQL that is used to change the data in a table.

datatype A characteristic assigned to each column in a table that defines what type of data can be stored in the column and its valid values.

declarative constraints Constraints that are not enforced. These constraints will have a state of `DISABLE NOVALIDATE`.

deferred constraint checking Constraint checking that is deferred to a transaction level. By default, constraints are checked at the statement level.

DUAL A dummy table in the Oracle database. DUAL has one column and one row. It is mainly used to query the system variables such as `SYSDATE` and `USER`.

E

environment variables Variables that define the SQL*Plus environment. These variables are set using the `SET` command. The `SHOW` command is used to display the value of the variables.

equality join (equijoin) A join in which two tables are joined with an equality operator or an `IN` operator. Natural joins and `JOIN ... USING` are examples of equality joins.

escape character A character used to prefix a pattern-matching character, such as % or _, to allow the inclusion of the pattern-matching character in the string.

exclusive lock A table or row lock that will block all changes to data and all other DML locks.

expression A combination of one or more values, operators, and SQL functions that results in a value.

F

foreign key A relationship between two tables. The foreign key defined on a table refers to the primary key or unique key of another table.

full outer join New to Oracle9i, a join between two tables that returns rows based on the matching condition, as well as unmatched rows from the table on the right and left of the `JOIN` clause.

function A PL/SQL program that returns a value and is called in an expression.

H

host string The database alias name used to connect to the Oracle database. You connect to the database by supplying a username, password, and a host string. The host string can be omitted if the database is local.

I

identifiers Names used in the database, such as table names, column names, and so on. An identifier must begin with an alphabetic character and can contain alphabetic characters, digits, and three special characters: #, $, and _.

index A data structure that physically organizes data from a table so as to improve table access speed.

inline view A subquery that appears in the `FROM` clause. This type of subquery is similar to selecting from a view.

inner join A join that selects only matching rows of both tables. This is the default type of join.

integrity constraints Constraints that protect the data integrity. They are business rules defined in the database.

iSQL*Plus The web interface to SQL*Plus. You do not need to install the client software to access the database. Using iSQL*Plus, all you need is a web browser and the URL of the Oracle HTTP server.

iSQL*Plus server The iSQL*Plus component that enables communication and authentication between the user interface and the Oracle9i database.

J

join A relationship between two tables specified by using common columns or a condition to join two tables together.

Julian date A date that refers to the number of days since January 1, 4712 BC.

K

key A distinct value in an index.

key-preserved A state of a table in a join view. A table in the join view is key-preserved if the primary and unique keys of the table are unique to the view's result set.

L

left outer join A join between two tables that returns rows based on the matching condition, as well as unmatched rows from the table to the left of the `JOIN` clause.

literals Values that represent a fixed value (constant). There are four types of literals: integer, character, number, and interval.

logical operators Operators that are used to combine the results of two comparison conditions to produce a single result or to reverse the result of a single comparison. `NOT`, `AND`, and `OR` are the logical operators.

M

multiple-column subquery A subquery that selects multiple columns in the subquery. Such subqueries are generally used in `UPDATE` statements or in the `WHERE` clause.

multiple-row subquery A subquery that returns no rows or more than one row.

multi-table join A join that joins more than two tables in a query.

N

National Language Support (NLS) Parameters and arguments that allow internationalization of the Oracle database system. NLS internationalizations include date representations, character sets, alphabets, and alphabetical ordering.

natural join A join that joins two tables using the columns with the same name and datatype in both tables.

nested subquery A subquery within another subquery.

NEXTVAL The sequence pseudo-column that will cause the generation of the next number from the sequence number generator.

nonequality join A join that joins two tables with a nonequality operator.

NULL A value that represents unknown or missing data. Most functions return NULL when called with a NULL argument.

O

object privilege A database privilege that allows the grantee to perform a specific operation on a database object, such as a SELECT, an UPDATE, or a DELETE operation on a table.

Oracle Net Networking software that establishes a connection between the Oracle database and a client session.

outer join A join used to select data from table even if there is no matching row in the joined table. These are the rows that are not returned by using a simple join. An outer join is specified by the outer-join operator (+) or the FULL|LEFT|RIGHT OUTER JOIN keywords.

P

package A container for bundling procedures, functions, and data structures.

password A secret word associated with each user ID to authenticate a database connection.

primary key A column or combination of column values that can identify a row uniquely. Primary key columns cannot have NULL values.

private synonym A restricted alias to another object.

procedure A stored program that is called as a statement.

profile A set of limits on database resources or password characteristics.

public synonym A global alias to another object.

R

right outer join A join between two tables that returns rows based on the matching condition, as well as unmatched rows from the table to the right of the `JOIN` clause.

role A set of privileges that can be granted to other roles or to user accounts.

role privilege A database privilege that, by proxy, gives the grantee any combination of object, system, or other role privileges. Some role privileges that are included with all Oracle databases are DBA, resource, and java_admin.

row exclusive lock A table lock that is implicitly acquired with an `INSERT`, an `UPDATE`, a `MERGE`, or a `DELETE` statement.

row share lock A table lock that is implicitly acquired with a `SELECT FOR UPDATE` statement.

ROWID A pseudo-column in every table that is the physical address of a row in the database.

S

savepoint An intermediate point within a transaction to which changes can be rolled back, without rolling back the entire transaction.

scalar subquery A subquery that returns one row and one column value. If the scalar subquery returns no rows, the resulting value is `NULL`.

script file One or more SQL and/or SQL*Plus commands saved in a file for reuse.

seed database The database that can be installed while installing the Oracle software to practice using Oracle9i with Oracle-supplied sample schemas.

SELECT The SQL statement used to query data. This is the most commonly used statement in Oracle.

self-join A join in which a table is joined to itself in a query.

sequence A named sequential number generator.

set operators Operators used to write compound queries. UNION, UNION ALL, MINUS, and INTERSECT are the set operators.

share lock A table lock that will block all changes to data and exclusive locks, but will allow other share locks.

share row exclusive lock A table lock that will block all changes to data and other locks, except other row share locks.

single-row functions Functions that operate on a single row at a time. These functions know how many arguments they will operate on at compile time, before any data is fetched.

single-row subquery A subquery that returns only one row.

SQL buffer A buffer where the previously executed SQL statement is stored. SQL in the buffer can be edited, or it can be run using the / command.

statement A single SQL command that can include subqueries.

subquery A query within another query. A subquery answers queries that have multiple parts. The subquery answers one part of the question, and the parent query answers the other part.

substitution variable A variable that will accept values from the user during execution of the SQL.

superaggregates Summary rows (created by the ROLLUP and CUBE clauses) containing NULL in the grouped expressions. The GROUPING function returns a 1 for these summary rows and a 0 for the nonsummary rows, and it is used to distinguish the summary rows from the nonsummary rows.

synonym An alias to another object.

SYSDATE A built-in function to get the current system date and time.

system privilege A database privilege that allows the grantee to perform a specific system operation, such as create a session or alter a table.

T

table The basic structure in the database to store data. Tables are defined with columns and contain rows of data.

table alias name An alias name for table in queries generally used to qualify ambiguous columns, to tell Oracle specifically to which table the column belongs.

time zone displacement The difference between the time zone and UTC (Coordinated Universal Time zone).

transaction One or more statements that constitute an atomic view of data or an atomic change to data.

U

Unicode A multibyte character set that can represent characters from any language. Unicode can, for example, represent characters from English, Greek, Urdu, and Japanese within a single character set.

updatable join view A view that queries from more than one table and can be used to update the base tables through the view.

username A unique identification to connect to the Oracle9i database.

V

view A customized representation of data from one or more tables. Views can be used to present a different perspective of data, to limit the data access, or to hide a complex query.

W

WHERE A clause used with SQL statements to limit the number of rows retrieved.

Index

Note to the Reader: Throughout this index **boldfaced** page numbers indicate primary discussions of a topic. *Italicized* page numbers indicate illustrations.

A

B

C

D

E

F

G

H

I

J

K

L

M

O

P

Q

R

S

T

U

V

W

Z